THE NOUN PHRASE IN BENGALI

TO THE LOVING MEMORY OF

MY FATHER

Narayan Chandra Sarkar

THE NOUN PHRASE IN BENGALI

Assignment of Role and the Kāraka Theory

MALAYA GANGOPADHYAY

MOTILAL BANARSIDASS
Delhi Varanasi Patna Bangalore Madras

First Edition : Delhi, 1990

MOTILAL BANARSIDASS
Bungalow Road, Jawahar Nagar, Delhi 110 007

ISBN: 81-208-0377-9

Branches
Chowk, Varanasi 221 001
Ashok Rajpath, Patna 800 004
24 Race Course Road, Bangalore 560 001
120 Royapettah High Road, Mylapore, Madras 600 004

PRINTED IN INDIA
BY JAINENDRA PRAKASH JAIN AT SHRI JAINENDRA PRESS, A-45 NARAINA INDUSTRIAL AREA, PHASE I, NEW DELHI 110 028 AND PUBLISHED BY NARENDRA PRAKASH JAIN FOR MOTILAL BANARSIDASS, DELHI 110 007.

PREFACE

THE PRESENT study represents a descriptive account of the noun phrase structure in Bengali and attempts to use the semantico-syntactic theory of *kāraka* for assigning roles to noun phrases.

Although 'roles' are to be understood from the viewpoint of universality, the ancient theory was based on one particular language. In my work the applicability of *kāraka* in mapping semantic-syntactic cross references is investigated. It is explored in the dimension of relation and that of manifestation.

The aim of this study is to show that the *kāraka-vācya* configuration, if understood the way it has been explicated, can be used as a useful axiom of semantic and syntactic cross reference. Following traditional grammar, it is suggested that minimization of factual reality and of certain semantic detail may be an appropriate directive for 'role' assignment. This restrictive criterion establishes a positive 'cut-off' point in role assignment.

The study criticizes the 'deep structure hypothesis' for confusing grammar and real world situations. It is argued that, in tracing the underlying factual and the psychological reality of structures, a grammatical analysis can easily be stretched too far.

The units and their relations are described in a basically structural framework. It is believed that, even though the multidimensional approach may be neutralized at the higher level description of syntax, various cross references which are pertinent need to be stated. Rigorous formalization and formulistic (symbolic) representations have not been favoured.

It is believed that the principle of economy is desirable in the sense that everything should be described in a concise manner, but this does not mean that variants and characteristics of language should be neglected.

There are four chapters. A list of verbs and three tables are given in Chapter III. All examples are put in the Appendixes. It is hoped that they will serve a useful purpose: the reader would be able to verify the occurrences of markers (including postpositions) with nominal expressions and their syntactical behaviour. In the transcription, the signs are those of the International Phonetic Association.

I wish to express my indebtedness to all those whose teachings and writings have contributed to the shaping of my ideas.

I would particularly like to mention Prof. U.G.E. Hammarström, who was my supervisor. I am greatly indebted to him for his advice and criticism. He has kindly written the Foreword. I convey my sincere thanks to the Authority of Monash University for awarding me a Graduate Scholarship for three years. The present study was awarded Ph.D. degree by

Monash University, Melbourne in 1976. I received invaluable help from the Main Library and the Departmental Library of Monash University.

Among others, I should mention Miss M. Lighfoot, Dr. P. Platt and Dr. P. Paul for their suggestions and discussions. I must acknowledge the forbearance and patience of my husband and our daughter, which they showed to me during the period of this study.

Due to my illness, it took a long time to revise the work and make it ready for the press. I know my limitations and feel responsible for any errors of analysis.

My labours will be amply rewarded if this study interests scholars and students in the field.

Melbourne MALAYA GANGOPADHYAY
March 1987

FOREWORD

DR. MALAYA GANGOPADHYAY's thesis is a thorough study of the noun phrase in Bengali with regard to both the expression structure and the various functions of the noun phrase. They are both dealt with in considerable detail.

It is obvious that the study should be of value to linguists interested in Bengali. I believe, however, that linguists interested in semantic and syntactic problems in general could read her work with profit. For scholars in the western tradition the use of the *kāraka* notion would be of particular interest.

Monash University U.G.E. HAMMARSTRÖM
March 1986

CONTENTS

INTRODUCTION

IN DESCRIBING the Bengali noun phrase including inflexion of the noun and the nominal compounds, our attempt will be to characterize various nominal expressions that can occur in a sentence or a clause. We shall concentrate on the following points:

(1) a description of the additive segments;
(2) a description of the structure of the noun phrase;
(3) an investigation of certain formal regularities;
(4) remarks on the semantic and functional aspects;
(5) remarks on the similarities and dissimilarities between the Bengali and English noun phrases in similar constructions.

Chapter 1 deals with different morphological markers as well as postpositions which function in a similar manner. In our discussion on noun modification, we shall occasionally refer to those inflexions which indicate differences in grammatical meaning ('case', definiteness, plurality). Basically, we understand 'case' or rather 'role' as the semantic relation between the verbal and the nominal groups.

Since the word order is more or less free in Bengali, inflexions on the noun phrase are very important to get the semantic relation of the nominal elements as well as their syntactic and semantic functions.

It will not be without interest to mention here that both in Sanskrit and in Bengali the relation of a nominal with the verb in a sentence is understood mostly by the inflexion on the noun and its determiner.

This semantic relation of the noun and the verb is referred to as the *kāraka* in Sanskrit and Bengali grammars ('case' relation = 'role'). Consider, for instance, a sentence in English: *Ram knows Shyām.* If the proper nouns in the above sentence change their positions, it will be altogether a different sentence, whereas in Bengali a sentence having the same meaning may be put in the following three different ways:

(1) *Rām Shyāmke jāne*;
(2) *Rām jāne Shyāmke*; and
(3) *Shyāmke Rām jāne*.

There are other possibilities also. We have taken here only three. Even though the nominal expressions occur in different positions in different sentences, the *kāraka* relations are considered to be the same, their subject-predicate functions also do not change. The prosodic feature may be changed. The difference between the sentences may be considered (*a*) as a statement; (*b*) as an assertion of the same statement; and (*c*) as an emphasis on the verb.

Obviously, the ending *-ke* is very important to get the correct interpretation of these sentences. From our collected examples, four types of morphological markers are found which express various grammatical meanings. A zero marker can be posited (where there is no such overt marker). Postpositions are included for identifying different grammatical meanings.

We suggest that 'case' should be looked at in a two-dimensional matrix: the form and the meaning (i.e. the semantic relation which has a syntactic function and which is expressed in a certain form).

In Chapters 2 and 3, we shall look at the noun phrases from two points of view—that of the expression and that of the function. We shall discuss the structure of simple as well as complex noun phrases and their functions. We shall try to show the association between their structural make-up and their functional role as shown by the corresponding markers.

We shall also discuss the Indian traditional concept of semantic as well as syntactic units. In Chapter 4 our investigation will be concentrated basically on the types of noun phrases that occur with different types of verbs in different types of sentences. We shall try to remark and discuss the similarities and dissimilarities between the English and the Bengali expressions mostly in Chapters 2 and 3.

In this study the selected criteria for identifying noun phrases are eleven:

(1) Noun phrases are expressions which have a noun as their head.
(2) Noun phrases may consist of a noun and any possible modifiers.
(3) Noun phrases may be parts of either a clause (which is a part of a sentence) or a sentence (which sometimes does not contain a full clause).
(4) The noun phrase will usually have an inflexional suffix (the exact detail will be given later) at the end.
(5) Sometimes more than one noun can act as the head of a noun phrase.
(6) All the components constituting the unit (the noun phrase) can form either an endocentric or an exocentric construction or both.
(7) Noun phrases hold semantic relations such as agent, instrument, etc.
(8) Noun in apposition and relative clause in apposition are included in the noun phrase.
(9) The noun phrase occurs either in subject part or in the predicate part in a clause or in a sentence.
(10) A single nominal can be considered as a noun phrase.
(11) A noun phrase may be the whole sentence (which consists of a noun unit, (i.e. NP only).

CHAPTER I

NOUN INFLEXION AND POSTPOSITION

[1.0] IN inflexional languages where the word order is rather flexible, one of the devices for semantic interpretation of a sentence is the inflexion of the categories (noun, verb, etc.). The interpretation of the sentence is related to the interpretation of its elements and the verb concord, on the one hand, and the noun inflexion, on the other.

In this chapter, we are mainly concerned with the inflexion and the postposition which occur with nominals. Nominals here are any noun with or without modifiers and pronouns. Not only the morphological markers but also the postpositions are considered to be a kind of marker occurring with the nominals and expressing different meanings. However, postpositions are free forms. The inflexional markers, on the other hand, being bound morphemes, are suffixed to a given nominal and express grammatical meaning like plurality, definiteness, case, etc. The postpositions likewise can express certain types of roles as well as other types of relations between nominals and verb.

We shall investigate those markers which have both semantic and syntactic functions, viz. the case markers. However, some markers which express meanings other than 'role' may come up in our discussion since they are fused with case markers. There are, for instance, such markers as those expressing difiniteness, plurality, possessive relations, etc.

[1.1.] If we use semantic criteria, then four distinct groups of morphological markers are evident:

(1) *ϕ* and other markers which are amalgams;
(2) *-ke*;
(3) *-r*, *-er*, *-der* (*-e*);
(4) *-e*, (*-te*) (see appendixes).

In Bengali, forms with these markers play multiple roles. The nominals with markers other than morphological markers which function in a similar way may be considered as complex forms. To investigate this in detail, we have collected about 800 examples of the use of the postpositions in Bengali sentences (see appendixes). Most of the sentences are from two Bengali daily newspapers and a literary weekly. A few sentences are taken from other sources.[1]

[1] *Ananda Bazar Patrika*, *Jugantar*, *Desh*, *Sandesh*, *Kishor Bharati*. These newspapers and magazines are chosen, because one could get the best examples of Bengali standard language in them.

[1.2.] We have set up the four forms just mentioned on the basis of four distinct inflexional markers found in our examples. In a large number of instances, 'roles' are normally expressed by morphological markers. They may also be expressed by nominals with a postposition. The particles correspond to English prepositions. As they occur after the nominals, they are generally called postpositions. These latter particles sometimes demand morphological markers like *-e*, *-te*, *-er*, *-der*, *-ke* which normally express locative, dative, genitive, etc.

A list of different postpositions that occur with noun and function similar to the morphological markers is given below. The noun is abbreviated here as N.

(1) N+*theke*
(2) N+*nie*
(3) N+*die* (*moddhe die*)
(4) N+*moddhe*
(5) N+*kore*
(6) N+*jonne* (*jonno*)
(7) N+*kāche*
(8) N+*nikoṭe*
(9) N+*hoite* (*hote*, *nikoṭ-hote*)
(10) N+*dārā*
(11) N+*rūpe*
(12) N+*dhore*
(13) N+*proti*
(14) N+*upor*(*e*)
(15) N+*bhitor*(*e*)
(16) N+*pokkhe*
(17) N+*khetre*

Most of the examples are from the literary weekly, *Desh*, and the list of postpositions below is made, according to the frequency of occurrence of the postpositions. Approximate percentage of occurrences is as below:

N+*kore*	22 per cent	N+*kāche*	6 per cent
N+*theke*	20 per cent	N+*hoite*	2 per cent
N+*nie*	12 per cent	N+*dārā*	4 per cent
		N+*proti*	2 per cent
N+*jonne*	11 per cent	N+*bhitor*(*e*)	1 per cent
N+*moddhe*	10 per cent	N+*upor*(*e*)	1 per cent
N+*die*	8 per cent		

The other five together may be considered as 1 per cent. Even though some are less frequent in *Desh*, they are commonly used in other papers already mentioned.

Postpositions which indicate 'roles' are to be considered as 'role' markers. They never precede the nominal. Further, they fulfil functions similar to the morphological markers, i.e. the 'roles' may be realized in this language partly by inflexions and partly by additional postpositions to the noun.

As the nominal expressions with postpositions function similar to a morphological form in Bengali, 'roles' cannot be profitably discussed if they are not included.

A few more can be added here, although they were not found in our materials. These are occasionally used in the language and share identical behaviour with other morphological markers. Their syntactical behaviour is similar. Therefore we add the postpositions:

(18) *dorun* 'because of, because'
(19) *koṭrik* 'by'
(20) *sɔṅge* 'with', 'accompanied by'
(21) *hoe* 'via', 'for'
(22) *bole* 'as' 'because'

Some of them signal 'roles'. However, there are morphemes which are homophonous with the above-mentioned postpositional ones which signal degree, comparison, etc. but do not indicate 'roles'. These can occur not only as postpositional segments but also as nouns. For instance, *theke* can express degree of comparison:

āmi tār-theke bɔṛo
I him than older
= I am older than he.
theke occurs as a noun,
theke theke mone hoe
Sometimes in mind comes
= Sometimes it appears to my mind.

A postpositional morpheme and a morphological ending can be compared as follows:

mukh-theke 'from the mouth'
mukh-e 'in or on the mouth—face; 'to the mouth'

We have set up four forms, according to the morphological markers. A fifth form may be added, i.e. a form which is represented by those nouns occurring with a postposition (N+postposition).

In Bengali, the English prepositional phrase can be translated as an inflexional form. A whole phrase would be like a compound. For instance, 'the shooting of the hunters' may take shape of a compound in Bengali translation: *sikārider sikār.*

This Bengali expression can take either morphological markers or postpositional markers such as *-ṭa, -ṭi, -e, -er, -ke, -theke, -nie,* etc.

It may be of some interest to mention here that, in some Bengali grammatical treatises, it is suggested that only the type of forms with morphological markers be considered as inflexional units.[2] It is observed that often the subject and object noun phrases are not marked with any kind of markers,

[2]S.K. Chatterjee, pp. 92-93.

whereas other noun phrases holding other 'roles' are always marked with a marker.

In Bengali a syntactic unit such as a noun with a marker or the longer unit consisting of more than one noun or a noun with modifers having marker can function in the same way.

[1.3] Traditionally, word-level and sentence-level units are analysed. A word in isolation is a lex, which is not necessarily to be considered as a syntactic unit. A word as a part of a sentence can be a syntactic unit. By definition, then, the lex as a part of a sentence is a grammatical form with or without overt inflexion, which is termed as *pada* in Indian grammar.[3]

The term *pada* corresponds to the English term 'a single word, a compound word or a smaller phrase in a given sentence'. Normally, certain kinds of morphophonemic changes occur in the internal structure of compounds and phrases which are called *sandhi* in Sanskrit as well as in Bengali grammars, even though there are differences in Sanskrit and Bengali *sandhi* processes.[4] The *sandhi* combines the elements into a single unit. The elements may be prefix+root, stem+suffix and two or more nominal stems etc.

The unit of nominal expression is either inflected with morphological marker or has a postpositional segment.

Even though exactly the same type of morphophonemic changes may not be observed in Bengali, in both languages a syntactic unit is bound by a marker and is separated by a juncture (phonetically). In syntactic and semantic interpretation, it is treated as a single unit. This unit is *pada*, a syntagm of a sentence; the markedness and internal juncture indicate the division of the syntagm in a sentence, and the external juncture (pause) indicates the sentence (i.e. the end of the sentence, boundary) or period whichever term one may use.

A syntactic nominal unit may consist of one nominal with marker or more than one nominal with marker. We consider both as inflexional units. We shall call them nominal units, in short NU.

[1.4] What is observed may thus be stated in the following:

Form I : Functions as agent and object;
Form II : Functions as object, dative and agent (rarely);
Form III: Functions as locative and instrumental;
Form IV: Functions as ablative, locative and instrumental;
Form V : Functions as agent (passive), locative, instrumental, object (rarely).

This implies that one 'role' may be represented by different markers and one marker may represent different 'roles'. As different markers can express

[3]Chatterjee, pp. 48-50. Also see Pāṇini, 1.4.14: '*Suptiṅantaṁ padam*'. That which ends in *sup* (case affix) or in *tiṅ* (tense affixes) is called a *pada* or inflected word.

[4]M.R. Kale, pp. 113-217; Chatterjee, pp. 30-44, 189-214.

the same 'role' and vice versa, the formal realization is ambiguous. Also, similar markers occur with all classes of nouns, irrespective of animate-inanimate differences when the agent or object functions are realized.[5]

Agent 'role' is expressed by a marker in active sentence,

Mong nāmlo = Mong got down (example no. 6, Appendix I)

Agent 'role' is expressed by marker II when the verb of the sentence occurs in a special aspect and sometimes with modal verb:

Jhunkāke jete hɔe (example no. 21, Appendix I)
= Jhunkā has to go. (Also see examples nos. 90, 96.)

Sometimes marker III with a nominal in the verb environment of *lāg- āch- hɔ-* (when these occur in impersonal form in a sentence), either affirmative or negative, may indicate agent or locative role of the nominal. For example:

Tār sukhe dukhe sɔmobhāb (example no. 89, Appendix I)
= His/her worries and ease same feeling.

If this Bengali sentence is translated as:

(1) He does not move in sorrow or in happiness;
(2) The same feeling occurs to him either in sorrow or in happiness;

then *he* in (1) and *to him* in (2) can be labelled as agent (including experiencer) and locative respectively.

Similar to agent the object (dative) occurs with I and II frequently in active sentences. For instance:

moŋger soŋkhipto jɔbāb (example no. 16, Appendix I)
Mong's precise answer (this is) Mong's precise answer.

The Bengali expressions with *r* in the above examples can be labelled as locative (tār) and modifier (moŋger). But if paraphrased as (1) and the other example as 'This is Mong's precise answer', then expression *tār* and the entire expression *moŋger jobāb* can be labelled as agent and object respectively. We shall discuss this problem in Chapters II and III.

Examples of this kind are to be found in the Appendix nos. 19, 25, 30, 35, 38, 40-44, 46-51, 58-61, 63-65, 67, 88, 92-95, 97, 98 and 100.

Instrumental expressed by IV is observed in example nos. 75, 78 and 79. Locative expressed by IV is observed in example nos. 72, 77, 80 and 83. Forms occurring with marker III may represent agent. In that case the noun is usually an animate noun. Forms occurring with the marker III

[5]Chatterjee, pp. 89-90.

may represent locative, and in that case the nominal is inanimate and usually indicates place, thing, etc. The dative takes the same marker as the object does, i.e. marker II. The ablative occurs with marker IV. Agent is expressed by V in passive only. Object, instrumental, locative, ablative, cause, source, benefactive, dative are expressed by V in active sentence construction. Ample expressions are to be found with marker V which expresses the above-mentioned 'roles' (see Appendix).

Marker V can express various meanings. For instance, nominals with *theke* can be interpreted as 'from', 'in', 'by' in different sentences. It depends on the meaning of the whole sentence and, in particular, the meaning of the nominal. It should be noted that when no reference is quoted, examples are not found in the corpus but constructed by the author.

Other postpositional markers such as *die* 'by', 'with', *jonne* 'for', 'because', *kāche* 'from', 'to', 'near', *moddhe* 'in', *sɔŋge* 'with', 'accompanied by', *kore* 'by', 'with', etc. express, according to different contexts, such meanings which may be termed as purposive, benefactive, reason, result, sociative and so on. It is often found that the marker indicates benefactive meaning if it is an animate noun. On the contrary, it indicates purpose or motive or cause if the nominal is inanimate in feature. Traditionally, in a similar context and with the same verb the function of the nominals would be considered the same in grammar. Otherwise, confusion with grammar and reality will arise.

In other words, if an animate noun occurs in the same context with same marker and same verb as an inanimate noun does, then both the animate and inanimate nouns can be assigned the same role.

Although we think aspects such as time, direction, location, etc. are to be included in the concept of locative 'role', it is not clear whether condition or state should be included in it or meanings such as 'between them', 'in relation to', 'in such condition', 'in such state', etc. should be included in the notion of 'role' at all.

There is an additional problem: nominals with homophonous morphemes such as *kore*, *nie*, etc. often constitute compound verbs (i.e. a nominal +auxiliary, viz. *lobh-kore*, 'being greedy', *jog-kore*, 'having added'). Sometimes such forms are manner adverbial. Sometimes the homophonous morphemes may be explained as non-finite verb forms. It depends on the other lexical items which occur in the sentence. It also depends on the syntactic unit divisions. The form which we call *pada* is a lexical morpheme plus another morpheme or marker which expresses the grammatical meaning of the form in a given sentence. Also there is a contextual enviornment which is relevant. In other words, the contextual environment—the internal juncture of the whole utterance—is important.

[1.5] For correct interpretation of a given sentence or period or utterance, one has to know the meaning of the items occurring in the structure and their related meaning. We believe that the grammatical 'roles' such as agent, object, etc. are basically identified on the basis of related meaning of the segments occurring in a given sentence. It will be argued later that the 'role' concept in the traditional grammar is not based on word semantics. Also, the types of grammatical relation, which are called syntactic function of a nominal, cannot merely be recognized from the form.

In traditional grammar, both Indian and Western, a few basic semantic relations are noted, which are commonly known as 'case' in Western grammar and *kāraka* in Indian tradition. In principle *kāraka* which, we consider, corresponds to the term 'case' is a complex notion. We prefer to define it from the viewpoint of both form and function (meaning). Lyons considers case as a morphosyntactic category.[6] Features like noun endings and prosodeme (intonation, unit division in utterance) are to be looked at.

To show the formal realization of various 'roles', which we consider as corresponding to the term *kāraka* in Bengali, we have concentrated on the meaning, expression and unit division. It is assumed that the expression itself provides relevant information for correct interpretation of a given sentence. Overt marker to the categories, agreement between the categories and the class of lexemes, determine their semantic and syntactic function.

[1.6] The 'forms' are established on the basis of modifications to the nominal. In English, the 'case-forms' are established on the basis of modifications to the noun.[7] The 'forms' in Bengali may be called 'case forms', although we prefer to call them *pada*.

The 'role' may be expressed by overt markers with the noun, i.e. inflexion, or preposition/postposition. In other words, different inflexional morphemes and other markers, such as preposition or postposition, to the noun (including expanded expression) constitute certain 'case forms'. Thus phonetic features may be important to establish a given case, and in some cases a zero marker may constitute a case.

Usually, in various languages, not all classes of nouns occur with the different case morphemes, nor does every language have the same number of markers for case. For instance, in Latin 'case forms' are nominative, accusative, dative, ablative, genitive and vocative. In Sanskrit, we find a similar system of six cases. However, vocative and genitive are not considered cases. Vocative is not related to the verb. The genitive behaves like an adjective since it is related to another noun and not to the verb.[8] Consequently, the definition of case has traditionally not been the same in Latin and in Sanskrit.

[6]John Lyons, *Introduction to Theoretical Linguistics*, pp. 289-302.

[7]C. T. Onions, *Modern English Syntax*, pp. 80-83.

[8]V. N. Misra, *The Descriptive Technique of Pāṇini*, pp. 116-17.

De Groot is of the opinion:

'...the vocative is a case like any other case, because it is in complementary syntagmatic distribution with other cases. A given noun in a sentence is either a nominative or genitive or a vocative, etc. but never two cases at the same time. Complementary syntagmatic distribution is part of the definition of any member of any inflexional category such as number, tense, mood, etc. There is no reason to say that in the case system, the vocative is 'on a different level' from the other cases....'[9]

De Groot's argument seems inadequate. Complementary distribution alone is not enough, as one needs some kind of similarity between the units in complementary distribution.

In Sanskrit grammar, *kāraka* relationships are considered to be of six types.[10] And these are expressed in morphological markers. Postpositions (postpositional markers) can also express *kāraka* relation.

Kāraka Relationship	Nominal Endings[11]			
	Singular		*Dual*	*Plural*
Sanskrit	Mas. Fem.	Nu.	Mas. Fem. Nu.	
(1) *kartṛ* (agent)	*-s*	*m*	*-au*	*-as -i*
(2) *karma* (goal, object)	*-am*			
(3) *karaṇa* (instrument)	*-ā*		*bhyām*	*bhis*
(4) *adhikaraṇa* (locative)	*-ī*		*-os*	*-su*
(5) *sampradāna* (indirect goal, dative, benefactive)	*-e*		*bhyām*	*bhyas*
(6) *apādāna* (ablation)	*-as*		*-bhyām*	*bhyas*

Bengali

kartṛ	marker I
karma/sampradāna	marker II, III
apādana/adhikaraṇa/karaṇa	marker IV

Genitive, which is considered as a relation other than a *kāraka*, has marker III (i.e. *-r*, *-er*, *-der*).

In Bengali we have four distinct case markers plus postpositions. *Kāraka* relationships are of six types as they are in Sanskrit.

In English we find genitive case markers and pronominal forms for different cases. The markers 's and as in man's, ladies', etc. are used in written language. In spoken language /s/, /z/, /iz/ correspond to 's and ϕ to apostrophe.

[9]De Groot, *Classification of Cases and Uses of Cases*, p. 187-94.

[10]Misra, pp. 116-17.

[11]A. A. Macdonell, *A Sanskrit Grammar for Students*, p. 33. See P. V. Naganatha Sastry, *Vaiyākoraṇa Siddhānta Kaumudī*, pp. 116-28 and M.R. Kale, pp. 34.

In English, prepositional phrases often have a function similar to 'roles'.[12]

The case paradigm of the noun-pronoun is usually found in its two dimensions of number and gender, and concomitantly it expresses the 'role'. The whole paradigm (i.e. different case markers) varies from language to language. In Bengali no gender distinction is made either in case markers or in the verb concord. Also, there are only four types of morphological markers to express the different 'roles'.

[1.7] The 'roles' are established on the basis of the syntagmatic relation of categories, i.e what function the particular nominal expression plays in a given syntactic environment is considered. A nominal expression like a noun with ending (morphological marker) or postposition can serve syntactic functions like subject-predicate or semantic functions such as agent, goal, etc. In the latter case we would prefer to use the term 'role'. 'Roles' may be comparatively universal.

Each form such as nominative, accusative, etc. has a function. Whether we look at the isolated forms, i.e. the whole case paradigm or the forms in a given syntactic environment, i.e. in a sentence, the nominal expressions express certain meanings.

It is obvious that the special formal expression, i.e. the inflexion and postposition, cannot be universal features of all languages. The functions ('roles') played by the expressions or the meaning expressed by the nominals, on the other hand, appears to be more or less the same in all languages.

The particular nominal expression considered as an abstract unit can be described as to the 'roles' it can fill within a sentence. This may be referred to as the meaning of a particular case. A case form as a set or abstraction (abstract unit) has many meanings and each meaning generally has a relation to a verb. The function of a case form, seen as an item, is a realization in a given syntactic environment.

As has been pointed out, 'role' of the case form is conditioned by the relation to other syntagms, often to the verb, i.e. the case form which is involved with the verb.[13]

The syntagmatic relation is bidirectional, i.e.

noun←———→*verb*

The meaning of the syntagmatically related categories is determined by the reciprocal influence of the categories themselves. In other words, the nominal expression signals the concord on the verb, and through the verb, concord features such as person of the nominal expression and its relative functions in a given environment are understood.

[12]Otto Jesperson, *Analytic Synatax*; *Essentials of English Grammar*, p. 138.

[13]C. J. Fillmore, *Lexical Entries for Verbs: Foundations of Language*, pp. 12-18.

[1.7.1] If the term 'case' is defined in such a way that both morphophonetic and syntactic features of noun are considered, then vocative may be considered as a 'case' in some languages.

In Latin, vocative has a separate marker, whereas in English there is no such marker. Vocative case form is paradigmatically related to other case forms in Latin. In English and Bengali there in no vocative case form.

From the point of view of certain features, one may say that, though the term of address has no special case marker either in English or in Bengali, it expresses a kind of attitude of the speaker.[14] This attitude in every language is probably expressed in a particular type of intonation. This prosodic feature may be taken into consideration to establish that all languages have the vocative 'role'.

However, in our analysis, we identify 'role' (or *kāraka*) on the basis of syntagmatic relation the nominal has to the verb. So, as has been said, we cannot include 'cases' like vocative and genitive which have no direct relation to the verb syntagm.

[1.7.2] From the point of view of the function, a nominal with marker I in Bengali can express: (*a*) agent or object function (semantic level); (*b*) exsubject or predicate function (syntactic level). For instance, a Bengali pression like

oi phulṭā	cā-i
that flower (obj)	want (I/we).

This example may be interpreted in the following ways:

(*a*) I/we want *that particular flower*;
(*b*) *That particular flower* is wanted.

The predicate and object functions in I (*a*), subject and object functions I (*b*) are understood from the meaning of the whole sentence. Therefore, we think that, even though the form can express (*a*) and (*b*) functions, it cannot signal any unless it occurs in a sentence with NU, VU.

Considering both syntactic and semantic points of view, when it is found that a particular form in Bengali can occur as subject in a sentence and can function either as agent or object, then one can attribute the traditional term 'nominative' to that nominal expression. We have seen the object function of the expression *phulṭā*. Let us see the agent function of the same:

phulṭā	*phuṭeche*
the flower	blossoms

We shall define the 'role' agent later. At this point, there is no reason to differentiate between nominative in the just-mentioned example and accusa-

[14]Groot, pp. 187-94.

tive in the other, even though the same form occurs as agent and object. On many occasions in many languages, there is no reason to make a difference between nominative and accusative or accusative and dative forms, since there are no separate markers. In this situation, it is preferable to use the term 'base form'.

For instance, in English sentences like

The boy did it
I gave *the boy* some money

the form *the boy* can be taken as the base form. In this sense, it is rather artificial to make differences such as nominative, accusative, dative, etc. (in pronominal forms, however, there are differences in English).

Some Bengali sentences may be considered:

āmi rām-ke jāni
I Ram know
(proper name)

=I know Ram (proper name occurs with-*ke* marker)

rām boi cāe
Ram book wants
=Ram wants a book (there is no marker on the object *boi*)

We suggest that a zero marker may be posited on the form *boi*. Thus, it may be written as *boi*ϕ. The base marker (ϕ) can signal: (*a*) syntactic items such as subject, direct object; and (*b*) roles. A nominal expression with *-ke* can be called accusative when it shows the function of object, goal, target, etc. In this situation, the nominal is to be considered influenced or affected by the verb but not vice versa.[15]

A nominal expression is to be considered locative when it expresses temporal, spatial, locational, directional significance of the verb.

A nominal expression is considered genitive when it expresses a relation with another nominal. It bears no direct connection to the verb (except certain verbs to be discussed later which occur only in impersonal form).

A nominal expression is considered instrumental when it expresses the effective means of a process.

A nominal expression is considered ablative when it indicates origin, source, or cause of a process.

Thus, the inflected form (nominal) expresses complex ideas and the function of that form indicates a relation mostly with the verb. An inflected form (a case form) in isolation indicates its inherent potentialities.

[15]Obviously the object nominal is indicated by the transitive verb.

However, I am tempted to equate (partially) the modern notion of 'role' with the functional aspect of *kāraka*. I am also tempted to use a few terms from Sanskrit (Bengali) grammar, such as : *kartṛ* = agent (subject); *karma* = direct or indirect object; *karaṇa* = instrument; *sampradāna* = dative, benefactive; *apādāna* = ablative, cause; and *adhikaraṇa* = locative.[16]

We think that it would be appropriate to the language under discussion to retain the traditional terminology.

A Bengali scholar, Prof. Ramendra Sundar, remarks that there should be assigned three forms (case forms) in Bengali, considering the distinct markers on the nominal. The nominative and accusative have distinct markers, and other cases are expressed by a common marker like *-e*/*-te*. Therefore only three case forms are to be distinguished: nominative, accusative and a common case.[17]

I have posited five markers (forms), because it is obvious from our observation that postpositions serve similar functions. We found also that one marker may express different 'roles', and different markers may signal the same 'role'. Thus, the determining criteria cannot be the markers only. Both in Sanskrit and in Bengali grammars, the *kāraka* is basically determined by the relation of the nominal and the verb in a sentence.

Kale remarks : 'The only portion of syntax treated separately in Sanskrit grammar is the *kārakaprakaraṇa* or the chapter on Government. *Kāraka* is the name given to the relation subsisting between a noun and a verb in a sentence.'[18]

Prof. Chatterjee says that the *kāraka* relationship is to be understood as the semantic relationship (at the sentence level). Therefore it depends how one interprets a given sentence. On the one hand, different 'roles' could be assigned to a particular nominal or nominal group if a sentence is interpreted differently. On the other hand, one may interpret sentences in such ways that there is more than one-to-one correspondence between meaning and form, and the same 'role' may be assigned in consideration of the form.[19]

A particular syntactic function of a form may be determined in different ways in different languages. In English, it is often the position in the sentence whereas in Sanskrit, Bengali, and other Indian languages cases determine the syntactic function.

Particularly the syntagmatic relation and the forms themselves indicate which nominal is to be considered as the subject and which as the object. The semantic function of a particular case form in understood by the interpretation of the whole sentence. We suggest that the term 'function' could be

[16]Chatterjee, p. 83; Misra, pp. 116-17.

[17]Chatterjee, pp. 102-3.

[18]Kale, p. 475.

[19]See Chatterjee, p. 83. The definition is translated by the author. The term 'role' is used here instead of the term 'case'.

equated with the term 'role'. Notionally, these two seem equivalent. If we consider 'role' as a certain kind of meaning expressed by a case form in reference to its syntagmatic relation with other categories, it may be of advantage to use the term '*role*' instead of case function. In English '*role*' is assigned to a certain category which is usually non-inflected but may be preceded by a preposition in the environment of certain types of verb. In Bengali '*role*' is assigned to the case form (category with inflexion), it may also be followed by a postposition in the environment of certain type of verbs.

The situation may be presented as:

(1) If *x* occurs with *y*, *x* is in the role 1,
or *x* functions in some particular way;
(2) If *x* occurs with *z*, *x* is in the role 2,
or *x* functions in some particular way.

Moreover, the same form may play multiple 'roles', and the same 'role' may be expressed by different forms. For instance, a diagrammatical presentation would be:

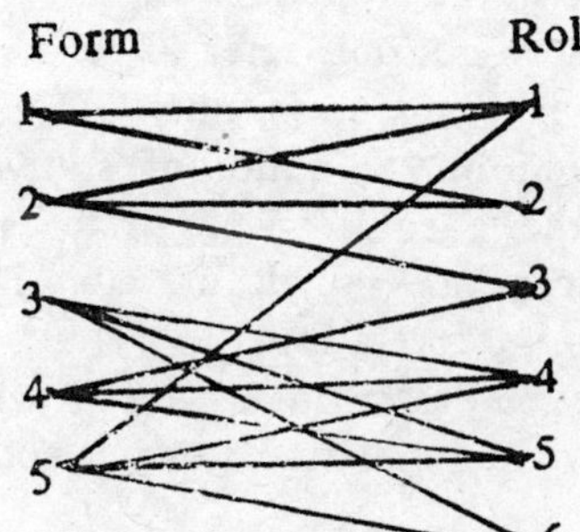

We have already mentioned five types of forms and the six basic 'roles'. The above diagram shows the related manifestation.

The syntagmatic relation may be of two types: the noun or pronoun may be either related to a syntagma shorter than a sentence or to the whole sentence.

The vocative may be shown as forming the whole sentence. It is a term of address. Sometimes the noun in vocative has no following syntagmas; it constitutes a complete utterance.

The syntagmatic relations differ in the attitude implied and the process envisaged. In that sense, one can group together the vocative and genitive under the label *non-process group*, and all the other cases in the *process group* with their relative involvement in the process. Each case differs from each other in its type of relation to the process.

A detailed discussion on cases later on will show case forms and different types of verbs in various types of expressions with different cases. We shall see later that, although the arrangement of the syntagmas in a sentence is not fixed syntactically as it is in English; the order within a syntagm or phrase is rather fixed and consequently is of grammatical significance. The system of concatenation and the network of relationship of the syntagmas semantically significant.

The 'roles' (the semantic functions) played by different forms usually are: agent, object, instrument, cause, source, origin, location, dative, benefactive. Obviously, many more 'roles' can be set up in the environment of different verbs. Fillmore and Langendon have discussed some more 'roles' than these.[20] We think that it is possible to discuss 'roles' in terms of this limited number of basic varieties. We perfer to include dative and benefactive in one. Likewise cause or origin may be taken as one, and source may be included in locative. Semantic features that determine the behaviour of nouns in relation to the verb syntagm could be summed up in these few 'roles'.

One can say that the 'roles' of agent, object, cause, instrument are more directly involved in the action of the verb than locative. At least this is so in many examples provided in the Appendixes.

By the action of the verb we not only refer to 'action' verbs but to 'stative' verbs as well. Verbs like 'be', 'stay', 'grow', 'happen', 'love' or 'hate', etc. also express a type of action. The notion of 'stative' verbs is some sort of condition or state of the agent. It may refer to the physical and abstract processes like perception, cognition, etc. This depends on the language concerned and its interpretation.

The 'role' of agent may be described as who or which does something, who or which is directly involved or stimulates the action indicated by the verb in a sentence.

The objective 'role' signifies an animate or an inanimate object which is affected, connected or indicated by the verb in relation to the agent. The locative is assigned to the relation of time, space, location, existence, etc. The cause 'role' prompts any action resulting in physical or metaphysical consequences. The notion of instrumental is semantically connected with effective animate or inanimate means. These semantic functions of cases may generally be derived from the syntagmatic relationship between the categories in a sentence. And this relationship determines, to an important extent, the syntactic function of the constituents in a sentence. Therefore, cases play a crucial role in the language under discussion.

In Bengali, Sanskrit and other Indian languages, the case forms and their involvement with the verb in a sentence determine (as has been discussed above) which nominal expressions should be considered as the agent,

[20]Fillmore, *Case for Case*, p. 32; Langendon. *Essentials of English Grammar*, p. 86.

target, instrument, etc. And the functions such as sociative, possessive are considered not as 'roles', but as adverbial (of manner) to the verb.

The expressions corresponding to *with me* and *to me* (*in relation to me*) are explained as a kind of modifier to the verb. As such they are adverbials.

Broadly speaking, in consideration of its syntactical behaviour the locative expression, may also be explained in the same way.

Eventually, we shall see that very often the syntactical subject and the semantic agent coincide in a sentence. And the 'roles' like locative, instrument, cause, etc. are never accepted as subject in Indian grammar.

This is probably one of the reasons for the Indian grammarians to stick to their principle of *kāraka relation* of the nominal expression in a given syntactic environment rather than defining the subject and predicate.

[1.8] In many languages inflexion is an important device to establish various kinds of grammatical relations among the items in a smaller as well as a bigger syntactic unit such as phrase, sentence. In Bengali

(1) Some 'roles' are distinguished morphologically and the markers used are constant for all nouns and pronouns.
(2) Other 'roles' are interdependent with definiteness, plurality, etc.
(3) Under certain circumstances some of the cases referred to in (1) or (2) may also be expressed by postpositions.

The morphemes like *upore, moddhe, bhitore, kāche, kore, theke, die*, etc. are not bound morphemes like *-e, -ke, -te,* and *-er*. The postpositional morphemes and *-er* can express case relation as well as other meanings. The postpositions like *moddhe, kāche, theke die*, etc. can also occur independently. Occurring with a nominal, they can express cases such as 'locative', 'ablative', 'instrumental', etc. They may also refer to certain other meanings and can occur in certain other constructions:

kāche kāche 'nearby',
theke theke 'sometimes'; 'in some interval'; 'constantly staying in';
moddhe moddhe 'occasionally'; 'leisurely';
kore 'having done'; 'as a result';
die 'having given'.

Considering the above-mentioned occurrences and meanings of the morphemes, we think that these morphemes are different from *-e, -te, -ke*, etc. But when both (the comparatively bigger like *theke*, etc. and smaller like *e, te*, etc.) occur with nominals and express 'roles' they are to be considered as similar.

Usually, in an English sentence except possessive-genitive, the noun shows its different relations by:[21] (*i*) its relevant position in the sentence; and (*ii*) the preposition which precedes the noun. It is thus evident that 'roles' are manifested in the following four different ways in English, Bengali and other Indian languages (both Indo-Aryan and Dravidian):

(*a*) By a distinct marker;

(*b*) By the position of the words;

(*c*) By a preceding preposition or following postposition;

(*d*) By classes of nouns.

It should be noted that the distinct markers on the nominals (noun inflexions) in Bengali can manifest role and such features of noun as plurality, definiteness, etc.

1.9 Some markers express meanings (functions) such as: definiteness, number, coordination, category changing indication, comparison and quality and quantity. We call these markers amalgams, because they express, those above-mentioned functions and the roles (i.e. the nominal is to be considered as a case form). When markers *-ṭā/-ṭi-khānā/-khāni*, *-gāchā/-gāchi*, *-ṭu/-ṭuku*, (*n/ni*) occur with a noun, they indicate singularity and definiteness.

Any semantic class of nouns with any of these markers can constitute Form I. The occurrence of the suffix *-ṭā/-ṭi* with animate nouns is not restricted.

However, when any mass noun is used in its unrestricted meaning, the suffix *-tā* generally appears with the nominal, which indicates definiteness but not singularity.

e deser *māṭi-ṭā* *bɔṛo* *sukno*
This country of the soil very dry
= The soil of this country is very dry.

When the suffix appears with an animate noun, it may either express an attitude of affection and tenderness or indifference and disrespect, depending on the contexts as well as the presence of certain lexemes and prosodic features like intonation. For instance:

lok-ṭā beś
the man (is) nice

Here *-ṭā* with the human noun can express either regard or disragard depending on the intonation.

The markers like *-ṭuku/-ṭuk*, *-ṭukun/ṭukuni* can be used with human

[21]Not to be confused with English pronouns which have different forms (to show different cases) for nominative, oblique, possessive-genitive.

inanimate and abstract nouns where any of these suffixes used with human nouns, in addition to definiteness, expresses either affection or appreciation.

These markers, with material nouns, indicate less quantity. For instance:

dudh-ṭuku the milk (*ṭuku* here implies small quantity)
cini ṭukuni the sugar (*ṭukuni* here implies little amount)

Suffixes like *ṭuku/-ṭuk* or *ṭu*, etc. can also occur with the numeral noun *ek* (one), in Bengali *æk* (with a context conditional assimilation) viz. *ek-ṭu/ek-ṭuku/ek-ṭu-khāni*—'a little', 'small qunantity'. In spoken Bengali *æk-rotti/æk-phoṭā*, etc. are commonly used in the same context. While *æk-ṭā/ek-ṭi* ('the one', 'that one', 'the particular one') are commonly used in both colloquial and literary Bengali.

In addition to definiteness, these expressions as a whole, can behave like adjectives, if they are followed by other nouns, e.g. *æk-ṭā boi* 'one book'. Otherwise the expression *æk-ṭā* can be considered as a caseform in N.P. and V.P. constructions.

æk-ṭā *æk-ṭā-kore* *rākho*
one after another keep
= keep one by one.

An adjective can be used as a noun when it is combined with suffixeg which indicate definiteness.[22] Thus it becomes a caseform.

ɔnek-ṭā *phaelā gælo*
much was wasted

Markers like *khānā/khāni, gācha/gāchi* are usually used with inanimate, and abstract nouns, viz.[23]

cithi-khānā 'the letter'
bhāb-khānā 'the attitude'
mālā-gāchi 'the garland'

These suffixes also occur with pronouns such as *ei-khānā* 'this one', *oigāchi/gācha* 'that one', etc. The interrogatives such as *kɔto* 'how much/how many', *kon* 'which', etc. can take most of the above-mentioned markers, although in some cases these occur as obligatory morphemes between the nominal and the 'role' marker. For instance:

kon-khānā-theke 'from which one'
kon-ṭā-te 'in which one'

Relative pronouns like *se* 'that', *tɔto* 'that much', *je* 'which (who)', etc. and a pronoun like *sɔb* 'all', take the above-mentioned markers and express

[22]Chatterjee, p. 280. [23]Chatterjee, p. 280.

definiteness. When these pronouns, with their suffixes precede other nominals, they behave like adjectives.[24] Otherwise, they denote definiteness and constitute caseforms like nominative and accusative, and function like agent and object. If other 'role' marker is added to them, they may express another 'role' as well, e.g.:

> *kon* 'which'; *kon-ṭā* 'which one';
> *kon-ṭā-ke* 'to which one'; *kon-ṭā-te* 'in which one';
> *kon-tā-r* 'of which one', etc.

These suffixes *ṭā*, *ṭi*, *khānā*, *khāni*, can also occur with any numeral noun and can be translated into English as 'piece(s) of', 'definitely that (those)', etc. For instance:

> *æk-khānā* 'one' (particular)
> *du-khānā* 'two' (particular)
> *æk-so-khānā* 'one hundred'

This (*khānā/khāni*) combination only refers to non-human entities. If an animate noun is referred to, the suffix *ṭā* or *jɔn* would occur, e.g.:

> *æk-ṭā-lok* 'one man'
> *æk-tā goru* 'one cow'
> *p̃āc-jon lok* 'five men/persons'

A similar type of expression occurs with human pronominals:

> Interrogative : *kɔjon/kɔtojon* 'how many (men)'
> *kon jon* 'who (that particular one)'
> Indefinite : *kɔek jon* 'a few'

These expressions can constitute caseforms and express 'roles'. If numeral nouns with such markers, either precede or follow a noun, they behave like an attributive to that noun; otherwise they constitute caseforms.

If a syntagm, with a marker, precedes or follows or if it is preceded or followed by another nominal, it can function as an attribute within the unit.

[1.9.1] Plurality is indicated in Bengali in four different ways:

(*a*) by morphological markers;
(*b*) by markers other than morphological markers, including numeral nouns;
(*c*) by repetition either of the noun or the attributive to the noun;
(*d*) by certain caseforms in certain contexts.

[24]Chatterjee, pp. 124-32.

(*a*) The morphological markers expressing plurality are the following:

> *-rā, -der, -gulā/-guli/-gulo, -bɔrgo,*
> *-brindo, -rāji, -āboli, -cɔe/-nicɔe, -dām*[25]

These suffixes are commonly used in both colloquial and literary Bengali. The suffixes *-rā. -der, -gulā/-guli/-gulo* are used both colloquially and literarily, but *-bɔrgo, -brindo, -rāji,* etc. are used only in literature.

The suffixes *rā, -der, -gulo/-guli, -brindo, -bɔrgo* occur with animate nouns. Except in certain styles, *-rā* and *-der* occur with noun having '+human' feature.

Expressions with *-der* constitute caseforms like genitive, dative, accusative. The suffixes *-rā* and *-der* can occur with neuter nouns in literary language. Expressions like the following can be found in poetry :

> *tārā-rā/tārā-der*
> stars stars of

The suffixes *-bɔrgo* and *-brindo* occur with a human noun which has the feature '+ common'. For instance :

> *bondhu-bɔrgo* 'the friends'
> *chāttro-brindo* 'the students'

The occurrence of *-gulā/-guli* is not restricted to animate nouns only. It can occur with inanimate and abstract nouns. It also occurs with interrogative, demonstrative, quantitative, and relative pronouns and these expressions can constitute caseforms.

Suffixes like *-gulā/-guli* can also constitute a caseform in combination with other plural adjectives, e.g.:

> *ɔnek-guli* *āche*
> many (plural suffix) exist
> = There are many.

The English expressions such as *all students, all chairs,* etc. may be compared with the following Bengali expressions:

> *sɔb chāttre-rā*
> all students
> *sɔb-guli ceār*
> all (plural marker) chair(s)

[25]Traditionally in Bengali grammar only *-rā/-der, -gulā/-guli* are considered as morphological markers and bound morphemes. It is found that the other plural markers such as *-rāji, -āboli, -bɔrgo, brindo,* etc. never occur independently. As a matter of fact they are also bound morphemes. This is a good reason for calling them suffix and to consider them similar to the other markers like *-rā, -der,* etc.

Where *all* corresponds to *sɔb* in an attributive sense, and nevertheless, the noun is marked for plurality. The difference between the expressions like *sɔb chāttro* and *sɔb chātre-rā* (all students) is that in the expression *sɔb chāttre-rā* the *sɔb* element denotes definiteness and *-ra* plurality, whereas in the other expression, *sɔb* indicates plurality and there is no other plural marker (morphological).

Where plurality is indicated by a numeral noun, no other plural affixation occurs with the following nominal:

pā̃c-ṭi āŋul = five fingers
five fingers

It should be noted here that by the term 'plurality' we also understand quantity in the case of mass nouns. Words like *ɔnek, sɔb, sɔmosto, sɔkol. kɔto, æto*, etc. when they occur before a nominal, which has one of the feature (*+mass, −count, +abstract*), indicate the meaning *much, all*, etc. (that is to say quantitative attribute).

We consider these words as plural attributives to the noun. They can either occur independently or in combination with morphological markers like *-rā/-der* and *-gulā/-guli*. The restrictions of different classes or nouns have been indicated in the previous paragraph.

The plural suffixes like *-raji, -āboli, -dām, -grām*, etc. occur with inanimate nouns, which have the feature '+count'.

(*b*) Attributes like *sɔb, sɔkol, ɔnek, sɔmudɔe somūho*, etc. are independent adjectives which indicate plurality. These adjectives except *somūho* can precede a noun and denote its plurality without a special plural marker on the noun. The morphome *somūho* follows the nominal and indicates plurality.

Adjectives like *sɔb, sɔkol, ɔnek*, can constitute caseforms with the morphological markers, *-ai, -e, -ke*, etc. Another type of plural attributes to the noun are independent nouns like *dɔl, mālā, kul, jutho, sreni, mɔhɔl, pāl, mondoli*, and adjectives like *rāsi, punjo, -gādā*, etc. Generally these words have meanings such as group, flock, bunch, heap, etc. They occur after a noun and indicate plurality of the nominal. Some of them can occur independently such as:

jutho bɔddho	*sreni bɔddho*
in groups	in rows

When they are in duplicated form some of them can precede the nominal and indicate its plurality.

rāsi rāsi phul
heaps of flower(s)
punjo punjo megh = layer after layer of cloud(s)

Usually these morphemes follow the nouns :

Jutho
hosti jutho = group of elephants
elephant group

Sreni
toru sreni = the rows of trees
tree row
monusso-sreni = the rows of men
man row

kul, pāl, dɔl
rɔmoni-kul = the women
woman group
chel-er-dɔl = the boys
boy of group
goru-r-pāl = the cows
cow of group

mɔhɔl and *moṇḍoli*
bondhu-mɔhɔl = the circle of friends
friend circle
poṇḍit mondoli = the group of scholars
scholar group

Among these, *pāl, dɔl* occur with inflected nominals while others do not.

The numeral noun (æk, dui, etc.) acts as determiner when it precedes the nominal, e.g.:

æk-gochā phul = a bunch of flowers
one bunch flower
pā̃c-gācha cuṛi = five pieces of bangles
five piece bangle

(*c*) Repetition of nouns or adjectives denote plurality. A noun can be repeated and express plurality with or without morphological markers:

either *ghɔr ghɔr* *ɔsukh*
house house illness
= in every house there is (illness)
disease
or *ghɔre ghɔre ɔsukh*

Reduplication in nominal expressions can denote plurality and location, whereas reduplication in adjective expressions (attributes) only indicates plurality of the following nominal:

bɔṛo bɔṛo ām
big big mango(es)

(*d*) When an adjective is used as a noun in a sentence, it indicates plurality.

ɔsɔt	*bissāsjoggo*	*nɔe*
dishonest	worthy to believe	not

= Dishonest (people) are not trustworthy

No plural marker can be added to the material nouns which cannot be counted. A word denoting the meaning 'all', 'much', etc. may precede the type of material noun, just mentioned, to indicate quantity. Material nouns such as *māṭi* 'soil', *jɔl* 'water', can occur with words like *ɔnekṭā* 'a good quantity', *sɔb/sɔbṭā* 'all', etc.

Plural expressions mentioned so far and the material nominal expressions just mentioned can constitute caseforms. Pluralization, by reduplication of noun, often coincides with locative.

[1.9.2] Forms with *-e/-te* marker express 'roles' like *goal*, *locative*, *instrumental* and *sociative*. When two nominals appear with this marker; the expression indicates plurality and coordination. For instance:

tomā-te-āmā-te	*kāj-ṭā korbo*
you (and) me	the work will finish

= you and I will do the work

The expression *tomā-te-āmā-te* is a coordinated subject with agent role.

When nominal expressions modify a verb in a sentence, those expressions should be considered as adverbials; automatically, they could be considered as a part of the predicate.

Adverbial expressions usually take the marker *-e/-te*, *-theke*, *-bhābe*, etc. For instance, if English expressions like happily, anxiously, spontaneously, etc. are translated into Bengali, the corresponding expressions would be:

sukh-e 'happily'
utkonṭhā-e } 'anxiously'
udbeg-e }
āpnā-theke } 'spontaneously'
sɔtosphurto-bhābe }

[1.9.3] Morphemes, which are bigger than a morphological marker and which have homophonous counterparts as lexes, and which express 'roles' and form adverbials occurring with nominals, are to be called postpositions. We have already said that, when they express 'roles' or form adverbials, they are bound elements.

The Morphome *theke/cee* expresses comparison in the example below:

se *āmār-theke/-cee* choṭo
he/she me than young
= He/she is younger than I.

Traditionally, considering their independent occurrence as lexes elsewhere, morphemes such as *jodi* 'if', *theke* 'from', etc. are called indeclinables. These are indeclinables, because they are neither segmental nor inflectional.[26]

The morpheme *sɔŋge* can signal the meaning 'with', 'between', 'among', if it occurs between two nouns:

āmār sɔŋge tomār...
me with you
= Between you and me
or *āmāder sɔŋge tomāder*
= Among us.

The morpheme can be used as noun, if it occurs without being preceded or followed by a noun:

sɔŋge thāko
company keep

The morpheme may be used as an adverbial:

sɔŋge sɔŋge kɔro
immediately do

[1.9.4] Adjectives behave like nouns when they appear with definite markers and determiners. For example, lexemes such as *ɔnek* 'many/much', *ɔrdhek* 'half', *mondo* 'bad', *chẽrā* 'torn', etc. can take the markers *-ṭā/-ṭi*, *-khānā/khāni* or *gulā/guli*, etc. and can constitute a caseform. Furthermore, they can take other case markers like *-ke*, *-te*, *-r*. For instance:

ɔnek-ṭā 'that much'
(in different context, it may mean 'to some extent' 'enough', etc.)
ɔnek-ṭā-r moddhe 'that much of'
ɔnekguli-r moddhe 'among that many',
'among them'

If the adjective, with definite marker is either preceded or followed by another adjective, then it cannot constitute a caseform. Reduplication of

[26]Chatterjee, p. 49, 51; Kale, pp. 223-35.

adjectives signals manner, if it occurs with an infinite form of verb, e.g. :

besi besi kore dāo
(in) much quantity give

[1.9.5] A sequence of syllables can be interpreted differently, if they are differently grouped together. In other words, an expression like the following can have two meanings:

duniā ṭākār bɔs

A distinct stress can fall either on the expression *ṭā* or on *kār*. Thus the unit division would be as follows:

(1) *duniā* *ṭākār bɔs*
(the) world the money of being controlled
= The money controls the world.
(2) *duniā-ṭā* *kār bɔs*
the world whose control?
= (under) whose control (is) the world?

From the examples given so for, it may be noted that the interpretation of a sentence depends, to some extent, on the context. The context can also indicate the unit division, the sequence of syllables which should go together and form a unit. For instance:

se *āmā-der nie jāe*
he/she us (usually) take/took

Either *niejāe* can be taken as a single verb unit or *nie* may be a postpositional marker to the noun *amā-der*. Thus, either the sentence is to be interpreted as 'he used to take us'/'he usually took us' or 'he usually goes with us'. If it is a part of a narrative, the tense expressed by verb form *jāe*, would be considered as historical past. The historical past tense form is often the same as with the present indefinite form. Considering this situation, we assume that for correct interpretation of a sentence, in addition to the marked feature, i.e. overt markers, the context, individual lexemes, the prosodic features (juncture, etc.) are equally important. In our investigation, we shall see later that to study the syntagmatic relations in a given sentence is no less important.

We assume that the necessary information provided by the sentence and the intuition of the native speaker are to be considered for grammatical analysis and interpretation of any given sentence of a language and no 'deep structure' will be posited. On this assumption, we shall try to find out whether the subject of any individual sentence—both in active and passive is indicated by certain types of relations which determine the 'roles' of the nominal expression.

The function of subject, which a nominal expression, with a given verb, represents in a given sentence, is often determined by the semantic relation existing between the nominal and the verb. The semantic potentiality of the head nominal can be characterized in terms of voice category. A syntactic notion such as subject can be considered as having semantic functions as below:

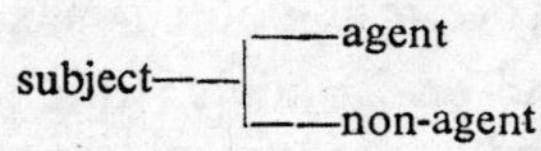

Further subsets may be represented in the following manner:

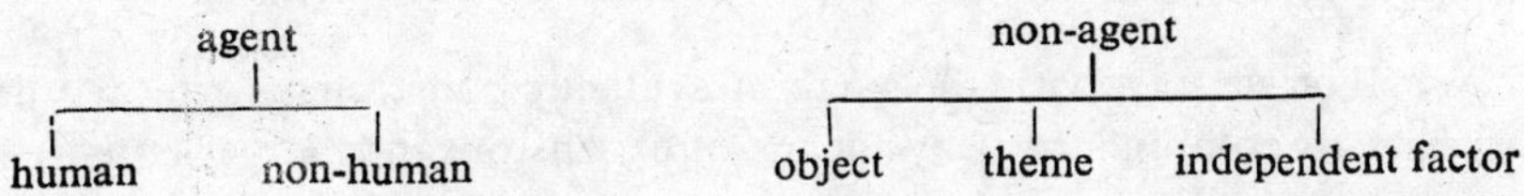

If one accepts this way of describing syntactic and semantic facts, one does not need the 'deep structure' hypothesis. We are neither going to use a generative transformational framework, nor are we taking the basic structure of sentence and their constituents to be modality plus propositions as suggested by Fillmore. We shall not follow 'case grammar' either. We shall deal with the nominal expression and its function. We shall, however, consider the verb as the pivot of the sentence assuming that the syntactic interpretation of nominal syntagms mostly depends on the semantic relation between the nominal syntagm and the verb. The positional occurrence of the subject in the initial position of a sentence or the positional occurrence of the predicate after the verb is not always maintained. In other words, the binary division of a sentence into subject and predicate which are mainly determined by their positions, may not always be relevant in Bengali and other Indian languages. We shall see that sometimes modifiers are discontinuous and the arrangement of syntagm is rather free in the language under discussion.

CHAPTER II

THE NOUN PHRASE

SIMPLE AND COMPLEX NOUN PHRASES

[2.0] In this chapter, we shall deal mainly with the structure of the nominal expressions and the Indian traditional concept of syntactic and semantic units.

In the first section, we shall treat the structure and the meaning.

[2.1] Whether we start with the smallest syntactic constituents, i.e. words, and proceed to combine them by means of expansions into larger constructions or we start with the largest constructions, i.e. sentences, and proceed to break them down by means of successive divisions into layers until the level of smallest constituents is reached, the ultimate aim is to establish structures, relations and functions of syntagms. Here syntagms mean the syntactic units within a sentence.

Following the Indian grammatical tradition,[1] we assume that the minimal syntactic constituents are usually inflected units which show mutual relation with each other and build up the sentence. These units are called *pada*. Syntactically *pada* presupposes both simple and compound units, and it implies nominal, verbal, adjectival and indeclinable words.

Only the nominal and verbal units can be inflected, in other words, these two categaries usually take markers or endings in Bengali. Here we are mainly concerned with the nominals. An inflected unit or a constituent in its minimal form is a lexeme, an obligatory stem optionally preceded or followed by affixes serving as the smallest constituent of a higher syntactic construction.

Where a syntactic constituent is not inflected, we posit a zero marker.

The term phrase corresponds to the term *pada* in its minimal form but not in its expanded form, i.e. when a phrase is understood as a syntactic constituent consisting of more than one word.

However, nominal compounds are considered to be a single form and a compound noun may be a *pada*. Kale remarks:

"In Sanskṛt simple words, whether substantives, adjectives, verbs or indeclinables, have the power of entering into combination with one another and forming what are called '*samāsas*', compound words or in short, compounds.

A compound thus formed may further be compounded with another

[1]Chatterjee, pp. 48-52.

simple or compound word and this again may become the member of a new compound.

In a compound, as a general rule, words are simply joined together, without any relation between the component parts being actually expressed, the whole compound word has the power to express the various relations that exist between the several parts. The last word only takes the case termination required by its grammatical position in a sentence, the remaining words (those ending in a consonant) generally assuming their crude forms before the consonantal case terminations; e.g.—राजन्+पुरुषः = राजपुरुषः, etc.

Final vowels or consonants (modified as mentioned above) of preceding members of compounds combine with the initial letters of the succeeding members according to the usual rules of *sandhi*'.[2]

The exceptions are also discussed by Kale. Considering the above remarks, we observe some differences in Bengali constructions where we find that the type of *sandhi* indicated here is not applicable, although there are many similarities between the *sandhi* rules of both the languages.

An interesting example can be taken from Prof. Chatterjee[3] where he shows the difference of *sandhi* between Bengali and Sanskrit. For instance:

(1) *gṛh-e* *āgɔta*
to the house arrived

This expression may be conveyed by a single word in Sanskrit, due to the internal *sandhi* or coalescence of the *e* and *a* vowels of the preceding and the following words, in Bengali the two should be considered as two separate entities or *padas*:

(2) *ɔdyɔ* *ɔpɔrāhṇhe*
today in the afternoon

In this example also, the two should be considered separate elements or *padas* in Bengali. It is contrary to the Sanskrit *sandhi* rule where these two should be *gṛhyāgata*, *ɔdyāpɔrāhṇhe* respectively.

So, in our analysis, we consider this kind of expression as a (complex) phrase, whereas in a combined form the elements can be considered as a single *pada* in Sanskrit.

Some nominal compounds are actually formed by discarding certain inflexional markers or by substituting some inflexional markers for a certain lexeme:

[2]M. Kale, p. 114. [3]Chatterjee, pp. 38-39.

(*a*) *rājā-r dɔrbār* *rājdɔrbār*
king's court king court

(*b*) *mukto-r mɔtɔ ɔkkhɔr* *muktākkhɔr*
pearl like writing pearl writing
(handwriting)

Fundamentally, there are two types of phrases: nominal phrases and verbal phrases. We have concentrated on the nominal phrase only. If we accept the concept of *pada*, there can be nominal *pada*, verbal *pada*, adjectival *pada*, and indeclinable *pada*[4] (*avyaya*). Some of the *padas* can be juxtaposed and by juxtaposition a syntactic unit can be expanded. In other words, an adjectival (an indeclinable word) can precede a noun and act as modifier. Therefore, a nominal *pada*, together with its immediate modifier or complement, may be bounded by a case marker. We call this a phrase which is a syntagm of a higher syntactic construction. It sometimes coincides with a simple sentence.

A nominal phrase, which we shall call nominal expression or nominal unit, is analysed in its smallest form as an obligatory stem optionally preceded or followed by affixes including case marker. The element which controls distribution and indicates the 'role' of the unit is the last element. It is characteristically a simple unit. For instance:

(3) *pākhiṭā-ke* *khā̃cā-e* *rākh-o*
the bird in the cage put

We consider that there are three phrases in this example. The markers *-ke*, *-e* indicate the 'roles' of the nominal units and *-o*, the agreement of the verbal unit with an unexpressed second person nominal unit. The 'roles' indicate the predicate distribution of the two nominal units.

Likewise, a complex unit may consist of two or more nouns. When all act as heads, it is considered as plural and all nouns take similar markers in that particular construction. There occurs a conjunction. For instance:

(4) *rām, śyām, jodu o modhu* *bāṛi* *jābe*
Ram, Syam, Jadu and Madhu home will go
(proper names)

A complex unit may also consist of one, two or more nouns with or without immediate modifiers; where one noun acts as the head and others stand in some sort of relationship to the head. Plurality is indicated by markers. For instance:

(5) *āmār meyer iskuler boi-guli* *tebile* *āche*
my daughter's school's books on the table are

[4]Ibid., pp. 49-51; Kale, pp. 223-237.

These modifiers normally occur before the head noun, but occurrence after or on both sides of the head is also found. These modifiers are attributes.

The *pada* division can incorporate this kind of discontinuous modifiers, like:

(6) *boi-guli* *ṭebile* *roeche*;
the books on the table exist
āmār *meyer* *iskuler*
my daughter's school (book)

Here, we think *boi-guli* and *āmār meyer iskuler* should be considered as separate phrases of which one acts as the complement of the other. In the above order of the segments, there would either occur a pause or an extra unit (*boi-guli/o-guli*) referring to the books. Expressions may be like the following :

(7) *meyeṭi* *āmār* *bier joggo*
the girl of mine marriageable age
hoeni *ækhono*
has not attained still now
is not yet
= My daughter has not yet attained
marriageable age.

The NU *meyeṭi āṃār* is an idiomatic use which is frequent in colloquial speech. The modifying element is occurring after the head noun, as:

(8) *toṃār* *ājkāl* *bɔṛo* *ṭākār* *ɔhoŋkār* *ār* *rūper* *bɔṛāi*
of you nowadays very of money proud and of beauty proud
hoeche
occurs
Money consciousness and beauty consciousness
appear to you recently
= You are very proud of wealth and beauty
nowadays.

The NU *tomār* and *bɔṛo ṭākār ɔhonkār ār rūper bɔṛāi* we consider a discontinuous phrase. We think *tomār* is the modifier or complement of the other part of the NU; *ājkāl* is a separate NU and *hoeche* is the verbal phrase. If the *pada* concept is followed, the unit division would be like:

tomār 'your'
ājkāl 'nowadays'
bɔṛo 'very'
ṭākār ɔhoŋkār 'pride for wealth',
'money conscious'

ār 'and'
rūper bɔṛāi 'pride for beauty'
'beauty conscious'
hɔeche 'is', 'becomes', 'occurs'

Where Indian grammar would establish several *padas* as in *tomār bɔṛo*, etc. structuralist grammar would have a phrase having discontinuous constituents. There are seven units or *padas* in the above sentence; the verb concord shows the agreement with the third person nominals, i.e. *ṭākɒr ɔhoŋkār* and *rūper bɔṛāi*.

We have remarked that the whole expression *bɔṛo ṭākār ɔhonkār ār rūper bɔṛāi* with its discontinuous modifying element *tomār* is to be considered as a complex NU. So far as we know the noun phrase in English is not discontinuous. If a compound noun occurs alone without any modifier, it is also considered as a complex unit. For instance:

(9) *bɔṭ-tɔlā theke chāpāno*
from bɔṭtɔlā is printed
(a place name)

(10) *pukhur-ghāṭe nāiche*
in the tank is bathing

(11) *sāstro-pāṭh hoche*
scripture chanting is occurring

(12) *jɔno-kolyān kɔro*
public work do

Here, the NU-s are considered as complex units.

We assume that the relations of the nominal units with the verbal units are basically of these types: they are either affected by the verb in some ways or they may affect the verb in one way or the other, or they may modify the verb.

Thus, the nominal units, showing the above-mentioned types of relationship with the verb, play the 'roles'. Where the influence is mutual between the nominal and the verbal units in the sentence, it may be termed as 'interselection'. Mostly the given NUs acquire their roles through combination with given VU in a sentence. And the overt markers on the NUs and on the VU indicate the semantic as well as syntactic function of the NUs.

It seems that either insertion of lexemes with more than one semantic interpretation, the lack of contextual reference, or lack of indication of the prosodic feature result in semantic ambiguity of the sentence.

We intend to give a structural description of the noun phrases or nominal units in Bengali sentences from the point of view of observable facts (and avoid hypothetical 'deep structures').

[2.2] A nominal unit as constituent has a stem, which is the nucleus. A simple nominal unit in its simplest form contains a nucleus with or without a marker:

(13) *pākhi* 'bird'
pākhi-ṭa 'the bird'

A simple NU has a simple nucleus (stem) whereas a complex NU can have a complex nucleus. It may be optionally preceded or followed by attributes and it may occur with or without marker.

A simple nucleus consists of a single stem; a complex nucleus consists of more than one stem (noun). The attributes may be related to one another in a fixed order, either in pre-nucleus or in post-nucleus position, or may not be related in a fixed order to one another. Attributes can also be inflected as:

(14) *āmā-r mā*
my mother

The expression *āmā-r* is an inflected attribute to the simple nucleus *mā*, and both constitute a complex NU. This complex NU can be further inflected:

āmār mā-ke
my mother to

An example of complex nucleus may be as follows:

āmār mā-bābā
my mother-father

Here *āmār* is the attribute, the expression *mā-bābā* is the complex nucleus with more than one stem. This whole NU can be inflected with case marker:

āmār mā-bābā-ke
my mother and father to

Note that a *pada* always maintains an order of occurrence within the compound, the attribute precedes the nucleus:

(15) *rāj-putro*
king son

The order should not be the other way. The higher unit such as a phrase is not mentioned in Sanskrit or Bengali grammar.

According to previous observation, markers like the *ṭa*/*ṭi*, etc. occur with either simple or complex nucleus and the whole expression can constitute a caseform. Either this singular definite marker or plural marker, together with another case marker are used.

[2.2.1] Nominal stems belong to three gender classes: masculine, feminine and neuter. The masculine and feminine are related to the sex of living beings. Beyond this no masculine/feminine gender distinction is maintained in any other class of nouns.

The masculine form has a corresponding feminine form. The *ɔ* ending masculine forms have *ī* ending feminine forms of the same root:

nɔrɔ *nārī*
man woman

The *ā* ending masculine forms also have some corresponding *ī* ending feminine forms of the same root:

rājā *rānī*
king queen

Many masculine forms have corresponding feminine forms from different roots:

bābā *mā*
father mother

Normally *ī, ā* and *u* are feminine markers. Examples of *ī, ā*, have already been given; for *u*, one may be provided:

khokā *khuku*
boy girl

Some stems determine some attributes, in particular, some adjectives which are inflected for gender concord. Otherwise, gender concord does neither concern the verb nor any attribute.

Though in personal pronouns the gender distinction is not relevant, there is, however, a distinction between reference to animate and inanimate nouns. For instance:

(16) *se* or *tini*
he, she (ordinary, formal) (honorific)

(17) *ihā* or *eṭā*
it, this one

The English three-way distinction in singular personal pronouns, viz. (*i*) he (him, his); (*ii*) she (her, hers); (*iii*) it (it, its), is basically a distinction of natural gender.

In Bengali we have:

se	(*tār*,	*tāke*)	
he/she	his/her	him/her	
tini	(*tā̃r*,	*tā̃ke*)	honorific
he/she	his/her	him/her	

We have a two-level distinction: honorific, non-honorific; both in the second person and in third person, both in singular and in plural forms. Furthermore, in second person another level is maintained in regard to inferior or close relation both in singular and in plural forms.

We have mentioned the semantic restriction of the occurrence of singular and plural markers with different classes of nouns. There is no such restriction to any class of noun which occurs as a nucleus of a nominal unit in a Bengali sentence.

ATTRIBUTES

Determiner: There is one type of determiner which corresponds to the English definite article *the*; the other type to the English demonstratives *this/these* and *that/those*. For instance:

(*i*) -*ṭā*: *boi-ṭā*
the book (a particular book)
-*guli*: *boi-guli*
the books (the particular books)

(ii) as above but with modifiers indicates
nearness or distance of the object referred to:

(18) (ei) *e boi-ṭā* 'this book'
(ei) *e boi-guli* 'these books'
(oi) *o boi-ṭā* 'that book'
(oi) *o boi-guli* 'those books'
e/ṭā/-guli corresponding to this/these and
o/ṭā/guli corresponding to that/those.

The basic forms and the forms with determiner indicate the contrast between specific and generic references, as in *boi-ṭā* ('the book/particular book') versus *boi* ('book, books'). The contrast is indicated by markers like *ṭā* or *guli* and by the non-occurrence of any singular or plural marker; in other words, inflected versus basic form of the category.

Attributes except determiners and numerals, occurring after the core, indicate an emotional colouring. An expression is made up of a numeral and a following noun. The numeral is followed by the determiner suffix, e.g.:

(19) *æk-ṭā boi*
one book

dɔs-jon *lok*
ten people

When plurality is indicated by a numeral, no other plural marker is used:

(20) *dɔs-ṭā* *boi*
ten pieces of book

The definite marker occurs with the numeral. Note the constrast with a demonstrative attribute:

boi-ṭā/boi-khāna
the book
or *oi boi-khāna/oi boi-ṭā*
that particular book

Note also the sequentially non-fixed occurrence of a numeral attribute:

(21) *boi dɔs-khānā*
book the -ten
oi boi dɔs-khāna *oi dɔs-khānā boi*
that book ten pieces that ten pieces (of) book

The demonstrative attribute always precedes the other elements in a nominal unit and gives an emphasis to 'those particular things'.

In the expressions like *dɔs-ṭā/dɔs-khānā boi*, the marker *ṭā/khānā* is determiner when there is no demonstrative. Similar features are observed with the plural marker *-guli*, as in *boi-guli* ('books').

Definiteness is indicated by a demonstrative or a relative pronoun, e.g.:

(22) *se boi-ṭā* 'that book' (distant)
se boi-guli 'those books' (distant)
o boi-ṭā 'that book' (proximate)
o boi-guli 'those books' (proximate)

When the pronouns *se/je* (relative), *o/e* (demonstrative), occur with the singular forms with the definite marker *ṭā/ṭi*, *khānā/khāni*, *jon*, etc. act as adjectives, i.e. attributes. But when they occur with plural forms, they indicate definiteness.

An interesting opposition is found with the adjective *sɔb* 'all'. Consider expressions like:

(23) *sɔb boi-ṭā* or *sɔb-ṭā boi*
the whole book
and *sɔb boi-guli*
sɔb-guli boi (all books)

The restriction with the construction *sɔb...ṭā* with (+human)—a noun with +human feature—cannot occur in that order, but can occur as *sɔb... guli/sɔb...kɔeṭā*. A demonstrative can also occur with constructions which indicate definiteness in that situation, e.g.:

(24) *oi sɔb boi-guli*
those all books

But a demonstrative never occurs with an indefinite plural pronoun such as *bes* 'a few', 'some'.

(25) *bes kɔetā boi*
a few books (a few particular books)
bes kɔtoguli boi
a few books

Demonstrative pronoun *e/o*, etc. never precedes such units. Normally, pronominal words, except personal pronouns and interrogative pronouns, are neutral in the sense that the same forms refer to both human and non-human.

These forms can substitute and modify any class of nouns irrespective of animate, inanimate and abstract features or the masculine and feminine distinction.

We have observed that definiteness may be indicated in Bengali in two ways: (*i*) by adding a marker to the nominal; or (*ii*) by a demonstrative or relative pronouns. Often these pronouns serve as attributes in such situations where definite markers occur simultaneously.

The constituents of a complex noun phrase are: (i) the prenominal and/or post-nominal attribute(s); and (ii) the head noun(s) with appropriate marker. These comparatively simple constructions can serve as indicated by the subject NU of the finite verb, the object NU of the transitive verb or the other predicate NU in a sentence.

However, in Bengali the copula is normally omitted when the sentence is in present tense and affirmative or interrogative sense. In that situation which NU should be considered as subject and which one is to be considered as predicate is understood from the total meaning of the sentence, e.g. *ei āmāder ghɔr* 'this our room'; *uni āmār bābā* 'he my father'.

Note that verbs such as *āche* 'exists', *hɔe* 'be', correspond to 'is' in English. For instance in English:

(26*a*) He is my father.
(27*a*) There is a book on the table.
(28*a*) He is angry.

These three sentences have the copula *is*.

If translated into Bengali these would be :

(26*b*) *tini* (*uni*) *āmār bābā* (without any copula)
he my father

(27*b*) *ṭebile ækkhānā boi āche* (the verb should be 'exist')
on the table one book exist

(28*b*) *tini rāg korechen*
he angry got (may be expressed in

(28*c*) *tā̃r rāg hoeche* different ways with
to him anger appear different verb)
or he became angry

However, a translation of 'he is angry' would be a nominal phrase, e.g.:

(28*d*) *tini rāgānnito*
he is angry

We have used the term attribute in a very simplified manner. All the components that modify the head noun are taken as attributes to the head and referred to as attribute.

Attributes may be either continuous or discontinuous. In a larger segment, there may be attributes of both kinds:

(29) *oi je boiguli ṭebile roeche sɔbi āmār*
those books on the table exist all mine
↑______________________________↑

We consider that these are discontinuous attributes. The attributes may either precede or follow the head in a larger segment:

bhālo boi ɔnekguli āmi dekhechi
good book many I have seen
↑__________↑

We consider that the two morphemes *bhālo* and *ɔnekguli* are respectively preceding and following the head *boi*.

Several types of attributes that can constitute the noun phrase with the head nouns are:

(1) determinative (*je boi-ṭā*)
which book

(2) demonstrative (*oi boi-ṭā*)
that book

(3) definitive (*sei boi-ṭā*)
that particular book

(4) quantitative (*ɔnek-guli boi*)
many books

(5) nominal	(*bilāti māl*) foreign goods
(6) pronominal (possessive and other)	(*tār boi*) his book (*jɔto boi*) so many books
(7) adjectival (qualitative)	(*bhāḷo bhāḷo boi*) good books
(8) verbal (gerundive)	(*deoā boi*) given book (*lok-dækhāno kāj*) show-off work
(9) negative	(*āḍhākā khābār*) not cover food (uncovered food)
(10) durative	(*cɔlonto gāṛi*) moving car
(11) numeral	(*pā̃ckhānā boi*) five books

The expansion is normally on the left side of the head. Frequently, the post-head adjectives and the nominal attributes are either predicative units or terms of address, emotional expression, etc.

These differences are similar to the one between:

(*a*) *the very good boy* and *the boy is very good*
which in Bengali corresponds to
khub bhālo chele-ṭi and *chele ṭi khub bhālo*

(*b*) *oṭho go mā āmār*
get up ↑ mother ↑

Both are terms of address (affectionate term with emotional stress) whereas an expression such as *āmār mā* simply means 'my mother'.

The Bengali structure with adjective (*bhālo*) together with adverb (*khub*) is, to some extent, similar to English *very good*, which in Bengali corresponds to adverb-adjective *khub bhālo*.

Other phrases where an adjective precedes the noun in English such as *tearful eyes*, *full moon*, etc. correspond to Bengali structures: *jɔl-bhɔrā cokh purno-cɔndro*, etc. But English phrases like, *full of misery*, *full of water*, etc. would have to be translated into Bengali as follows :

dukkho-bhɔrā, *jɔl-bhɔrā*, etc.

In other words, both types of English structures correspond to one type of structure in Bengali.

English	*Bengali*
tearful full of tears	jɔl-bhɔrā

The Bengali expression *jɔl-bhɔrā/jɔl-purno* can be paraphrased as *jɔl-e bhɔrā/jɔl-e purno* 'full with water'. It may be noticed that the compound expression *jcl-bhɔrā* and the phrasal expression *jɔl-ebhɔrā* have little difference. It may be said that the noun phrase is nominalized by discarding the marker *-e*. Conversely, it may also be said that a compound noun is a nominalized version of a noun phrase by discarding certain lex, as in the expression below:

c̃āder	*moto*	*mukh*
(of moon	like	face)

This phrase can be condensed as *c̃ād-mukh* 'moon faced'.

From our observations, we found that the internal structure of nominal units are of the following types:

Simple Units

(1) single head = noun ϕ[5]
(2) single head + determiner = noun + *-ṭā/-khānā*, etc.
(3) single head + plural marker = noun + *-rā/-guli*, etc.
(4) single head + *-der* + determiner (singular or plural) = noun + *-der* + *-ṭā/-guli.*
For instance: *chele-der-ṭā* = the thing that belongs to the boys = the thing that is meant for the boys.
(5) single head + plural marker + overt case marker = noun + *-der* + postposition.
For instance: *chele-der dike/chele-der nie*, etc.
to the boys/with the boys

Complex Units

(1) single head + attribute = noun + attribute
(ϕ, determiner, plural marker)
(2) single head + more than one attribute = noun + attributes
(ϕ, determiner, plural marker).
(3) complex head[6]
(*a*) noun + noun + connective
(*b*) compound noun (ϕ, determiner, plural marker, overt case marker).

[5]To make explicit, ϕ is overtly marked.

[6]If a core is a derived noun, it can occur with derivative marker and considered to be single; but it would be considered complex if it is a combination of more than one noun.

(4) complex head+attribute = noun+noun+attribute (ϕ, determiner, plural marker, overt marker).

(5) complex head+more than one attribute = noun+noun+attributes (ϕ, determiner, plural marker, overt case marker).

Examples

(1) without any overt marker

āmār mā (ϕ)
my mother

with an emphatic marker

āmār mā-i
my mother indeed

with a modulator, intonational particle

āmār mā nāto!
is not my mother!

(2) *oi āmāder bāṛir goru* (*-ṭā/gulo*)
that our domestic cow
(*a*) *...goru-ṭā-ke* (*-guli-ke*)
(*b*) *...goru-ṭā-ke-nā* (*gulo-ke-nā*)
(*c*) *...goru-ṭā-ke-o* (*gulo-ke-o/i*)

(3) (*a*) *rām, śyām o dulāl*
Ram, Shyam and Dulal (proper names). Other classes of nouns can also have this structure. Occurrence of such markers as *-ṭā*, *-guli*, etc. with different classes of nouns has already been discussed in the first chapter. Any type of other markers such as cases, emphatic, etc. can occur with this type of structures:

(*i*) *rām, syām o dulāl-ke*
(*ii*) *...-ke-nā*
...-ke-o

(*b*) *gɔŋgā-jɔl* ϕ
(the) Ganges water (water of the Ganges)

(*i*) *gɔŋgā-jɔlṭā*
water of the Ganges (of that particular, of particular place, etc.)

(*ii*) *gɔŋgā-jɔl-e*
to the Ganges water

(*iii*) *gɔŋgā-jɔl-ṭā-ke*
that particular Ganges water

(*iv*) *gɔŋgā-jɔl-i*
the Ganges water indeed

(*v*) *gɔŋgā-jɔl-o*
the Ganges water also

(*vi*) *gɔŋgā-jɔl-nā* (*to*)
the Ganges water!

(4) *bisudho gɔŋgā-jɔl*
pure Ganges water
Different markers can be added as well as in other examples.

(5) *ei ɔcintopurbo cittākɔrsɔk nɔbbɔ Hindi film* (+case marker)
this unthinkable interesting new Hindi film
Other markers can be added to the head. Note that the attributes are not connected with any connective marker.

An expanded phrase can contain many attributes together with a head noun which constituting a complex unit, usually as follows:

demonstrative+relative+attributes which are connected+ numeral+adverb+adjectival+head noun+different markers, e.g.:

(30) *oi* + *je* + *sei* + *āmār* + *bɔṛo* + *bhāier* +
that that that my elder brothers of the
grāmer + *bāṛir* + *dotolār* + *ghɔrer* +
village home of second floor of room
ækṭā + *khub* + *boṛo* + *uttormukhi* +
one very big north faced
bhāŋā + *dɔrjātā* + *no*
broken door that emphatic marker.

May be some more insertions are possible in the form of:

purono, *segunkāṭher toiri*, etc
old of teak wood made

This expanded phrase is very different from a corresponding one in English. The English translation would contain some relative clauses.

This kind of expanded noun phrase satisfies most of the criteria we set up in identifying a noun phrase which is complex in nature. These elements cannot be put haphazardly the relative order should be maintained to get the relevant meaning.

Our example shows that the relative order of occurrence of the head is normally at the end. But it may occur in other positions too.

A simplified order of occurrence of the elements in a complex nominal unit is something like the following:

d = demonstrative
r = relative
p = possessive (noun/pronoun): attributes with connectives
n = numeral (quantifier, qualifier, indefinite, numeral)

a = adjective (adverb, indeclinable word, adjective)

h = head noun (stem, nucleus)

d = determiner

m = (1) singular (coincides with determiner)
plural (coincides with possessive when it is passive and plural)
(2) case marker (ϕ, etc.)
(3) emphatic marker (emphatic marker *i*, *o*, *nā*; modulator *nā/to/nāto*)

Further the whole nominal expression can be preceded by a negative morpheme *nā* if it is a negative NU.

The numeral can be substituted by an interrogative, relative or indefinite pronoun. The adjective immediately before the head noun can be substituted by another adjective, and the head noun may be pluralized either by adding a plural marker or by reduplicating the other adjective preceding the head. Ordinal and cardinal numerals can occur after the possessive attribute.

All the elements that modify the head one after another, constitute a complex unit, and come under the syntactic function of either subject part or predicate part in a sentence.

We would like to point out that this type of expanded syntactic unit is not mentioned in Indian grammar. The *pada* (word) and *vākya* (sentence) are however mentioned.[7]

We are not dealing primarily with different classes of nouns in this work, so we are not going into detail about pronominal, adjectival, gerundival, infinitival words that can occur either as a head or as an attribute in different structures.

[2.2.2] However, a short discussion on the nominal compound and its paraphrase may be of some interest. We have mentioned before that nominal compounds can be considered as noun phrases, nominalised by discarding certain inflexional markers or by substituting some inflexional marker for a certain lexeme.

For instance, a compound word *gɔŋgā-jɔl* means 'the water of the Ganges'. But the two in isolation, i.e. *gangā* and *jɔl*, refer to 'the Ganges' (a particular river) and 'water' in general.

Basically, in Sanskrit as well as in Bengali grammar, a compound does not only depend on the semantic structure but also on its phonetic structure. Normally, some internal coalescence of sounds gives a different shape to the compound than to the noun phrase when both are expressing a similar meaning.[8]

[7]Chatterjee, p. 48; M.R. Kale, pp. 113, 475.

[8]M. R. Kale, p. 113; Chatterjee, p. 189.

Kale explains :

> In Sanskṛt simple words, whether substantives, adjectives, verbs or indeclinables, have the power of entering into combination with one another and forming what are called *samāsas*....
>
> A compound thus formed may further be compounded with another simple or compound word....
>
> Final vowels or consonants (modified as mentioned above) of preceding members of compounds combine with the initial letters of the succeeding members according to the usual rules of *sandhi*....
>
> The expounding of a *samāsa* (i.e. giving its *vigṛahavākya*) consists in the expression of the various relations existing between the objects or ideas devoted by the various members of a *samāsa* by means of the proper cases or subordinate sentences....
>
> Compounds are divided into four principal classes: (1) *dwandwa* or copulative; (2) *tatpuruṣa* or determinative; (3) *bahuvrīhi* or attributive; and (4) *avyayibhāva* or adverbial.[9]

The English term 'compound' corresponds to the Sanskrit term *samāsa*.[10]

Besides these above-mentioned types of *samāsa* in Sanskrit, *sahasupāsamāsa*, *aluk-samāsa*, and *nitya-samāsa* are mentioned in *Sidhānta Kaumudi*. In a footnote, Kale mentions the varieties of constructions, i.e. a noun can be compounded with another noun, a preceding member of a compound may retain case endings (i.e. *aluk-samāsa* and a paraphrase may not be possible of some compounds (i.e. *nitya-samāsa*).

Sengupta maintains that more than one word related to each other can express a particular meaning, and that particular meaning may be expressed by one word.[11] It seems to me that he describes a paraphrase of a word, or he links up a word with its paraphrase, in other words, a comparatively longer syntactic unit and a rather shorter unit (a word) can express a similar meaning (refer to the same 'thing').

Also he explains that a compound signals a particular meaning in addition to the lexical meaning of the items compounded. He gives two examples: the word *rājapuruṣa* is a combination of two words, *rājan* 'king' and *puruṣa* 'man', but the compound signals the meaning 'a person related (in one way or other) to the king'; *caturānana* means 'lord Bramha' not just four (*cutuḥ*) and face (*ānana*) but who has four faces.[11]

Even though the isolated meaning of the lexes in compound does not change and there is no difference in structure, 'the collective sense of the

[9]Kale, pp. 114-15.

[10]S. N. Sengupta *Sanskṛta Sabdasāstrer Mulkathā*, 1957 p. 73.

[11]Sengupta, p. 73.

whole compound[12] in many cases, is more prominent than the isolated meaning of the lexes. For instance:

(31) *kṛṣṇa-sarpa*[13]
black snake

If one takes the isolated meaning, then the compound means black snake, i.e. a snake which is black in colour. But actually this compound phrase does not mean it at all; it means a particular type of snake which is very poisonous.

One may compare our example *kṛṣṇa-sarpa* with an English example, *black-berry* and say that the morph (lex) semes all add up to form the compound semes. i.e. in *blackberry* one recognizes the meaning 'black' and the meaning 'berry', although the combination of the two does not just mean a berry which is black.

It seems that compounds are considered as a new word class due to their structures and the type of meaning they convey, even though the lexeme is not different, and often no considerable change in structure is obvious in relation to a simple word.

In Bengali six types of compound are classified :[14] (1) *dwandwa*, (2) *tatpuruṣa*, (3) *bahnrīhi*, (4) *avyayībhāva*, (5) *dwigu*, and (6) *karma-dhāraya*.

Prof. Chatterjee mentions that even though Pāṇini mentioned only four types of *samāsa*, the other two are mentioned in many Sanskrit *treaties*, such as '*Bṛihaddevatā*' and '*Śabdaśaktiprakāśikā*'.

Although Prof. Chatterjee remarks that these latter two can be treated as a variety of *tatpuruṣa*, he deals with them separately. According to Kale: 'A dwandwa compound consists of two or more nouns which, if not compounded, would be connected by the copulative particle च (and); as रामकृष्ण which is equal to रामः च कृष्णः च.[15] Prof. Chatterjee explains in a similar fashion that in paraphrases one has to use a connective word (morph) *o*, *ebŋ*, *ār*, *tɔthā*, etc.[16]

As to whether in Bengali this type of compound is just a sequence of two consecutive nominals seem to be a borderline case, since there is no phonetic change as in Sanskrit. For instance, *mā-bāp* 'mother and father'.

The *aluk-samāsa* deserves a separate explanation. This type of compound should perhaps not be called compound at all, because there is no coalescence of phones in the two consecutive lexes. The situation is similar both in Bengali and in Sanskrit. The case marker of the preceding lex is not dropped. There is neither any phonetic change nor any distinct meaning conveyed, other than the lexical with some marker, by the com-

[12]Kale, p. 116. [13]Chatterjee, pp. 214-15. [14]Chatterjee, p. 191, f.n. [15]Kale p115..
[16]Chatterjee, p. 192.

pound (*aluk*). For instance, the two nouns occur with the *-e* marker and the marker indicates locative meaning in the examples below:

(32) *āge-piche*[17]
in the front, in the back

(33) *buke-piṭhe*[18]
on/in the chest, on/in the back

In some cases, even though a morphological marker seems to 'break up' with the construction (as the first *-e* in the above two examples, which traditionally are thought of as compounds. Here we would refer to the construction just mentioned above, that the construction is not a compound. This type of combination of more than one element is considered as compound on the semantic ground. When two words occur in a successive order and in combination indicating certain meaning in addition to the meaning of both lexemes, it is called *nitya samāsa*[19], for instance, *kṛṣṇa-sarpa*.

It seems that generally where one cannot distinguish between the sequence of two words and a compound of two words either in relation to meaning or in relation to form, then one should not assume that the sequence is a compound.

Other *samāsas*, namely, *tatpuruṣa*, *bahuvrīhi*, *karmadhārayā*, *avyībhāva* are established on semantic grounds. Examples:

(34) *tatpuruṣa*: *bilāt-pherot*[20]
western country returned
As a compound, it means 'returned from a foreign country'. The compound can be paraphrased as *bilāt theke pherot* 'returned from a foreign country'

(35) *bahuvrīhi*: *sonāmukhī*[21]
gold face (*ī* feminine marker)
As a compound it means a girl whose face is as bright as gold. The compound can be paraphrased as
sonār moto ujjɔl mukh jāhār
gold like bright face whose

(36) *karmadhāraya* : *lonā-jɔl*[22]
salty water
It can be paraphrased as *lonā je jɔl* 'the water which is salty'.

[17]Chatterjee, pp. 213-14. [18]Chatterjee, pp. 213-214. [19]Chatterjee, pp. 213-14.
[20]Chatterjee, p. 93. [21]Chatterjee, p. 207 .[22]Chatterjee, p. 200.

(37) *avyībhāva*: *upakul*[23]
the bank

It can be paraphrased as *kuler somīpe* 'near the bank' (of the river or sea). Normally, an indeclinable morpheme (word) precedes the other noun with which it is compounded.

(38) *protidin*[24]
every day
It can be paraphrased as *dine dine* 'day by day'.

(39) *jɔthāsokti*[25]
as capacity
It can be paraphrased as *soktike ɔtikrɔm nā koriā* 'not beyond the capacity'.

Besides these there are two other *samāsas* mentioned in many Sanskrit and Bengali grammars :[26] *dwigu* and *dwandwa*. When the first member of a compound is a numeral adjective and the other one is a nominal, the two together are called a *dwigusamāsa*, e.g.:

(40) *cou-rāstā*[27]
four street
It can be paraphrased as *cāri rāstār jog* 'the intersection of four roads'.

We have already mentioned *dwandwa*. In the above examples of compound, it is observed that an expanded phrase can be compared with a compound which is affiliated in meaning. Sometimes comparisons are possible with a full sentence and a phrase or compound, e.g.:

(41) *gācher prān āche*; *jībonto gāch/gāch jībonto*
of tree life exists; living tree
= A tree has life.

(42) *jībone ɔnek dukkho āche*: *dukkho mɔe jībon*
in life many sufferings are; sorrowful life
= There are many sufferings in life.

In the above examples, a verb occurs in both the sentences but it does not occur in the other expressions. The subject becomes the attribute of the other nominal in that expression. The locative function of *gācher* and *jībone* no longer remains locative in the condensed expression. It becomes nominative and has the function of topic.

[23]Chatterjee, p. 213. [24]Chatterjee, p. 213. [25]Chatterjee, p. 213.
[26]Chatterjee, p. 191, f.n. Kale, p. 115, 141. [27]Chatterjee, p. 204.

In this language, a sentence can occur without a verb. For instance:

se khub bhālo chele
he very good boy
=He is a very good boy.

We think that the kind of expressions containing more than one morpheme can be considered as a complex phrase. A complex phrase and a compound seems structurally the same if there is no morphological coalescence.

The examples given in connection with the compounds would make it clear that the term *samāsa* in traditional Indian grammar includes differences at the semantic as well as at the phonetic level.[28]

The differences at the semantic level are to be characterized as :

(*i*) The amalgamated meaning of the two or more items combined;
(*ii*) The non-amalgamated meaning of the two or more items combined.

The differences at the phonetic level are :

(*i*) Coalescence takes place either in the form of *sandhi* or dropping of marker or lex;
(*ii*) The consecutive lexes do not coalesce.

In most cases, the amalgamation and coalescence coincide in Indian grammatical analysis. Where one is missing, the label of *samāsa* can still be justified by one of two criteria mentioned above.

[2.3] At this stage we would like to deal with the semantic aspects of the units. In the preceding discussion we have pointed out that the smaller units of a larger unit in Indian grammar are called *pada*. Thus, a *pada* refers to the syntactic constituent of a higher syntactic construction. A *samastapada* or a compound is also a single unit.

By definition a *pada* is a syntactic unit which has an isolated as well as related meaning, i.e. isolated meaning as a single lex or a compound word and related meaning as a syntagm of the sentence.[29] This related meaning refers to the grammatical function of the unit in reference to the other *padas* of the sentence.

An important view held by the Indian grammarians is that a lexeme or a word has two types of significatory power. The primary one refers to the isolated meaning of a lexeme and the secondary one refers to the relational meaning, i.e. when a lexeme occurs in a sentence with or without modification (i.e. with or without marker or an attribute, etc.) becomes a part of a whole, it becomes a *pada* of a sentence. A lex as a part of a given sentence (normally inflected forms) conveys its syntagmatic, paradig-

[28]Kale, pp. 114-15. [29]Chatterjee, pp. 48-49.

matic relations as well as functions (i.e. agent, object, etc.). The technical term *pada* comprises these essential inherent potentialities of a lexeme.[30]

The *padas* (generally the smaller units of a larger unit) are established on the basis of three factors: mutual expectancy, logical consistency and contiguity.[31]

It was argued that an utterance is to be called a sentence, if it expresses a complete sense through the chosen item or items.[32]

Both the syntactic and semantic unity of any given sentence are dependent on the inherent significatory power of lexemes and the basic factors with which the lexemes are chosen and conditioned to express a complete sense.

The *pada* with one lexeme or more than one is itself a syntactically relevant and semantically compatible unit of a sentence. Therefore, there is no place for an ungrammatical sentence in a grammatical discussion. However, it is not unreasonable to assume that discussion of an ungrammatical sentence may provide suggestion for the descriptions of grammatical sentences.

We assume that syntactic and semantic units coexist in smaller units as well as larger units. The whole sentence is to be considered as a set of units related to each other. The meaning of an utterance is the total meaning expressed by the units in relation. These views comprise the theory of *sphoṭa*[33], an important theory developed by Indian scholars belonging to the various schools of thought who discussed linguistic problems.[34]

The terms 'mutual expectancy', 'logical consistency' and 'contiguity' need explanation. The relevant technical terms employed by Indian linguists are *ākāṅkṣā*, *yogyatā*, *sannidhi/āsatti*, and *tātparyajñāna*.

We take the last term first. This term refers to the fact that both the speaker and the hearer must understand the language to be used for communication.

The term *ākāṅkṣā* refers to the fact that in every language certain words necessarily require certain other words to convey a complete sense. A noun normally requires a verb to express the complete meaning; similarly a verb normally requires some other nominals to complete the sense of the speaker or writer's sentence. Thus, *ākāṅkṣā* refers to the interdependence of the *padas*.

For instance, in a Bengali expression such as:

(43) *āmi kāl*
I tomorrow

[30]S.K. Chatterjee, pp. 48-49, 75-77.

[31]K. Kunjunni Raja *Indian Theories of Meaning*, pp. 154-68.

[32]SK Chatterjee, p. 291. [33]Kunjunni Raja, pp. 135-148.

[34]Chatterjee, pp. 291-301; Bhattacharya, pp. 10-18.

one expects a verbal *pada* to complete the sense intended by the speaker or writer. The *pada kāl* indicates that the verbal *pada* should be conjugated in future tense.

The term *yogyatā* refers to the grammatical as well as to the semantic compatibility or logical consistency among the *padas* in a sentence, e.g.:

(44) *rāttre sūrjo oṭhe*
night at sun rises
= The sun rises at night

Here the idea is logically inconsistent, since the sun does not rise at night (although it may happen in some geographical region); the word 'night' itself means that part of the day when there is no sun. It may not be a universally accepted idea, but in Indian culture things are understood in that way. And the sentence is not acceptable, as it is not at all a sentence according to Indian tradition.[35] Metaphorically such types of utterances may be considered as sentences in some special contexts, but in traditional grammar false sentences are not treated.

The term *āsatti* or *sannidhi* refers to the order of the components within the unit as well as to the arrangement of the constituents and the accepted order of their occurrence in a sentence.

The different *padas* occurring in a sentence may be sometimes juxtaposed which does not affect the sentence significantly. For instance, a verbal or a nominal unit may take several positions as there is no rigid or fixed word order in Bengali. But the order within the unit is rather fixed. The meaning of the unit depends mostly on the order of the elements. For example, in a Bengali sentence like:

(45) *āmi ekhāne dubɔchorer opor āchi*
I here more than two years live (am)
= I am here more than two years,

the units may be juxtaposed but the internal relation or arrangements of a unit can neither be broken up nor be changed as in:

(45*a*) *āmi du ekhāne opor āchi bɔchorer*
I two here more am years of, etc.

Since the numeral *du* modifies the nominal *bɔchorer*, both elements should occur in successive order. The element *opor* is a postpositional affix to be affixed after the element having the connective marker *-er*. The postpositional affix occurs at the end and thus shows the segment of the unit. Hence the three constitute one single unit.

[35]Chatterjee, p. 292.

From several definitions given in different treatises,[36] it is understood that the sentence was considered as a divisible larger unit denoting a single complete idea.

The term '*vākya*' refers to the larger syntactic unit containing several smaller syntactic units which have given relation to each other. They convey the total meaning of the whole. We find the terms *vākya* and *pada* but we do not see any term to label the intermediate syntactic unit such as phrase in traditional Indian grammar. The compound (*samāsa*) corresponds to the phrase in many cases.

In short, a definition of a word is grammatically well formed, semantically compatible and indispensable in its particular situation to complete the sense. The word which occurs in an acceptable order in a sequence to make the intended sense comprehensible is the suitable word for the sentence.

The *padas* must have mutual expectancy (in other words, one item must be semantically and syntactically relevant to the other) through which they constitute a larger syntactic and semantic unit—a sentence. The semantic and syntactic units are interdependent; therefore they coexist in smaller as well as larger expressions.

Semantically, there are two parts in a larger syntactic unit, i.e. a sentence can basically be divided into two parts: *uddeśya* and *vidheya*, which correspond to the terms subject and predicate.[37]

Sometimes a single verbal unit may indicate both subject and predicate; sometimes one or more nominal units may indicate subject and predicate without any verbal unit.[38] The following three types of constructions can occur in Bengali and other Indian languages: a construction containing verbal and nominal units, a construction having verbal unit only, and a construction with one or more nominal units only. They can be considered as sentences.

We will suggest that constructions with NU only or VU only should not be divided as subject and predicate. Rather they should be called 'unit having sentence building function'.

[2.4] We assume that to identify the units of the subject part and the predicate part, the meaning of the lexical items and the marker on them play an important role.

The structure of the unit helps to get the meaning of the unit and its relation to other units. The correct interpretation of a sentence is obtained from the structure and the meaning of the units in relation to the larger structural unit.

[36]*Kātantrapariśiṣṭa*, *Sāhityadarpaṇa* and *Arthaśāstra* quoted in Chatterjee, p. 291; See Kunjunni Raja, p. 152 for quotations from *Mīmāṃsāsūtra*.

[37]Chatterjee, p. 293.

[38]Chatterjee, pp. 293, 300-01.

The *pada* concept, which is mentioned in traditional grammar, seems an alternative to the phrase concept. When directly related constituent elements are discontinuous (positionally) in a given sentence, this may be explained either as two *padas* or a discontinuous phrase. For instance:

(46) *oguli choṭobolāe āmār chilo skuler boi*
those in childhood mine were of school books
= Those were my school books in the childhood.

The expressions *āmār* and *skuler boi* are discontinuous elements of a nominal phrase which correspond to English:

my school books.

In English, a verbal phrase may be discontinuous like:

Did you *find* it ?

The expressions *did* and *find* both constitute a verbal construction which is discontinuous. So far we have not noticed any discontinuous nominal phrase in English. A smaller unit rather than an expanded phrase can be accommodated in the *pada* concept. For instance:

(47) *oi pɔkkokes brdho lokṭi bollen*
that gray hair old man said (it)

One may consider *lokṭi* '(the) man' as subject rather than the whole expanded phrase.

There is no doubt that the whole phrase should be considered as the subject part of the above sentence. The ending of the noun phrase normally indicates the function of it, i.e. the case marker contributes to indicate the grammatical meaning of the unit. Different 'roles' of the unit 'are determined by correlating differences in syntactic form with differences in grammatical meaning'.[39]

The nominal units, in any given sentence are to be analysed on the basis of their relation to the verb unit. We have already mentioned the types of relation held by the nominal unit in relation to a verbal unit in a sentence.

One type of relation held by the NU is overtly manifested by the verbal concord.[40] The others are not manifested by the verbal concord; the mark on the nominal unit itself identifies the type of relation in most cases.

[39]C.R. Longyear, *Linguistically Determined Categories of Meanings,* p. 35.

[40]Here the term 'concord' is to be understood as the personal marker on the verb form. The verb concord differs in first person, second person, and in third person. There are three sets of markers indicating different tenses.

The structural description of the sentence would come close to the suggestion of Staal 's——(NP, VP)'.[41]

In this framework without postulating any fixed ordering, we rather write a complete sentence——(subj. VU). The two types of significatory power which we explained before are considered to be inherent in each item. Thereby the syntactic and semantic units are established and the meaning of the whole sentence is conveyed which in turn signals the functions of the NU-s.

[2.5] We shall discuss the 'roles' in the following chapter. Here we intend to consider the fact that even though languages refer to the real world, the grammatical notions do not always coincide with facts of the real world.

It is a fact that animate beings can have experience and knowledge of things and actions, etc. But when one analyses sentences in grammar and categorises the functions of different classes of nouns, the criteria chosen may 'contradict' the event of the real world. Consider, for instance:

The family loves him.
The audience reacted.
The company is closed.
The boy loves reading.

If one labels similarly the initial NU-s of the above-mentioned examples or the expressions *him* and *reading*, one would not be thought of being too far off the mark.

One can show the difference between the classes of noun such as *family*, *company*, *audience*, *boy* and *reading*. These nouns have different referents in the real world. But that does not necessarily negate the possibility of treating them similarly in grammar, if their syntactic and semantic functions happen to be similar.

It seems to be a confusion if, on the other hand, they are treated differently in syntax (grammatical analysis) because of their referents in the real world. They may be classified as collective, verbal nouns and animate pronominal form as the case may be at the word level analysis.

If, in a similar construction, the same verb can agree with an animate and inanimate noun, we assume that a similar relation can be thought of in grammar between the NU-s and VU-s in respective sentences. For instance, in English we can have: *the boy is growing* and *the tree is growing*. We believe both should be labelled similarly. In the kind of semantics (sentence semantics), which is directly relatable to syntax, the two examples are not different; the only difference is that the two lexes refer to different referents in the real world.

[41]J.F. Staal, 'Introduction', '*Word Order in Sanskrit and Universal Grammar*', p. 8.

As a matter of fact, many intransitive sentences can be arranged in a different way by means of using the intransitive verb as subject of the *be* verb in Bengali. Often the actual doer/actor, referred to by the nominal in intransitive sentence, appears to be the modifier of the subject (verbal noun) which shows agreement with the *be* verb. For instance:

(48) *rām* *douṛāe*
Ram runs (intransitive, present
(proper indefinite)
name)

It can be changed into another construction as follows:

(49) *rāmer douṛ* *hɔe*
Ram's run(ning) occurs

In the above two examples, the person in the real world (Ram) is the same so is the action (running).

Both the above-mentioned sentences are affiliated in meaning, but they differ in syntactical arrangement. And this difference leads to the difference in function of the NU in the two sentences.

A transitive verb *pɔṛā* 'reading'; *pɔṛ-* 'read' can be used in constructions as follows:

(50) *āmi boi poṛechi*
I book have read
and *āmār boi-pɔṛā hoeche*
my book reading is finished
(to me) (study)
or *āmār boi pɔṛā hoeche*
I book has been read
(to me)

These three are affiliated in meaning. They are communicating, more or less the same information in three different ways. In the real world, *I/me/my* the referent of these expressions is the actual reader or performer of the action *reading*. The real event does not directly determine the labelization of the subject NU in the above-mentioned sentences. The expressions *āmi*, *boi-pɔṛā* and *boi* are subjects in the respective constructions. Expressions having *er/r* marker indicate their link with the following expressions. Their isolated and grammatical meaning shows their potentiality to form a single unit in combination with the following elements. Thus, they constitute single VU in respective examples. And the head nominal of the expanded expression shows agreement with the following VU in respective examples. The verb is a *be* verb, and the head nominal is a verbal noun.

The NU, VU do not show the performer relation. The subject nominal is not to be assigned as agent in any case.

If, on the contrary, an expression is like.

(51) *rāmer gāṛi douṛāe*
'Ram's car runs,'

then the expression *rāmer gāṛi* may be assigned as 'agent', in view of consideration that the relation between the NU and VU is the performer relation. The term '*performer*' is to be understood as a linguistic term. The verb *douṛāe* is to be considered as the action performed by the noun *gāṛi*, although in the real world the noun may refer to an inanimate object and therefore requires somebody's driving.[42]

[2.6] Presumably, the assignment of any semantic function such as agent 'role' (or other 'roles') to the NU depends on the (*i*) unit division and (*ii*) on the interpretation of the whole sentence.

We cannot assign an agent 'role' to the expression *rāmer* or *āmār* in the above-mentioned examples. A possessor 'role' may be assigned to *rāmer* in *rāmer gāṛi* in the sense that 'the car belongs to Ram' which will 'coincide' with the reality. The same 'role' cannot be appropriate to the expression *āmār* even though the noun has similar feature and marker on it. It seems that the criterion of semantic feature constraint should not be taken as a reliable guide in assigning the 'role' of a nominal unit.

We have observed that nominals having both animate and inanimate features can show *performer* relation, if similar verbs occur with both types of nominals. Agent can be animate agent and inanimate agent. The latter can be called 'inanimate agent'. In modern linguistic analysis, the notion of 'agent'[43] refers usually to the animate agent only.

We suggest that in English sentences like

Ram runs
This car runs well
He runs the business well

the difference lies not exactly in the animate and inanimate features of the nouns 'Ram' and 'Car' but in the sense of the verb '*run*'. If one considers the total meaning of the two sentences and limits the importance of lexical meanings, 'Ram' and 'Car' can be labelled as agent in grammar.

One can classify the verbs of any language. The features of the verb like activity, state, etc. and also the transitive and intransitive use of the verb may be accounted for. Similarly, nouns of any language can be classified and the features like living, non-living, animate, inanimate, abstract, etc.

[42]P. Acharya, pp. 96-97; Chatterjee, pp. 83-86.
[43]Fillmore, p. 243 Langendon, p. 64.

may be taken into account. We consider that this is useful to the word levei analysis. At the syntactic level and the sentence semantic level which is directly related to syntax, only the minimum is to be taken into account. In other words, verbs are to be taken as verbs, nouns as nouns, etc.[44] in assigning the functions such as 'roles' of agent, object, etc. and the functions such as subject and predicate.

In Indian grammar, the subject NU is defined in terms of verb agreement in most cases. In the non-copulative sentence, the subject is defined within the total meaning of the sentence. Even though in most cases, the NU-s showing different 'roles' are marked overtly, the 'roles' are assigned to the NU-s on the basis of their relation to the verbal unit in a given sentence.

Sometimes the structural similarity is proved to be ambiguous.

Compare the following two sets of sentences:

(52) *Set (A)*
āmār eṭā bhālo lāge
to me good strikes it
=I like it/it appears good to me
tomār...
to you
tār...
to him
Set (B)
āmār boi āche
to me book exists
=I have a book/A book exists to me.
tomār...
to you
tār...
to him

The above-mentioned Set (A) can have affiliated expressions as follows:

(53) *āmi pɔchondo kori/bhālobāśi*
I like
tumi...... ɔro/bāso
you
se...... ɔre/bāse
he/she

We call these affiliated in the sense that they have the same referent. In Set (A), the verbs are to be considered impersonal (*lāge*) since the same form occurs with three different personal pronouns. Either

[44] Chatterjee, p. 83.

one should say that the verb agrees with pronouns (*āmār, tomār, tār*), or one should consider that the verb agrees with the adjective *bhālo.* The affiliated constructions of Set (A) are different—the pronominals occur in nominative and the verb shows appropriate concord on it.

If one postulates a deep structure and correlates both constructions with it, then one nominal seems depository of more than one case, i.e. one deep and another surface case. In other words, if

(54) *āmār bhālo lāge*
me good strikes
= To me/in relation to me it strikes good

is considered as passive expression and

amibhālobāsi/pcchondo kori
I like (it)

as active expression of a given referent which is exact 'deep structure form', then one will posit *āmi* or *āmār*, of which *āmi* can be considered as agent (or experiencer) and *āmār* locative/dative.

The Set (B) cannot have any other construction; in other words, the meaning expressed in the construction cannot be expressed in any other construction as it happens in the case of Set (A). The expressions *āmār, tomār, tār* in Set (B) should either be considered as locative or possessive, according to the interpretation of the sentences.

Thus, it is assumed that the type of complications observed in the above examples implies,

(*i*) the structural similarity may not always signal the same 'role' of the nominals (compare sets (A) and (B));

(*ii*) the active and passive test in our opinion signals the semantic affiliation of both sentences and it is not very helpful in establishing 'roles' (compare the active and passive constructions of Set (A));

(*iii*) the 'deep structure' seems to indicate the real world event. It can be omitted in grammar. To indicate the real world events or the facts or the reality, one often creates confusion in grammatical analysis.

If the expression is interpreted as *'to me'* in Sets (A) and (B), one can assign *locative* to *āmār* in both sets. If the real world situation is considered one has to assign the 'role' *experiencer* to *āmār* in Set (A) If the expressions in Set (B) are compared with reality, one has to assign *possessor* 'role' to *āmār* in Set (B). Otherwise, *āmār* can be interpreted as *to me/in relation to me*, and thus it should be assigned 'locative' in our opinion.

In traditional Indian grammar, the possessive/genitive forms are not considered as having any semantic function such as 'role'. In Bengali, the form with *-er/-r/-der* in most cases shows a direct connection with the other nominal. Therefore it acts as modifier, but in special cases, as in Sets (A) and (B), it shows semantic functions like locative (and other 'roles' if it is interpreted differently).

One can apply transformations in active and passive constructions. But causative cannot be transformed, if transformations are not allowed to change the meaning. For instance

(55) *bɔrṣāe sosso nɔṣṭo holo*
due to rain corn is spoilt/ruined.

We consider the expression *bɔrṣāe* as 'cause' and thus the sentence as a causative sentence. We do not think it is derived from a non-causative sentence like *sosso nɔṣṭo holo 'corn is spoilt'*.

We do not think generally that transformations can maintain the grammatical meaning invariantly. For instance, if the active construction like.

(56) *āmi mālā gathi*
I garland make

is changed to a passive construction like

(57) *mālāṭi āmār dārā gāthā holo*
the garland by me was made (is being made)

one must admit that the grammatical meaning is changed by transformation as:

in active	*in passive*
āmi: subject—agent	*mālāṭi* subject—object
mālā: object—predicate	*āmār dārā*: predicate adverbial (of agent); actor/doer in the real world.

The forms and the structure are changed; automatically there occurs semantic change.

We set up a few basic semantic relations of the NU following the traditional Indian *kāraka* theory, which we think reasonably include various types of 'roles' presented by NU-s in our language.

We shall try to show which 'roles' can occur in the subject of most sentences which are structurally NU and VU. We shall also observe in the following chapters that actual expressions provide necessary information for grammatical analysis, and there is no need for any hypothetical structural representation ('deep structure') for identifying and establishing semantic relation (function) of the NU-s in a given sentence.

The *kārakas* automatically refer to both subject and predicate functions of different NU-s.

It would also be observed that the so-called universal phenomenon of NP-VP in sentence structure is not suitable in about 1 per cent of the sentences in Bengali. We have already mentioned that sentence structures in Bengali are of three types, viz. (*i*) NP-VP; (*ii*) NP-NP; and (*iii*) VP.

The syntactic function, such as subject can be defined as topic in the sentence which is structurally NP-NP. There may not be any subject at all in the sentence which is structurally VP. A sentence which is structurally NP-VP, may be subjectless if the NP is not in agreement with the VP. Therefore, in our opinion, neither the structure NP-VP nor the binary division of subject and predicate can be taken as universal phenomenon of a sentence.

CHAPTER III

DIFFERENT FUNCTIONS OF THE NOUN PHRASES

THE KĀRAKA

[3.0] In this chapter, the semantic functions of the noun phrase will be treated following traditional Indian grammar.

We have mentioned that a syntactic unit[1] may either end in a marker or be terminated by a 'break'.[2] We posit a marker where there is no overt ending. Different types of markers are found with nominal items[3] which indicate the relation of one nominal item with another and the relation of a nominal unit (NU) with the verbal unit (VU) in a sentence.

Thus, these markers serve an important function in the language. A group of words becomes a meaningful sentence when the meaning of these words is interrelated to the meaning of the markers and other syntactic devices.

The relation between the nominal and the verbal[4] in a sentence is traditionally called *kāraka*.[5] In all Sanskrit and Bengali grammars, the term *kāraka* is defined as a kind of relation which involves the verbal and the nominal in a sentence. Faddegon interprets Pāṇini:

By *kāraka* Pāṇini understands the logical or ideational relation between a noun and a verb or more precisely between an object or anything conceived after the analogy of an object and an action or anything conceived after the analogy of an action'[6]

We have tried to draw attention to the fact that the theory of *kāraka* is to some extent similar to the idea of 'role' (case). Fillmore says: 'By labelled relation I mean the relation of an NP to a sentence or to a VP, which is mediated by a pseudo category label, such as Manner, Extent, Location, Agent.'[7]

[1]Syntactic unit here means a syntactical construction smaller than a sentence. It may consist of one segment or more than one.

[2]A pause within a sentence.

[3]The term *pada* which we have used in the previous chapter, has more or less the meaning of the term syntactic *item* (a word including a compound). It corresponds to some extent to the term *item* used by Hammarstrom in *Linguistic Units, Acts and Items*, p. 5.

[4]The terms 'nominal' and 'verbal' refer to the noun and the verb respectively, but not to their modifiers.

[5]Kale, p. 475. Chatterjee, p. 83; N. Vidyabhushan, p. 49; P. Acharya, p. 90. Also Pānini, Aṣṭādhyāyī, 1.4.23. Sengupta, p. 35.

[6]Quoted by Staal, p. 37.

[7]*Universals in Linguistic Theory*, p. 16; Langeondon, p. 64.

In fact, in establishing the *kāraka* relation the involvement between the NP and VP is taken into account irrespective of the semantic features and the lexical items—nouns occurring with the same verb and showing the same involvement, are labelled similarly. In the traditional Indian approach, there is no such distinction made as action verb, stative verb, motion verb, etc. when the *kāraka* is established.[8]

Both in Sanskrit and Bengali grammars it is maintained that verbs not only mean action like doing something, but also actions like becoming, living, happening, or growing, etc. as well.[9]

The term '*kāraka*' is interpreted as 'case' by Rammohun Roy in his *Gourio Vyākaran*, and Rajsekhar Basu also considers these two as corresponding ideas. Both were Sanskrit scholars.[10] In Bengali to English and English to Bengali dictionaries, the term '*kāraka*' is taken as equivalent to the term 'case' in (English) grammar.[11]

However, the theory of *kāraka* seems to be only partially equivalent to the notion of case. Even though nobody has compared *kāraka* and *case* elaborately in Bengali, scholars such as Haraprasad and Rāmendrasundar have discussed the difference between the theory of *kāraka* and case. They maintain that, in Sanskrit and Bengali, *kāraka* refers to the relation of nominal to the verbal in a sentence. Unless the nominal is somehow connected with the verbal or it modifies the verb, it cannot be said to be in *kāraka*.[12] In other words, no *kāraka* can be established if the NU is not connected with the VU. Sengupta maintains that, according to the grammarians, the important item is the verb in a sentence. The other *padas* (items) make the meaning of the verb explicit. The relations of the other *padas* with the verb may be called *kāraka* relation.[13]

In Bengali, following the Sanskrit grammar, the possessive or genitive and vocative are not recognized as *kāraka*. Since these have no direct connection with a verb and while possessive is connected with another noun, vocative can constitute a sentence alone. These are considered as case in Latin and other languages as well. Generally, these are considered different from *kāraka* relation in Indian grammar.[14]

As a matter of fact, the Bengali scholars mentioned above disagree with the Sanskrit grammarians in many respects. Applying an argument similar to the one about possessive and vocative, they did not agree to accept *apādāna* as a *kāraka*. They also maintain that *sampradāna* should not be

[8]Chatterjee, p. 83.

[9]Chatterjee, p. 83.

[10]Chatterjee, p. 105; Rajsekhar Basu, *Calantikā*, p. 614.

[11]*Dev's Concise Dictionary*, p. 183; *Samsad English-Bengali Dictionary*, p. 195.

[12]Chatterjee, p. 104; Kale, p. 475.

[13]Sengupta, p. 35. The author has translated from the original.

[14]Chatterjee, p. 104; Kale, p. 496.

considered to be different from *karma*.[15] Ravindranath[16] also is of this opinion.

We shall discuss this point in detail later. Although most of the Bengali scholars noticed that the nature of the Bengali language is different from that of Sanskrit in many respects[17] and although they disagree with the Sanskrit grammarians regarding the six basic *kāraka* relations established by the latter, we find that the six *kāraka* relations are discussed in all Bengali grammars.

[3.1] A sentence in which *kāraka* padas appear may be symbolized as NU-VU. Sentences without NU-VU constructions cannot have *kāraka*.

It is imaginable that this *kāraka* conception would lead to the establishment of a ϕ copula in a sentence where there is no verb (unit), and a ϕ nominal (which is in agreement with the verb) where there is no such nominal or no nominal at all.

However, the ϕ copula or ϕ nominal are not postulated in Sanskrit or in Bengali grammar, but a very similar idea is found there. The verb or noun is realized in terms of unexpressed verb or unexpressed noun, i.e. where there is no verb item or noun item, it should be understood as unexpressed.[18]

In Bengali, usually, the *be* verb is understood in such a situation, and unexpressed nominal is understood according to the verb concord. For instance:

(*a*)	*ki*	*vicitra*	*ei*	*desh*
	how	strange	this	country

A copula such as *hɔe* 'is' to be understood in analysing the above example. In grammatical analysis, it could be:

(*b*)	*ki*	*vicitra*	(*hɔe*)	*ei*	*deś*[19]
	how	strange	is	this	country

Normally it is called *a ujjha kriyā* 'unexpressed verb'.

Similarly a nominal can be called *ujjha kartā* 'unexpressed subject' in the following example:

jābo
will go

There is no first person pronominal item that should be understood

15Chatterjee, pp. 93, 103; Acharya, pp. 101-03.

16Ravindranath Tagore, 'Sabdatattwa' in *Ravīndra Racanāvalī* (vol. 14), pp. 94-95.

17Chatterjee, pp. 101-03, 322; 'Sabdatattwa' in *Ravīndra Racanāvali* (Vol. 14), pp. 94-95.

18Chatterjee, p. 301.

19Vidyabhushan, p. 50.

considering the first personal marker, i.e. concord on the verb expression. It may be in singular or in plural, because the verb form does not change in number in Bengali.

The expression *jā-b-o* may be explained in a different way. Instead of saying that an unexpressed subject nominal should be understood, one can say that the overt personal marker indicates the first person and that since it incorporates the idea in the verb form itself, there is no need to posit an unexpressed nominal.

Traditionally in Indian grammar to establish *kāraka*, in particular the *kartā*, where there is no nominal or where there is one or more than one nominal but none of them is in agreement with the verb, an unexpressed agreeable nominal (*ujjha kartā*)[20] usually is understood. Often it is either a first person or a second person pronoun.

The controversy whether we have to understand an unexpressed verb such as *hɔe* in case of a sentence where there is no verb unit, started in ancient India.[21] The grammarians and the logicians disagreed on this point. The logicians were of the opinion that a sentence may contain the nominal only (which is the *uddeśya*)[22] and the meaning intended may be fully understood without any verb in that particular sentence. But the grammarians were of the opinion that the verb is the 'pivot' of the sentence, a sentence can never be completed without a verb (*tiṅantaṃ padam* 'finite verb'). If there is no expressed verbal item, we should understand an unexpressed verb.[23]

Since, in Bengali and in many other languages, sentences without any verb are frequent and seem quite natural and the meaning is fully expressed by the nominal unit or units, we prefer to follow the logicians here as explained above. For instance, in Bengali there may be sentences like the following:

(1) *sɔrotkāl*
autumn
= It is autumn.

(2) *cɔmotkār* *sɔrotkāler* *sɔkālti*
wonderful of autumn the morning
= It is a wonderful morning of autumn.

(3) *uni* *āmār* *ɔdhyāpɔk*
he my professor (teacher)
= He is my professor.

[20]Acharya, p. 96.

[21]*Śabdaśaktiprakāśikā* of Jagadish and *Śaktivāda* and *Vyutpattivāda* of Gadadhar are the books where these controversial points are discussed. See Dinesh Chandra Bhattacharya, *Baṅge Nyāya Carcā*, pp. 168-200.

[22]Chatterjee, p. 301.

[23]Chatterjee, p. 301. Note that most of the Indian languages can have such types of sentences metioned above.

(4) *dhɔrme* *āmrā* *hindu*
in religion we Hindu
= We are Hindu in religion/Our religion is Hinduism.

(5) *āmi* *ækjon* *chāttro*
I one student
= I am a student.

(6) *ākāse* *sonār ālo*
in the sky golden light
= There is golden light in the sky.

These sentences show that the Bengali sentence structure can be NP or NP-NP. Not only other Indo-Aryan languages but also the Dravidian languages have this sentence structure. For instance, in Tamil we can have

	avar	*enuraia*	*āsiriar*
	he	my	professor
or	*nān*	*oru*	*mānavi*
	I	one	student/female
	nān	*oru*	*mānavan*
	I	one	student/male.

The above-mentioned sentences communicate the intended meaning, because the meaning of the words and the markers on them, their syntactic structure and order of the related words are known to the native speaker and hearer.

It seems that in those types of sentences one need not try either to posit a verb or to establish the subject-predicate division. We would prefer to say that the nouns have 'sentence building function'.

In a similar way a sentence, with a verbal unit only can express a complete idea. Recall our example, *Jābo* 'will go'; some more can be added:

(7) *je-o* (with a second person marker)
go

(8) *jā-o* (with a second person marker)
go

Even though both No. 7 and No. 8 have second person markers, the prosodic feature makes the difference in meaning. No. 7 is a request, whereas No. 8 is either a command or permission (the difference is conditioned by the difference between *e* and *ā*). Similarly, the following No. 9 can either express disgust or a kind of unhappy feeling. This is due to the prosodic feature.

(9) *jāe jāk* (with a third person marker)
(if) goes let—go
= If (he/they/one) goes, let him (them) go.

In these examples, the verbal expression incorporates a morpheme with the meaning of first, second and third persons. The number of the person is not clear. Observing these facts, one can say that there are three basic structures of the Bengali sentences. Here we mean the simple sentence only. The basic structures are:

(*a*) Sentence with one or more nominal units and one verbal unit;
(*b*) Sentence with one or more nominal units but no verbal unit;
(*c*) Sentence with one or more verbal units only and no nominal.

We can abbreviate the nominal unit as NU, and verbal unit as VU, and define these three situations as :

(*a*) NU-VU
(*b*) NU
(*c*) VU

In addition to a finite verb, there can be a non-finite verbal form in a sentence which is structurally NU-VU. For instance:

kothāo pɔth nā-pee tomār kāche esechi[24]
anywhere way not finding to you have come
= Finding no other way, (I/we) have come to you.

In this example, the expression *esechi* is the finite verb. The non-finite form is *nā-pee* and there is no subject nominal which agrees with the verb.

[3.2] In Sanskrit, six basic *kāraka* relations are established and this set of *kāraka* (as explained) concerns the subject-predicate division of a sentence. In all grammars, it is said that the *kāraka* concept depends on the meaning, and that the relation should be understood from the meaning of the whole sentence.[25]

For instance, a sentence like the following can have two interpretations, although both interpretations involve *kāraka*.

(10) *bipɔde* *more* *rokkha kɔro*
in danger/from danger me save
= (1) Save me in time of difficulty (danger).
(2) Save me from the difficulty or help me to overcome the difficulty.

When such different interpretations are possible, one has to understand the intended meaning from the context.

According to the grammarians, the first interpretation establishes *adhikaraṇa-kāraka* involving the NU *bipɔde* and the second interpretation

[24]Chatterjee, p. 316. [25]Chatterjee, p. 83.

establishes *apādāna* involving the same nominal.[26] However, in both cases there is no such NU which is in agreement with the VU.

[3.2.1] The six *kārakas* are: (1) *kartṛ-kāraka*; (2) *karma-kāraka* (3) *karaṇa-kāraka*; (4) *sampradāna-kāraka*; (5) *apādāna-kāraka*; (6) *adhikaraṇa-kāraka*.[27]

Kale says:

> There are six *kārakas* in Sanskrit belonging to the first seven cases, except the Genitive.... The nominative, as in English and other languages is simply the naming case; its office, when used by itself, is to express the crude form of a word, gender, measure and number and nothing more. When used with a verb it forms its subject.[28]

And he quotes Pāṇini II.3.46 to indicate that in these situations the nominal takes a certain type of marker.

But he neither explains clearly the *kartṛ-kāraka* relation nor does he give any example of this *kāraka* in different voices.

The term *kartā* is taken as equivalent to the English term 'subject' in the *Practical Sanskrit-English Dictionary* by Apte.[29] Prof. Chatterjee used another term *kartṛpada* 'kartā element' in addition to the term *kartā*.[30]

The terms *kartā* and '*kartṛpada*' are thus defined by Prof. Chatterjee: When a nominal performs (completes, does or accomplishes) the action indicated by the verb in a sentence, that nominal should be taken as *kartā* of the sentence and the NU be called *kartṛpada*, i.e. *kartā* unit or element. The performer relation between the NU and the VU is called *kartṛ-kāraka* (in Sanskrit as well as in Bengali grammars).[31]

P. Acharya maintains that the *kartā* independently performs the action. The term *kartā* is explained by him as the nominal which performs (accomplishes) the action indicated by the verb in a sentence.[32]

Since I could not find a better term for the Bengali word '*sɔmpādon kɔrā*'[33] I have used the word 'perform' in my translation. The Bengali term is explained in *Calantikā*[34] and the equivalent terms given only in other dictionaries are:[35]

[26]Chatterjee, p. 94.

[27]Chatterjee, p. 83; Vidyabhushan, p. 49; Acharya, p. 91.

[28]Kale, p. 475.

[29]V.S. Apte, p. 452.

[30]Chatterjee, p. 83; Acharya, p. 93.

[31]Chatterjee, pp. 83, 103. (The author has translated from the Bengali original.)

[32]Acharya, p. 95.

[33]Each of the Bengali grammarians, previously mentioned, have used the term.

[34]Rajsekhar Basu, *A Bengali to Bengali dictionary* (8th ed.), 1955.

[35]*Dev's Concise Dictionary*; Bengali to English, pp. 128, 375, 598; *Calantikā* (3rd ed.) 1955, pp. 74, 580; *Samsad English-Bengali Dictionary*, (2nd. ed.), 1963, pp. 11, 464, 264, 985.

to perform; to accomplish; to execute;
to complete; to carry into effect; to do.

From various examples given in Bengali grammars and in Bengali dictionaries, one understands that it includes the idea of agreement of nominal with the verb which is manifested by the verbal concord.[36]

P. Acharya also explains that the *kartā* performs the action independently. He says that the *kartā* is independent in the sense that it performs itself the action and not to be used as an instrument by an agent. He provides an example:

(11) (1) *ei trisul*
this trident
(2) *pātālgɔrbho hoite*
from the inferno
(3) *utthito hoiā*
arising
(4) *medini bidārɔkpurbɔk*
having pierced the earth
(5) *ākās*
the sky
(6) *biddho koriteche*
is piercing
= This trident is piercing the sky, having pierced the earth, and it has come from the bottom of (the) hell.

There are six segments in the example. No. 1 is that NU which performs the action indicated by the VU, No. 4 segment. No. 1 is independently doing the action. Even though the noun refers to an inanimate thing, it takes such a verb that can occur with an animate noun also. No. 1 segment is considered as *kartā* by P. Acharya. We assume that the term *kartā* implies the subject and the agent.

The fact is, in most cases in all languages, the agent (which is also the subject) refers probably to an animate noun. And very often it is not accepted that the term 'agent' does not necessarily imply an animate noun. Particularly, in traditional Indian grammar, 'agent' is a grammmatical term; the agent function of the subject NU is assigned on the basis of the performer relation involved between the NU and the VU in a given sentence. From the examples given by all Bengali grammarians and scholars mentioned in our work, it seems clear that the term *kartā* which corresponds to subject and agent does not necessarily refer to an animate noun.

[36]Here 'concord' means the marker on the verb which indicates the person of the nominal with which the verb is in agreement.

Obviously, the term 'agent' is defined in a different way in modern linguistic analysis. Langeondon defines it in the following way:

For someone or something to be an agent, it must be capable of acting on its own volition and since inanimate physical objects or abstract ideas normally cannot do so, it is generally odd to use a nominal expression which refers to an inanimate object or abstract idea as an agent.[37]

Though Prof. Chatterjee, N. Vidyabhushan and P. Acharya define *kartṛ-kāraka* in a similar way, there are some differences in their descriptions. N. Vidyabhushan and P. Acharya have not mentioned that *kartā* includes the notion of subject. They have given different types of *kartā* and have indicated different markers that appear on the *kartā* nominal. Though Prof. Chatterjee has discussed the voices elaborately, he has not mentioned the *kartā* except in active voice. Often he has used the term '*uddeśya*' which corresponds to the term 'subject'. He explains that the *uddeśya* has agreement with the verb in all voices. Though N. Vidyabhushan has discussed the voices of verbs, he has not mentioned that grammatical device of agreement and concord indicates the subject function of the nominal.

Prof. Chatterjee has said that the predicative verb takes the person marker, according to the subject nominal.[38] Thus, from the verbal concord, the subject nominal can be established in most cases, excepting the type of verb construction which does not show agreement with any subject nominal. We shall discuss this point in some detail later in this chapter.

Prof. Chatterjee has not used the term '*kartā*' while discussing neuter voice. He has explained:[39]

(*a*) When the nominal referring to the actual doer (animate doer) in the real world is the subject of the verb, the verb is in active voice;

(*b*) When a *potential object* of a transitive verb acts as the *kartā* (here he means that subject NU which is in agreement with the verb) of the sentence, i.e. when the NU shows agreement with the verb, the verb is in passive voice;

(*c*) When the subject of the predicative verb indicates a theme of *an action*, i.e. when the subject NU is a verbal noun and the finite verb of the sentence is in agreement with that subject, the verb should be considered to be in neuter voice:

(*d*) When the subject NU refers to an object of the real world, the verb should be considered to be in reflexive voice.

In Bengali (Sanskrit and all modern Indian languages), when the physical things such as cloud, rain, current, etc. as well as machine, trident, etc. appear to be the performer of the action indicated by the verb, we call

[37]Langeondon, *Essentials of English Grammar*, p. 64.

[38]Chatterjee, pp. 83, 319-327.

[39]S.K. Chatterjee, pp. 319-327.

them agent. Considering their inanimate feature, they may be called inanimate or non-animate agent.

None of the grammarians, mentioned earlier, have used the term 'metaphorical agent' or 'inanimate/non-animate agent', since they consider the subject NU as agent in the sense of performer of the action without considering the semantic features of the NU. Differences may be established in terms of voice and syntactic structure of the sentence. The grammarians also employ the term *kartṛpada* in the sense of the subject NU, the leading element in the sentence irrespective of active, passive neuter or reflexive voice and syntactic structure of the sentence.

No attention is drawn to the fact that some *kartā* could, perhaps have the function of animate agent and others, the function of non-animate agent.

Although P. Acharya does not give any example of neuter voice, i.e. he does not mention the different voices of verbs and the *kartā* nominals occurring in different voices, he gives examples which make it clear that irrespective of the semantic features of the nominal, it can be considered as *kartā* if it shows agreement with the verb in a sentence. The following examples may be considered:

(12) *mondire* *sankha* *bājā-uṭhilo*
in the temple the conchshell rang
= *The conchshell* rang in the temple (kartā: sankha)

(13) *jɔntro* *āsiā* *mānuṣer hāter-kāj*
the machine having coming the work of men
kāṛiā loiāche
snatched away
= The machine has seized the (role of) human labour (kartā: jɔntro)

(14) *se æmon kthā bolte pāre biswās hɔenā*
he such word can say cannot be believed
(*kartā*: se)[40]

P. Acharya thinks that the expression *se...pāre* is the *kartā* of the verbal expression *biswās hɔenā*.

It is obvious that he refers to the grammatical factor of agreement. We think that one may wonder if the clause *se...pāre* in the last example should be taken as object, as he thinks it is. In our opinion, the whole expression can be substituted as *ihā* which corresponds to the English term *it*. A similar sentence would be :

ihā biswās hɔenā
it cannot be believed.

[40]Acharya, pp. 96-97.

Prof. Chatterjee's examples of active voice are the following:

(15) *koto sthāne gāri thāmilo*
several places the vehicle stopped.

He considers that the expression *gāṛi* is the *kartā* and the verb is in active voice. It seems that *gāṛi* itself stopped.

(16) *koto nuton lok āsilo*
many new person(s) came

(17) *srot āmāder noukā ulṭāiā dilo*
the current our boat turned over

Prof. Chatterjee considers that the expressions *gāṛi*, *lok* and *srot* are to be taken as *kartā*, because they are showing the same type of relationship to the verb in respective sentences. All these nominal expressions show *kartṛ* relation. Thus they should be called *kartā*.[41]

It should be noted that (*i*) the grammatical devices of the verb ending indicates explicitly the subject function of the NU in the above-mentioned examples, and (*ii*) that the *kartā* which is the subject includes animate and inanimate nouns. It also includes a verbal noun, thus an abstract idea. See the sentence below:

(18) *mohāsoer thākā hoe kothāe*
of the person living is where
= Where do you live?
or *ækhon pherā jāk*
now return let be done
= Now let us return.

In such a situation, Prof. Chatterjee thinks the expressions *thākā* 'living', *pherā* 'return' should be the subject of the respective verbs. He does not use the term *kartā* but the term '*uddeśyapada* which corresponds to the English term subject.[42] In consideration of the argument forwarded by him, we believe that the term '*uddeśyapada*' and '*kartṛipada*' are equivalent. But the *kartṛpada* which refers to a verbal noun, cannot be said to be in *kartṛ-kāraka*, because the verb and nominal do not show the kind of involvement, readily noticeable in other examples, with other verbs and animate or inanimate nominals. From the viewpoint of the sentence semantics, we consider that the *trisul* (trident), *saṅkha* (conchshell), *srot* (current), *gāṛi* (vehicle), *mohāsoe* (person), etc. in the examples are agents. The actions indicated by the verbs are being done by the nouns referring to different animate beings and inanimate or physical things in respective

[41]Chatterjee, pp. 84-85. [42]Chatterjee, p. 323.

sentences. We consider their functions as similar, because these nouns can occur with the same verbs and agree with them in a similar fashion. In other words, an inanimate noun can occur with the type of verbs which occur with animate nouns and can agree with the verbs in a similar fashion as the animate noun does.

Inanimate things or physical phenomena are not the same kind of agents as the living beings. Even though things like plants and trees fulfil the basic qualities of living species, they are not recognized as agents in English grammar; but in Sanskrit and Bengali grammars they are.[43]

There is no doubt that physical phenomena such as water, wind, volcano, thunder, etc. and things such as machine, gun, train, etc. can be considered as performing something on their own force, although they may not perform on their 'own volition'.

In English, it may be said metaphorically that *nature does as it wishes*, or *the volcano is alive again*. But in any Indian language, the translation of these expressions will be more natural—not simply stylistic or metaphorical (figure or speech). In such cases we use the term agent. Considering the word semantics, this type of agent may be further indicated as inanimate agent. This implies that the language difference conditions the idea of agent in Bengali and in English.

In Bengali animate, inanimate and abstract nouns can take similar verbs:

mānuṣ cintā kɔre
man thinks
trisul biddho kɔre
(the) trident pierce
ākāśe megh kɔre
in the sky clouds come

But there are some combinatory rules. We find that on the one hand, a non-agent often occurs with the 'be' verb *hɔ-*; and that, on the other hand, an inanimate agent does not comply with such verbs as *likh-* 'write', *bɔl-* 'speak', etc. unlesss the noun is personified. Here we may utilize the idea of 'having brain' and 'having no brain'.[44]

The above-mentioned verb forms—*cintā kɔre*, *biddho kɔre*, and *kɔre-* show that *kɔr-* 'do' can occur as a full principal verb as well as an auxiliary.

Many verbs can be used with either animate or inanimate nouns in Bengali. Because of that we prefer to label animate and inanimate nouns with the same label.

[43]Various examples can be found in Sanskrit and Bengali literatures. See Kale, p. 476.

[44]This biological term can make the difference between the inanimate agent and the animate agent quite clear.

An abstract idea also can be labelled as *kartā*, i.e. agent, in many occurrences. An abstract noun can have agreement either with *be* verb or with verbs such as *bādh-* 'yield', 'happen', *jāg-* 'wake', 'come', 'rise', *ghɔt-* 'happen', occur', etc.

(19) *juddho bādhlo*
the war began (started)

(20) *ghɔṭonā ghoṭlo*
the incident occurred

These two verbs can occur with an animate noun only in causative. For instance:

(21) *rājā juddho bādhālen*
the king the war caused

Whereas the verbs, *jāg-* 'wake' and *lāg-* 'strike', 'put', can occur in the same form with animate and inanimate nouns as:

(22) *khokā jāge*
the child wakes up

(23) *sūrjo jāge*
the sun rises

(24) *dāzā jāge*
the land rises

Bengali and Sanskrit grammars agree that the nominal expressions of the above-mentioned examples should be considered as *kartā*, because they are believed to be showing *kartṛ* relation to the verbs in the respective sentences.

[3.2.2] Even though the subject which refers to an action can have agreement with the *be* verb in Bengali only, it is described as *uddeśyapada* which we think, corresponds to *kartṛpada*. No Bengali grammar explains the *kāraka* relation of such an NU.

In Bengali grammar, the *kāraka* relation is described as basically a semantic relation.[45] Its syntactic implication is given in the *vācya* category which corresponds partially to the idea of voice. The semantic functions of the nominals are categorised in the *kāraka* notion and the syntactic functions of the nominals are categorised in the *vācya* notion in traditional Indian grammar.

Kale says:

'Syntax deals with the mode of arranging words in sentences. Of the three

[45]Chatterjee, p. 83. (f.n.).

divisions of syntax—concord, government and order—the syntax of Sanskrit is mainly concerned with the first two, syntax in English depends principally upon the last".[46]

Kale describes *kāraka* and *concord* in the section of syntax and he thinks *kāraka* implies 'government'. 'The only portion of syntax treated separately in Sanskrit grammars is the *kārakaprakaraṇa* or the chapter on government,'[47] whereas Prof. Chatterjee and other Bengali scholars put *kāraka* in the section of semantics.[48]

The term *kāraka* is translated as 'case-relation' by Bahulikar,[49] and *kārake* (in *kāraka*) is established 'when there is a factor affecting verbal activity'.[50]

It seems to me that in sentence analysis the traditional Indian grammars put *kāraka* in two levels of semantics and syntax. Semantically, the idea defines the basic relations involving the nominal and verbal syntagms in a sentence. The basic relations are six in number, and they are labelled to the nominal expressions. Syntactically, the related syntagms are smaller syntactic units of a larger unit such as *vākya*[51] which corresponds to the term 'sentence'. Thus, *kāraka* includes the syntactic relation between two smaller syntactic units, and describes the subject-focusing by a verb. Furthermore, different *kārakas* indicate the different syntactic functions of the nominals such as subject and predicate in different *vācyas* of the sentence.

The *kāraka* relations are established on the basis of the total meaning of the sentence which we call sentence semantics. The sub-functions of the *kāraka* (as well as the sub-functions of the subject) and the category of *vācya* are defined on the basis of word semantics. Also the *vācya* concept implies the subject-focusing and the constructional differences of the sentences.

We suggest that the *kāraka* concept may be taken as a useful method to analyse also sentences of other languages.

[3.2.2.1] Although the *kāraka* relation of the subject—referring to a verbal noun is not indicated by Bengali grammarians, it is accommodated to the sub-function and the *vācya* category. Some concepts which are provided by the traditional Indian grammarians are not to be found in Western grammar. The traditional Indian grammar identifies the causative subject and causative object affiliations of sentences. The passive subject which is the object of the transitive verb is called *anuktakartā*;[52] likewise the causative subject as *prayojakakartā* and causative object or instrument as *prayojyakartā*. These can be translated as:

[46]Kale, p. 468. [47]Kale, p. 475. [48]Chatterjee, p. 83, f.n.
[49]Bahulikar, *Indian Linguistics*, vol. 34, no. 2, June 1973, p. 89.
[50]*Ibid.* [51]Chatterjee, pp. 291-301. [52]Acharya, pp. 96-97.

anuktakartā	'unspecified subject'
prayojakakartā	'causative agent' (subject)
prayojyakartā	'provoked agent'

For instance:

tumi āmāke ār bokio nā
you me any more do not cause to speak

The expression *tumi* is considered as 'causative agent' (subject) and the expression *āmāke* is considered as 'provoked agent'.

Prof. Krishnamurti uses the terms 'controller agent' and 'performer agent'.[53] It seems to me that the 'controller agent' can be either cause or performer (see examples below). So I translate the term '*prayojaka*' as '*causative agent*' i.e. as agent of the causative verb. The 'performer agent' no doubt performs the action simultaneously in the causative sentence but he is the instrument, in other words he is provoked by the '*causative agent*'. Therefore, we think 'provoked agent' or 'instrumental agent' is more appropriate translation of the term '*prayojyakartā*'. We prefer to use the term '*provoked*' to avoid any confusion with the term 'instrument'.

We have not found anyone saying that the grammatical device of agreement between nominal and verbal should also be a criterion to set up the *kartā* which is also a *kartṛpada* in some sentences, although Prof. Chatterjee maintains that the *uddeśyapada*, i.e. the subject of the sentence, controls the verbal concord.[54]

P. Acharya classifies different types of *kartā* as follows:

(*a*) *Kartā of active voice*
(*b*) *Kartā of passive voice*
(*c*) *Kartā of Reflexive voice*
(*d*) *Kartā of Causative Verb*:

(25) *tini aṁae pɔṛān*
he/she me teaches

(*e*) *Cognative Kartā*:

(26) *rādhuni rādhe*
the female cook cooks

(*f*) *Sociative Kartā* (*coordinate*)

(27) *māe-jhie jhɔgṛā kɔre*
mother-daughter quarrel

(*g*) *A Phrase as Kartā*

(28) *tomār amon kāj kɔrāṭā ɔnnāy hoeche*
your such work doing was wrong

[53] Linguistic Seminar on 10 October 1974, Monash. [54] Chatterjee, p. 319.

(*h*) *A Clause as Kartā*

(29) *se æmon kɔthā bolte pāre biswās hɔenā*
he such word could speak cannot be believed

(*i*) *Unexpressed Kartā*

(30) *tomāe sājābo jɔtone*
(to) you (I) will cause to dress carefully

(*j*) *One Kartā of Many Verbs in a Sentence*

(31) *jɔl chuṭiteche nāciteche kulukulu gān gāhiteche*
the water is running dancing murmuring

(*k*) *Many Kartā of One Verb*

(32) *kiser jonno binɔy, badol o dinesh*
what for Binoy, Badol and Dinesh
mṛttubɔron korilo
embraced death

(*l*) *Kartā of a Non-Finite Verb or Impersonal Kartā*

(33) *sūrjo uṭhile . āmrā jātrā korilām*
the sun when rose we started journey

The expression *uṭhile* is the non-finite verb form and the subject of the form s the expression *sūrjo* 'sun'. So it is defined as *impersonal kartā* of the verb *uṭhile* ('when rose').

(*m*) *A Means as Kartā*

(34) *omni tāhār lekhoni colitɔ lāgilo*
immediately his pen begun to move

(*n*) *Provoked or Instigated Kartā*

(35) *āmāke tumi ār bokionā*
me you anymore cause to speak (not)
= (do not cause to speak)

These fourteen examples of different types of *kartā* have been taken from P. Acharya. The present author has translated the following words: *samadhātuja* as *cognate* (this word 'cognate' is also used to express the same by Prof. S.K. Chatterjee, p.87); *vyātihāra* as *coordinate* or *sociative* (see *Samsad* English-Bengali *Dictionary* p. 1129 and *Dev's Concise Dictionary* p. 481); *sādhana* as *means* (*see Dev's Concise Dictionary* p. 609); *prayojya as provoked/instigated* (see *Dev's Concise Dictionary*, p. 426). To the present author, it seems reasonable to combine *vyātihāra* and *sahayogikartā*. As a matter of fact, these two are same.

There is no complete agreement about this classification and the number of the items in the classification. Prof. Chatterjee does not consider that the provoked agent (No. 35) is different from the indirect object. So far as we understand, Prof. Chatterjee includes that type of *kartā* under the label of indirect object (*gauṇa karma*) or instrumental (*karaṇa*) considering the causative verb form, the form of the particular noun, and the total meaning of the given sentence. On the other hand, N. Vidyabhushan and P. Acharya consider that the action by both nominal expressions of a two-place causative sentence can be simultaneous, which implies that there are two kinds of agent (compare example nos. 25 and 35 above). A three-place causative sentence like the following can be compared:

(36) *mātā* *śiśuke* *cād*
the mother to the child the moon
daekhāitechilen
caused to see (= was showing)

The verb form is causative in past progressive tense. This example is given by N. Vidyabhushan. The expression *mātā* should be called *prayojakakartā* which is the subject of the causative verb form in the sentence. The expression *śiśuke* which is defined as indirect object by Prof. Chatterjee is considered as *prayojyakartā* by N. Vidyabushan. The idea of *prayojyakartā* is explained by both P. Acharya and N. Vidyabhushan. It is interesting to note that the well-known syntactic criterion that the indirect object never becomes a subject in another affiliated sentence fails in the case of a language like Bengali, where a causative verb has a relation to three nominal units (example no. 36).

If a corresponding non-causative is compared, it would be observed that the indirect object of the corresponding causative (*śiśuke*) becomes the subject in the non-causative sentence.

śiśu *cad* *daekhe*
the child the moon sees

The example no. 36 shows that the expression *mātā* is to be considered as subject; the expression *cād* as direct object; and the expression *śiśuke* as indirect object.

It would be a mistake if one interprets that theoretically the causative and non-causative affiliations and the provoked/instigated agent conception are based on the 'deep structure' hypothesis. It is believed that the causative verb implies simultaneous action both by the mother and the child. Therefore both are to be considered as agents. Somebody might argue against the interpretation maintaining that the mother can show or be the cause of seeing but the child may not see or may refuse to see. However, the meaning of *daekhāno*, show implies that this verb cannot be used for such a situation. In other words, a causative verb such as *daekhāno* includes the idea that someone shows and the other one (other party) sees. This simultaneous action is to be understood.

The example (no. 35) indicates that someone is speaking having been instigated by another. The simultaneous action of provoking and being provoked can be labelled as two separate agents. One is the cause and the other is the caused. In a sense, the caused one may be called object also in addition to its agent function. Perhaps, in this case, one can say that an NU can be 'depository of two cases'.

P. Acharya defines the provoked (instigated) agent as follows: 'If one does anything being provoked by another person, the one who does the action should be considered as the provoked agent.'[55]

This kind of agent (*kartā*) can be compared with 'accusative with infinitive' in Western tradition, as the 'subject part, has often the function of agent as *him* in the following sentence. *I want him to do it*. In this example, both the verb and the noun form the object. If one paraphrases the object part, one will get a sentence: *He should do it*.

It seems the above non-causative *I want him to do it* is quite different from the Bengali example nos. 25, 35. Rather than equating the *provoked agent* with 'accusative with infinitive' we find another type of sentence in Bengali which is quite comparable with the English one. For instance:

āmi	*ke*	*obolte*	*dilām*
I	him	to speak	allowed (gave)

Perhaps the object part *oke bolte* 'him to speak' can be considered as similar to the English construction *him to do it*. And the expression *oke bolte* may be paraphrased as *he should speak*.

As far as the number of different *kartās* is concerned, Prof. Chatterjee does not present the same numbers as P. Acharya or N. Vidyabhushan does. Prof. Chatterjee presents the classification of *kartā* in voice, although he does not mention the subject as *kartā* in *bhāvavācya*. P. Acharya establishes fifteen types of *kartā* and N. Vidyabhushan, seven.[56]

Structurally, all types of sentences occurring in four different voices, can be grouped into two, i.e. the verb is active or passive including causative.

Here, structurally, active means that the verb is in active and there is no adverbial of agent; passive means that the verb form is in passive, and there occurs an adverbial unit which is potentially agent and may be either animate or inanimate. For instance:

(37)	*pitā*	*putroke*	*tiroskrto korilen*	(active)
	the father	the son	scolded	

[55]Acharya, pp. 96-97.

[56]Acharya, pp. 96-97; Vidyabhushan, pp. 50-51; Chatterjee, pp. 319-327.

(38)	*putro*	*pitākottṛk*	*tiroskṛto hoilen*	(passive)
	the son	by the father	was being scolded	

The verb construction is different in the sense that one auxiliary is a '*do*' verb, the other is the '*be*' verb. There is an adverbial of agent unit with a certain marker in the passive construction. And the object of the active becomes the subject of the passive.

P. Acharya defines that if a noun for an instrument, which is actually used by somebody, seems to perform the action indicated by the verb, then the noun should be considered as m-type *kartā*. It seems that he accounts for the nominal classification also, in addition to the voice difference, i.e. by indicating the term '*means*' he identifies a given class of noun and its semantic feature. Prof. Chatterjee differentiates the voices only. However, agent should be assigned on the basis of performer relation between verb and noun. The '*means*' *as kartā* and many others which refer to inanimate objects are called *kartā* of the *karmakartṛvācya* both by Prof. Chatterjee and N. Vidyabhushan.[57]

Scholars such as Ramendrasundar and Rabindranath point out that the nature of the Bengali language is different from Sanskrit. We should not always expect correspondence between both the languages. Prof. Chatterjee is of the opinion that one should not deal with the markers in Bengali in the way the markers are dealt with in Sanskrit.[58]

The relatedness of active and passive constructions leads to the idea of two cases in one expression in Sanskrit grammar as well as in Bengali grammar.

Following Sanskrit grammar, P. Acharya and N. Vidyabhushan define *anukta* and *ukta kartā* in affiliated sentences such as active and passive. Examples (nos. 37 and 38) contain two items in different forms in respective active and passive constructions.

P. Acharya considers that the item *pitā* in active is *uktokartā* and *pitākottṛk* is *anuktokartā* in passive. Similarly *putroke* is *anuktokartā* in active and *putro* is *uktokartā* in passive. We think that in consideration of corresponding affiliated sentence the idea of connecting the corresponding active or passive with each other and to consider one item as the depository of more than one relation (i.e. 'case') is similar to the idea of Starosta who also thinks that an item can be depository of two cases.[59]

One can show that quite different relations exist between verb and noun in expressions such as *pitā* and *pitākottṛk* in both active and passive, and *putroke* and *putro* in respective sentences of active and passive.

[57]Chatterjee, pp. 83-85, 319-27; Vidyabhushan, pp. 81-82.

[58]Chatterjee, p. 92.

[59]*Working Papers in Linguistics,* Hawaii University, Vol. 4, No. 1, January-March 1972, pp. 71-118.

Prof. Chatterjee uses the term *kartā* and *karma* to identify *pitā* and *putroke* in active, whereas *putro* and *pitākottṛk* should be identified as *kartā* (syntactic subject) in semantic relation to *karma* and adverbial to the expression *pitākottṛk* in respective passive. For instance, compare his example:[60]

(39) *dāktār* *rogīke* *dekhechen* (active)
the doctor the patient has checked

(40) *dāktārer* *rogī* *daekha hoeche*
of the doctor the patient has been checked
= The patient has been checked by the doctor.

One can say that the expressions *rogīke* and *rogī* in the above examples should be called direct object in active and subject: object in passive respectively. Similarly, the expressions *dāktār* and *dāktārer* can be called subject agent in active and adverbial of agent in passive. Or one may call the latter two expressions *uktakartā* and *anuktakartā*.

The term *uktakartā* includes both subject-agent and subject-object, whereas the term *anuktakartā* includes object (animate) which is potentially the subject of the affiliated passive and the adverbial of agent which is the potential agent and subject of affiliated active sentence.

We believe that, if, in the classification of *kartā* P. Acharya can maintain that a clause can be considered as *kartā* (no. 29), then a verbal noun can also be called *kartā*. For instance in a sentence like

jāoā hɔbe nā
going will not occur

the term '*kartā*' implies both syntactic subject and a semantic 'role' such as agent.

Prof. Chatterjee points out that the grammatical *kartā* and the doer in the real world are not synonymous.[61] He furnishes an example:

(41) *purohit-kottṛk* *śāstrānusāre*
by the priest according to the scripture
pūjā *sɔmpɔnno hoilo*
the worship was accomplished
= The rites were performed (accomplished) by
the priest according to the scripture.

Prof. Chatterjee explains that though *the priest* is the actor in the real world, i.e. the agent (in grammatical term), the expression *by the priest* is to be explained as adverbial in the above sentence. Since it does not show agreement with the verb, it cannot be taken as subject. Neither does

[60]Chatterjee, p. 326. [61]Chatterjee, p. 85 (f.n.).

it show performer relation to the verb in the example no. 41. What corresponds to the doer in the real world is an NU which has a kind of modificatory relation to the verb. We can assume that there are mainly two functions of *kartā*:

(*a*) the nominal is the agent of the verb (including inanimate agent);
(*b*) the nominal is non-agent.

Now (*b*) can be subdivided further into:

(*i*) the nominal is the patient or object of the verb;
(*ii*) the nominal does not signal object.

And (*ii*) can be further subdivided into:

(*a*) Independent factor;
(*b*) Theme.

As far as we know, the sub-functions of *kartā* are not clearly mentioned in any Bengali grammar. In Bengali most of the verbs occur with both animate and inanimate nouns and can show agreement in third person irrespective of the animate-inanimate distinction of the noun.

We have said before that, though Prof. Chatterjee, P. Acharya, N. Vidyabhushan define *kartṛ-kāraka* in a similar way, some confusion arises when they provide examples.

None of them has given any *kartā* status to the verbal noun which is in agreement with the verb (in the neuter voice). In Sanskrit grammar too, it is not mentioned whether the verbal noun should be given *kartā* status.[62] Prof. Chatterjee has mentioned that the verbal noun which is in agreement with the *be* verb is to be considered as subject (*uddeśya*) of the neuter voice.[63] Kale maintains that this type of construction is a kind of passive in Sanskrit *bhāve proyoga*,[64] because the verb forms are constructed similarly. In Bengali, however, the *bhāva* and *karmakartṛ* sentences are structurally similar to the *kartā* (agent-subject) sentence.

Historically, many passive verb forms become the active in Bengali, so in synchronic description one cannot expect one-to-one correspondences in Bengali and Sanskrit.

We maintain that *kartā* is that nominal which is in agreement with the verb in a sentence and the term *kartā* implies both *kartṛ-kāraka* and *kartṛ-pada*. Otherwise the definition and examples given by Prof. Chatterjee, P. Acharya, and N. Vidyabhushan would seem defective, because they say that the *kartā* accomplishes or performs the verb in a given sentence.

Following scholars such as Ramendrasundar Trivedi, Prof. Chatterjee and all others mentioned in this work, we assume that the notion of *kartṛ kāraka*

[62]S. Banerjee, p. 57. [63]Chatterjee, pp. 323-24. [64]Kale, p. 360.

implies the idea of agent of a verb, even though this *kāraka* is established on the basis of performer relation between the NU and the verb. The other implication of *kartā* is *kartṛpada*, and it is identified mainly by the grammatical device of agreement and concord. We have also mentioned that, in establishing the *kāraka* and a syntactic function such as subject and predicate, the total meaning of the whole sentence is one of the grammatical devices.

In summing up, we can say that the term '*kartā*' implies both the semantic and syntactic functions of the nominals. Our assumption of subfunctions of *kartā* gives a good account of the fact. The total meaning of a sentence, nominal relation to the verb and the devices of agreement-concord are equally important to establish the *kartṛ-kāraka* relation and *kartā* function of a nominal in a given sentence.

The grammarians employ the term *kartā* in a wider sense which includes the performer relation (some performers may be the actual doers in the real world), the agreement-concord, the topicalization of the subject. We have already said.

(*i*) When the syntactic subject has the semantic function of agent and it refers to an animate noun which is the referent in the real world, it is the actual doer or actor. In this case the real world situation and the grammar 'coincide'.

(*ii*) The term 'performer relation' is to be understood as a grammatical term.

(*iii*) The topicalization of the subject implies the identification of the subject on the basis of sentence semantics.

We intend to point out that in traditional Indian grammar in establishing *kāraka* (roles) the word semantic features (details such as animate-inanimate distinction, etc.) are not used as criteria. On the other hand, in a more global way sentence semantics based on the meanings of words is taken into consideration.

[3.3] Interestingly, in modern linguistic analysis, the 'roles' (the labelled relations) suggested by Fillmore and others are based on word feature semantics rather than sentence semantics.[65] Occasionally, the stress on word semantics leads to the error of confusing grammar and real world situation. Fillmore maintains: 'Chicago is windy' and 'It is windy in Chicago'; both *Chicago* and *in Chicago* are in the same case or 'role', i.e. locative. This idea of locative seems to be based on the fact that Chicago has a feature 'place name'. The thought that a place name denotes a place in the real world seems then to influence the grammatical interpretation, so that not only *in Chicago* is (correctly) called locative but also *Chicago* (in 'Chicago windy') is (incorrectly) called locative.

[65]Fillmore, *Case for Case*, p. 25; Langendoen, *Essentials of English Grammar*, p. 64.

If one indicates the potential cause, instrumental or locative function of any nominal which in a given sentence occurs in a similar environment as an agent (animate noun) does, then we believe, the type of error just mentioned is made.

It should be observed that an animate noun can also be the cause, instrument or location in a particular construction. In other words an animate noun can play such 'roles' in some constructions depending on the verb and the total meaning of the given sentence; not on the animate, inanimate, or abstract features of the noun or the place name, etc.

In this sense, we believe, Indian traditional grammar suggests a better solution than some modern linguistic semantic theories (case grammar, Fillmore and others). Another suggestion in Indian traditional grammar concerns the classification of verbs. All classes of verbs are taken as verb only and not as stative, dynamic, etc. Similarly, in establishing semantic 'role' or function in a given sentence, all classes of nouns are taken as noun only and not as animate, inanimate, count, abstract, etc.

It seems that if the distinction of verbs—static, dynamic, lexical, etc.,—and the distinction of nouns animate, inanimate, etc.—are taken into account while labelling case or 'role' to the NU, then the grammar and real world situation will not be kept distinct.

In traditional grammar all kinds of verbs are treated similarly and so are all kinds of nouns also.

For instance, *leaves* fall down, *the river* flows, *the train* stopped, etc. or *peace* prevails, *the eating* is going on, *the sky* is blue, *I am* old, etc. the underlined nouns in italics should be considered as *kartā* of the respective sentences, according to the traditional grammar. It is clear that all of them are not showing performer relation with the action indicated by the verbs in respective sentences. And except the last one, none of them are animate nouns. The nouns referring to human, plant, animal, physical objects, inanimate things, abstract ideas and action can occur as *kartā* if they show direct relation with the verb in a sentence. We suggest that this direct relation can be defined in terms of the grammatical device of agreement.

This direct connection can be of two types: (*i*) agent relation; and (*ii*) non-agent relation. The agent function of a noun is to be established when it shows performer relation with the verb in a sentence. In the case of non-agent function of any kind of noun performer relation[66] is not shown.

We have already mentioned different classification of the subject noun in Bengali grammar. In the opinion of the present author, all kinds of *kartā* subject can be semantically divided into two groups mentioned above. the performer relation applies to active and causative sentences. Thus, the

[66]The latter type includes sentences which are structurally NU-VU or NU. The sentence which is structurally NU can have a subject which is identified on the basis of the total meaning of the sentence only.

subject of these two sentences can be labelled under the agent function. This way the agent and non-agent functions of the subject nominal include active, passive and causative construction. To make the point clear example nos. 35, 37 and 38 appearing above, are repealed:

(37) *pitā* *putroke* *tiroskrto korilen* (active)
the father the son scolded
(performer = agent)

(38) *putro* *pitākottṛk* *tiroṣkṛto hoilen* (passive)
the son by the father was being scolded
(non-agent)

(35) *āmāke* *tumi* *ār* *bokio nā* (causative)
me you anymore cause to speak not
(do not cause to speak)
(agent = actor + object) (performer = agent + cause)

Here it should be noticed that (*i*) some causative *kartā* can function as cause + actor (such as *tumi* in *āmāke tumi*) (*ii*) the provoked *kartā* can function either as object + actor = agent, or instrument + actor = agent (as *āmāke* in *āmāke tumi...* is an example of object + agent).

For instrument + actor = agent, compare the following:

(42) *tumi* *kāhākediā* *bhāt* *rādhāiācho*[66a]
you by whom rice cause to cook

The expression *tumi* is subject and cause + agent and the expression *kāhākediā* is instrument + agent.

The *anuktakartā*, i.e. the agent in a passive sentence can be treated syntactically as adverbial. The passive subject, which is semantically the object of the verb, can come under the label of non-agent function of the nominal (*kartā*).

It would seem that, if one takes facts of the real world into consideration, one may be tempted to establish underlying structures of the sentence. For instance, consider the following sentences:

(43) *rām* *rāvanke* *mārilen*
Rāma Rāvaṇa killed

(44) *rāvan* *rāmer* *hāte* *morilen*
Rāvaṇa of Rāma in the hand died (was killed)

66a Chatterjee, p. 139-140.

(45) *rāvaner mṛttu* *hoilo* *rāmer hāte/rāmkottṛk*
the death of Rāvaṇa occurred in the hand of Rāma/by Rāma

These three syntactic constructions communicate the same event or fact of the real world. To correlate these three, we may say that they are affiliated in meaning or they have the same referent. But syntactically and semantically they are different.

For the purpose of grammar and basic sentence semantics, it seems sufficient to establish two kinds of verb meaning—
- a full verb
- a be verb

So far we understand that this type of verb classification was taken into account in traditional grammar.[67]

Let us consider the syntactic deviancy of the last three examples:

	Subject	*Predicate*
(43)	*rām*	*rāvanke mārilen*
(44)	*rāvan*	*rāmer hāte morilen*
(45)	*rāvaner mṛttu*	*hoilo rāmer hāte/rāmkottṛk*

The forms change, emphasis changes, the semantic and syntactic functions change, although the event referred to remains the same. The above sentences are affiliated, because they have the same basic sentence meaning. This may be abbreviated as BSM.

In this context, we would like to quote Chomsky who says that 'the deep structure of a sentence is in general not identical to its surface structure, but is a much more abstract representation of grammatical relations and syntactic organisation.'[68] In practice deep structure seems to be rather arbitrary and different linguists represent the deep structure differently. To show this, I quote James D. McCawley:[69]

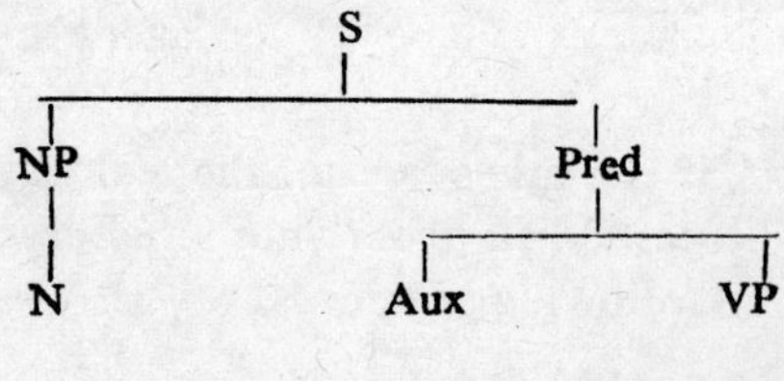

Also I quote Fillmore: 'Let us consider sentences derivable from the deep structure [diagram]'.[70]

[67]Chatterjee, p. 83.

[68]Chomsky, *Current Trends in Linguistics* (Vol. III.) p. 21.

[69]Bach, E. and Harms, R.T. (eds.), *Universals in Linguistic Theory*, p. 127.

[70]Bach, E. and Harms, R.T. (eds.), Fillmore, 'Case for Case' in *Universal in Linguistic Theory*, p. 68.

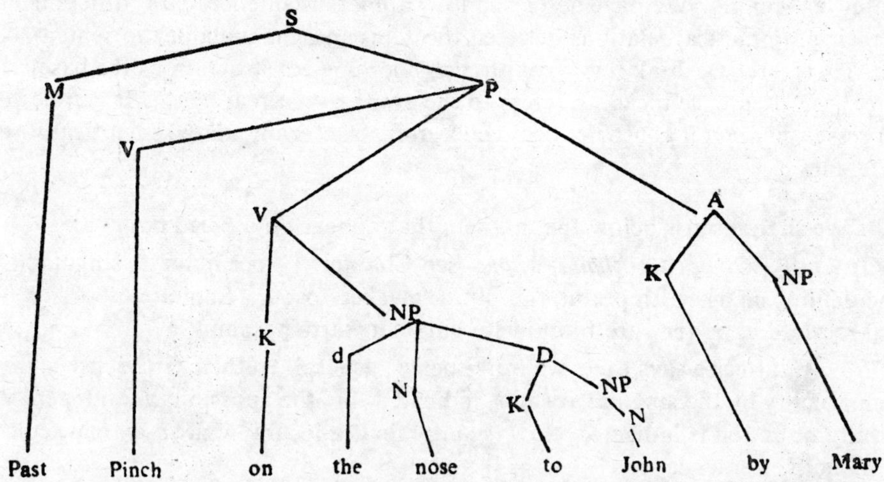

One thing seems clear from the above diagram [deep structure] that, even though Chomsky remarks that deep structure representation indicates grammatical relations and syntactic organization, none of the two are really represented fully. McCawley does not mention grammatical relation such as subject, and Fillmore's modality+proposition does not indicate the syntactic organisation.

If every linguist follows or invents his own deep structure, one may be more tempted than ever to follow the traditional representation of subject and predicate division of a sentence. As a matter of fact, we do not believe that any sentence should have any surface different from its deep structure. Rather a normal sentence should just be said to have its structure. Theoretically, there is no doubt that every sentence has a syntactic structure as well as a semantic structure. And such senseless expression as 'colorless green ideas sleep furiously' cannot be considered as a sentence, because the semantic structure is unacceptable. We agree with Dixon that such sequence does not follow the rule of collocation.[71]

We do not think that the description of a sentence in its two levels of grammar, i.e. on the levels of syntax and semantics, is a very new idea. Both in Indian and in Western traditions these, two levels of grammatical analysis are well established. The representation of a syntactic structure in a tree diagram is also not invented by the generativists. Bjorn Collinder points out that this type of diagram was used already in 1883.[72]

We do not believe that a passive construction should be considered as a construction derived from the active, even though both have the same basic

[71]Dixon, 1963, p. 75.

[72]Bjorn Collinder, 'Noam Chomsky Und Die Generative Grammatik', *Acta Universitatis Upsaliensis*, Acta Socientatis Linguisticae Upsaliensis Nova, Series 2:1, Uppsala, 1970, p. 6.

sentence meaning. We have described how affiliated sentences are different in their grammatical relations between the items and the units of the sentences. Therefore, we think it is wrongto consider one construction as the base. The basic sentence meaning refers to the event of the real world. It can be expressed in several constructions which are structurally and semantically different.

[3.4] We shall discuss below the markers that appear on a *kartā* nominal.

Generally, *O*, *-ṭā/-ṭi*, *-khānā/-khāni* (see Chapter I) occur as a singular and definite marker. In plural, the plural markers occur. Sometimes *-e/-te* and rarely *-ke*, *-r* (*er*) are found with singular kartā nominal.

Prof. Chatterjee says that, where either a general truth and a sense of commonalty by the singular form is indicated or the possibility and perpetuity of action is indicated, the *kartā* nominal appears with *-e-te* marker in an active sentence, e.g.[73]

(46)	*mānuṣ-e*	*bhābe*	*aek*	*hɔe*	*ārek*[73]
	man	thinks	one	happens	something different

Not one man only but the entire human race is indicated by the singular form with *-e* marker. One may givea non-individual or non-definite indication by the marker *-e*.

Sometimes, the marker singals perpetuity (constancy) of the action, a general truth.

(47)	*cor-e*	*curi kore*
	(the) thief	steals

It is the nature of a thief and it is a common quality of thieves.

Rajsekhar Basu says that when the nature of the species is indicated by the nominal, it takes *-e/-te* marker. He furnishes the following example:

(48) *chāgole ki nā khāe*[74]
(a) goat what not eats
= What a goat does not eat,
i.e. a goat eats everything.

This statement says something about the nature of a goat.

Both Prof. Chatterjee and Rajsekhar Basu point out that to indicate cooperative actve, i.e. the action shared by two the *kartā* nominals take *-e/ -te* marker. The two can be two individuals or a party/group, etc. For instance:

[73]Chatterjee, p. 84-85.
[74]*Calantikā*, p. 616.

(49) *tomāte-āmāte* *kājṭi* *koriā phelibo*[75]
you (and) me the work will do (accomplish)

(50) *poṇḍite-poṇḍite* *tɔrko korchen*[76]
scholar with scholar are debating
= The scholars are debating.

We find that in spoken language the *-e* marker is used with *kartā*, when it is a kinship term,[77] to indicate a definite person. In conversation, in a dialogue of a drama one finds sentences such as,

(51) *bāpe* *mereche*
(the) father has beaten

(52) *māe* *bole thāke*
(the) mother usually says so

Here *bāpe* or *māe* indicates a particular person who has close relation to somebody about whom something has been said before.

Rajsekhar Basu maintains that if the *kartā* with an *-e* marker is not definite, it seems to signal a species.

(53) *pokāe* *keṭeche*[78]
(the) insect has cut (it)

He also says that if there is a sense of either instrumental or cause in the expression of *kartā*, it takes *-e*/ *-te* marker, as:

(54) *mɔde* *sɔrlonās korle*[79]
the wine (liquor) had spoilt (him)
= He was finished by drinking liquor.

It can also indicate locative meaning, for instance:

(55) *bede* *bɔle*[80]
the Veda says

If one interprets the sentence *mɔde sɔrbonās korle* as 'he/she or they are corrupted by liquor' and *bede bɔle* as 'it is written in the Veda', then the cause/instrumental or locative meaning can be obtained. But we think it

[75]Chatterjee, p. 85.

[76]*Calantikā*, p. 616.

[77]In some East Bengali dialects, it is commonly used both with kinship term and proper name.

[78]*Calantikā*, p. 616.

[79]*Calantikā*. I have translated from the original. So far as I understand, the term *karaṇa* includes both cause and instrumental.

[80]*Calantikā*, p. 616.

is wrong to interpret these two sentences in any way other than 'the liquor had spoilt him' and 'the Veda says' and analyse them accordingly.

Neither Prof. Chatterjee has dealt with *-ke*, *-r* and postpositional marker in *kartā*, nor Rajsekhar Basu has given any example of *kartā* with these markers.

N. Vidyabhushan and P. Acharya have given examples such as:

(56) *tomā-ke gān korite hoibe*[81]
you have to sing

(57) *ɔmɔr-ke bhāt khāite hoibe*[82]
Amar rice has to eat

(58) *megh-ke jɔl dite hɔbe* (doggeral verse)
(the) cloud water has to give

The verb in the sentences expresses a certain aspect and tense in the above examples. It has agreement with the *-ke* marker 'nominal, so the *-ke* marker nominal is considered as *kartā* of the respective sentence.

It is debatable whether the *-r* marker nominal can be considered as *kartā* in the following examples given by P. Acharya and N. Vidyabhushan:

(59) *āmār thieṭāre hārmonium bājāno cāi*[83]
me in theatre harmonium playing wish
= I wish to play harmonium in the theatre.

We think that the verb indicates no direct relation with the expression *āmār*. Rather it shows agreement with the verbal noun *bājāno* 'playing'. P. Acharya describes *āmār* as *kartā*. It seems that *āmār* may be 'the *kartā* of the real world', i.e. the actor or doer of the action in the real world event. But it should not be considered as a grammatical *kartā*. Similarly, we find no direct relation between the verb and *āmār* in the following

(60) *āmār jāoā hɔbenā*[84]
me/my going will not occur, happen

In the same type of sentence, Prof. Chatterjee states that the agreement is between the *verbal noun* and the *be* verb. He provides the example:

(61) *āmār nāoā hoiāche*[85]
my bath is finished

[81] Acharya, p. 97.
[82] Vidyabhushan, p. 50.
[83] Acharya, p. 98.
[84] Vidyabhushan, p. 50.
[85] Chatterjee, p. 323.

Prof. Chatterjee maintains that historically it corresponds to the Hindi verb *cāhie* 'is wanted'.[86] Perhaps here, too, the verb *cai* and the animate noun *āmār* should be explained as *to me* playing harmonium *is desired* (is a must).

It seems that a nominal with *-r* marker can be considered as *kartā* when it shows direct relation with the finite verb. Some verbs occur with *-r* nominal as subject (*kartā*) such as *lāg-* 'strike', *hɔ-* 'be', *cāh-* 'want, like wish'. Otherwise, a complex verb, similar to the other ones that occur with *-ke* marker nominals, takes *-r* marker nominal as subject.
Compare the following with example nos. 56, 57 and 58:

(62) *āmār je sɔb dite hɔbe*[87]
me those all have to give

Structural differences should be considered, if the meaning of the verb is to be correctly interpreted. The expression *jāoā hɔbe nā* in example no. 60 does not constitute a complex verbal construction as the expression *dite hɔbe* (see example no. 62) which is a complex construction of a verb and constitutes one single unit.

The verbal noun *jāoā* is in agreement with the verb *hɔbe nā* (example no. 60). No one seems to have termed such an agreeable nominal as '*kartā* nominal'. Prof. Chatterjee mentions that the *uddeśyapada* 'the subject nominal' and the *kartṛpada* are equivalent.[88] He considers the verbal noun which is in agreement with the *be* verb as *uddeśyapada*. So we think it is not unreasonable to consider the verbal noun as *kartā*. It seems justified, since *be* verbs shows similar agreement with the abstract, animate and inanimate nouns.

The involvement between the subject noun and the verb may be of different types. From the point of view of semantics they may be classified as: performer and non-performer. The non-performer relation or involvement may be further indicated as: cause, independent factor, theme, topic, object.

We have already noticed that P. Acharya and N. Vidyabhushan have used the term *kartā* for a phrase, clause, etc. N. Vidyabhushan has dealt with such sentences where he considers a verbal noun indicating an action as *kartā*. He furnishes the following example:

(63) *ɔlpo ālote boi pɔṛā bhālo nɔe*[89]
in dim light book reading good is not
= It is not good to read a book in dim light.

[86] *Ibid.*
[87] Tagore, *Gītabitān*, p. 190.
[88] Chatterjee, p. 174.
[89] Vidyabhushan, p. 66.

N. Vidyabhushan considers that the expression *pɔṛā* 'reading' is the *kartā* of the sentence and it shows *kartṛ* relation with the negative verb *nɔe* 'is not'; the expression *boi* is the object.

From the examples given so far, we assume that *kartā* can be any noun irrespective of its semantic feature, if it shows agreement with any verb irrespective of its classification such as action stative, etc.

It is also observed that in some causative sentences the second animate nominal with *-ke* marker can be explained as object. But if simultaneous action is indicated by the verb, then the second nominal should be considered as being in performer relation and thus agent (see example no. 35).

[3.5] We have collected five hundred examples from Tagore.[89] Eighty per cent of the sentences of this collection contain a *kartā* NU or subject, and twenty per cent of the sentences, though structurally NU—VU, do not contain such an NU which shows agreement with the VU. These twenty per cent are subjectless sentences.

In the eighty per cent of the collected sentences which contain a subject, i.e. an agreeable NU, the percentage of different classes of nouns as the subject, i.e. *kartṛ Pada* or *kartā*, is as follows:

(1)	animate nouns	49 per cent (195 examples)
(2)	nouns indicating body parts and inanimate things	10 per cent (40 examples)
(3)	nouns indicating physical objects including plants	10 per cent (40 examples)
(4)	nouns indicating abstract ideas	26 per cent (105 examples)
(5)	nouns derived from verbs indicating action	5 per cent (20 examples)

[89]a *Rabīndra Racānavalī*, Vol. 7. Names of the stories: *Ghāṭer Kothā*, 'The Story of the Bathing Place', p. 3-10; *Mukuṭ*, 'The Crown, p. 14-15; Denāpāonā, 'The Liabilities and Assets', p. 29-34; Poṣṭmāṣṭār, 'The Postmaster', p. 34-39.

The style of the language, (i.e. our collected examples are from written language), is not very far from the educated and cultivated standard spoken form, except the verbal forms.

There are four hundred and twenty-six sentences on the twenty-one pages of the book mentioned. Some of them are compound and complex in construction. I have taken simple sentences and a few compound sentences breaking them into two simple constructions. For instance:

ɔbośeṣe	*ækdin*	*niru*	*sɔbinɔe*	*śāśurike*	
at last	one day	Niru	with modesty	to the mother-	
bolilo;	*'bābāke*	*ār*	*āmār*	*bhāider*	*dekhbo*
-in-law said	father	and	my	brothers	will see
mā'	(I wish to see (visit) my father and brothers)				
mother					

Even though it seems one big sentence, I have broken the sentence into two. The collected examples are given in the appendix.

In our text, we find that the percentages of the sub-functions of *kartā*, such as agent and non-agent functions of the subject NU, are as follows:

(*a*)	agent	35 per cent
(*b*)	non-agent	65 per cent

This can be further described as follows:

(*i*)	animate noun+performer relation with the verb	30 per cent
(*ii*)	inanimate noun+performer relation with the verb	5 per cent
(*iii*)	animate, inanimate and abstract noun + non-performer relation with the verb	65 per cent

It is found that in the non-agent function the percentage of the occurrence of different classes of noun is as follows:

(*a*)	animate noun as *kartā* (non-agent)	14 per cent
(*b*)	inanimate things and object	46 per cent
(*c*)	abstract noun as *kārtā*	32 per cent
(*d*)	verbal noun as *kartā*	8 per cent

In Bengali, we have more than eight hundred verbs. The following are found in our examples collected from *Rabīndra Racanāvālī* (Vol. 7). We have listed only the verb roots (including stems), not the exact verb forms which occurred in the sentences. Verbs are alphabetically arranged as follows:[90]

(1) *ās*, come; appear; arise
(2) *āche*, remain; stay; is; exist
(3) *ālokɔr*, make light; make glow
(4) *āstede*, allow to come; give permission to come
(5) *ān*, bring
(6) *āk̃*, draw; paint; print
(7) *ābṛtti kɔr*, recite; read; utter
(8) *āghāt kɔr*, touch; wound; give pain; hit; hurt
(9) *ālocɔnā kɔr*, discuss
(10) *bhul*, mistake
(11) *bækul hɔ*, be restless; anxious
(12) *bɔh*, flow; blow
(13) *bhed kɔr*, pierce; penetrate

[90]There are different types of verbs which have been discussed in some detail in the following pages.

(14) *bodh hɔ*, feel; guess
(15) *bissrām kɔr*, rest; take rest
(16) *bæthito hɔ*, be wounded; offended; feel pain
(17) *bhālo lāg*, like; be fond of
(18) *bhālobās*, like; love; be fond of
(19) *bānā*, make; prepare
(20) *bakto kɔr*, express
(21) *bissās kɔr*, believe; trust
(22) *bɔddhomul hɔ*, take firm root; confirm
(23) *bās kɔr*, live; remain; stay
(24) *bhuliā jā*, forget
(25) *birɔkto hɔ*, be annoyed; vex
(26) *bhās*, float; throw
(27) *bɔbosthā kɔr*, make arrangement
(28) *bikrɔe kɔr*, sell
(29) *bɔndho kɔr*, stop; close; give up; shut
(30) *bhāb*, think; remember
(31) *bāki thāk*, be unpaid; remain
(32) *bɔndhok rākh*, mortgage; keep in mortgage
(33) *bhikkhā cā*, beg; request
(34) *bibāhɔ kɔr*, marry
(35) *bujh*, understand; realize
(36) *bādhiā jā*, stagnate
(37) *bāhiā jā*, to run; flow; glide
(38) *bɔl*, speak; tell; say
(39) *bhāŋ̮*, break; split
(40) *bikosito hɔ*, blossom
(41) *bāhir hɔ*, come out; expose
(42) *bāṛite thāk*, remain increase
(43) *bhoriā uṭh*, to fill up; full
(44) *bājā*, ring; to make sound; give sound
(45) *bāsā kɔr*, make house; build nest
(46) *bɔs*, sit
(47) *chɔlchɔl kɔr*, be in tears; murmur
(48) *cāh*, look; want; opening out of the eyes
(49) *cɔl*, move; run; go
(50) *cāhiā kɔr*, demand; claim
(51) *cāpā*, fell; burden
(52) *ceṣṭā kɔr*, try
(53) *cintā kɔr*, think; decide
(54) *citrito kɔr*, paint; draw; print; decorate
(55) *chāṛ*, leave; to give up
(56) *cetɔnā hɔ*, be conscious
(57) *dækhā de*, be in sight; be in vision

(58) *ḍāk*, call
(59) *dɔrkhāsto kɔr*, apply; make a petition
(60) *dābi kɔr*, claim; demand
(61) *dā̃ṛā*, stand; become
(62) *dækhā kar*, see; meet
(63) *de*, give; pay
(64) *dūr hɔ*, be away; fade; get away
(65) *golmāl hɔ*, be upset
(66) *ghūc*, remove; pass over; overcome
(67) *ghumā*, sleep
(68) *ghuriā berā*, give round; travel
(69) *hɔ*, be; is; become
(70) *hās*, smile; laugh
(71) *icchā kɔr*, wish; desire
(72) *jɔṛāiā dhɔr*, hold firmly; embrace
(73) *jwɔl*, light on
(74) *jāg*, rise; awake
(75) *juṛā*, adjust; fix up; yoke; affix
(76) *jānā*, 'know'; realize
(77) *jɔtno hɔ*, take care of
(78) *jiggāsā kɔr*, ask; enquire
(79) *jɔnmā*, born; arrive; grow
(80) *jhul*, hang
(81) *jā*, go
(82) *khelā kɔr*, play
(83) *kādiā uṭh*, began to cry; weep
(84) *kɔh*, speak; say; tell
(85) *khoj kɔr*, search; find; look for
(86) *kɔrā jā*, can do
(87) *khoṭā de*, blame
(88) *kādiā pɔṛ*, implore
(89) *kɔr*, do
(90) *kāṭia jā*, run away; pass
(91) *khāite pā*, get to eat
(92) *kuṇḍolāito hɔ*, be roll
(93) *khā*, eat
(94) *khul*, open
(95) *lāg*, strike; touch; take root
(96) *lābh kɔr*, gain; obtain
(97) *lek*, write
(98) *lɔ*, take; carry
(99) *lāl hɔ*, be red; be rich; angry
(100) *mone hɔ*, think; decide; remind; make impression
(101) *mon-de*, pay attention; give mind;

(102) *miṭ*, fulfil
(103) *mukh thākā*, remain way
(104) *mɔr*, die
(105) *mone pɔr*, come in mind; remember
(106) *niṣkṛti pā*, get relief
(107) *niṣiḍdho hɔ*, prohibit; cancel
(108) *nissās phel*, take breath
(109) *nirās hɔ*, be disappointed
(110) *nie ās*, bring; make view
(111) *nāi*, not exist
(112) *nikɔṭ hɔ*, be near; close
(113) *nāmiā pɔṛ*, come down; start; begin; get down; decrease
(114) *ɔpekkhā kɔr*, wait
(115) *ɔgocɔr thāk*, remain unknown
(116) *ɔsɔnmān kɔr*, disrespect
(117) *ɔbāddho hɔ*, be disobedient
(118) *ɔbɔlɔmbɔn kɔr*, take help; follow
(119) *ɔbohelā kɔr*, neglect; not take notice of
(120) *ɔbbhās kɔr*, practise
(121) *ɔbāk hɔ*, wonder; surprise
(122) *ɔnubhɔb kɔr*, feel
(123) *odhikār thāk*, possess the right
(124) *pher*, return; turn
(125) *polāyɔn kɔr*, flee; go away
(126) *prottāśā kɔr*, expect
(127) *phuṭ*, be express; blossom; boil
(128) *pāṭh kɔr*, read; read out; recite
(129) *pāṭhā*, send
(130) *protiggā kɔr*, promise
(131) *phāṭ*, crack; break
(132) *prokāś hɔ*, be reveal; come into light
(133) *phāki de*, deceive
(134) *pā*, get; obtain
(135) *poṛiā jā*, began to fall; decrease; become low
(136) *probeś kɔr*, enter; penetrate
(137) *prosārito hɔ*, be opened; expand; spread
(138) *protipholito hɔ*, be reflected
(139) *poribortito hɔ*, be changed
(140) *protipotti hɔ*, be famous; renowned; be powerful
(141) *pɔṛ*, fall; read
(142) *rɔconā kɔr*, make; compose; write
(143) *rāṣṭro hɔ*, be spread out; disclose; be exposed
(144) *rākh*, keep; maintain
(145) *rākhite pār*, be able to keep; maintain; keep under control

(146) *rɔ*, remain; exist; live; endure; last
(147) *ruc*, taste
(148) *ruddho kɔr*, obstruct; choke; shut
(149) *śihoriā uṭh*, tremble; move; shiver
(150) *śu*, lie down; sleep
(151) *śekhā*, teach
(152) *śikh*, to learn
(153) *sāj*, be dressed; make dress; dress up; be ready; arrange
(154) *śɔkh hɔ*, wish; desire
(155) *sākkhāt kɔr*, see; meet
(156) *śikkhā hɔ*, take lesson
(157) *sthogit ro*, postpone; make stay
(158) *sɔnmɔto hɔ*, agree; be in terms
(159) *sɔmpɔnno hɔ*, be performed
(160) *śodh kɔr*, repay
(161) *sun*, hear; listen; pay attention
(162) *sɔncār hɔ*, accummulate
(163) *sɔndhān kɔr*, search; find
(164) *śeṣ hɔ*, be end; finish; complete
(165) *sɔh*, tolerate; bear
(166) *sthir kɔr*, decide
(167) *sāmlā*, to evade; avoid carefully; control; manage
(168) *sthāpon kɔr*, build; construct; make foundation
(169) *sɔmbɔndho kɔr*, make negotiation
(170) *tul*, pull
(171) *ṭɔlmɔl kɔr*, shake
(172) *ṭer pā*, can understand; take notice of; smell
(173) *ṭānāṭāni pɔṛ*, fall short
(174) *thām*, stop; check
(175) *uccārito hɔ*, be uttered
(176) *uṭh*, rise; awake; get up; be alive
(177) *uposthit hɔ*, be present; arrive
(178) *ullekh kɔr*, mention
(179) *upojukto hɔ*, be fit; be deserving; be appropriate
(180) *udɔe hɔ*, appear; rise; arrive
(181) *unān dhɔrā*, fire on the oven; make fire
(182) *uttīrno hɔ*, crossover; complete
(183) *uṛ*, fly

Among these one hundred and eighty-three verbs, the following can show performer relation when they occur with a *kartā* (subject):

(1) *āste de*, give permission to come (4)
(2) *āghāt kɔr*, hit; wound (8)

(3) *ān*, bring (5)
(4) *āk*, draw; paint; print (6)
(5) *ālocɔnā kɔr*, discuss (9)
(6) *ābṛtti kɔr*, recite (7)
(7) *bāsā kɔr*, make house; build nest (45)
(8) *bāhir hɔ*, come out (41)
(9) *bhāŋ*, break; split (39)
(10) *bɔl*, speak; say (38)
(11) *bujh*, understand; realise (35)
(12) *bibāho kɔr*, marry; get wed (34)
(13) *bɔndhok rākh*, keep in mortgage (32)
(14) *bhikkhā cā*, beg; request (33)
(15) *bhāb*, think; remember (30)
(16) *bɔndho kɔr*, stop; check; give up; shut; close down (29)
(17) *bikrɔe kɔr*, sell (28)
(18) *bɔbosthā kɔr*, make arrangement (27)
(19) *bhuliā jā*, forget (24)
(20) *bās kɔr*, live (23)
(21) *bissās kɔr*, believe; trust; keep faith (21)
(22) *bakto kɔr*, express (20)
(23) *bānā*, make; prepare (19)
(24) *bhās*, float; swim (26)
(25) *bhālobās*, love; be affectionate (18)
(26) *bɔh*, flow; blow; tolerate (12)
(27) *bhed kɔr*, pierce; hit; penetrate (13)
(28) *bhul*, forget (24, 10)
(29) *bisrām kɔr*, take rest (15)
(30) *bāhiā jā*, run the show; run (37)
(31) *chāṛ*, leave; give up (55)
(32) *citrito kɔr*, paint; draw; decorate (54)
(33) *cintā kɔr*, think; realise; understand (53)
(34) *ceṣṭā kɔr*, try (52)
(35) *cāhiā bɔs*, demand; claim (50)
(36) *cɔd*, move; run (49)
(37) *cāh*, look; see (48)
(38) *dūr hɔ*, be away; get away (64)
(39) *de*, give (63)
(40) *dekhā kɔr*, see; meet; get introduced; call on; visit (62)
(41) *dāṛā*, stand; wait; stop (61)
(42) *dābi kɔr*, demand; make a claim (60)
(43) *ḍāk*, call (58)
(44) *dɔrkhāsto kɔr*, apply; make petition (59)
(45) *dekhā de*, be in sight; grant an interview (57)
(46) *ghumā*, sleep; get sleep (67)

(47) *hās*, smile; laugh (70)
(48) *icchā kɔr*, wish; desire (71)
(49) *jāg*, awake; rise (74)
(50) *juṛā*, adjust; yoke; fix up (75)
(51) *jiggāsā kɔr*, ask; enquire (78)
(52) *jɔnmā*, born; grow (79)
(53) *jhul*, hang (80)
(54) *jɔṛātā dhɔr*, hold firmly; embrace (72)
(55) *kādiā uṭh*, began to cry; weep (83)
(56) *khelā kɔr*, play (82)
(57) *kɔh*, speak; say; tell (84)
(58) *khoj kɔr*, search; find; look for (85)
(59) *kādiā pɔr*, implore (88)
(60) *khotā de*, blame (87)
(61) *khā*, eat (93)
(62) *kɔr*, do (89)
(63) *khul*, open (94)
(64) *lekh*, write (97)
(65) *lɔ*, take; carry (98)
(66) *mon de*, give mind; pay attention (101)
(67) *nie ās*, bring (110)
(68) *nikɔṭ hɔ*, be close; come nearer (112)
(69) *nāmiā pɔṛ*, get down (113)
(70) *ɔbāddho hɔ*, be disobedient (117)
(71) *ɔbɔlɔmbɔn kɔr*, follow; take path (118)
(72) *ɔbbhās kɔr*, practise (120)
(73) *ɔnubhɔb kɔr*, feel (122)
(74) *ɔbohaelā kɔr*, neglect (119)
(75) *ɔsɔnmān kɔr*, show disrespect; disrespect (116)
(76) *ɔpekkhā kɔr*, wait (114)
(77) *probeś kɔr*, enter (136)
(78) *poriā jā*, fall down (135)
(79) *phāki de*, deceive (133)
(80) *pāṭhā*, send (129)
(81) *pāṭh kɔr*, read out; recite (128)
(82) *pɔlāyɔn kɔr*, flee; go away (125)
(83) *protiggā kɔr*, promise (130)
(84) *pher*, turn; return (124)
(85) *pā*, get; obtain (134)
(86) *ruddho kɔr*, shut; obstruct (148)
(87) *rākhite pār*, keep under control; keep in possession; maintain; be able to keep (145)
(88) *rākh*, keep; maintain (144)
(89) *rɔconā kɔr*, compose; make; write (142)

(90) *śihoriā uṭh*, tremble; shiver (149)
(91) *śu*, lie down; sleep (150)
(92) *śekhā*, teach (151)
(93) *śikh*, learn (152)
(94) *sāj*, dress up; be ready; make dress (153)
(95) *śun*, listen; hear; pay attention (161)
(96) *sɔnmɔto hɔ*, agree; give consent (158)
(97) *śodh kɔr*, repay; pay back (160)
(98) *sɔh*, tolerate (165)
(99) *sāmlā*, avoid carefully; manage (167)
(100) *sākkhāt kɔr*, meet; see (155)
(101) *sɔmbɔndho kɔr*, negotiate (169)
(102) *sthāpon kɔr*, build; construct; make foundation (168)
(103) *tul*, pull (170)
(104) *ṭɔlmɔl kɔr*, move; shake; tremble (171)
(105) *thām*, stop; check (174)
(106) *uṭh*, rise; get up; awake (176)
(107) *uposthit hɔ*, be present; arrive (177)
(108) *ullekh kɔr*, mention; make note (178)
(109) *udɔe hɔ*, arise; arrive; appear (180)
(110) *uṛ*, fly (183)

Among these above-mentioned one hundred and ten verbs, some take only animate noun as subject; some can occur with both animate and inanimate. In all such cases, irrespective of the semantic feature of the subject nouns, they are to be labelled on the same label which is to be established on the basis of the relationship subsisting between the nominal and the verb. For instance, the verb no. 56 (82) can take either an animate or an inanimate noun as subject. In both the cases, the relationship should be understood as performer; as such the function of the NU is to be called agent. At a higher level, there is perhaps no need to make differences such as *animate agent* and *inanimate agent.*

As a matter of fact, the verb allosemes, the meaning of the subject nominal and the meaning of the other items—all these come in 'play' to establish the 'role' of a nominal. All these together can indicate performer or non-performer relationship. The performance may be active or non-active. This active non-active type of difference may be shown at a lower level of semantic syntactic description rather than at the sentence level. Using the minimum of word semantics, the 'role' of a nominal can be labelled which, we think, can be limited within the boundary of sentence level.

A verb can have different allosemes; the sentence meaning may differ because of different word allosemes.

In some situations, the same verb and the same subject occur but other lexical items may differ. Taking a verb form *thāki* and a subject pronoun *āmi*, one can see how the alloseme of the verb is selected by the other lexical item in the following examples:

(64) *āmi ekhāne thāki*
I here live
= I live here

(65) *āmi sɔkāle thāki*
I in the morning remain (stay)
= I stay (at home) in the morning

(66) *āmi bhālo thāki kājer moddhe*
I good remain (feel) in work
= I feel better when I work.

It seems that the different allosemes (live, remain, feel) of the verb *thāki* are selected by the lexical items *ekhāne*, *sɔkāle* and *bhālo* in the above examples. And due to that the sentence meanings differ. Considering these sentence meanings, one can label the subject nominal differently. On the contrary, one may not label the subject nominal differently. As such, one can label the expressions *āmi* in the above three situations as *non-agent* or *agent* as the case may be. In a more abstract way, the same label (non-agent) seems appropriate. At one level we may not consider different word allosemes.

From our observations we can say:

(1) Even though the subject nominal and the verb remain the same, other items can cause a difference in the total meaning.

(2) The same verb may occur in different sentences, but the meaning of such sentences may differ due to the different allosemes of the verb.

(3) If the sentences semantics implies same type of involvement existing between the subject and the verb in different sentences, subject nominals can be labelled similarly.

The following points should, perhaps, be particularly emphasized. Broadly speaking, a noun refers to something; theoretically, it should be considered as a reference. A verb either connects two or more lexical items, or indicates action and other items refer to state, quality, condition, means, place, etc. Considering these as basic points, all examples so far given may be semantically represented in an abstract way as follows:

a reference—a link or—a state/quality/
action condition/means/place/time, etc. and (or) a
reference

The grammatical device of concord and agreement signals the subject function of a noun unit ('a reference') in a given sentence. Different markers, together with the lexical items, express the meaning of a unit. The lexical meaning, together with the relational meaning, expresses the total meaning of a given sentence.

Sometimes a simple verb is compounded with a noun and expresses several meanings. For instance, the simple verb *lāge* (strike) in Bengali has allosemes as follows:

when the verb *lāge* acts as an auxiliary in different contexts:

(*a*) *mɔne* *lāge*
in mind strikes
(*i*) 'like', 'prefer', '(it) strikes,
(*ii*) 'offend', wound', 'hurt', 'cause pain'

(*b*) *gāe* *lāge*
on the body
'pains', 'hurts'

(*c*) *cokhe* *lāge*
in the eye
(*i*) 'seem colourful', 'dazzle', 'reflect'
(*ii*) 'seem offensive', 'not look nice'

Therefore, we think that the establishment of the basic 'roles' of the NU depends mostly on the sentence semantics.

[3.6] The active, passive and causative subjects can be identified by the verbal construction of the given sentence.

In our text we have noted that some of the active subjects show the agent function and some do not. We have already mentioned that the latter subjects should be called non-agent subjects and they include both active and passive.

Sentences can be defined structurally in terms of verbal construction. The verbal construction in Bengali can be characterized in three different ways:

(*a*) The aspect, tense and person markers appear directly on the root.

kɔr 'do'; *kor-i* 'I do'

(*b*) The above-mentioned markers appear on the auxiliary *be* verb and not on the root. The root is nominalized with a derivative marker.

dhɔr- 'catch', *dhɔr-ā* 'catching'
māch dhorā+hocche
fish is being caught

(*c*) There occurs no auxiliary *be* verb. The root is affixed with a causative marker. The aspect, tense and person markers appear on the secondary root.

kɔr- 'do'; *kɔr-ā-* 'cause to do'
tumi kɔrāo
you make (someone) to do (it)

The sentences are to be classified as follows:

Active

(*i*) The subject usually appears without any marker and semantically it is either agent or non-agent. The verb is A (constructionally).

rām dækhe
Rām sees

(*ii*) The subject is non-agent: theme. The verb is A and always a *be* verb. The doer of the real world appears as the complement or in attributive relation to the subject.

rāmer dækhā	*hocche*
the seeing of Rām	occurs (is occurring)

(*iii*) The subject is non-agent: causative, theme.

rāmer (-ke) dækhāno hocche	
Ram's	showing occurs/is done checking (is being done)

Note that in (*ii*) and in (*iii*) the verb is structurally A and it is considered to be impersonal because it agrees with the theme, and it is conjugated in the third person.

Passive

(*iv*) There occurs a subject which is object of the verb.

tumi	*dāktār*	*dekhiecho*
you	(by) the doctor	have been checked?

(*v*) The subject is semantically object of the verb. The verb is structurally B. The agent of the verb appears with certain markers, syntactically the unit is adverbial of agent.

jeleder	*māch*	*dhɔra hocche*
(by) the fishermen	the fish	is being caught

Causative

(*vi*) There may occur no agent (adverbial of agent) NU in the sentence. The verb is structurally B, and semantically causative
The marker '*no*' indicates causative meaning.

māch	*dhɔrā-no hocche*
the fish	is being caught

(*vii*) There occurs a provoked agent in addition to the agent of the causative verb.
Structurally the verb is C. The provoked agent appears with certain marker.

tumi	*āmāke*	*bɔkāccho*
you	me	cause to speak

Note that the above-mentioned (*vi*) has no subject NU. A type of passive sentence can be subjectless. Consider the following sentence:

rām-ke	*dhɔne*	*bɔs kɔrā gælo*
Rām	by wealth	was being tempted (controlled, overpowered)

The verb is structurally B and semantically passive. There occur both instrumental and object NU-s, but no agent and subject.

Kale maintains that 'there are three kinds of passive verbs' in Sanskrit.[91] Bengali verb construction is somewhat different from that of Sanskrit. The above-mentioned (*vi*) and (*vii*) have semantically causative, structurally B-type and C-type verbs respectively. Also (*ii*) and (*iii*) have A-type verbs which are focusing agent and theme subjects. A verb which agrees with a theme or an adjective, etc., always appears in impersonal form. Impersonal form means the verb is appearing with third person marker. In Sanskrit, the latter type of sentence is considered as passive by Kale.[92]

We have just mentioned that there are differences in Sanskrit and Bengali passive constructions. Even though from the semantic point of view the Bengali scholars follow the Sanskrit grammar and establish four types of *vācya* (voice) considering the type of subjects focused by the verb, they hesitate to call the sentence structurally passive where the subjects are theme (including causative theme with active verb) and object (with causative verb).[93]

[91]Kale, p. 360.

[92]Kale, p. 360.

[93]Chatterjee, p. 324. Kale uses the term '*prayoga*' as the corresponding term for 'voice' (p. 238) while others use the term '*vācya*' as the corresponding term. See Banerjee, p. 57, and Chatterjee, (p. 319).

The passive verb is a complex construction of a verbal noun or a nominal with an auxiliary. The auxiliary is often the *be* verb, otherwise *pɔṛ* 'fall'. etc.

Even though the verb construction in passive is complex, a complex verbal construction with *do* as an auxiliary often should not be considered as passive at all. The following construction with *kɔr* 'do' cannot be considered so:

(67) *rogī* *dækhā koreche*
the patient has met (the doctor)

A passive construction with *pɔṛ* would be as follows:

(68) (*tumi*) *dhɔrā poṛiācho bondhu*[94]
you have been exposed my friend
= My friend, you have been correctly understood (by others).

A difference can be observed between two verbal constructions with the *be* verb *hɔ* and *poṛ* and with *kɔṛ* and *āch*. We have already given examples of all except with *āch*. We have mentioned before that the unit division also plays a very important part in establishing function, construction and meaning of the units in a sentence. For instance, a construction, such as.

(69) *tomār jāṇā āche*
your knowing exists

is an active construction even though the expression *jānā* is a verbal noun and followed by the verb *āch*. It seems structurally similar to example no. 68, but the unit division in no. 69 is different from the other. The verbal noun *jānā* is a separate item and it is the subject with which the verb *āch* is in agreement. Though Prof. Chatterjee mentions in another context that this type of verb

se *kɔthā* *āmār* *jānā ache*[95]
that word (story) to me is known

is a passive verb which would be more like no. 68, it depends on the sentence semantics. A stylistically better English translation of the sentence would be 'It is known to me'.

[3.6.1] An interesting comparison can be made between Bengali, Punjabi and Hindi. What Comrie considers as ergative in Punjabi,[96] is traditionally to be considered passive. Comrie's example of Punjabi:

[94]Tagore, 'Vidāe Abhiśāp', Vol. V, p. 479.

[95]Chatterjee, p. 326.

[96]Bernard Comrie, 'The Ergative Variations on a Theme', *Lingua* 32, 1973. p. 239-53.

(*a*) *daktār* (mac. sg) *ne efylma* (fem. pl.) *vekhiā* (fem. pl) . *hoṅgiā* "doctor erg. part. these films seen will be (the doctor will have seen these films)".

can be translated in Hindi and Bengali as follows:

Hindi

(*b*) *dāktar ne in fylmoko dekh liā hogā*
The doctor will have seen these films

(*c*) Bengali
dāktārer oi filmguli dækhā hoe thākbe/
hoe gie thākbe/hoe gie che

We believe that the above three examples from the three different languages show that the agreement of the verb is either with the expressions *efilmā, infylmoko, oi filmguli* or with *vekhiā, dekh, dæhā,* respectively. Traditionally, this type of subject and verb agreements is considered to be characteristic of a passive construction. If the verb focuses on subject: object, the verb is said to be in *karmavācya.*[97] If the verb focuses on subject: theme (verbal noun), the verb is said to be in *bhāvavācya.*[98] Both *karmavācya* and *bhāvavācya* are considered as passive by Kale.[99]

Kellogg maintains: 'The passive voice is much less used in Hindi than in English. Its place is largely taken by neuter verbs. It is to be remembered, however, that the construction of the past tenses of transitive verbs with ने is in reality a passive construction.[100] He further says that 'even [sic] neuter verb may be thus conjugated passively. Thus हम से आया नहीं जाता 'I can not come", lit. "it can not be come by me"...[101]

Some historical facts may be of interest. Many active verb forms in modern Indo-Aryan languages have developed from the passive of Sanskrit·[102] Also, perhaps, the *ne* marker in other modern Indo-Aryan (hereafter M.I.A.) languages except in Bengali is the residue of the Sanskrit *eṇa* marker, the third marker of *kartā* in passive construction (Sanskrit).[103] The tendency of M.I.A. languages is to avoid the type of passive which in Sanskrit was very frequent and from which the active verbs developed in M.I.A. languages. As far as Bengali is concerned, the third marker of *kartā* (*en*) was retained in Old Bengali as e.[104] This exists no more in Bengali. We believe that it still exists as *ne* in other M.I.A. languages, in particular in Punjabi and Hindi.

[97]Chatterjee, p. 322; Banerjee, p. 57.
[98]Chatterjee, p. 323; Banerjee, p. 57.
[99]Kale, p. 360.
[100]Kellogg, *Grammar of Hindi Language*, 1965, p. 251.
[101]Ibid., pp. 478-479.
[102]*Rabindra Racanāvatī*, Vol. 14, p 98.
[103]Kale, p. 482, f.n.
[104]Chatterjee, The Origin and Development of the Bengali Language Vol. II, pp. 742-43.

If we do not take into account the historical point of view, synchronically the *ne* marker in Punjabi and Hindi can be compared with the Bengali *-r* (*-er*) marker which usually appears on the agent noun in passive construction and in a sentence where the non-agent theme or object is the subject.

It may be of interest to compare the Hindi and Bengali sentences below:

Hindi

(70) (*a*) *ham-ne kitāb paṛliā*
by me (to..) the book have (has) read (has been read)
= I have read the book

(*b*) *tum-ne...*
by you
= You have read the book

(*c*) *dāktar-ne...*
by the doctor
= The doctor has read the book.

It seems to me that these constructions are similar to certain Bengali constructions.

Bengali

(*a*) *āmā-r boi pɔṛā hoeche*
to me the book (have read) has been read
= The book has been read by me/I have read the book

(*b*) *tomā-r...*
to (by) you
= You have read the book/the book has been read by you.

(*c*) *dāktār-er...*
to (by) the doctor
= The doctor has read the book/The book has been read by the doctor.

It is relevant to mention here that the English sentence given by Comrie, 'The doctor will have seen these films', if translated into Hindi would be the same as above.

We think that the Punjabi sentence and the corresponding Hindi and Bengali sentences can be treated similarly. The verb is impersonal and its agreement is either with the object or with the verbal noun (which we call 'theme').

There are two possibilities:

(1) In terms of semantics, on the basis of subject focusing the above examples can be called passive traditionally.

(2) Syntactically, the *ne* or *-r* marked nominal is in modifying relation with the verb.

(*a*) The verb is in a complex construction.

(*b*) The nominal with *ne/-r* marker can be described as adverbial of agent, locative or dative (with the meaning: 'in relation to me/you/doctor, etc.' in case of locative and dative

The term 'ergative' is employed differently by different linguists. For instance, Fillmore establishes it on the basis of the semantic 'role' of noun phrases, (1968 p. 53-55). Lyons describes it as a type of relation between the subject of an intransitive verb and the object of the same verb used transitively in another construction with an animate subject noun;[105] whereas Comrie defines this notion in syntactic terms: 'I have defined ergativity in essentially syntactic terms.[106]

The different morphological expressions of the subject of a transitive verb and the subject of an intransitive verb have been taken as the criteria for an ergative language by Comrie.[107] He also suggests that Punjabi is an ergative language. Both suggestions seem unacceptable. We have argued that the morphological marker taken into account by Comrie can be historically described as the residue of some marker of the parent language. In a synchronic description, this type of marker should not be explained as ergative marker. It does not occur with transitive verbs only, but the subject of an intransitive verb appears with the same marker when the intransitive (or transitive) is conjugated in certain aspects and tenses.

Not only the *ne* marker in Hindi and *-r* marker in Bengali but also other markers are found with subject (agent) in active sentence in Hindi as well as in Bengali, such as *-e* marker both in Bengali and Hindi and *-ke* in Bengali and *-ko* in Hindi. For instance:

Bengali

(71) *āmāke/āmāe jete hɔbe* (intransitive)
me have to go

=I have to go.

āmāke/āmāe dite hɔbe (transitive)[108]
me have to give

[105]Lyons, p. 342, 351-52.

[106]Comrie, *Lingua*, 32, 1973, p. 240.

[107]Comrie, p. 240.

[108]Note that the example is ambiguous, because the context is not given here.

=(1) I have to give (something).
(2) (Something) should be given to me.

Compare the subject with *-ke/-e* marker and an object with *-ke/-e* in the following examples:

(72) *mā* *āmāke/āmāe* *bhālobāsen*
mother me loves

(73) *rājā* *dɔridro* *brāmhan-ke* *upohār* *dilen*
the king (to) the poor Brahmin gift gave
Hindi

(74) *mujhe/hamko* *jānā* *pɔṛegā*
me have to go
=I have to go.

Compare with

(75) *maĩne giā* (intransitive)
=I want/I have gone

(76) *maĩne kiā* (transitive)
=I have done (this)/I did (it).

Considering the above-mentioned examples, one can say that Comrie's definition of ergative cannot effectively be applied to the M.I.A. languages such as Hindi and Bengali because the type of example provided by him is passive.

It may be of interest to add some quotations here. A.H. Hasley mentions:

When the Hindusthani verb in a sentence is transitive, i.e. takes a direct object, and is in one of the past tenses, the subject is put in the oblique form with *ne* the agent sign, which marks the subject as the source of the action affecting the direct object, the verb is then made to agree in gender and number with the direct object:

ws-ne cytṭhi lykhi; *bandər-ne wskā hāth kāṭā*
he a letter wrote; a monkey his hand bit

This construction is based according to one theory on an old passive form different from the modern passive form.[109]

Again to quote from Kale:

'The past passive participles are often used impersonally, tbe agent being put in the instrumental case; प्रद्युतितं or प्रद्योतितं सूर्येण it is shone by the sun.

109Hasley, *Colloquial Hindusthani*, p. 33.

The past passive participle agrees adjectively with the object in gender, number and case, the agent being put in the instrumental, while the past active participle is treated exactly like the verb in the past tense; तेन कार्यं कृतं "by him the work was done", तेन बन्धनानि छिन्नानि "by him the bonds were cut".[110]

We have already given our suggestion in favour of the historical explanation of these markers. Synchronically the marked subject in M.I.A. language cannot be described as ergative. The marker appears on subject(s) irrespective of the transitive intransitive verb situation. So the restrictive occurrence cannot be used as an argument in establishing ergative notion.

[3.6.2.] Prof. Chatterjee considers that the marker is 'instrumental nominative' which existed in Old Bengali as -ए marker.[111]

It may be called instrumental marker on the agent noun. A form can either be nominative or instrumental, but not both. It may be nominative in form and can show instrumental relation. From the point of view of the above-mentioned authors, we confirm that the *ne* marker which is the relic of Sanskrit *-eṇa* and is originally instrumental as it was in Old Bengali in Hindi and Punjabi is comparable to the Bengali *-r* marker either in passive construction or the active. In most of the examples treated here, the nominal with *-ne* and *-r* does not agree with the verb. Therefore it (nominal with *ne* and *-r* marker) cannot be considered as subject in those sentences. Where it agrees with the verb (conjugated in certain aspect and tense), in our opinion no corresponding transitive sentence of the intransitive or vice versa is possible in respective languages. For instance:

āmāke/āmāe jete hɔbe
me have to go

This intransitive verb cannot be used transitively in any construction. Similarly, the transitive verb *dite hɔbe* 'have to give' in a construction, such as

āmāke/āmāe dite hɔbe
me have to give

cannot be changed into an intransitive. If another noun is added to this construction, the resultant construction would be something like:

tāke āmāe dite hɔbe
him/her me have to give (something)

110Kale, p. 512.

111Chatterjee, p. 724. 'Evidence of western Hindi and the eastern languages would show that the northern India from the Punjab and midland eastwards, the instrumental assumed the place of the lost nominative.' Also see p. 743.

In this situation also, it is an ambiguous utterance like the above one. Either it means 'He has to give me (something)' or 'I have to give him (something)'.

Whether it is one-place, two-place or three-place verb, such as *de-* 'give' or *bɔl-* 'speak', they have more than one meaning when they express certain aspect, mood and tense. The intended meaning depends on the context of the utterance.

However, the *ne* marker in Punjabi and Hindi and *-r* marker in Bengali occur with the adverbial of agent in a passive construction. The Punjabi example given by Comrie is passive since the verb construction is different and it focuses the subject:object and not the agent. As a matter of fact, Prof. Chatterjee considers that the *-r* marker agent is the characteristic construction of Bengali syntax (modern).

We prefer to consider the Punjabi and Hindi sentences have impersonal verbs constructions like Bengali as a kind of passive; but not the construction which expresses certain aspect, mood and tense of the verb which has agreement with *-ke, -e, -ko, -r, -ne* marked noun as active. We have said before that the active-passive differences basically depend on both semantic and syntactic implications of subject focusing, verbal construction, including the meaning of the verb and the manifestation of the agent with certain markers.

Kale maintains that the neuter and reflexive voices are also passive in Sanskrit. 'There are three kinds of passive verbs: (1) the passive properly so called (कर्मणि प्र०), as रामेण द्रव्यं दीयते; (2) an impersonal passive (थावे प्र०) as गम्यते 'it is gone'; and (3) a reflexive (कर्मकर्तरि प्र०) as (आदेन पच्यते) 'rice is cooked'.[112]

In Sanskrit these three verbs are constructionally similar. So it may be appropriate to group them under one label of passive. We shall discuss, in some detail later the notion of *vācya* which is partially similar to the notion of *voice*.

The situation in different languages (M.I.A.) are, to some extent, different from Sanskrit. In Sanskrit, the three verbs are constructionally similar when they focus different subjects. So Kale can describe them as different types of passive verbs. In Bengali, the 'object/subject' is focused by a type of verb which can only be called passive in construction. The verbs focusing *bhāva* or *karmakartṛ* subjects are constructionally the same as active verbs. Thus, the neuter and reflexive voices in Bengali are not structurally passive.[113] This may be the reason why sometimes the attempt of the Bengali grammarians to correlate the two languages has failed.[114]

[112]Kale, p. 360.
[113]Chatterjee, p. 326.
[114]*Rabindra Racanāvalī*, Vol. 14, p. 94.

In summing up, we can remark that Comrie's assumption of 'ergative' is not acceptable. Neither syntactic nor semantic characterization of the 'ergative configuration' is fully applicable to the languages mentioned. What Comrie meant as ergative in Punjabi is passive syntactically and semantically. Not only in Punjabi but also in other M.I.A. languages, the situation appears to be the same.

Historically, certain markers in M.I.A. languages are residues of certain markers of Sanskrit. Synchronically, certain markers can either occur in passive or in active construction of the languages mentioned. The devices of subject focusing agreement-concord and the total meaning of the sentence and the verbal structure; certain aspects, mood and tense expressed by the verb—all these should have to be accounted for in establishing any distinct labels to sentences.

[3.6.3.] Besides this we intend to mention the idea of 'depository of two cases' in one item. It seems in some affiliated sentences this type of 'role' can be found. If the active and corresponding passive constructions contain two animate nominals and if the verb of the affiliated sentence are two-place or three-place verb and the two nominals are animate in feature, then two can be explained as depository of two cases.

Similarly, two sentences, of which one has a causative and the other has a non-causative verb, can also be described as 'depository of two cases'.

(77) *śrīkṛṣṇa arjunke biśwarūp dækhāiāchilen*
Lord Krishna to Arjun the universal truth showed (cause to see past tense)

The expression *Śrīkṛṣṇa* is to be considered as 'cause-agent'/'provoker agent' and the expression *arjunke* is to be considered as *karma* of the verb and in turn the '*provoked* agent'.[115] This problem has been dealt with in some detail later.

The other sentence would be

(77a) *arjun biśwarūp dekhiāchilen*
Arjun the universal truth saw

In this sentence the expression *arjun* is the agent and subject of the non-causative verb.

This type of 'depository roles' or cases may be shown where either the two sentences are affiliated or the sentence contains a causative verb. We assume that the semantic and syntactic affiliation of active-passive constructions can show one expression that is used in both, and can be a

[115]Vidyabhushan, p. 51; Acharya, p. 96; Chatterjee, p. 139-140 The term 'suppressed agent' is the author's translation. The terms 'provoker' ·cause' provoked' agent are the author's translation.

criterion to think of the expression as the depository of two cases. Also the causative verb can signal the simultaneous action by two animate nouns which can be taken as the criterion for establishing two cases on one expression.

[3.7.] The second type of relation, which is called *karma* in Indian grammar, corresponds to the object relation in western grammar. Pāṇini defines *karma* as: 'That which is most desired by the agent is *karma*'.[116] Saudamini Bahulikar translates as follows:

(*i*) *Karma* in the case of verbs *krudh* and *druh* when preceded by prepositions;

(*ii*) In the case of *du*, *karma* as well;

(*iii*) *Karma* in the case of verb *śī*, *sthā*, *as*, when preceded by the preposition *adhi*, and in the case of *viś* when preceded by the preposition *abhi+ni*; in the case of the verb *vas* when preceded by *upa*, *anu*, *adhi*, *an*.

Paṇini's definition is taken up by N. Vidyabhushan when he defines *karma* in Bengali and adds: what is done, eaten, seen, heard, understood, given, taken, brought, read, spoken, etc. In other words, that which undergoes the action of all transitive verbs accomplished by the *kartā*, or that for which an action is performed; that which results from the action upon an undergoer—when these are expressed by a noun or NU or its equivalent, that noun or its equivalent is *karma* (*karma-kāraka*).[117]

Other Pāṇinian definitions (*sūtra* 'rule') of *karma* are not taken up by the Bengali grammarians mentioned earlier, who are of the opinion that these rules are not applicable in toto to Bengali.[118]

Prof. Chatterjee, N. Vidyabhusan, and P. Acharya explain approximately the same thing as Pāṇini's. But other details are not mentioned since some verbs have different meanings in Bengali and some words are constructed differently. For instance, a word like *abhinibeś* is not explained as *abhi+ni*...but the Bengali unit as a whole is derived from Sanskrit. Therefore, all rules are not applicable in toto to Bengali.

According to Prof. Chatterjec's definition, that which is accomplished or done, that which is the topic of the action indicated by the verb in a sentence is to be called *karma*. A noun or pronoun which expresses this kind of topic is to be called *karmapada* or should be understood as having *karma* relation, i.e. *karma-kāraka*.[119]

P. Acharya maintains that, that which is done or accomplished by the *kartā* when it is expressed in a form (of a noun or pronoun or equivalent to it) should be called *karma*, i.e. it has *karma* relation (*karma-kāraka*).[120]

[116]*Aṣṭādhyāyi* 1.4 49. *karturīpsitatamaṃ karma*. Soudamini Bahulikar's translation in *Indian Linguistics*, Vol. 34, no. 2, June 1973, pp. 84-85.

[117]Vidyabhushan, pp. 51-53.

[118]Chatterjee, pp. 92-93, f.n.

[119]Chatterjee, p. 86.

[120]Acharya, p. 98. The author has translated from the original.

Each of the above-mentioned authors considers that the subject (*kartṛ-pada*) of the passive sentence is basically an object (*karma*) of the transitive verb.

Each of them agrees that intransitive verbs also can have an object (*karma*) when the object noun is derived from the same root of the intransitive verb. Some relevant quotations can be cited from western grammars:

Sweet says: 'The accusative or "direct object case" serves to complete the meaning of a transitive verb.[121] Onions speaks of:

> ... an object, which denotes the person or thing to which the action of the verb passes over.
>
> (*i*) The person to whom or thing to which something is done ... (they murdered the king);
>
> (*ii*) The result of an action or process (the people elected a king);
>
> (*iii*) That which is done (I dreamed a horrid dream).

'An object of the third kind (which denotes the action itself) is called a cognate object because it is of kindred meaning with the verb....

'The object denotes the person or thing with respect to which an action takes place, or it serves to point out how far, i.e. to whom or what the action of the verb extends.

'Thus it is in origin of the nature of an adverb or (as we say) expresses an adverbial relation. It is no longer, however, distinctly felt as an adverbial part of the sentence but simply as denoting the person or thing that is affected. The character of the object can nevertheless change the meaning of the verb.'[122]

Jespersen explains:

'An object is a primary which is intimately connected with the verb of the sentence (or clause) though less intimately so than the subject ... to find the object by asking whom, or what with the subject and the form of the verb actually used; thus we find the objects of the two sentences:

She eats an apple every morning.
What does she eat? An apple.

The mystery puzzled us a great deal.
Whom did the mystery puzzle? Us.'[123]

It seems to me that Prof. Chatterjee's explanation is similar to the one given by Jespersen.

[121]*New English Grammar*, Vol. I, pp. 49-50. As a matter of fact, there is no accusative form in English.

[122]*Modern English Syntax*, pp. 6, 31, 1971.

[123]*Essentials of English Grammar*, p. 108, 1933.

In general the notion of *karma-kāraka* in Indian grammar and the notion of object in Western grammar is more or less similar. The idea of direct object corresponds to that of *mukhya karma*; the indirect object corresponds to the idea of *gauṇa karma* and cognate object to *samadhātuja karma* respectively in Western and Indian traditional grammars. The idea of complement corresponds to the idea of *paripūraka*.[124]

[3.7.1.] A similar event can be expressed in many different constructions. The active or passive can have different stylistic values. Like the subject, the direct objects have different subfunctions: 'target', 'goal', 'object of result', 'object of quality', 'cognate object', etc.

[3.7.2.] Usually verbs like *kɔrā gæhe* 'has been done', *deā holo* 'was given', literally 'giving done', *bɔlā gæche* 'has been told'/'was told', etc. occur with such nominal in sentences which can be labelled as object. Tagore has mentioned this type of subjectless sentence,[125] and P. Acharya has given some examples:

(78) *durotter jonno nɔkkhɔtrogulike æto choṭo*
for distance the stars so small (is shown so small
dekhāe
are looking

The verb construction here is rather causative. P. Acharya considers the expression *nɔkkhɔtrogulike* as object.

(79) *sutɔpāke nutɔnsāṛite bhāri sundor dekhāitechilo*
Sutapa in new clothes very nice was looking.

The verb construction here is like causative. P. Acharya considers the expression *sutɔpā-ke* 'Sutapa' (a proper name) is the object. The object function should be understood from the sentence semantics.[126] In our opinion this type of object may be called 'object of quality'.

[3.7.3] Prof. Chatterjee, P. Acharya and N. Vidybhushan maintain that some transitive verbs can have two objects. Usually the direct object is unmarked and it is an inanimate noun. The indirect object is usually marked and it is an animate noun.

Verbs which express meanings such as 'speak', 'give', 'write', 'ask', 'send', 'see', 'hit', etc. and all causative verbs which are derived from transitive verbs can have two objects.[127]

[124]Chatterjee, pp. 86-90; Acharya, pp. 98-99; Vidyabhushan, pp. 51-53.
[125]*Ravindra Racanāvali*, Vol. 14, p. 94.
[126]Acharya, p. 99.
[127]Vidyabhushan, p. 52.

Semantically, a verbal noun can have objects, such as:

(80) *sɔtpāttre* *kɔnyādān* *kɔro*
to an honest groom the daughter-giving (you) do

The verbal noun *dān* 'giving', 'the act of giving away', has two objects: (1) *kɔnyā*; (2) *sɔtpāttre*. Interestingly both the objects refer to the animate nouns: the direct one is unmarked and the indirect one is marked. And the whole segment from the beginning to *dān* is the object of the finite verb *kɔro* 'do'.[128]

A non-finite verb form can have an object.[129] For instance:

(81) *cheleṭi chobi-ā̃kite śikhiāche*
the boy picture to draw has learnt

The expression *śikhiāche* 'has learnt' is the finite verb and its object is the segment *chobi-ā̃kite* 'to draw picture', whereas *chobi* 'picture' is the object of the infinite form of the verb *ā̃ki-te* 'to draw'. An example can be considered with an animate noun and a complement:

(82) *tumi āmāke pɔrom bondhu monekoro*[130]
you me (as) real friend think
= you consider me as a real friend.

Although the expression *āmāke pɔrom bondhu* 'me (as) real friend' structurally occurs in a unit which can be segmented from *tumi* and *monekoro*, positionally it seems similar to the position of *sɔtpāttre kɔnyādān*. But they are expressing different sorts of relation. The two here are in attributive relation; the expression, *pɔrom bondhu* is a complement of the preceding expression *āmāke* 'me'. It is noticed that the preceding head nominal (animate expression) is marked and the complement is unmarked.

The animate direct object usually takes the marker:

(83) *āmi rāmke dekhiāchi*
I Rām (marked) have seen

and the inanimate direct object does not take *-ke* marker:

āmi boiṭā poṛiāchi
I the book have read

An interesting difference may be observed between the explanation of Prof. Chatterjee and the descriptions given by N. Vidyabhushan and P. Acharya. For the same example:

[128] Vidyabhushan, p. 52.
[129] Chatterjee, p. 180.
[130] Acharya, p. 98.

mātā	*śiśuke*	*cā̃d*	*dækhāitechen*
the mother	the child	the moon	is showing

Prof. Chatterjee explains that *mātā* is *kartā* (agent) and *cā̃d* is the *mukhyā karma* (direct object) and *śiśuke* is the *gauṇa karma* (indirect object),[131] whereas N. Vidyabhushan gives a different explanation. He describes *śiśuke* asprovoked *kartā* (provoked agent). He argues that the verb is causative (in the Bengali construction) and both *mātā* and *śiśu* carry out a simultaneous action. Like N. Vidyabhushan, P. Acharya also maintains that when an action is done by the provocation of another person, both the persons, the one who provokes and the other one who is provoked, are in action; in other words, when one causes other to do, the person who provokes is one type of agent and the other one who is provoked is also another type of agent. The simultaneous actions of seeing and showing are included in the idea of the verb *dækhāitechen.* Unless both are concerned, the idea of the particular verb is not fulfilled. A comparable explanation is found:

> 'Apart from concord, there are other ways in which the choice of one element within a sentence may affect the choice of another:
>
> | | | |
> |---|---|---|
> | The men scattered; | not | The man scattered. |
> | Police dispersed the rioters; | not | Police dispersed the rioter. |
> | The cars collided; | not | The car collided. |

Each of the above pairs shows how a particular verb requires a particular type of subject or object: collide (unless accompanied by a with phrase) requires a plural subject; scatter and disperse require a plural 'affected' participant, i.e. a plural subject when used intransitively or a plural object when used transitively.'[132]

One can say that in the above-mentioned Bengali example (no. 36) the idea of simultaneous action is something like the idea of Jacendoff's reciprocity of action in 'buy' and 'sell' verbs or of Dr. Platt's idea of 'kiss' and 'love' verbs in a sentence such as: 'John kisses Mary'.

One can say that in the description of both the Bengali and English examples, the real world situation influences the grammatical analysis. Our argument is that the verb 'kiss' is an active verb and the simultaneous action may not be applicable to it, because one can kiss someone, and the other partner may remain uninvolved. Both can be considered as involved if they are emotionally attached. Also the expression itself shows that the initiative is taken by John, so Mary can be considered as object and not the agent, whereas in the Bengali construction the verb itself is a causative verb and by definition it indicates a simultaneous action in most cases.

131Chatterjee, p. 88.

132*A Grammar of Contemporary English*, p. 371.

In particular, the verb *dækhāno* signals the simultaneous action of both. P. Acharya and N. Vidyabhushan describe the situation in this way and find a grammatical feature as the point of such explanation. It is evident that the structure of the verb considers with the difference in meaning.

[3.7.4] The definition of active is given by Prof. Chatterjee as follows: Where the subject of the sentence is the agent of the verb (doer in the real world) in other words, where the subject is agent—the verb is to be called active verb, i.e. the verb is in active voice.[133]

N. Vidyabhushan maintains (following the definition given in Sanskrit grammar) that in active voice the verb agrees with the agent; in other words, the verb takes the person concord according to the person of the agent (actual doer).[134]

The definition of passive is given by Prof. Chatterjee as follows: where the object is the subject of the sentence and the verb agrees with the object in person, the verb is to be considered to be in passive voice.[135]

N. Vidyabhushan maintains that in passive voice the object of the transitive verb is prominent and the verb agrees with it; in other words, it takes the person concord according to the person of the object.[136]

The two examples given by both the authors are:

puliśer hāte *cor* *dhɔrā poṛeche*
in the hand of the police the thief is captured (being caught)
(S.K. Chatterjee, p. 322)

āmi āhɔto holām
I wounded was
(N. Vidyabhushan, p. 82)

So far we understand from the above two examples that both the verbal construction and the verb meaning are equally important to label the passive verb.

Sometimes it is difficult to differentiate between active and passive on the basis of the verb construction, and the active-passive differences can only be established from the total meaning of the whole sentence. For instance:

Active:
(*a*) *āmi kāpoṛ cāi* (S.K. Chatterjee, p. 323)
I cloth want

Passive:
(*b*) *āmār kāpoṛ cāi* (S.K. Chatterjee, p. 323)
to me cloth is wanted (needed)

133Chatterjee, pp. 84, 321.
134Vidyabhushan, p. 81.
135Chatterjee, p. 322.
136Vidyabhushan, p. 82.

The two forms are different; the form *cāi* in (*a*) is active; the form *cāi* in (*b*) is passive in the sense that the verb is impersonal. Both the active and passive sentences contain a homophonous verb form. The subject of the active is the agent and the verb agrees with it; the subject of the passive is the expression *kāpoṛ* which is the object. Even though these two sentences have almost the same lexical items[137], they are considered to be different, i.e. the way native speakers percieve the meaning.

The meaning of the verb and its focuses on different subjects indicate the active and passive difference. An event of the real world can be expressed in two or more different constructions or in stylistic variants. They are affiliated in the sense that they have the same basic meaning.

The traditional Indian grammarians treat the subject of the passive and reflexive as the object. Jespersen mentions 'active-passive' use of some verbs.[138] He gives such examples are:

'The book sells well'.
'It feels cold indoors'.
'The meat cooks all the better if you cook it slow'.

We see that Jespersen's term 'active-passive' means 'notionally passive though formally active'. We also see that a passive construction of the kind which is called new construction by him in English does not necessarliy contain an agent with the preposition 'by'. Consider Jespersen's examples:

I was never frightened of you.
She was quite ready to be fallen in love with.

Jespersen remarks that 'very often the passive term is used without any express indication of what in the corresponding active construction would be the subject; it is believed (people believe), it is generally believed (most people believe).'[139]

Jespersen also describes other examples:

He was difficult to find

He is the grammatical subject of *was*, but the notional object of the verb *find*. In the construction with a passive infinitive, *he* may be said to be the subject of *was* (*difficult*) and of *to be found* at the same time.[140] This seems to be a case of subject: object (matter). The other sentence is not actually the corresponding active of the above sentence.

137After all *āmi* and *āmar* are different.
138Jespersen, *A Modern English Grammar*, pt. iii, I Syntax (2nd Vol.), pp. 347-352.
139Jespersen, p. 137.
140Jespersen, p. 228. 'He was difficult to be found.'

It seems that the identification of grammatical subject and notional object is one of the main criteria of 'passive' as explained by Jespersen. Voice is defined in *A Grammar of Contemporary English* as:

'... a grammatical category which makes it possible to view the action of a sentence in two ways, without change in the facts reported:

(*a*) The butler murdered the detective.
(*b*) The detective was murdered by the butler.

Sentence (*a*) is in the active voice and sentence (*b*) in the passive voice. The active-passive relation involves two grammatical 'levels': the verb phrase and the clause'.[141]

The notion of voice in Western grammar which is considered to be equivalent to the idea of *vācya* in traditional Indian grammar,[142] is to some extent different. The idea of *karma* which corresponds to the English term 'object' is basically the semantic idea in traditional Indian grammar. Jespersen sometimes distinguishes the notional object from direct and indirect object.[143] He gives a list of verbs 'whose relation to their various objects is similar'.[144] In the example; *He was difficult to find*, Jespersen labels *he* as subject of the verb *was* and notional object of the verb *find*, and says that in a passive construction, such as *he was difficult to be found*, *he* is the subject of both *was* (*difficult*) and *to be found*.
In sentences such as:

'This cost him a lot of money'
or 'I have bet Scaife twenty pounds'

Jespersen calls *a lot of money* and *twenty pounds* direct objects, and *him* and *Scaife* indirect objects.

These two examples would be treated as having locative and instrumental rather than object relation to the verb in corresponding Bengali constructions. The Bengali translation of the English sentence, *this cost him a lot of money*, would be:

(*a*) *er jonno* *tāke* *ɔnek ṭākā*
for this him (he) a lot of money
khɔroc korte holo (*hocche*)
has to spend

or (*b*) *etc* *tār* *ɔnek ṭākā* *khɔroc hocche* (*holo*)
in it him (to him) a lot of money cost

141 *A Grammar of Contemporary English*, p. 801.
142 Chatterjee, pp. 319-327; Banerjee, p. 57.
143 Jespersen, p. 228.
144 Jespersen, pp. 238-252.

The expression *tāke* in (*a*) is subject: agent; in (*b*) the expression *ɔnek ṭākā* is subject: object and *tār* may be called source, locative, etc. Even though the two expressions communicate the same event of the real world, the grammatical relations expressed by the nominal syntagmas are different: *tāke* and *tār* cannot be called similar in grammar. They show different relation to the verbs in respective construction.

The expression *tāke* may be considered as either the subject or the object in the above example. If one considers it as the object, one breaks the verb construction into the separate units *khɔroc* and *korte holo*. Thereby one can interpret the meaning as, 'spending has (to do) be done', and then one can establish the object status to the nominal expression *tāke* in that example.

But to us, the verb expression is a single complex unit. And it cannot be explained in the above-mentioned way, because the aspect of the verb is expressed in that complex construction. The initial element is a nominal, the medial one is a participal form of the VU, and the final one is the auxiliary verb. We are not concerned with the structure of the VU, so we are not going into the detail of it in this work.

Following the traditional analysis, we prefer to take the above-mentioned verbal expression as a single unit with the meaning 'has to spend', and not as 'spending has to do/has done'. We have said before that the participle occurs to express certain aspects of the verb and in that situation the agent: subject takes *-ke -e* marker. Usually the participle appears on the root. The verb may be either a 'primitive root' or a 'derivative root'.[145] In the above-mentioned VU, the verb is a derivative verb.

Similarly, the other sentence, if translated into Bengali, would be as follows:

scepher sɔyge	*āmi*	*beṭ dhorechi*	*kuṛi pāuṇḍ*
with Scaife	I	*have bet*	twenty pounds

Here *Scaife* may be considered as coordinated subject and *twenty pounds* as object in Bengali construction.

From the comparison it appears that the idea of object relation is based on the sentence semantics or, broadly speaking, on the total meaning of the sentence. And this semantic criterion is one of the main points in identifying the *kartṛ* and *karmavācya*.

Besides these two, there are two other types of *vācya* or *voice* of verb: *bhāva* 'theme', and *karmakartṛ* 'object as agent'.[146]

[3.8] Though they are not equivalent, the two terms '*voice*' (English)

[145]The terminologies in Bengali or Sanskrit grammar are *siddha* (*maulika*) and *sādhita*. See Chatterjee, p. 134; Vidyabhushan, p. 64. Kale uses the term 'primitive root' and 'derivative root' corresponding to *siddha dhātu* and *sādhita dhātu*. See *A Higher Sanskrit Grammar*, p. 238.

[146]Chatterjee, pp. 319-27; Kale, pp. 238, 359-60; Vidyabhushan, pp. 80-82.

and '*vācya*' (Sanskrit) have partially the same meaning in the sense that roughly the same grammatical category is implied.

However, the Western as well as Indian scholars who discuss the category *vācya*, use the term 'active-passive' in parenthesis, although in different Sanskrit-English dictionaries we find that partially different meanings are given. For instance, Apte makes *vācya* and *voice* equivalent, whereas the meaning of *vācya* is given as 'that of which anything is predictable' (A Practical Sanskrit—English Dictionary, p. 275.)[147]

J.S. Speijer says: 'The Sanskrit verb has three voices: the active (परस्मैपदम्), the medial (आत्मनेपदम्), and the passive. Of these, the active is formally different from the other two, but the medial and passive voice have many forms in common.''[148]

In English grammars the verbal construction, the agreement with the subject, and the reversibility of subject and object (in two affiliated sentences) are considered to be the main point in the grammatical category (or in the notion) of voice.[149]

Different types of passive sentences (which are constructionally different) are also taken into account:

(*i*) Agentive passives

(*a*) with expressed agents (examples 1, 2, 3)

(*b*) without expressed agents (examples 4, 13b)

(*ii*) Quasi-passive (examples 5, 6).

(*iii*) Non-agentive/intensive active complement construction (examples 7, 13).[150]

The term *vācya* is defined by N. Vidyabhushan: 'The verb (with its structural differences) focuses different subjects, such as *kartā*, *bhāva*, *karma* etc. The structural difference of the verb itself indicates with which subject the verb is directly related and in agreement. This focus and the different structure of the verb are included in the idea of *vācya*.''[151]

[147]Arthur A. Macdonell, *A Practical Sanskrit Dictionary*, Oxford University Press (1929), reprinted 1954. Also see Sir M.M. Williams, *Sanskrit-English Dictionary*, New Edition, pp. 937.

[148]*Sanskrit Syntax*, p. 235.

[149]Quirk and Leech, *A Grammar of Contemporary English*, pp. 943-944, and G.O. Curme, *Parts of Speech and Accidence*, pp. 203, 217-23.

[150]*A Grammar of Contemporary English*, p. 808-811. Examples: (1) This violin was made by my father; (2) This conclusion is hardly justified by the results; (3) Coal has been replaced by oil; (4) This difficulty can be avoided in several ways; (5) We are encouraged to go on with the project; (6) John was interested in linguistics; (7) The modern world becomes more highly industrialized and mechanized; (13) The house is already sold; (13b.) The house has already been sold.

[151]Vidyabhushan, p. 81.

Vācya seems analogous to 'that of which anything is predictable'. The main point in *vācya* seems to be the focus of the verb on different subjects and the verbal construction by which the agreement is identified. Kale does not define *vācya*, but he says: 'There are three kinds of passive verbs.'[152]

Prof. Chatterjee and other Bengali grammarians mention that there are four types of *vācyas* of verbs: (1) *kartṛ*; (2) *karma;* (3) *bhāva*; and (4) *karmakartṛ*[153] In other words, four types of subject-verb relation or identification are established in the category of *vācya*. The subject of causative verb is also included in *kartṛvacya*.

It appears from the definition of active given by the Bengali grammarians that the verb structure and its focus on the agent: subject are implied by the term *kartṛvācya*.

Similarly the *karmavācya* is defined by N. Vidyabhushan: 'When the potential object of the transitive verb is the subject of the verb (the verb agrees with it in person), the verb is to be considered in *karmavācya*.'[154]

Prof. Chatterjee provides the definitions: 'When the predicative verb takes its object as subject in a sentence, it is to be understood that the verb is in *karmavācya* (passive voice)".[155]

The third type of *vācya* is defined by N. Vidyabhushan: In the *bhāvavācya*, the meaning of the intransitive verb is the dominant factor.[156]

Prof. Chatterjee says that when the meaning of the predicative verb in a sentence is the subject (theme), the verb is to be considered as *bhāvavācya* (neuter voice). In his example;

tomār	*ghumāno*	*hoiāche*[157]
your	sleeping	has finished (occurred)

=Did you sleep?
Have you Slept?

the verbal noun *ghumāno* is considered as the theme and the predicative verb is *hoiāche*.

To the examples below one can apply the just mentioned definition of *bhavavācya* by N. Vidyabhushan:

āmār	*jāoā*	*hoibenā*[158]
my (to me) going		will not be possible
(will not occur)		

152Kale, p. 360.
153Chatterjee, pp. 319-627; Vidyabhushan, pp. 81-82.
154Vidyabhushan, p. 82.
155Chatterjee, p. 322.
156Vidyabhusan, p. 82.
157Chatterjee, p. 323.
158Vidyabhusan, p. 82.

The definition of *karmakartṛvācya* is as follows: where it is difficult to identify the *karta* where the *object* seems to act on itself as *kārta*, the verb is in *karmakartṛvācya* (reflexive voice). This is the way Prof. Chatterjee defines. His examples are:

śīt kɔre
cold appears (cold feels) = It is cold.
bṛṣṭi hɔe[159]
the rain occurs = It rains.

On the other hand, N. Vidyabhushan defines that in *karmakartṛvācya* the potential object of the transitive verb seems to be the subject of the sentence or the *kartā* of the verb.[160] He furnishes examples:

śīt koriteche
cold is feeling (is appearing)
kāpoṛ chaẽṛe
cloth tears (wears)
boikhāni bhālo kāṭiteche
the book good is selling (sells)
śiśiṭā bhāŋiāgælo
the bottle broke

The verbs in the above examples given by N. Vidyabhushan can be transitive, but the *be* verb *hɔ* in the example given by Prof. Chatterjee does not seem to be transitive at all.

In Sanskrit the three other types besides *kartṛvācya* are same in structure. In this sense it is appropriate to call them passive. The difference is established on the basis of their different subject focussing.

In Bengali the three types of verb occurring in *kartṛ*, *bhāva* and *karmakartṛ* are structurally similar, so the *bhāva* and *karmakartṛ* are not considered as a type of passive.[161]

From our discussion and illustrations it is clear that the sentence semantics comes into full play in establishing both the *kāraka* to the nominal (NU) and the *vācya* to the verb (VU). The theory of *kāraka* which to a greater extent similar to the idea of labelled relation, i.e., 'role', and the theory of *vācya* which also to some extent corresponds to the notion of 'voice' can adequately be defined and explained in terms of sentence semantics.

We have argued in favour of the idea that the *kāraka* is to be understood in its two dimensions, i.e. in the dimension of relation and the dimension

159Chatterjee, pp. 324-325 (the present author has translated from the Bengali original.).
160Vidyabhusan, p. 82.
161Chatterjee, pp. 325-326.

of the manifestation. The *vācya* also should be understood in its two dimensions.

On the one hand, *vācya* includes the grammatical factor of subject focussing, on the other hand it is manifested in different constructions of the sentence as a whole, where the verb structure and overt markers on different nominals appear in different ways.

The subjects of sentences can function differently. A subject nominal can have *kartṛ-kāraka* which corresponds to the term 'agent'. It can have *karma-kāraka* relation. Besides these *kartṛ* and *karma*, we have established other functions of the subject as well. They are: *bhāva* which corresponds to the theme of the verb, and (1) *karma* which refers to the object of the verb and it seems acts on itself. The subject of *link* verbs, *be* verbs and any other copula which do not come under any other label, is here called *independent factor* subject on the basis of sentence semantics. In our analysis the (1) *karma* is included in *independent factor*.

Following the traditional definition (given by N. Vidyabhushan) one can say that the subject which functions as object and the (1) *karma* which refers to the thing of the world can be grouped in one. And the two subjects may be called passive considering the sentence semantics even though the verb structures are not similar is these two types of sentences.

It is noticed that in traditional Indian grammar the syntactic reversion of subject and object in the two affiliated sentences is not given much importance, even though the possible reversibility is mentioned in the way that the agent (*kartā*)/subject takes a certain marker and occurs as an adverbial in a *karmavācya* sentence when the verb focuses the object: subject.

The cross reference between the two notions can be represented as:

(1) semantic function:)
kāraka (roles)) sentence
) semantics
(2) syntactic function:) ←——→ voice: *vācya* of
kartṛpada (subject) the VU
of the NU

↓ ↓

(*a*) agent/subject:
kartr-karaka/kartṛpada (active) [162]*kartṛvācya*
(*b*) object/subject:
karma-kāraka/kartṛpada (passive) *karmavācya*

[162]I have provided the terms 'active' and 'passive' (in parenthesis) because it is more comprehensive. Here (*a*, *c*, *d* are similar in construction in that sense, they are labelled as active. The Indian terms *krtṛvācya*, *karmavācya*; *bhāvavācya* and *karmakartṛvācya* do not just mean the constructional difference, these indicate something more, which have already been described.

(*c*) theme/subject: *bhāva* (ideational relation) *kartṛpada* — (active) *bhāvavācya*

(d) independent factor/ subject: *kartṛpada* — (active) *karma-kartṛvācya*

The double-headed arrow represents the co-relation of the two notions both of which fall under sentence semantics. The sentence is structurally NU- VU. The NU which occurs in the subject part is alone considered in establishing voices of the VU. The term 'subject' implies the syntactic function of the NU which corresponds to the term '*kartṛpada*.' The term 'role' implies the semantic function of the NU which corresponds to *kāraka*. Some of the (*d*) subjects are not *karma,* such as *uni āmār kākā hɔn* 'he is my uncle'. The sentence is an active one. The subject is to be considered as 'independent factor'.

Further, the relation can be described from the point of view of the VU:

(1) The VU that focuses the agent/subject is in *kartṛvācya.*

(2) The VU that focuses the object/subject is in *karmavācya.*

(3) The VU that focuses the theme/subject is in *bhāvavācya.*

(4) The VU that focuses the other subjects including some independent factor/is in *karma-kartṛvācya.*

Sentences which are not structurally NU-VU, have been excluded from this discussion. The notion of voice or the notion of semantic function, such as agent and object, cannot be established in such sentences. Traditionally sentences with *link*-verb, *be*-verb or any other copula in which the semantic functions such as *kartṛ* and *karma* relations cannot be established to the subject nominal, usually come under the labels of *karmakartṛ* and *bhāva* on the basis of sentence semantics. In some cases, the voices of the verb have not been explained.

We think that the type of description given here in regard to the cross reference between the two notions of semantic and syntactic functions and the voice may be useful in the description of other living languages as well.

The passive 'scale' set up in English grammar[163] seems to me basically a classification of the structural differences of passive sentences. Certain examples of 'awkward passive' may be quoted:

> 'The verb and the two phrases from a very close idiomatic unit, which has two passive analogues when either of the noun phrases can become the subject of a passive sentence:
>
> The owner had made a mess of the house (C2C)

[163] *A Grammar of Contemporary English*, p. 808.

or | A mess had been made of the house (2C')
| The house had been made a mess of (2C")

Other examples of the latter kind of passive are:

Many realized she was being made fun of.

Her beauty was made much of.

Pretty girls will always be taken notice of.

The children were taken good care of.

There is a tendency to use the regular passive, if the head of the prepositional phrase is premodified by an open-class adjective (and hence the idiomatic nature of the construction is weakened). *Considerable allowance will be made for special cases* rather than special cases will be made considerable allowance for. The (2C') passive is often felt to be more formal than (2C"). In some cases it is unacceptable or rare. Compare:

This possibility was hardly even made use of.
? Use was hardly even made of this possibility.'[164]

The above quotation seems to make clear that in English grammar the notion of *voice* is mainly explained in the reversibility of two phrases in affiliated sentences and the structural side of the syntactic units. Whereas we think in the notion of *vācya* the stress is put on the subject focus, and it includes the semantic function of the subject NU which is focused by the verb.

The way N. Vidyabhushan defines seems adequate. He does not give any example with *be* verb.

We can consider Prof. Chatterjee's example:

bṛṣṭi hɔe
rain pours (is)
= It rains, the rain pours, it is raining, etc.

The verb *hɔe* here seems equivalent to *occur* in English. One can interpret as 'what pours', this way the object (*karma*) status of the expression *bṛṣṭi* may be established. Here it seems the potential object (*karma*) of the transitive verb acts on itself. From the sentence semantics the subject can be labelled as agent, in the sense it is acting, it is happening etc. although this agent is different from the other agent. In traditional grammar, the verb which focuses such agent-subject is called 'the verb of *karmakartṛvācya*'.[165] Applying this definition it is observed that some of the independent subjects do not co-occur with a verb which can be labelled under *karmakartṛvācya*. For instance:

164*Ibid.*, p. 848.
165Vidyabhushan, p. 82.

(84) *ākāś meghlā āche*
sky cloudy is
= The sky is cloudy.

The expression *ākāś* may be labelled as *independent factor*, but the verb *āche* does not signal any action which is done on the nominal itself.[166] Obviously the four types of *vācya* mentioned, do not cover all possible sentences in the language under discussion.

However, on the basis of construction, this type of sentence can be called active, thus syntactically it can be incorporated.

[3.8.1] The transitive intransitive distinction of the verb can differentiate the type of subjects which we refer to as the *karma-kartṛ subject*, the *kartṛ subject* and *bhāva subject*, *karma subject* and those *independent factor subjects* which do not come under the *karma-kartṛ* label.

We have mentioned that the voice category should be looked at in its two dimensions. We have discussed one already. The other seems to be the construction of the sentence occurring in different *vācya* (voice). From the point of view of the verb construction, there are two types of sentences in different voices: (*a*) simple or complex construction of active verb; and (*b*) complex construction of passive verb.

In *kartṛ*, *bhāba* and *karmakartṛ* the verb is conjugated without any passive marker. From the point of view of certain markers the three voices have similar type of verb structure, whereas in *karmavācya* the verb is always conjugated with passive marker. In addition to that, the *karmavācya sentence* has a segment in adverbial form, which is not the subject. The *kartrivācya sentence* has the agent in the form of subject of the sentence. It can appear with certain marker or without any marker on it. The *bhābavācya sentence* has a segment in the subject part, which appears as the modifier to the subject. It has a link marker which connects it with the subject of the sentence and takes a neutral position. The *karmakartṛvācya* sentence has no agent in the proper sense and the subject itself is an independent factor in relation to the verb. This independent factor may seem to be something like a pseudo-agent (originator) as:

bristi hoe
= It rains
or *kɔlɔsi bhɔreni*
= The pitcher is not filled up.

There occurs no other unit which can be syntactically referred to as adverbial of agent or a neutral agent. It appears that structurally there are

[166]Chatterjee, p. 324.

great variations in sentences in Bengali, but from the point of view of the verb (construction) Prof. Chatterjee classified them in two: active and passive.[167]

We think that these four voices cannot be adequately classified exclusively in terms of either syntactic or semantic criteria:

(1) The *kartṛ*, *bhāva*, and *karmakartṛ* sentences are similar in verb structure, which is a syntactic criterion.

(2) The *karma* sentence is different in verb structure.

(3) The *kartṛ* subject is different from the *karma* subject. The *karma-kartṛ* subject may be shown as a variety of *karma* as well as *kartṛ* (pseudo-agent/potential object). The *bhāva* subject is different from *kartṛ* as well as *karma*. These differences are established in terms of semantics.

(4) The fourth types of sentences have some other semantic and syntactic peculiarities on their whole constructions which we have already mentioned.

These sentences are different in their construction: the focus, stress, meaning and grammatical relations, etc. are different from the point of view of NU, VU and VU, NU in these constructions.

[3.8.2] It is interesting to note that those sentences which are explained as agentive passive, quasi passive, awkward passive[168] in English grammar seems comparable with the *karmavācya* sentences in Bengali. The non-agentive passive of English also should be called passive in Bengali. The 'non-agentive intensive active complement construction'[169] in English may be called *karma-kartṛ* in our grammar. Conversely, there seems to be no attempt in English grammar to classify the type of sentence containing a subject which is a verbal noun, although in English it may be possible to have a sentence such as: 'In this situation *saving* is not possible.'

In G.O. Curme's words: 'There are two voices, the active and the passive. The active voice indicates that the subject does something, is or is becoming something. The passive voice represents the subject as acted upon'.[170]

He also describes the forms and remarks that 'some forms of the second group—the participle, the infinitive, the gerund—are infinite.... The forms of the second group do not have inflectional endings hence they can never indicate their agreement with the subject.'[171]

[167]Chatterjee, pp. 319-25.

[168]*A Grammar of Contemporary English*, pp. 848, 808-81.

[169]*Ibid.*

[170]G.O. Curme, *Parts of Speech and Accidence*, pp. 203, 217, 223.

[171]*Ibid.*

From the above discussion and quotations it is clear that the verbal structure, the whole sentence construction, the agreement of the verb with the subject or the subject focusing by the verb, reversibility of subject-predicate, and the meaning (in Curme's terms) are considered to be the basic factors of the grammatical category of voice by grammarians of both the East and the West.

In the traditional Indian grammar the focus of the verb to different types of subjects is thought to be the main criterion of the voices of the verb. The subjects are classified on the basis of sentence semantics. It is noticeable that neither in establishing *kāraka* (roles) nor in establishing *vācya* (voices) the details of word level differences are taken into consideration.

[3.8.2.1.] Once again we would like to take up the problem of ergative construction. Comrie defines it 'in essentially syntactic terms' (above) which means that he stresses the morphological expression of the subject of transitive versus intransitive verb. Lyons explains: 'The term that is generally employed by linguists for the syntactic relationship that holds between (1) and (3) is ergative'.[172]

He further explains that

> ... the subject of an intransitive verb 'becomes' the object of a corresponding transitive verb, and a new ergative subject is introduced as the agent (or cause) of the action referred to. This suggests that a transitive sentence like (3) may be derived syntactically from an intransitive sentence like (1) by means of an ergative or causative transformation (the term "ergative" was coined from a Greek verb meaning "cause", "bring out", 'create'). It will also be observed that the causative or ergative agent in (3) is an animate noun. We have already noted that the tendency for the subjects of transitive verbs to be animate.'[173]

It seems that some linguists describe the term 'ergative' in relation to the markers of the subjects of the transitive verb and intransitive verb, and that some employ the term in regard to the syntactic relationship of two sentences (one having intransitive and another having transitive verb). The relationship is established since the subject of one sentence becomes the object of a corresponding transitive sentence.

Then the idea of ergative relationship is based on the syntactic point that the subject of an intransitive verb becomes the object of a transitive sentence, when the same verb is used transitively in another construction. The argument for establishing any syntactic ergative relationship between the two separate sentences seems to be weak.

The active and passive sentences have affiliation in meaning and syntactic

[172](*i*) The stone moved; (*ii*) John moved; (*iii*) John moved thestone. See Lyons, p. 351.
[173]Lyons, pp. 351-52.

reversibility of the function of the nominals. In the notion of 'ergative' the verb (transitive-intransitive) seems important rather than the subject and object relation or the marker (on the nominal) of the same nominal occurring in two different constructions.

We would like to point out that, even though the transitive verb often occurs with an animate subject, it is not always the case as a transitive verb can occur with an inanimate subject in Bengali (as in other languages). For instance:

(85) *āgun joliā uṭhiā sɔb grāskorilo*
the fire lighted up all caught
(being lighted up)
or *ei trisul ākās biddhokoriteche*
this trident sky is piercing

Either the various markers, the reversion of one item in a different syntactic position, etc. come under consideration or like the active and passive sentences the two independent sentences which are considered having ergative relation should be affiliated in meaning. We believe that 'ergative' cannot be explained in terms of such affiliation or syntactic reversion. It is also questionable whether transitive and intransitive use of a verb should be taken as a criterion to establish relationship between two independent sentences. The notion of ergative relation seems not profitably applicable to languages which use inanimate subject nominal with transitive verb in sentences.

[3.8.3.] In the first chapter we have set up five markers, which usually appear on the NU in Bengali. We have already described the types of markers which appear on the *kartā* and *karma* nominals. In Sanskrit as well as in Bengali grammars, the notion of *vācya* is defined in the fashion we have explained above. Now we shall deal with the markers on *kartā* and *karma* nominals and given verbal constructions.

	Sanskrit	*Bengali*
(1) In *kartṛvācya* (active) the *kartā* (subject) takes (agent: subject)	*prothomā bivakti* (termination)	usually ϕ, plural marker sometimes -e, rarely -ke, -r
The *karma* (object) of that *vācya* takes	*dwitiā bivakti* (termination)	usually -ke, ϕ, plural marker
The verb takes the person marker according to the agent: subject		

(2) In *karmavācya* (passive)	*Sanskrit*	*Bengali*
the subject is the object: subject and it takes the	*prothomā bivakti*	ϕ or plural marker
The agent appears as the adverbial and it takes	*tritiā bivakti*	usually -r/-er, dārā/dia, kottrik/hāte/kāche, etc.

The verb takes person marker according to the karma (object) subject. In Bengali the verb conjugates with passive marker. In Sanskrit the verb form is complicated (most roots are conjugated in 'atmane-pada').[174]

(3) In *bhāvavācya* (passive: an impersonal passive according to Kale, and according to Prof. Chatterjee neuter voice) the verbal theme (idea) is the subject. The *bhāva kartā* (the theme subject) appears in tritiā bivakti in Sanskrit and the verbal form is impersonal in the sense that there is no change in the forms of verbs according to the number and person.
In Bengali the *bhāva kartā* (the theme-subject) takes ϕ marker and the actual doer or agent appears with a link marker -r (plural -der). It takes a neutral position of modifier to the subject nominal (here the *bhāva kartā*).
There can occur a *karma* (object) which appears as usual with either -ke, -e or ϕ marker. The verbal form is similar to the active form in Bengali. Usually it is a *be* verb and conjugated in third person.

(4) In *karmakartṛvācya* (reflexive according to both S. K. Chatterjee and Kāle) the subject is the potential object of the transitive verb (refers the same thing in the real world) or the subject is independent factor. If the word semantic level is considered one can say that the *karmakartṛ* subject is always an inanimate noun. Whereas the *kartrivācya* subject can be either animate or inanimate. In *karmakartṛvācya,* the subject appears with prothomā bivakti in Sanskrit and in Bengali the usual marker is ϕ or plural. In Sanskrit the verb form is like passive, whereas in Bengali it is similar to active.

It follows from the above enumeration that the subjects of Bengali or Sanskrit sentences show mostly either the agent (including the subfunctions of agent) function or the object function. And the theme subjects are typical of these languages. However, the nominals or nominal units holding other roles or *kāraka* relations do not occur as subject but they are always to be considered as part of the predicate. The complexity arises with the role of

[174]Kale, pp. 239, 359, 360, f. n.

cause. This is not discussed as *kāraka* in Bengali grammar. But *svaṭantra*-subject and *hetu*-subject are mentioned in Pāṇiṇi.[175]

However, the *kāraka* relation of the nominal and its occurrence as subject can be diagrammatically shown as:

(1) AGENT

Performer Agent (*kartṛkāraka*), non-performer agent	the subject of active voice

(2) OBJECT

Object of the Verb: *karmakāraka*	the subject of passive voice
object/pseudo agent	the subject of reflexive voice

We have already pointed out that the *theme subject* and the *independent factor subject* do not come under the *kāraka* relation, although some independent factor subjects are considered as agent by N. Vidyabhushan (see (p. 122-23).

The *hetu subject* (the cause) occurs in Bengali, the sentence is structurally active.

The *bhāvavācya* sentence (sentence which has *theme* subject) is structurally active and notionally different from both active or passive.

The *karmakartṛvācya* sentences are structurally active but notionally most of them are passive in the sense that the subject often is a potential object of the transitive verb. However, few independent factor subjects which are not the potential object of the transitive verb and animate in semantic feature may be considered as notionally active. The latter type of sentences are enumerated as *kartṛvācya*.

All these complexities of *vācya, kāraka, uddesya* (subject), *vidheya* (predicate) and different markers on the subject NU can be shown in the tables below Nos. I and II. It may be interesting to consider briefly the traditional fashion of classification of verbs.

Structurally, verbs are classified as follows:[176]

(1) *A radical stem*+inflection: *kɔr* 'do', *ami kori* 'I do'.

(2) *A derived stem* (i.e., radical stem+marker)+inflection: *dekh* 'see' > 'show' *dækhā* 'seeing'

[175]Soudāmini Bahulikar, *Indian Linguistics*, Vol. 34, No. 2, June 1973 pp. 84-86.
[176]Chatterjee, p. 134-38., Vidyabhushan, p. 63-64.

se chobi dækhāiteche
he picture is showing (cause to see)

(3) *A compound stem,* i.e., radical stem with a participle+an auxiliary with inflection:
bɔl 'speak', *bɔl+ite=bolite+lāg* 'began to speak'. The radical+participle=infinitive+auxiliary:

se bolite lāgilo
he began to speak (started speaking)

The above no. 2 can be further classified from the point of view of structure and from the point of view of function. From the point of view of structure they are conjugated like nos. 1, 2 or 3. From the derivational point of view the verbs under no. 2 are of three types:

a. verb
b¹. noun
b². onomatopoeia

From the point of view of function the derived verbs can be classified as follows:

(*i*) *causative function*
(*ii*) *passive function*

(*i*) *Causative*
(*a*) *khā* 'eat' 〉 *khāoā* 'eating' 〉 *khāoā-e* 'cause to eat', 'feed'.
Radical stem 〉 derived stem 〉 *derived stem+inflection*. It is conjugated like no. 1.
(*b*) *khā-* 〉 *khāoā* 〉 *khaoā+te khāoā+te+de+ilām*
'(I) allowed to cause to eat', '(I) allowed (him) to feed'
Radical stem 〉 derived stem 〉derived stem+participle 〉 *infinite +auxiliary+inflection*. It is conjugated like no. 3.
(*ii*) *Passive*
khā- 〉 *khāoā+hɔ+iāche=khāoā hoiāche*[177]
'has been eaten'.
Radical 〉 derived (=verbal noun)+auxiliary+inflection.

The *ā* appears both on causative and passive. The (*i*) (*b*) causative verb is taking a participle whereas (*i*) (*a*) causative does not take any participle or auxiliary. The passive takes *ā* marker on the main verb and auxiliary occurs with appropriate inflexion.

177This type of verbal expression is often neutralized with perfective form of verb.

The no. 3 may also come from different sources as follows (a) (*i*) noun; (*ii*) onomatopoeiacal segment (*b*) adjective.

At the semantic level the verbs may be used actively, passively or causatively. At the syntactic level they may be used transitively and intransitively. Structurally, they are of three types mentioned above.

Likewise, the subject nominal of a sentence can be described. At the semantic level subjects are classified as: (1) agent; (2) non-agent. These can be sub-classified:

(1) *agent*
- (a) animate
- (b) inanimate

(2) *non-agent*
- (a) cause (source)
- (b) originator (source)
- (c) experiencer
- (d) object — potential object of the transitive verb object: *karmakāraka* (direct and indirect objects)
- (e) verbal theme
- (f) independent factor — animate / inanimate

The explication of originator, experiencer, etc. allo-functions, obviously are based on the semantic feature of the nominal and some of them are established on the basis of verb classification in Western grammar. As a matter of fact, our classification of different subjects is based on a higher semantic level than that of word semantics or the sentence semantic, undoubtedly, the word meaning comes into play, but not the details of semantic features of either the nominal or the verbal.

It is to be noticed that the subject such as theme is not coming under any *kāraka* relation.

In traditional grammar, some of the independent factor subjects which have animate feature are called agents which pose some problems. Since in traditional grammar they are considered to have the agent (*kartṛkāraka*) function, the verb occurring with that subject is considered to be focussing the agent subject (*kartṛvācya*).

Besides these, when the verb focuses a causative subject, it can also be taken as in *kartṛvācya*. The causative subject is provoker-agent and the verb has agreement with it. Presumably sentences which have no subjects, or which are not structurally NU, VU, cannot be included in the enumeration of *vācya*.

TABLE 1

A SENTENCE WHICH IS STRUCTURALLY NUVU

	Nominal in agreement with the verb, marker on the unit		*Verb*	*Semantic function or roles of the subject nominal*	*Syntactic Function of the Nominals*
1	2	3	4	5	6
Voices of the verb : the verb *is katṛvācya* (active)	(1) Animate or inanimate	Definite, singular, plural, -a-e/-te; emphatic; optionally -e/te or conjunction if co-ordinated subject :	All types except the passive	Agent function : *kartṛkāraka* relation	The unit which is in agreement with the verb : subject (*kartṛpada*); any other NU occurring to that sentence functionally may be *karma*, *karaṇa*, *adhikaraṇa*, *apādāna*, these to be considered as part of the predicate of the sentence.
	(2) Animate	-Ke in rare cases to express definite aspect			
The verb is in *karmavācya* (passive)	(1) Animate/ inanimate	Singular, definite, plural, emphatic	The passive verb only, obligatorily transitive transitive	Object function : *karmakāraka* relation. It has agreement with the verb	The NU holding *karmakāraka* relation is the syntactic subject. Other NU's occurring in that sentence functionally may be agent, *adhikaraṇa*, *apadānā*, *karaṇa*, *samprudāna*. Syntactically all these come in the predicate part.

1	2	3	4	5	6
The verb is in *bhāvavācya*	(1) Inanimate : abstract-theme	Definite, emphatic	Intransitive or transistive *be* verb	*Bhāva* (theme) or ideational relation	The *bhāva* NU has agreement with the verb : the syntactic subject. The doer in the real world occurs as a modifier to the subject. Other NU's occur in the predicate part.
The verb is in *karmakartṛ vācya*	(1) Inanimate, animate	Definite, plural emphatic	Usually either transitive or intransitive	The potential object of transitive verb; independent factor	The subject, other NU's occurring in the sentence from the predicate part.

TABLE II

A SENTENCE WITH MORE THAN ONE NOMINAL UNIT AND A VERBAL UNIT WHICH HAS AGREEMENT WITH A CAUSATIVE SUBJECT NU

The verb is in *kartṛvācya**	Subject NU is animate/ inanimate	The verb is causative verb	Semantic function; provoker agent/ cause	Syntactic function of the provoker or cause NU is subject: *kartṛpada*. Other NU's including the *provoked agent* are to be considered in the predicate part of the sentence.

NU (s) occurring in the predicate part of various types of sentences (including the causative) usually take the following markers:

—der, ,0 -e, ke	in *karma*,
r, -der, -e, te	different post-positions in *adhikaraṇa* and *apādāna*,
-der, -e, -ke	*in provoked agent*,
-e, -ke	in *sampradāna*,
0, -e, -ke	different post-positions in *karaṇa*,

The adverbial of agent usually occurs with post-positions. The actor NU as modifier to the subject which may be called neutral agent, occurs with -r, -der (plural). This NU syntactically comes under the subject part, but the adverbial of agent syntactically should be considered in the predicate part.

*See Acharya, p. 96.

[3.9] It seems obvious that the appropriateness of considering 'one voice in terms of the other',[178]—does not apply to all languages. Modern Indo-Aryan languages have different types of subject focussing, and, accordingly, four voices are recognized in traditional grammar of these languages.

Structurally, the passive and causative are different from active, further causative is different from passive. Presumably, one need not be thought of as a conversion of a corresponding other (of other voice) sentence. It is wrong to think that all passives can have a corresponding active in Bengali.

[178]Jan Svartrik, *On Voice in English Verb*, p. 3.

Some passives can be converted to actives and vice versa as has been shown above.

We have tried to point out that the subject-object conversion or the structure of the verb, the whole sentence construction, etc. come under the dimension of manifestation (presentation).

A subject of an active sentence may be converted into a modifier in another sentence; there may not be slight structural change in regard to the verb structure, even though the verb can focus a different subject. The voice should be understood in accordance with different subject form. For instance, the Bengali sentence:

86. *āpni kothāe jāben*
you where will go
= Where will you go?

has a 'basic' meaning which may be communicated by another independent sentence:

āpnār kothāe jāoa hɔbe
you where going will be

No doubt, both are interrogative sentences having the same meaning. In these two constructions, there is little difference in the sense that both have the same lexical items (more or less) but in a slightly different form. The differences are:

(*i*) The predicative verb in respective sentences:
(*ii*) The focus on the type of subject in respective sentences;
(*iii*) The relation between the lexical items in respective sentences.

The type of nominalized verbal subject (*jāoā*) shown above is a characteristic feature of all Indian languages.

To map up this kind of difference the classification of four *vācya* of the verb (according to its subject focus) is more an appropriate method rather than the active-passive labels. Sentences containing different types of subjects which show different semantic relations with the verb are taken as independent wholes. And the particular type of subject of a sentence determines the *vācya* (voice) of the verb. Even though Curme and others define the term voice in semantic terms and Jespersen gives an account of 'the notional passive', it seems that the syntactical relationship of active-passive is more stressed in Western grammar. And the structural differences are given more importance than defining the term voice from the point of view of the verb in relation to its subject focus, and labelling the voice of verbs in terms of their focus on different subjects. We believe that the Indian way could be tried in describing other languages also.

So far we know no one has pointed out the difference in emphasis between the concept of *vācya* (in Sanskrit) and *voice* (Western grammar) in Bengali grammar. Many Eastern and Western scholars have maintained that the two concepts are corresponding. We have mentioned before that a few Bengali scholars pointed out the difference between the concept of *kāraka* in Sanskrit and 'case' in Western grammar, even though we do not find any elaborate comparison.

In Sanskrit grammar written by Western as well as Indian scholars in the nineteenth and twentieth centuries, the term 'voice' is commonly used rather than the term *vācya*. And in most of the grammars on modern Indian languages written in this century both terms are taken as equivalent.

M.R. Kāle, in his *A Higher Sanskrit Grammar* does, not use the term *vācya*. Instead he mentions 'the use of verb' (voice).[179]

In fact, Prof. Chatterjee equates reflexive voice and neuter voice with *karmakartṛvācya* and *bhāvavācya* in Bengali, and Kāle described *bhābe proyoga* as impersonal passive and *karmakartṛ proyoga* as reflexive passive.

It seems that the meaning and not the expression is the ground of similarity in these two concepts. On that basis one can say the two concepts are partially similar.

Poutsma describes:

'The meaning of the reflexive voice maintains itself best when the subject denotes a material body perceptible to the sense, the imagination being inclined to ascribe to that body itself a force to originate the activity when the real acting force is imperceptible or incomprehensible...The cigar dropping on the empty hearth, burned itself out....'[180]

The reflexive voice is mostly defined as a sentence containing a reflexive pronoun or reciprocal pronoun as object. Also it is defined in terms of the subject function either as animate or inanimate originator.[181]

The subject of *karmakartṛ* is similar to that extent with the subject of a reflexive construction that both refer to an inanimate originator. The animate originator is not taken into account in *karmakartṛ*. The verb always shows third person concord both in *bhāva* and *karmakartṛ*. In the Bengali constructions and possibly in those of all other Indian languages, the occurrence of a reflexive pronoun is not one of the criteria for labelling the sentence in reflexive voice, whereas in English it is.

From the point of view of the meaning there is great similarity between the *karmakartṛ* and reflexive, but from the point of view of expression structure they are different. Bengali examples given below may be compared with Poutsma's description:

179Speijer, pp. 235-41; Banerjee, p. 57, Chatterjee, pp. 319-27; Vidyabhushan, pp. 81-82, Kale, pp. 359-60, 238.

180Poutsma, pp. 143-58.

181Lyons, p. 361; Poutsma, pp. 143-58.

(87) *gāe* *ækhono* *sā̃kh bāje*
in the village still now the conchshell rings
or *māthā dhoreche*
the head (aches) pains

In fact, in recent English grammar the existence of the reflexive voice is not separately mentioned but it is considered as a variety of active.[182] A quotation can be given:

'Co-reference between subject and nominal object blocks the passive transformation, and occurs with (*a*) reflexive, (*b*) reciprocal, and (*c*) possessive pronouns in the object. Normally, however, transitive verbs with other nominal objects *Passivize*....

'*Note*: Since reflexive and reciprocal pronouns are objective case replacements, it would be unexpected anyway to have such a pronoun in the subject position of a passive.[183]

Poutsma says; 'A passive meaning may also seldom be observed in verbs that have thrown off the reflexive pronoun and have consequently become intransitive...'Her eyes filled with tears...when an opportunity offered'.[184] The nominals occurring in respective sentences have chosen or selected the alloseme of the verb and the verb also selects the alloseme of the nominal. As such dependency is in both-ways and the verb is not actually the dominant factor. The meaning of the whole sentence is understood when the allosemes are selected.

To quote from Jespersen:

It is important here as elsewhere to distinguish between syntactic and notional categories. Whether a verb is syntactically active or passive depends on its *form* alone; but the same idea may be expressed sometimes by an active, sometimes by a passive form...There is thus nothing in the ideas themselves to stamp verbs as active or passive. And yet we may speak of 'active' and 'passive' as notional as well as syntactic categories, but only as applied to the meaning of each verb separately and—what is very important—only in case of a transposition of the relation of the subject (and object if there is one) to the verb itself. "Jill is loved by Jack" and "as wird gelanzt" are notionally as well as syntactically in the passive, because the subjects are different from those in "Jack loves Jill" and "sietarzen". In other cases there is disagreement between the syntactic and the notional active or passive.

[182] *A Grammar of Contemporary English*, pp. 613-14, 967.
[183] *Ibid.*, p. 805.
[184] Poutsma, p. 158.

'Thus if we take the two sentences, "he sells the book" and "the book sells well" we must say that active form sells in the former is a *notional active*, and in the latter a *notional passive*, because what in one is the object in the other is the subject. In the same way we have other verbs (in some languages more, in others fewer), which are used idiomatically as notional active and notional passive, thus

Persia began the war.
The war began.

Other English examples: He opened the door; the door opened....It is rare to find verbs with passive forms that may be used in both these ways.[185]

We have noticed before how these types of sentences are treated in traditional Indian grammar. A comparable English example may be *the book appears today* (with Jespersen's *the book sells well*). One can say that *sell* could just have an "intransitive" alloseme: "have such a quality that one can sell it easily." If so *book* is not an object in the sense it is an object in the other sentence, 'he sells the book' (object).

Also in the other examples given by Jespersen, we believe that the verb *began* in just 'intransitive' with the meaning "had a beginning". Thus *the war began, continued, finished, lasted, was cruel,* etc. and *the door opened* or *closed,* etc. do not necessarily indicate the object function of the nominals. They are object in the sense that they refer something, some idea; they are also the potential object of a transitive verb. These types of subject are called "independent factor" in our analysis following the traditional Indian grammar. And they can be aptly categorized as *karmakartṛ vācya.*

Similar problems are the current issues in Generative grammar. We quote from Jackendoff:

'The feature of underlying syntactic structure that presumably relates to functional structure is the system of grammatical relations, that is, the structural relations obtaining between verbs and the noun phrases, adjective phrases, prepositional phrases, and sentence complements that they strictly subcategorize. Much of the justification of transformations involves arguments about understood grammatical relations and their representation in deep structure. Yet the "natural" grammatical relations such as subject and object do not correspond in any simple fashion to the understood semantic relations. Consider these well known examples:

(2.1) The door opened.
(2.2) Charlie opened the door.

[185]Jespersen, *The Philosophy of Grammar*, 1924, pp. 165-66.

(2.3) Fred *bought* some hashish from Reuben.
(2.4) Reuben *sold* some hashish to Fred.

In the traditional sense of grammatical relations, (2.1)-(2.4) have their underlying grammatical relations expressed in the surface as well; the sentences have undergone no movement transformation that would alter the underlying positions. But the grammatical relations do not express certain obvious semantic facts. The door has the same semantic function in (2.1) and (2.2) although it is the subject in one and the object in the other. In both (2.3) and (2.4) the relation between Fred and Reuben is recipient-donor. Yet in (2.3) Fred is subject and Reuben is in a prepositional phrase; and the reverse holds in (2.4).'[186]

Here we think that, firstly, the object is the direct object in (2.2), and the subject of (2.1) can be explained as independent factor. Secondly, the *recipient-donor* relation of Fred and Reuben is the (matter) event of the real world. Probably, the subject-direct object relation is enough in grammatical analysis. Even though the recipient-donor relation can be explained at the semantic level of a grammatical analysis, it may not necessarily be the basis for establishing syntactic relations between the two independent sentences.

Jackendoff further says:

'The existence of numerous examples like (2.1)-(2.4) has led many grammarians to feel that something is seriously wrong with the traditional notion of grammatical relations. Their feeling is substantiated in a theory of grammar which includes the strong form of the Katz-Postal Hypothesis. For if all semantic information is contained in deep structure the "natural" deep structure (2.1)-(2.4) cannot be the real deep structures. In the real 'deep structure', the door would occupy the same position in (2.1) and (2.2) and Fred and Reuben would occupy the same respective position in (2.3) and (2.4).

'If we assume the strong Katz-Postal Hypothesis, then we are forced to give up the "natural" deep structures of (2.1)-(2.4) in favour of some more "abstract" representation. The original notion of deep structure as a representation of syntactic distributional patterns must thus be rejected in favour of a more semantically based conception.

'Alternatively, one could retain a notion of deep structure in the spirit of syntactic structures, adopting the "natural" deep structures for (2.1)-(2.4), and give up the strong Katz-Postal Hypothesis. Thus deep structures and semantic representations will not be isomorphic; we will have to find a mapping relating them. The problem then is to decide which of these alternatives to choose in order to arrive at an adequate description of (2.1)-(2.4).

'There have been two rather different lines of approach within the constraints of the strong Katz-Postal Hypothesis. One approach, proposed by

[186]Jackendoff, *Semantic Interpretation in Generative Grammar*, p. 25.

Lakoff (1971) and taken up and developed by the generative semanticists is to break off parts of the semantic reading and express them as higher pro-verbs that must eventually be deleted. For example, the similarity of (2.1) and (2.2) would be represented by the deep structure (2.5) and (2.6). In (2.6) a transformation raises open into the position of the causative, pro-verb, leaving no trace of the pro-verb; then various roles are deleted, leaving the "natural" surface structure for (2.2). The presence of the clause the door open in (2.5) and (2.6) explains the semantic relation between (2.1) and (2.2).

'A number of objects can be made to this approach mostly concerned with the nature of the proposed pro-verbs. First, it should be noticed that it is substantial increase of power in the syntax to allow lexical items which never appear in the surface, and which always must be deleted by a particular transformation (which in turn is used only to delete pro-verbs). Lakoff presents other, more precedented, cases of lexical items which must undergo particular transformations, then proposes a formalism to handle them called a positive absolute exception. But in each of these other cases, two

(2.5)

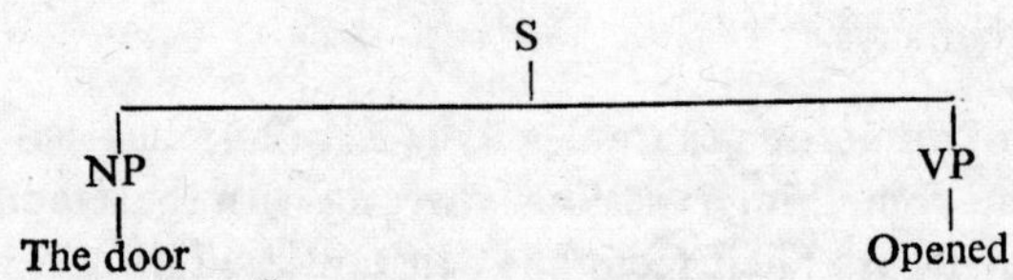

(2.6)

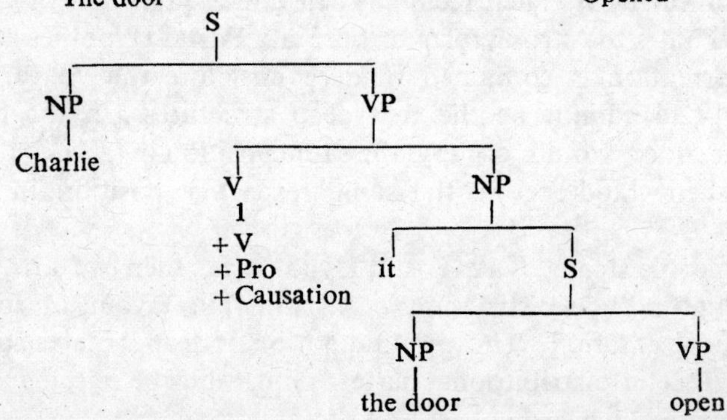

other conditions hold: the lexical items do not delete, and the transformations they must undergo also apply to other lexical items optionally. Hence these cases differ significantly from the hypothetical pro-verbs. In applying the notion positive absolute exception to hypothetical pro-verbs, Lakoff shows that he has chosen a device far more powerful than is necessary to handle his original data....

'One might attempt to meet this objection in part by claiming that the main verb in (2.6) is not a hypothetical pro-verb, but the real verb cause (or bring about). It would thus be claimed that Charlie opened the door and

Charlie caused the door to open have the same deep structure, that is, are synonymous. But this cannot in general be the case....

'In (2.7) and (2.8), drop has a paradigm similar to open:

(2.7) The glass dropped to the floor.
(2.8) Floyd dropped the glass to the floor.

Thus we would incorrectly predict that (2.9) and (2.10) are synonymous:

(2.9) Floyd caused the glass to drop to the floor by tickling Sally, who was holding it.
(2.10) Floyd dropped the glass to the floor by tickling Sally, who was holding it.

'The causation implied in (2.2) and (2.8) is of a more direct nature than seems to be expressible by any verb in English. Therefore it cannot be due to the deletion of any real item, the verb must be the hypothetical form that Lakoff posits, and the original objection stands....

'Another way of expressing the semantic relations of (2.1)-(2.4) in deep structure has been discussed by Fillmore (1968); a somewhat different version of the same theory is given in Mathews (1968). Instead of expanding deep structures of sentences into additional clauses, Fillmore puts more deep structure information into the clause itself, in the form of a system of case relations. The deep structure of (2.1) and (2.2) are (2.11) and (2.12) respectively.

(2.11)

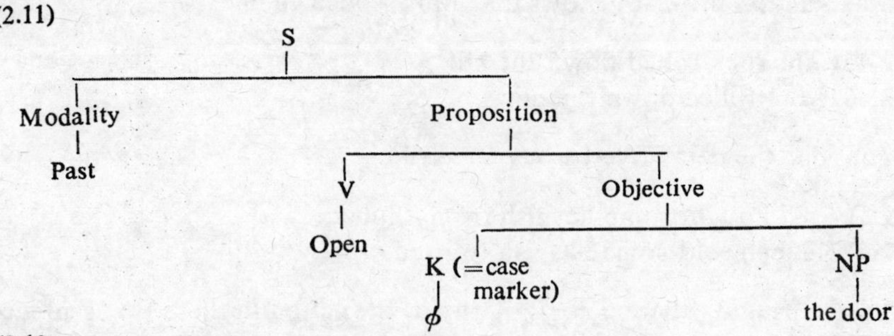

(2.12)

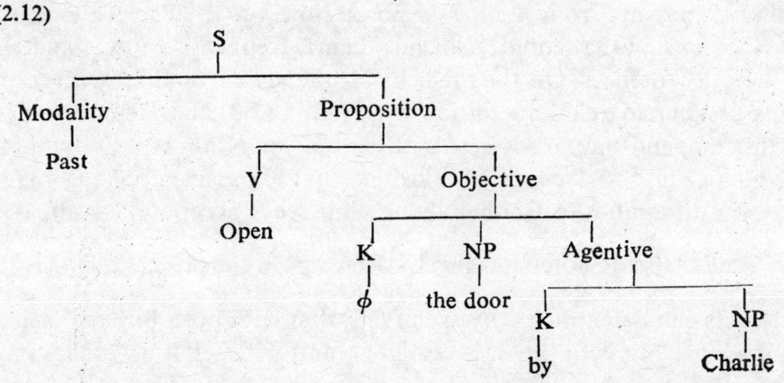

The surface forms are created by transformations which move exactly one NP into subject position and delete its case marker. The semantic similarity of (2.1) and (2.2) is expressed in the case relations; the surface disparity is explained by the application of the transformations that create subjects. As in Lakoff's approach, the traditional notion of underlying grammatical relations is of no importance.

Fillmore's approach makes the interesting claim that there is a relatively small class of case relations, and that they are universal. One extremely interesting question that it poses, then, is what the right case relations are for expressing the observed semantic and syntactic generalizations.

I will propose here a third way of accounting for (2.1) (2.4). It is based on a system of semantic relations developed by Jeffrey S. Gruber in his dissertation and other work (Gruber, 1965, 1967a).

This system of semantic relations looks superficially like a possible realisation of Fillmore's case system....It seems to me that there is one crucial difference between the two...this difference argues that case grammar cannot be altogether correct......the deep structures differ from surface structures in word order and in the addition of case nodes and case markers. However, the number of noun phrases in the deep and surface structure is the same: each surface structure noun phrase is assumed to have exactly one deep structure case. On the other hand, in Gruber's system of thermatic relations, noun phrases can function in more than one thermatic role within the same sentence. For example, in (2.45) the rock is theme; the semantic similarity of Max's action in (2.46) shows that Max is also theme.

(2.45) The rock rolled down the hill.
(2.46) Max rolled down the hill.

Or consider the pair of verbs buy and sell:

(2.3) Fred bought some hashish from Reuben.
(2.4) Reuben sold some hashish to Fred.

On one hand, there is a similarity in the action in these two sentences: the hashish is passing from Reuben's possession to Fred's. This can be expressed by saying that some hashish is theme, Reuben is source, and Fred is goal in both sentences. On the other hand, the sentences differ with respect to who is designated as taking initiative—Fred in (2.3) and Reuben in (2.4). To see this, append on purpose to both sentences. Note especially that if Fred is moved into surface subject position by the passive applying to (2.4) on purpose still applies to Reuben if the sentence is acceptable at all.

(2.47) Fred was sold some hashish by Reuben on purpose.

These facts can be captured by specifying that with both buy and sell the subject is agent, but with buy it is also goal, and with sell it is also source.

There is no convenient way in a case grammar to simultaneously express the reciprocity of the source-goal pattern and the agent status of the subject. To show that agent is not the only relation which can combine with others, we turn to a more complicated example, which involves some semantic relations not discussed by Gruber. Consider the verb trade, which takes a direct object, an optional phrase with to, and an obligatory phrase with for.

(2.48) Esau traded his birthright (to Jacob) for a mess of pottage.

'This sentence describes two related actions. The first is the change of hands of the birthright from Esau to Jacob. The direct object is theme, the subject is source, and the to-object is goal. Also there is what I will call the secondary action, the changing of hands of the mess of pottage in the other direction. In this action, the for-phrase is secondary theme, the subject is secondary goal, and the to-phrase is secondary source.'[187]

We have quoted a very long passage, but it is very characteristic of recent generalistic view points.

Jespersen generalized differences in *he sells the book* and *the book sells well* as notional active and notional passive; on the other hand *Jack loves Jill* and *Jill is loved by Jack* as syntactical active and syntactical passive.

Fillmore and others establish a deep structure. The main issue here is whether it is reasonable to postulate any hypothetical structure for a given grammatical expression.

It is clear that an event of reality or an idea can be expressed in a language in different ways. Why, then, should the syntactic differences on the expression side be related to a hypothetical structure?

We have repeatedly pointed out that any structure of a language should be treated as an independent structure. We take it for granted that in languages there are constructionally three types of sentences: active, passive and causative. Each may have syntactical relations with some other construction, and they may be affiliated in meaning.

Some of the active and passive constructions are syntactically reversible. The difference between active and passive is mainly that the same words are arranged differently and have different markers. For instance:

Active	Passive
A, B, C————→	A + B + C + or B + A + C + etc.

Here the + sign signals a certain type of marker on the lexical item, i.e., the grammatical form. For instance, A, B, C may be taken as the substitutes of two nominal units and a verbal unit.

We consider that the constructions are affiliated in meaning. The labelled relation is to be established both in passive and active considering the total meaning expressed by the NU, VU in respective sentences. The syntactic

[187] *Ibid.*, pp. 25-35.

reversion changes the syntactic function of A, B in relation to C, here A, B are NU and C is VU. The semantic function (relations) such as agent, object persists, although the morphological or postpositional markers will be different. The VU also will be structurally different in active and in passive. The causative is structurally different in the sense that the verb structure differs from the active and the passive. The same verb can be used as causative, non-causative or passive. Therefore, we assume that these constructions are independent.

The "deep structure" is not intuitively present in the speaker of hearer's mind, but some deep structures are close to a description of the real world.

Deep structure (—real world event)

active (by given rules) | passive (by given rules)

We have already mentioned the peculiarities of the language under discussion. Some passives will not necessarily have to be thought of in terms of active. Some actives can never be transformed into passives. All the problems and difficulties discussed by Jackendoff and others disappear if "deep structure" is not posited. But still semantic syntactic explication is possible and languages can be described. All active subjects do not have the same role, i.e., sentences which have the same structure may structurally be put under the same label but they may have different subjects which have semantically different roles. Considering these differences it seems proper to establish two parallel levels of grammar, i.e., the syntactic level and the semantic level.

In this respect, the traditional grammars described languages very satisfactorily and elaborately. And it is not an exaggeration to say that the theory developed in Indian traditional grammar in the ancient time is still adequately applicable to the description of the present stage of Indian languages.

In traditional grammar, the semantic and syntactic generalizations are made in two parallel levels and a correlation is often observed, though one-to-one correspondence were not found out. In the *kāraka* and *vācya*, theories, the syntactic and semantic relation was impressively co-related.

We do not follow the transformational theory or the deep structure hypothesis, and many remarks by Fillmore and others do not seem appropriate for our language.

Fillmore's remark that 'each case relationship occurs only once in a simple sentence'[188] cannot map the simple sentence:

(88) *āmār ār khukur ghɔrer jānlāe*
mine and khuku's room's on the window

[188]Fillmore, *Case for Case*, p. 21.

duipāllāte *ækjoṛā* *pākhi* *bose*
on the doorpang one pair of birds having sat
muṛi *ār keker ṭukroguli*
the rice bubble and the pieces of cakes
khũṭe khuṭe khācche
in the manner of picking up are eating

It is a simple sentence since there occurs only one finite verb. And there occurs more than one NU which holds the same case relation (labelled relation), i.e., there are two locatives in the above sentence, the expressions *jānlāe* and *duipāllāte.* Sentences can have more than one locative or instrumental or object or agent in one, sometimes the two locatives are co-referential.[189]
For instance:

(89) *āpni bāṛite* *kɔlerjɔle* *snānkorben nāki*
you at home with tap water would bath or
nodite *sroterjɔle*
in the river with current water (the water that has current =fresh water)

We think the expressions *bāṛite* and *nodite* are locative and the expressions *kɔlerjɔle* and *sroterjɔle* are instrumental.

(90) *āmi rāmke jāni* *ebɔŋ* *rāmer* *bābākeo*
I Ram know and Ram's father

In this sentence the expressions *rāmke ebɔŋ rāmer bābākeo* may be taken as a discontinuous noun phrase which has object role semantically.

(91) *chuṭir dine* *khuku* *khæla korte, ganbajna korte*
in the holidays khuku to play to sing
bhālobase
likes

This simple sentence occurs with two objects: *khælākorte, gānbājnākorte*; there occurs no conjunction between these two expressions. They are separated because each expression occurs with a break and a marker.

In a causative sentence there can occur two agents. The above examples make it clear that a case or "role" may occur more than once in a simple sentence in many languages.

[189]See S. Starosta, 'Case forms and case Relations in Sora', in *Working Papers in Linguistics*, Vol. V, No. 1 January-March 1973.

Note also Jackendoff's belief that 'there is no convenient way in a case grammar to simultaneously express the reciprocity of the source-goal pattern and the agent status of the subject'.[190] Also Gruber did not notice relations which can combine with others.[191] He thinks he can establish primary and secondary actions:

(*i*) *Primary Action*
The change of hands of the birth right
from Esau to Jacob;
The direct object is theme;
The subject is source;
The to-object is goal;

(*ii*) *Secondary Action*
The *for*-phrase is secondary theme;
The subject is secondary goal;
The *to* phrase is secondary source.

A suggestion by Starosta is similar to Jackendoff's idea; Starosta mentions the reciprocity of cases in one unit,[192] i.e., he admits that one unit can have two "cases". The idea of primary and secondary action does not seem acceptable. As soon as the secondary actions are taken into account instead of the primary one, we consider the result of the event in the real world, but a grammar should not include such consideration.

Simultaneous reciprocity may be understood as a relation between syntactic units such as subject and semantic units such as agent, object, theme, etc. In other words a subject can be an agent, object, theme, etc.

[3.10] Prof. Chatterjee has explained that the meaning of *sampradāna* is to give something to somebody else relinquishing one's right so that the thing cannot be taken back. The nominal which is to be labelled *sampradāna kāraka* (in Bengali, Sanskrit) considering the above-mentioned relation with the verb (meaning 'give' or 'offer') always refers to an animate recipient who receives the gift.[193] N. Vidyabhushan also makes a similar statement: 'When something has been willingly given, the recipient is in *sampradāna kāraka*.'[194]

All Bengali scholars have had a similar idea in reference to Sanskrit. In the present author's translation of Chatterjee's words, it would be something like: 'The person who receives the gift is to be called in *sampradāna*

[190]Jackendoff, p. 35.
[191]*Ibid.*
[192]Stanley Starosta, pp. 133-51.
[193]Chatterjee, pp. 91-92.
[194]Vidyabhushan, p. 53.

kāraka.'[195] Further, one may quote: ... with verbs which indicate such meaning as "to offer", "pray", "salute", "to give", "to respect", "to show devotion", etc. The person affected by the verb is to be considered as *sampradāna* in Bengali and Sanskrit.'[196]

Kale says: 'The primary sense of the dative case is *sampradāna*. The indirect object of the root *dā* is called *sampradāna*, also the person or thing with reference to whom or which an action is done: *biprāya gāŋ dadāti* 'he gives a cow to a Brahmana'; *judhaya saŋnajhati* 'prepares for battle...'[197] And in a footnote Kale quotes Pāṇiṇi: *karmanayam abhiprāiti sa sampradānam*.[198]

This Sanskrit rule (*śūtra*) is connected with other rules (*śūtras*), and is translated by Saudamini Bahulikaras:

(32) The person whom one wishes to connect with the object is *sampradāna*;
(33) In the case of verbs meaning 'to please', the one who is to be pleased;
(34) In the case of *šlagh, hnu, stha*, and *šap*, the one who is intended to be informed;
(35) In the case of the causative of *dhṛ*, the creditor;
(36) In the case of spṛh, that which is desired;
(37) In the verbs having the meaning *krodh* 'to be angry', *druh* 'to injure', *irśya* 'to envy', *asūya* 'to be antagonistic', the one against whom anger is directed;
(44) Optionally *sampradāna* in the case of *parikrayana* ('employing on stipulated wages').[199]

We believe that the idea of *sampradāna* in Indian grammar is similar to some extent to the idea of dative is Western grammar. More exactly *sampradāna* can be said to correspond to a kind of 'dative' but all datives are not *sampradāna*.

The two Sanskrit examples given by Kale may be described as "dative of person" in *biprāya*... (*a*) to a 'brahmana' (animate), and dative of abstract noun in *judhāya*.... (*b*) 'for battle' (abstract idea).

In modern English grammar, however, we find an idea of dative which is more restricted. The dative is considered as 'recipient participant' as in the following passage:

"I found a place for the magnolia tree" "I found a place for Mrs. Jones" appear to be equivalent utterance, only the one can be transformed into a

[195]Chatterjee, pp. 93. The present author has translated the above definitions from the original.

[196]Acharya, p. 101.

[197]Kale, pp. 485-86.

[198]*Ibid*.

[199]*Indian Linguistics*, Vol. 34, No. 2, June 1973, p. 84-85.

clause with indirect object: I have found Mrs. Jones a place, not 'I have found the magnolia tree a place. This is because the magnolia tree is not animate and therefore does not qualify for the recipient role.'[200]

Thus modern English grammar restricts the idea of dative to the animate participant only. It does not say anything about the type of verb. It also says nothing about the form of the dative syntagma, whereas in Sanskrit a *sampradāna* syntagma may refer to an abstract idea like war or an animate noun such as *bipra* 'brahmana'.

We do not believe that it is a good solution to make *for the magnolia tree* and *for Mrs. Jones* difference in grammar. We think that the two expressions may have different relations to other constructions without being different as constructions.

Kale further says that in the case of other verb roots the object may be in instrumental or accusative form, but it should still be considered as *karma* (object) and not *sampradāna* (dative).[201] It is apparent that the verb meaning refers to the *sampradāna* role of the particular nominal affected by the verb.

It seems to me that in Sanskrit the *sampradāna*, which is considered to be concerned with some particular verb roots as well as a particular marker on the noun, includes a wide range of nouns, whereas in English the dative concerns 'animate participant' only.

The *sampradāna* in Bengali grammar always refers to an animate noun. (In Sanskrit this is not so.) The Bengali *sampradāna* seems to be similar to *benefactive* in English, which means *for someone's benefit*. The *dative* and the *benefactive* in English grammar depend very much on the animate semantic feature of the lexical item.

The question is whether it is worthwhile to assign a separate label to the expression *for the magnolia tree* in English grammar or a separate label such as *sampradāna* in Bengali, which is in form similar to *karma* (object). In other words, considering the particular relation between the affected animate noun and a particular verb should the *sampradāna kāraka* be mentioned separately from *karma*?

As a matter of fact, most Bengali scholars are of the opinion that *sampradāna* can be described as a variety of *karma* (object). Generally, the indirect object is an animate noun. The indirect object of a verb like *da-*'give/offer' is to be considered as *sampradāna* if it means a gift, and if it is a voluntary action. From the point of view of sentence semantics, *sampradāna* can be assigned on the basis of the meaning of the verb (give) and the type of relation existing between the nominal and the verbal. For instance:

doridroke ɔkātɔre ɔrtho bitɔrɔnkɔro
to the poor freely money distribute

[200] *A Grammar of Contemporary English*, p. 350.
[201] Kale, p. 485-86.

joggobɔre *kɔnyā* *dānkɔrāucit*[202]
to a deserving groom the daughter give away
is proper

The expressions *dɔridroke* and *bɔre* are considered as *sampradāna kāraka* in Bengali grammar following the Sanskrit.

The verb *btiɔrɔnkɔrā* includes meanings such as 'to distribute', 'to give away', 'to supply', etc. and the verb *dānkɔrā* includes meanings such as 'to make a gift', 'to present', 'to bestow', 'to give away', 'to give alms', etc. All these meanings may be simply rendered as 'to give', which may be expressed in Bengali with a verb *dā*-'give'.

We wish to point out that the particular alloseme of the verb is not dominant in such expressions; the alloseme does not select the meaning of the other lexical items. The semantic feature of the nominal in particular is not prominent either.

In Bengali language, a noun referring to a mortal being and a noun referring to personified beings are considered to be the same in semantic features, even though words like God, spirit, sun, etc. are not animate nouns in the sense 'I', 'you' or an 'animal' are. The *sampradāna kāraka* may correspond to 'recipient' or 'affected participant' or benefactive in English. Syntactically, its behaviour is similar to the indirect object.

At the level of word semantics, the *sampradāna* and *indirect object* are similar, i.e., both are animate nouns.

The difference which is found at the level of sentence semantics: the *sampradāna—recipient* receives something unconditionally and the giver gives voluntarily. There is no compulsion or pressure or claim. The affected person is benefited. Furthermore, in *sampradāna* the thing received by the affected participant cannot be returned. For instance, in the sentences below the particular expressions cannot be considered *sampradāna,* according to both Bengali and Sanskrit grammar.

(92) *projā* *rājāke* *kɔr* *dæe*
the subject to the king tax gives

The expression *rājāke* may be called dative or benefactive but not *sampradāna* as there is no voluntary action; it is done by compulsory rule.

An English sentence can be compared:

(93) Give the dress *to the dry-cleaner.*

The expression *to the dry-cleaner* cannot be considered as *sampradāna* since *the dress* is not a gift and *the dress* can be taken back. The action may be voluntary, the 'affected recipient' is benefited. Therefore, the expression *to the dry-cleaner* may be either called dative or benefactive.

[202]Chatterjee, p. 92.

Prof. Chatterjee and other Bengali scholars prefer to include *sampradāna* in the more basic idea of object.[203] And it may be a better solution to show *sampradāna* (which corresponds partially to the idea of dative and benefactive) as a subfunction of the basic function of indirect object. In this language, the indirect object very often refers to an animate noun. The *sampradāna* includes:

(*i*) Recipient participant;
(*ii*) Simultaneous reciprocity of the recipient's unconditional gift and the giver's willingness or voluntary action;
(*iii*) The recipient's benefit.

Thus, it includes the idea of dative and benefective in addition to the idea that the action is voluntary and the gift unconditional.

If one considers the reciprocity of action to which Jackendoff refers, it is doubtful if this reciprocity belongs to grammar. Apparently, it is in many examples a part of our knowledge of the real world event only, but not directly expressed in the sentence.

In terms of grammatical function, the expressions in the above-mentioned examples as *dɔridroke, joggobɔre, rājāke, to the dry cleaner*—are to be treated similarly. They seem to function as indirect object. Prof. Chatterjee would refer to them as indirect object.[204]

If in Bengali the dative, benefactive and the idea of *sampradāna* are taken as the variety of indirect object, then they can be tabulated in a way similar to the one we have used for subject.

indirect object ——|—dative
|—benefactive
|—sampradāna

Alternatively, one can establish *sampradāna* separately rather than considering it as a variety of the indirect object. In any case, the *sampradāna* NU appears with *-ke/e* marker, which is the same as for *karma*; the sentence which contains a *sampradāna* NU, contains also a *karma* NU which is inanimate. The verb of this sentence indicates the meaning 'to give' (in a wide range) in Bengali. The particular type of involvement between the nominal and the verbal (in that type of sentence) has already been mentioned. We have mentioned the difference between the notions of *dative, benefactive,* and *sampradāna*. Both *dative* and *sampradāna* occur with the same marker in Bengali. Usually, benefactive occurs with *-r/-er* together with the V marker (post-positional segment). Normally, these three roles are labelled to animate nominals.

203Chatterjee, p. 93, Acharya, p. 102-03.
204Chatterjee, p. 92.

[3.11.0] Following Prof. Chatterjee, I put *apādāna kāraka* in the fourth place, but Kale, N. Vidyabhushan, P. Acharya, have put it in the fifth. It is explained that the source of a thing, cause of an action, a place from which a thing or person has departed, or has fallen, cause of an experience, etc. which are expressed in a nominal unit with certain markers are labelled as *apādāna kāraka* in Sanskrit and Bengali grammars.[205]

It is found that whichever the marker is the expression should be translated into English with the preposition *from* to get the *apādāna* meaning. The *apādāna kāraka* is exemplified in the following sentences:

bije gāch jɔnme
from the seed the tree grows
kukɔrme nirɔstrɔhɔo
from misdeed desists (you)[206]

94. *se chād hoite poṛiāche*
he/she from the roof has fallen

The expressions in the above-mentioned examples *bije*, *kukɔrme* and *chād-hoite* are considered as *apādāna*.[207]

Kale also maintains that the expressions such as 'motion away from', 'protection from fear', 'that from which or whom the fear proceeds, when concealment is to be had recourse to. . ."[208] should be understood as the *apādāna kāraka.*

Even though sometimes it is difficult to differentiate *apādāna* and *locative*, the definition of *apādāna* would be meaningful if one considers sentence semantics. The above example contains the *apādāna* nominal *chād hoite*; the expression is to be considered *apādāna* because by definition it signals '*detachment*', '*fall*', and *away from*', etc.

Prof. Chatterjee points out that the distance or range of time, range of place should not be considered as *kāraka* relation. For instance:

cɔkrotirtha hoite bālu ghai projonto
from Cakratirtha to Balughai
unisso āṭānno sāl hoite unisso couṣoṭṭi.
from the year 1958 to 1964
brikkho ɔntorāl hoite/brikkho
being behind the tree/from the
ɔntorale thākia[209]
behind of the tree

[205]Chatterjee, p. 94.
[206]*Ibid.*
[207]*Ibid.*
[208]Kale, pp. 491-93.
[209]Chatterjee, p. 95; Vidyabhushan, pp. 54-55.

are not to be taken as *kāraka* relation, because the verb does not indicate any separation or fall, or source, or origin, cause, cessation, abstention, a leaving off, repose, etc.

It is quite clear then that the expression *chād hoite* 'from the roof' and *bije* 'from the seed' are not considered as locative, because the relation involved in the respective sentences does not indicate the location of the verb; instead it indicates the meaning 'leaving off' and 'source'. Even though 'from a place' and 'source' come close to the idea of locative to some extent, we think that, unless the sentence semantics signals the location of the action indicated by the verb, the nominal expression with a marker which can indicate *apādāna* or locative cannot be considered as locative. At the word semantics level the lexical item may well refer to a place, but this is not sufficient. There are differences in description between Prof. Chatterjee and P. Acharya.

Bahulikar translates Pāṇiṇi:

> That which remains stable in case of separation is *apādana*; in the case of verbs meaning 'to fear', and 'to protect', that which causes fear; in the case of the verb *ji-* with the preposition *parā*, that which is unbearable; in the case of verbs meaning 'to ward off' that which is desired; in the case of verbs meaning 'to hide oneself', that from whom one wishes to hide; the teacher in the case of learning; the origin in respect to that which arises therefrom; the source in respect to that which springs therefrom.'[210]

Kale says:

> The principal sense of the ablative case is अपादान or "motion away from"; hence the noun from which the motion, real or conceived takes place is put in the ablative case; ग्रामादायन्ति 'comes from a village"....
>
> '(*a*) Words having the sense of जुगुप्ला, बिराम or cessation, pause and प्रमाद "swerving from" also govern the ablative case. पापाद जुगुपलते "he hates sin". . . .
>
> 'In the case of words expressing fear or protection from fear, that from which or whom the fear proceeds is put in the ablative case; चोरादिभेति 'is afraid of a thief'. . .
>
> 'That from which one is kept off is also put in the ablative; पापान्निवारयति wards off from sin. . . .
>
> 'In the case of जि with परा the thing unbearable is put in the ablative case; अध्यनान्पराजयते finds study unbearable or difficult. . . .
>
> 'When one wants to express concealment, that whose sight one desires to avoid is put in the ablative case; मातुर्निलीयते कृष्ण: 'Krishna conceals himself from his mother'. . .

[210]Indian Linguistics, Vol. 34, No. 2, June 1973, p. 85.

'(*a*) The teacher from whom something is learnt regularly is put in the ablative case उपाध्यायादधीते learns from the preceptor. . . .
'(*b*) Similarly the prime or original cause in the case of जन् to be born, and the source in the case of भू are put in the ablative ब्रह्मण: प्रजा: प्रजयन्ते the creation proceeds from Brahman. . .हिमवतो गङ्गा प्रभवति. The Ganges rises from the Himalayas. . .
Note: Verbs meaning to be born, or to be begotten upon are often used with the locative. . . .'[211]

P. Acharya further describes such divisions as:

(*i*) *ādhār bā sthānbāc ɔkɔpādān* (ablative of place)
sākhā hote phul jhorepɔṛe
from the branch the flower has fallen
(*ii*) *ɔbosthābācok ɔpādān* (ablative of state)
jānlā theke dekhbe cee cee
being at the window will see (time to time)
(*iii*) *kālbācɔk ɔpādān* (ablative of time)
sɔkāl theke bādol holo phurie elo bælā
since the morning it rained ends the day

He also argues in favour of the difference between distance and comparison.

(*iv*) *udɔepurtheke pā̃c krosh dur hɔbe nāhɔrāmuŋra*
from Udoypur 5 *krosh* distance will be Naharamungra
= the place Naharamungra is about 10 miles from Udoypur.
(*v*) *rāmer ɔpekkhā syāmer bɔyes besi*[212]
Ram than Syam's age more
= Shyam is older than Ram.

We have pointed out that Prof. Chatterjee does not favour to call 'role' *kāraka* of the noun phrase which expresses distance or comparison.

Ramendrasundar is of the opinion that the argument which is given in the Sanskrit grammar regarding the possessive is also applicable to the *apādāna*. The *apādāna*, in his opinion, has no direct relation to the verb as it has in the case of *kartṛ* and *karma*. It only qualifies the action, and the function may be considered as similar to manner, time, and place adverbial. He finds the *apādāna* is comparable with the adverbial.[213]

[3.12] Following Prof. Chatterjee, I put the *karaṇa kāraka* in the fifth place. It corresponds to the English term 'instrumental case'. The definitions given

[211]Kale, pp. 491-92.
[212]Acharya, pp. 103-04.
[213]Chatterjee, p. 103.

by Prof. Chatterjee and others are as follows: 'That by which or using which or by the means of which the agent accomplishes or performs, does the action, is to be understood as *karaṇa* 'instrument.'[214]

P. Acharya includes the way an indication or sign and the cause by which the action is accomplished or something is resulted.[215] The following are examples:

(1) The means or thing by which the action is done:

se kɔlomdiā lekhe
he/she with a pen (using a pen) writes

The expression *kɔlomdiā* is *karaṇa.*

(2) The way by which the action is accomplished:

ruperdārā kichu hɔena
beauty (with) by anything cannot be achieved
guṇer-dārā mon jɔe kɔrājāe
quality by (with) the heart/mind can be won
= One can win a heart by quality and not by beauty.

The expressions *ruperdāra, guṇerdārā* are to be understood as *karaṇa.*

(3) An indication/sign by which something can be detected:

gõph-die cenājāe
by the moustache (he) can be recognized

The expression *goph-die* is to be considered as *karana.*

(4) The cause of some effect:

dukkhe tāhār cokkhe jɔl āsilo
due to grief to his/her eyes water came
= Tears came to her eyes due to grief.

The expression *dukhe* is *karaṇa.*

Soudāmini Bahulikar translates Pāṇiṇi's idea of *karaṇa*: 'That which is most effective in producing an action is *karaṇa.*'[216]

It can be a means, a way, a cause, an indication. Prof. Chatterjee's examples:[217]

āmrā cokhe dekhi
we through the eyes see

[214]Chatterjee, p. 96.
[215]Acharya, p. 100.
[216]*Indian Linguistics*, Vol. 34, No. 2, June 1973, p. 84-85.
[217]Chatterjee, pp. 96-98.

The expression *cokhe* is considered as *karaṇa*. The noun refers to body parts (inanimate in feature), it is the means by which the action is accomplished.

lok die *ciṭhi* *pāṭhābo*
by a messenger the letter shall send (I)

The expression *lok die* is considered as *karaṇa*. The noun refers to a person (animate noun).

jār-bɔle *tumi* *boli*
through whose strength you (are) strong
Through whose strength do you consider yourself strong.

The expression *bɔle* is an abstract noun, it is considered as *karaṇa*.

jātite *āmrā* *bāŋāli*
in identity (as a race) we Bengali

(The noun as such seems to mean identity). The expression *jātite* is considered as *karaṇa*.

In addition to that Prof. Chatterjee considers that duration of time can be *karaṇa* in such examples as:

ækmāse *vyākɔrɔn* *sāriāche*
within a month grammar studied (he/she)

[3.13] Saudāmini Bahulikar translates the definition of *adhikaraṇa* of Pāṇini as: 'The site of an action is adhikaraṇa'.[218]

Kale says:

'The place where an action takes place with reference to the subject or object is called *adhikaraṇa* and is put in the locative case. . . the locative also denotes the time when an action takes place. . . .

Verbs having the sense of love, regard for, attachment to. . . generally govern the locative...verbs of acting, behaving towards...and of throwing . . . govern locative, गुरुषु विनयेन वृत्ति कार्या one should act modestly, towards respectable persons.'[219]

The Sanskrit word *ādhār* is translated as 'site' by Bahulikar and Kale used the word 'place', whereas Bengali grammarians used the term *ādhār* and Prof. Chatterjee defines *adhikaraṇa* as: '*Adhikaraṇakāraka* indicates the ādhāra of the verb.'[220]

[218]Indian Linguistics, Vol. 34, No. 2, pp. 84-85.
[219]Kale, pp. 503-506.
[220]Chatterjee. 98-99.

Further, he says that *ādhāra* means the place, the person, the time, the subject matter of the action; in other words, which site or place or the matter is the receptacle of the action when any action takes place or finished or exists or expresses.[221]

It may be of three types:

(1) *desādhikaraṇ*: the corresponding English term may be 'place-locative' or *locative of place*
(2) *kālādhikaraṇ*: *locative of time*
(3) *bisɔādhikaraṇ*: *locative of matter*

N. Vidyabhushan differs in naming the first and the third type of *adhikaraṇ*. He terms these (1) *ādhārādhikaraṇ*, (3) *bhāvādhikaraṇ* and he explains that in understanding these types of *adhikaraṇa* one should give stress to the meaning of the verb. He further divides the type (1) into four:

(*i*) *samipya-ādhār* (nearness of the place)
(*ii*) *ækdes-ādhār* (the country, place name)
(*iii*) *bæpti-ādhār* (pervading locative, over-spreadness, locative of diffusion)
(*iv*) *bisɔe-ādhār* (locative of matter)[222]

N. Vidyabhushan's examples:

(*i*) *gɔngāsāgore prokānḍo mælā hɔe*
on (near) the bank of the river (confluence of Ganges and others) a big fete occurs
= There occurs a big fair at the confluence of the river Ganges and others

(*ii*) *uṛissār* *cilkānāme hrɔd* *āche*
in (a place of) Orissa a lake named Cilka exists
= There exists a lake named Cilka in certain place of Orissa.

(*iii*) *sɔmudrojɔle lɔbɔn āche*
in sea-water salt exist
= Salt pervades in sea water.

(*iv*) *dhɔrme* *bhokti* *āche*[223]
in religious matter (matter) respect has (he)

In the above four subdivisions, the (*i*), (*ii*) and (*iii*) are to be considered as *desādhikaraṇ* and the (*iv*) as a separate main devision of locative and not as a subdivision.

Both authors define *kālādhikaraṇa* as one of the main divisions of locative. *Kālādhikaraṇa* can appropriately be translated as the *locative of time*.

[221]Chatterjee, p. 98-99. The present author has translated from the original.
[222]Vidyabhushan, pp. 55-57.
[223]Vidyabhushan, p. 56.

The other main division besides the *desādhikaraṇa* and *kālādhikaraṇa* is *bhāvādhikaraṇa*. N. Vidyabhushan considers that where an indication of relative activity is expressed by the NU, the NU should be understood to be in *bhāvādhikaraṇa*. For instance:

cɔndrodɔe *ɔndhokār soriagælo*
due to the rising of the moon the darkness removed
= After the moon rising the darkness has gone.

However, we think that the distinction of *bhāvādhikaraṇa* or the four subdivisions of *ādhārādhikaraṇ* are maintained essentially on the basis of sentence semantics, which is no doubt derived through the interselection of the alloseme of the lexical items occurring in a sentence. Prof. Chatterjee's examples

ækmāse *vyākɔrɔn sāriāchi*
within a month grammar studied

may be labelled as *locative of time* rather than *karaṇa* (instrumental).

Careful observation of the meaning of the examples given for ablative, instrumental and locative will make sure that these notions do modify the verb in one way or the other.

The 'source', 'cause', 'sign' meaning can be accommodated in the more basic idea of *apādāna*. One can say that 'source' is a kind of locative, it can be described as 'from some given place. We consider source in the sense of something originated or resulted or an information transmitted. In the real world a given place or person or object may be the referent. The *apādāna* can incorporate source.[224] Similarly, the 'cause' and 'sign' can also be accommodated in it rather than in *karaṇa*.

It seems that the basic difference between the notions of *apadāna* and *adhikaraṇa* is that the *apādāna* (cause, source, indication) does not imply the place where the action has taken place. On the other hand, *adhikaraṇa* (locative) implies the place of action indicated by the verb in a given sentence.

Thereby, the semantic roles can be accounted for within the range of six basic types. The definitions of the basic roles would explicitly indicate the type of grammatical relations included in them.

If one imagined that each different kind of meaning expressed by NU's ought to be mentioned separately, then there would not be any 'cut-off point'. We have pointed out that not all NU's can be assigned a role. Some of them are automatically excluded from the list of roles as they are not related to the verbal syntagm in one way or other (of course, if we wish to

[224]Chatterjee, p. 97.

define role as a semantic relation and consider that this relation is derived on the basis of noun-verbs involvement in a given sentence).

[3.14] None of the above-mentioned authors uses examples which show '*adhikaraṇa*' to be an animate noun. But in Sanskrit there are ample examples of animate *adhikaraṇa* form.[225] And Prof. Chatterjee mentions 'the person' while explaining the meaning of the term *ādhāra*.[226]

We think that in our language too we have animate *adhikaraṇa*.

> *manuserpɔre bissās hārāno pāp* (Tagore)
> on the man faith to lose sin
> =It is a sin to lose faith in man.

It seems that word semantics unconsciously plays a distinct role in the case concept, although the grammarians try to analyse their concept on the basis of sentence semantics.

As a matter of fact, it is often found when one differentiates examples like the following as dative, locative, and possessor that the distinctions are due to word semantics or, sometimes, to circumstances in the real world:

BENGALI

> (95) *āmār* *boi* *āche*
> to me (in relation to me) (a) book exists
> =I have a book/in relation to me (a) book exists

If the role of possessor is assigned to *āmār* this role is perhaps conditioned by the real world circumstances.

In English the following sentences can occur:

> (*a*) Send a telegram *to me* (Send me a telegram)
> Write a letter *to me*

The above expression *to me* would be considered as dative, considering the animate noun, whereas *to the Department* or *to Channel* 7 below would perhaps be considered as locative:

> (*b*) Give a ring *to the department* (Telephone to the Department)
> Write a letter *to Channel* 7

When one labels *dative* to, *to me* and locative to, *to the Department* or *to Channel* 7 detailed word semantics predominates.

Kale remarks: 'The genitive......is not a *kāraka* case. It therefore expresses simply the relation of one noun to another in a sentence'.[227] The relation

[225]Kale, pp. 504-05.
[226]Chatterjee, pp. 98.
[227]Kale, p. 496. Also see Chatterjee, pp. 104-07.

mentioned by Kale has been used by us (above) to establish one of the cut-off points for establishing roles. In other words, when the NU is related to another NU (and not to a verb) a role need not be established.

In our definition the 'source', 'cause', 'sign' are included in *apādāna*. In a sense *adhikaraṇa*, *apādāna* are syntactically comparable with adverbial.

[3.14.1] From the above discussion on the *kāraka* in Sanskrit and Bengali grammars and the case notion in English grammar in general and the case grammar suggested by Fillmore, so far one thing seems clear: in establishing semantic roles the total meaning of the sentence is not always given stress in English, whereas the principle is maintained in traditional Indian grammar.

In establishing the agent and the dative the animate feature of the noun is given prime importance, particularly in the casegrammar and modern English grammar, whereas in traditional grammar, both Indian and Western, the animate-inanimate distinction is not made in identifying the agent. Animation is one of the required features of 'agent role' in modern analysis. It is also required of 'dative role' and the animate feature is required for instrumental and locative in modern linguistic analysis.[228] These requirements are characteristically different from Indian traditional theory and the definition of *kārakas*.

[3.14.2] We may say that the elaborate and explicit semantic description is the characteristic feature of a casegrammar suggested by Fillmore.

A good picture of the case relations suggested by Fillmore may be quoted:

'The Case for Case' Fillmore (1971: 250-52)

Agent	Source and Goal (in terms of earlier and later locations, earlier and later states or earlier and later point of time)
Experiencer	
Instrument	Place
Object	Time

We have defined the basic roles and established the following functions of the noun phrase in Bengali with the option that some of them can be shown as subfunction:

(1) Agent (kartṛ)
(2) Object (karman)
(3) Instrument (*karaṇa*)
(4) Locative (*adhikaraṇa*)
(5) Ablative (*apādāna*)

[228]Fillmore, *A Grammar of Contemporary English*, 1968; Jackendoff and Langendoen, *Essentials of English Grammar*.

(6) *Sampradāna*
(7) *Svatantrah* (independent factor)
(8) *Hetu* (cause)

The *sampradāna* can be included in the more basic role of object and can be shown as subfunction of object. In no Bengali grammar the *hetu:kartā* or *svatantrah:kartā* are either established or described. The *hetu* and *svatantrah* can be shown as subfunctions of agent. Some of the *hetu* and *svatantrah* are borderline cases. A *hetu* NU which is subject can be a subfunction of agent. A *hetu* which is in predicate should be grouped differently.

In our opinion, various roles may be grouped together as variants of a basic meaning:

(1) The goal, affective, factitive, can be included in the basic meaning of *object* in English;
(2) The source, place and time can constitute one or two basic roles (which may be subdivided as source, place and time);
(3) The agent and experiencer can be grouped in one;
(4) A topic and a matter can be included in independent factor;
(5) The cause may be included in *apādāna*.

Stressing the sentence semantics one can limit the number of roles, and these roles may be applicable to other languages also.

A Bengali sentence which is structurally NU, VU and is divided into subject, predicate, can be diagrammed in regard to kāraka (role) and syntactic function (subject-predicate) in the following way:

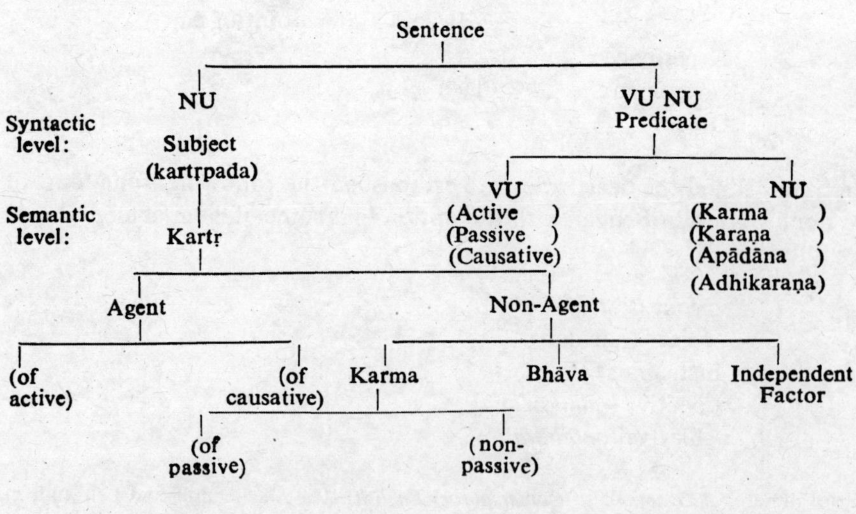

The non-agent subject covers a wider range of meaning variants than that of the agent subject. Though in most Bengali grammars the *hetu* relation established by Pāṇini is not taken into account, it may be considered as a subfunction of agent in active construction. The semantic relation *hetu* may be labelled to a particular type of NU occurring in a particular situation in a given sentence. For example:

96. *tumi ghɔr bʰāŋle*
you family broke

In this sentence the expression *tumi* is an agent, because it does something actively. One can think that the verb alloseme of *broke* indicates the *splitting up of the family,* in that sense the agent is doing something and the activity is understood as the *splitting up*. The agent also includes the meaning *cause.* We think that the *agent* is here the more basic idea. Thus, cause which corresponds to the term *hetu* can be taken as a subfunction of agent in Bengali.

Thus, one can say that in Bengali the active construction can have agent including the subfunctions and the non-agent subfunctions of *hetu, bhāva, independent factor* (Svatantra) subjects. The non-active constructions can have agent (in a causative sentence) and non-agent-karma subjects.

A major confusion arises due to Indian traditional terminology relating to *kartā*. So far we know no-one except Prof. Chatterjee has dealt with this problem, but he has only dealt with the application of term *kartā*.

We have mentioned that the term *kartṛ* implies both semantic function such as *agent* and the syntactic function such as *subject*. The other term *karma* also implies the semantic function such as *object* and the syntactic function such as *subject* (of passive) and the subject of *karma-kartṛvācya* sentence.

It is found in Bengali that in most cases a nominal unit which holds either *kartṛ* (including svatantrah and hetu) or *karma* relation functions as subject. Other relations of the NU's do not occur as the subject of the sentence. We have already mentioned the cross reference of the syntactic and semantic functions of the NU's in Bengali sentences.

We feel that the 'labelled relations' suggested by Fillmore are partially similar to the traditional theory of *kāraka,* and it seems proper to say that the semantic and syntactic functions of the NU's can be accounted for without positing any 'deep structure'. It may not be out of place to quote Fillmore here:

'The notion of subject is identified 'as the relation between an NP and an immediately dominatings,' while the notion "direct object" can be equated with the relation that holds between an NP and an immediately dominating VP. Where the relation 'subject of' is understood to hold between elements of the deep structure, one speaks of the deep structure subject; where it is understood to hold between elements of the (Prestylistic) surface structure, one speaks of the surface structure subject. This distinction appears to correspond to the traditional one between 'logical subject' and 'grammatical subject'.

By 'labelled' relation I mean the relation of an NP to the sentence or to a VP, which is mediated by a pseudo-category label such as manner, extent, location, agent.

It is clear that if all transformations which create surface subjects have the effect of attaching an NP directly to an S, under conditions which guarantee that no other NP is also directly subjoined to the same S, and if it always turns out that only one NP is subjoined to a VP in the prestylistic surface structure, then these two 'pure' relations are exactly what determine the most typical occurrences of the case categories 'nominative' and 'accusative' in languages of a certain type. For remaining case forms, the determination is either on the basis of idiosyncratic properties of specific governing words, or on the basis of a labelled relation, as when the choice of by is determined by reference to the dominating category extent in the extent phrase of sentence like 17. He missed the target by two miles.

In my earlier paper [Fillmore, 1966] I pointed out that no semantically constant value is associated with the notion 'subject of' (unless it is possible to make sense of the expression 'the thing being talked about', and if that can be done, to determine whether such a concept has any connection with the relation 'subject'), and that no semantically relevant relations reside in the surface relation which are not somewhere also expressible by 'labelled' relations. The conclusion I have drawn from this is that all semantically relevant syntactic relations between NP's and the structures which contain them must be of the 'labelled' type. The consequences of this decision include (*a*) the elimination of the category VP, and (*b*) the addition to some grammars of a rule or system of rules, for creating 'subjects'. The relation 'subject' in other words is now seen as exclusively a surface-structure phenomenon.[229]

We understand that what Fillmore meant by 'labelled' relation seems similar to the *kāraka* notion in traditional Indian grammar. It seems meaningless to define anything in terms of the dominating S, etc. because unless one knows the subject to start with one does not know what NP should be said to be dominated by the S. Unless one knows the lexical meanings and the meanings of the markers, the sentence meaning would not be known. After knowing the meaning of the whole sentence, grammatical relations like 'labelled' relation or 'pure' relation can be described. 'Labelled' relation can be

[229]Fillmore, 'Case for Case', pp. 16-17.

thought of but cannot be assigned to any NP unless the meaning is understood in given sentence. We assume that the basic interdependence of syntax and semantics lies here. The subject of a sentence can be perfectly identified by the concord of the VU in Bengali (and in all Indian languages). We have found that 90 per cent of the sentences are structurally NU, VU where we can apply the labelled relation and identify the subject on the basis of the grammatical concord.

It seems that the use of the term *subject* to mean things as different as 'logical subject', 'grammatical subject', or 'surface subject', 'deep subject' is inappropriate.

For the time being, let us forget the term 'subject' and the use of 'transformations', and let us consider a language which is structurally different from English. Pāṇiṇi characterised the *kāraka* relation of the nominals in his Sanskrit data of a particular time (4000 B.C.).[230]

Fortunately, his theory is still applicable to the description of the daughter languages of Sanskrit. The theory of *kāraka* and the theory of *vācya*, we think, can adequately describe the semantic relation of NU's, their syntactic functions in a construction and the interplay of the semantic relation and the syntactic function of any Indian language. We have already described the possible co-reference of *kāraka* and *vācya*. The four semantically different kinds of subjects establish four *vācya* of the verb.

The *kāraka* notion is mainly characterized as a grammatical relation involved between the NU and the VU in a syntactic construction (sentence) of a language. This grammatical relation is understood on the basis of the semantic relations such as:

(*a*) Doer of an action, performer of an action;
(*b*) Affected person or thing or the target of the action or the goal of an action;
(*c*) Where, in which direction or place or subject of an action, the time when an action occurred;
(*d*) What is indicated by the action;
(*e*) What is the cause of an action or the Origin (source) of an action;
(*f*) What is used as the means by the doer (performer) to perform the action.

Approximately, these are the relations identified as *kāraka* relations in Indian traditional grammar.[230a] A partial similarity with these may be found in the following quotation from Fillmore:

'The case notions compromise a set of universal, presumably innate, concepts which identify certain types of judgments human beings are cap-

[230]Pānini, *Astadhyai*, Sandamini Bahulikar's (tr.) *Indian Linguistics*, 1973; Kale, McDonald, etc.

[230a]Chatterjee, pp. 83-103; Vidyabhushan, pp. 49-65; P. Acharya, pp. 92-107.

able of making about the events that are going on around them, judgments about such matters as who did it, who it happened to, and what got changed. The cases that appear to be needed include:

AGENTIVE (A), the case of the typically animate perceived instigator of the action identified by the verb.

INSTRUMENT (I), the case of the inanimate force or object causally involved in the action or state identified by the verb.

DATIVE (D), the case of the animate being affected by the state or action identified by the verb.

FACTITIVE (F), the case of the object or being resulting from the action or state identified by the verb, or understood as a part of the meaning of the verb.

LOCATIVE (L), the case which identifies the location or spatial orientation of the state or action identified by the verb.

OBJECTIVE (O), the semantically most neutral case, the case of anything representable by a noun whose role in the action or state identified by the verb is identified by the semantic interpretation of the verb itself; conceivably the concept should be limited to things which are affected by the action or state identified by the verb. The term is not to be confused with the notion of direct object, nor with the name of the surface case synonymous with accusative.'[231]

[3.14.3] We have already mentioned in what respect we disagree with Fillmore. We have pointed out Jackendoff's confusion of grammar and the real world event in his idea of "simultaneous reciprocity" such as the identification of primary and secondary action in the same grammatical expression. One may have to start from the real world event in a more psychological analysis of language, but we do not think that this kind of analysis has any place in grammar.

We disagree with Fillmore's formula 'any N in an A or D phrase must contain the feature (+animate), N—(+animate) A, D (x-x).'[232] When we consider different languages, the very concept of 'dative' and 'agentive' seems different in the grammar of different languages. Fillmore's formula may be applicable when the A and D phrases contain an animate noun. The A phrase, however, does not contain an animate noun always. Thus, the formula may be partly acceptable and partly suitable to describe 'agentive' phrases of different languages.

According to Fillmore, the formula of '(-locative)' should be applied to all abstract nouns. We believe, however, that an abstract noun can be locative as in 'in my opinion'.

[231]Fillmore, *Case for Case*, pp. 24-25.
[232]*Ibid.*, pp. 26-27.

We would like to point out that any 'frame feature' of a verb is a contradiction of the labelled identification, which is based on the meaning of the whole sentence. In other words, the sentence semantics is the very basis of the label assignment and is not to be the word feature such as animate, inanimate, etc.

The 'horizontal' as well as 'vertical' relations, in other words, both the syntagmatic and paradigmatic relations can be shown in the assignment of label. For instance, one can group an animate, inanimate and abstract together considering their horizontal and vertical level relations. Consider *he*, *the stone*, and *the war* in:

> *He* killed John.
> *The stone* killed the snake.
> *The war* killed the soldier.

On the one hand, one can establish the same 'role' (relationship) to these nominals considering their similar mutual relationship in the expression (in the environment of the same verb); on the other hand, the verb can also be classified according to its acceptance of case (role) as subject. We have already mentioned the cross references of the semantic and syntactic functions of the NU's.

[3.15.0] It may be of some interest if we compare some examples of English and Bengali with German. English sentences such as:

> The king destroyed the village.
> The avalanche destroyed several villages

can be translated into Bengali as:

> *rājā grāmṭi dhɔŋsokorlen*
> himobāhɔ bohu grām dhɔŋsokorlo.

These can be translated into German as:

> Der könig zerstörte das Dorf
> Die lawine zerstörte mehrere Häuser

According to the traditional German grammar, both *Der könig* and *Die lawine* are agentive; in form they are nominative, they are subjects of respective sentences.

Both the expressions *das Dorf* and *mehrere Häuser* are nominative/accusative in form, and they are objects of the active verb in the above sentences.[232]

[232]F. Hinze, *Deutsche Schulgrammatik*, Klettverlag, Stuttgart, 1960 (*passim*).

The grammar of Sanskrit, Bengali and other Indian languages will be similar to German grammar. Moreover, they would mention that *himobāhɔ* (the avalanche) is to be considered as subject: agent.

In English grammar *the avalanche* is, however, considered as instrumental.[233] The active construction (in English) with an inanimate subject such as *the avalanche* destroyed several houses is explained as instrumental: 'Apart from its agentive function, the subject frequently has an instrumental role; that is, it expresses the unwitting (generally inanimate) material cause of an event.[234]

However, according to what has been explained above, one should rather speak of cause than instrumental in cases where there is no agent.

Even though it seems that traditionally distinctions such as animate-inanimate agent are not generally made in German, the 'psychological subject', 'psychological object' are mentioned. The 'psychological' entities seem, however, to fit the real world situation better than the grammar of the actual utterance. However, despite the comparisons just provided, we do not believe that translation from one language to another can always be helpful. An event may not even be expressible in another language, if such an event is not experienced by the speakers of the language.

It is a very common thing in a tropical country to hear the rumbling sound of the clouds, even though there is no flash of lightning that immediately follows. We express such an event as *megh ḍākā* 'roaring of the clouds'. Therefore, it is perfectly natural,[235] acceptable and grammatical to say in Bengali:

megh ḍākche
the cloud roars (rumbling sound)
= There is a sound in the sky.

It is not surprising that this kind of sentence cannot be translated into German, since that type of event is not experienced by Europeans. It is typically a characteristic of tropical nature.

A Bengali sentence

briṣṭi poṛche
the rain is pouring
= It rains

can be translated in German as *Es regent*. The construction seems similar to English *it rains. Es* is to be considered as subject. It is an active sentence. The verb is intransitive and passivization is not possible. This type of dummy

[233] Girk *et al*, *The Grammar of Contemporary English*, p. 351.
[234] *Ibid.*, p. 35.
[235] So far I know in other Indian languages also, this type of sentence would be natural.

subject does not occur in Bengali. There is no such dummy subject in any Indian language.

Some active sentences with inanimate subject can be expressed in passive construction also. And it is a common feature in Bengali that the same inanimate noun (subject) of an active sentence can be labelled as object of another active sentence where the verb is used transitively. This kind of syntactical relationship is considered as 'ergative' by Lyons and others. We have given our arguments before and we prefer to call this type of inanimate or animate subject *independent factor* (Svatantra). We tabulate it as a subfunction of non-agent subject.

(1) Active (intransitive use of verb)
kɔlosi *b^hɔreni*
the pitcher is not full

(2) Active (transitive use of the same verb)
se *kɔlosi* *b^hɔreni*
he/she the pitcher did not fill up

The expression *kɔlosi* in active (1) is considered as the potential object of the verb (used transitively) in a corresponding transitive sentence active (2). The noun is an inanimate noun, and in this particular sentence it seems the action is done automatically; in other words it seems that the potential object (*kɔlosi*) itself does the action upon it. This type of subject is called the subject of a voice which is different from the animate agent subject. In Sanskrit this voice is called *karmakartṛ*.

The above-mentioned Bengali sentence may be translated into German as:

Der krug ist noch nicht voll

In traditional German grammar *Derkrug* is described as subject, and no such description is given as 'agent' or 'instrument' or 'cause'. However, some recent authors[236] consider that it should be labelled as 'benefactive' or 'objective'. It might be of interest to note that in traditional Indian grammar it is considered as 'objective' (potential object of the transitive verb), but its occurrence with the intransitive verb has given it a status which corresponds to the one of animate subject with transitive verb.

We have established the *independent factor* subject in Bengali considering the sentence semantics. Irrespective of the animate-inanimate feature of the subject noun, the above-mentioned subfunction can be labelled to the subject noun considering its involvement with the verb of the sentence. It can be a *copula*, an *intransitive verb*, or a *be* verb.

[235]I had a personal discussion with Dr. P. Paul, Lecturer in Linguistics, Monash University, on 9 July, 1974 and he has kindly supplied all the German translations and checked the traditional German grammar.

This type of approach does not seem unsuitable to a language such as English or German. We believe that the English or German translation of the Bengali sentence may be described in a similar fashion. The English expression, *the pitcher* in the sentence *the pitcher is not full*, and the German expression *Der krug* in the sentence *Der krug ist noch nicht voll* can be labelled as *independent factor*.

In Bengali there is no verb corresponding to English *have*. An English sentence such as *I have a book* will be translated in Bengali (and in most Indian languages) with a neutral agent. The subject will be *the book*. The verb does not agree with the animate noun which may be called neutral agent. It will be something like the following:

āmār boi āche
to me a book exists

In German it will be *Das Buch gehört mir*, the verb is an active verb and *mir* is a dative expression in German. The Bengali construction also is an active one. Considering the meaning of the expression *āmār*, we think it is appropriate to label it as locative.

We have pointed out that the possessive is not considered as a role (*kāraka* relation) in Indian grammar.[237]

Following this directive we may not assign any label to the Bengali expression *āmār* (*boi*) which corresponds to English *my* (*book*). This *āmār* functions like an attribute to the following *boi*. It, therefore, expresses simply the relation of one noun to another in a sentence.[238]

We find that translation from one language to another does not always help in analysing the first language. One can translate in many different ways. One can use non-corresponding lexical item and non-corresponding constructions in translating an item from one language to another. For instance, if *āmār boi ache* is translated into English as *I have a book* or *I possess a book*, then Fillmore's possessor role would seem appropriate to *āmār*; but this procedure is obviously meaningless.

Compare an example given by N. Vidyabhushan, which shows a structurally similar expression, even though the two nouns (*āmār* in the above example and *uṛissār* in the example below) differ in semantic components which we think can be labelled similarly in grammar:

uṛissār cilkānāme hrɔd ache
in Orissa by name Chilka (a) lake exists
= There is a lake named Cilkal at (in)
Orissa (state)

237Chatterjee, pp. 104-47; Vidyabhushan, pp. 57-60; Kale, pp. 496-503.

238Kale, p. 496. See *Pāṇini*, II 3·50 and *Sidhanta Kaumundi*.

N. Vidyabhushan considers *uṛissār* as locative. There is no doubt it is so, because of the place name and also because of the way the native speaker understands the information communicated by the expression. Therefore the expression *āmār* in *āmār boi ache* should be described in the way that a native speaker understands.

In Bengali both in causative and in passive the *a* marker happens to occur on the verb root. But there is a difference because the passive takes another auxiliary, and it is possible that the passive verbal construction may be segmented into two parts. For instance, a verb root like *dekh* 'to see', 'look', becomes causative with the *a* marker:

> dekh+ā = dækhā+inflection (+tense mark+person marker)
> = *dækhāibo*
> (I) would show (would cause to see)

The same verb becomes passive with the same marker:

> dekh+ā = dækhā+auxiliary (*be*)+inflection (tense+person)
> (*rogi*) *dækhāhoiteche*
> (the patient) is being seen

This passive verbal construction may be segmented into two parts:

dækhā	*hoiteche*
seeing	is being done

Sometimes another marker may be found on the expression *dækha* which makes the meaning causative: *dækhāno* 'showing'.

If the verb unit is like *dækhano hoiteche* 'showing is being done', then we consider it as causative-passive. If it is segmented as *dækhāno* 'showing' *hoiteche* '(is being done)', then the first part is the subject. Same is the case in *daekhā* 'seeing' *hoiteche* 'is going on (is being done)'. The first part is the subject of the verb.

The two expressions just mentioned, which we described as having *bhāva-subject* in Bengali, because the *be* verb agrees with the verbal noun, have no equivalent in English, German and other languages. It is considered as a neutral form of the verb. This kind of neutrality can also be found with animate subject and a verb like *lag*.

Compare some verbal expressions below:

> *upokar-kɔrā* 'to help'

It is a compound verb. The nominal is used as verb with the help of auxiliary and the first element cannot be segmented from the following element.

āmi āpnār upokār-korechi
I (to) you did help (helped)
= I helped you.

In passive also they cannot be segmented, even though the first element is not in neutral form:

upokrito-hɔn
being helped is
= 'were benefitted', 'were helped'
āmār dārā (kāche) āpni upokrito-hɔn
by me/to me you were benefitted

The same idea can be expressed in the following way, where the neutral form of the verb is the subject with which the following *be* verb has agreement:

āmārdārā (kāche) āpnār upokār hoeche
by me/to me your (to you) benefit (help)
has done (has occurred)

Many other sentences which are thought to be subjectless seem to have this kind of verbal construction.

bɔs kɔrā-gælo
control has been done
temptation has occurred

It seems to be a similar example as the one we described in the previous paragraph. The difference lies in the verb construction. Here it is a passive verb whareas in the previous sentence it is an active form of verb. The idea can be expressed in a different way which will still be considered passive:

tini bosibhutohɔn
he was controlled/was tempted

The verb unit cannot be segmented, it is passive in meaning. The sentence semantics would give passive status to the sentence with such verb construction (and meaning).

One can say that the subject element is to be found in the passive VU itself. In some cases this description may seem correct, since the initial nominal or adjectival element can be segmented without much change to the meaning of the verb syntagma. But in many cases this description may not be appropriate.

Even though the verb unit *bɔlā gælo* seems to be the same type of construction and it is passive, this verb unit cannot be separated. There are innumerable instances in Bengali verbs where the preceding nominal or adjectival (adverbial) is a part of the verbal unit and cannot be separated.

[3.15.1] A grammatical theory develops from the detailed and minute observation of the facts of a language, and preconceived theories will fail to incorporate many peculiarities of the language.[239]

This is one of the reasons why we disagree with the principle of economy in linguistics. We agree that in analysis things should be defined and described as precisely as possible. But very often to follow this principle the language peculiarities, characteristics are overlooked to fit preconceived theories and their symbolic representation. The linguist may seek validity in a coherent and consistent linguistic theory and develop a technique of language description, but it is debatable if for the sake of such theory and technique language characteristics can be overlooked.

We believe in the multilevel theories of grammatical structure, and we identify the grammatical relations on the basis of sentence semantics without considering detailed word semantic level.

The inconsistency, observable in the *kāraka* notion in traditional Indian grammar, is mostly due to a confusion between the real world situation and the grammar. Paradoxically, a similar type of confusion is also to be noticed in very recent linguistic analysis.

However, we believe that basically our idea of case (role) is to some extent similar to Fillmore's, where he differs will be clear from the quotation and discussion below:

'The propositional care of a simple sentence consists of a predicator (verb, adjective or noun) in construction with one or more entities, each of these related to the predicator in one of the semantic functions known as (deep structure) *cases*. These cases identify the roles which the entities serve in the predication, these roles taken from a repertory defined once and for all for human languages and including that of the instigator of an action, that of the experiencer of a psychological event, that of an object which undergoes a change or movement, that of location of an event and so on. (I recognise the emptiness of this assumption in the absence of a coherent grammatical theory in which the cases play a crucial role).

'The cases exist in a hierarchy, and this hierarchy serves to guide the operation of certain syntactic processes, in particular that of subject selection. It figures in subject selection by determining which noun phrase is to become the subject of the sentence in the "unmarked" instance. That case in a sentence which, according to the hierarchy of cases, outranks the others is the one which has the noun phrase it is associated with, selected as the subject of the sentence.

[239]Chatterjee, pp. 6-7.

'Certain predicators have their own lexically determined subject choices, and there are furthermore certain subject choice options provided by the language—among them that provided in English by the passive transformation'.[240]

The cases of nouns were identified as 'roles' on the basis of the related semantic function (excluding the relation of one noun to another noun) in the traditional Indian grammar. In a certain way it was indicated in Western grammar too. But, generally, no deep structure was thought of, although the notions such as 'logical' or psychological subject have similarity with recent deep structure notions.

Claims such as 'once and for all' would come under criticism. Note that only some of the languages of the world have been described in any detail. Many languages are completely unknown.

The subject selection is partly decided by the grammatical device of concord and partly by the sentence meaning in Indian languages. Wherever the sentence contains an NU and VU the subject, selection is entirely based on the agreement of the NU, VU and the overt marker on the VU.

Indian grammar discards classification of verbs as 'psychological', mental involvement, etc. and semantic features of the nominal such as animate, inanimate, etc. as a basis for identifying roles of the nominal units.

If the 'hierarchy of cases' simply refers to the percentage of occurrence, then it is applicable to Indian languages. It is true that certain predicators have their own lexically determined subject choice. It is also true that certain subjects have their verb choice. But it would be a mistake to invent some expressions which are grammatically unacceptable, and then to remark that the result is produced by the application of 'the principle of contrast'.

Consider Fillmore's examples, when he maintains that mixtures of cases is not possible:

'It is alright to say (John and Fred are both sad) or (my sweater and your jacket are both very warm), but not (John and the movie both become very sad near the end) or (my sweater and I are both nice and warm)'.[241]

One would perhaps say that *John and movie, my sweater and I* have the same function, and what is 'wrong' is the predicate which implies different allosemes for different subjects and that makes a strange impression.[242]

It seems to me that Fillmore assigns case of a noun on the basis of its word semantic features. Unless *John* and *Fred* occur in an actual sentence no one can establish any 'role' or 'case' of the two nouns. Likewise, the

240Fillmore, Some Problems for Case Grammar' in *Working Papers in Linguistics*, March, 1971 pp. 4-5.

241*Ibid.*, p. 10.

242A. Culter, 'A Note on a Reference by J. D. McCawley to Adjectives Denoting Temperature', *Talanya*, I, (1972), pp. 47-49. She did not use the term allosemes, she describes the ambiguity of the lexical items and says; ...but note that in each language a possible centre value is always subject to selection restrictions—e.g., tepid, lukewarm, law, lawwarm.'

lexical item *movie* cannot be considered as having any 'case', unless it occurs in an appropriate situation. There is no way to assign *instrument* role either to the isolated lexical item *jacket* or *sweater* or *movie*. One can say: *John and the movie were actually equally old* or *I and my sweater became blue with paint*, etc. Note that in this case the adjectives (*old* and *blue*) have each an alloseme which fits both subjects.

Fillmore's principles of complementarity says:

'Sometimes we find in different sentences semantic functions which in detail are partly alike and partly different, their differences being systematically relatable to differences in the semantic properties of the lexical material they are in construction with.

'With verbs of motion, like for example (go), we can specify a starting point and a destination, as in a sentence like (He went from the top of the hill to the cemetery gate); for transformation verbs we can specify the earlier state and the later state, as in a sentence like (He changed from a 96-pound weakling into a famous football hero); and for verbs of temporal lapse we can talk about the starting and ending point of a time period, as in (The pageant lasted from sundown until midnight). My inclination is to refer to the two points identified in all of these earlier/later indications as different instances of the same cases, namely Source and Goal. Depending on the type of predicator, the Source and Goal are interpreted as earlier and later locations, earlier and later states, or earlier and later time points'.[243]

We disagree here with Fillmore. Neither do we classify verbs in the fashion he classifies them, nor do we think that the above expressions, (*i*) 'from a 96-pound weakling into a famous football hero' and (*ii*) 'from sundown until midnight' have semantic function such as 'source and goal'. No. (*i*) is in attributive relation to the noun *he*, and (*ii*) has an adverbial relation to the verb *lasted*.

It cannot be denied that somehow there is a point of time. We would rather like to put the 'role' at the higher level of sentence semantics where 'adverbial of time' belongs and we would speak of a clearly delimited stretch of time. But source and goal does not seem to fit. One may have lower subdivisions: point of time (from—to, during, etc.). The starting and ending does not seem to be the same thing as source and goal, nor does the change from one state to another.

Further, Fillmore points out that given noun phrases occur with certain predicators, such as:

'We can say either (He walked from the top of the hill to the cemetery gate) or (He walked from noon until sundown).... We cannot say (He

[243]Fillmore, 'Some Problems for Casegrammar' in *Working Papers in Linguistics*, March 1971, p. 11.

walked from the top of the hill to the cemetery gate from noon until sundown); nor can we say (He walked from the cemetery gate until midnight) or (He walked from noon to the zoo). To account for these facts we must either (*i*) increase the number of cases by positing both spatial and temporal source and goal cases and introduce some constraints on their co-occurrence possibilities in single clauses, or (*ii*) re-analyze sentences with (walk), (swim), (run), (drive), etc. as referring either to types of activities, describable in terms of their durations or to types of movements describable in terms of their paths.'[244]

Many manner adverbial expressions can be included in the broader label of 'locative'. The expressions (*i*) 'from the top of the hill to the cemetery gate', and (*ii*) from noon until sundown' can either be labelled as adverbial or locative, because the expressions signal the time (duration) of walking and the place (space) of walking. In this sense the two expressions modify the verb: therefore, they are adverbial.

It seems possible to argue that Fillmore's mixed sentences may be grammatically correct but nonsensical. The fact that the content does not correspond to 'reality' is not a grammatical problem.

The adverbial expressions can be described in another way: the expressions which signal the spatio-temporal state of the verb syntagma can be said to have locative relation with the VU.

Fillmore says:

'The whole thing makes sense only if there are good reasons to believe that there is an irreducible number of role types by which grammatical theory makes its contribution to semantic interpretation; if it turns out that this number is small; if there are reasonable principles according to which these role types can be identified, and if grammars in which they are incorporated into underlying representations are superior to those in which they are not. There are certain criteria that I have appealed to in attempting to determine the cases, and I will speak of them now....

First of all I make the assumption that there is in a single clause at most one noun phrase (which may, however, be compound) serving a given case role....

Sometimes a single predicator takes noun-phrases of different cases, occurring in one sentence with one choice of cases, in another with a different choice... . There should be a natural *stopping point* in any attempt to classify these semantic functions.'[245]

244Fillmore, p. 12. If earlier and later indication of a verb has to be taken into consideration, then one cannot neglect the aspect of a verb.

245Fillmore, pp. 6-9.

We think the traditional Indian grammar appropriately limits the number of the basic roles within the range of six. In many sentences the noun phrases expressing range of time, quantity, distance of place or path, etc. cannot be considered as *kāraka,* because they are not directly attached to the verb and they should be labelled as adverbial, or 'clause adverbial' or, in the word of Jespersen, 'adjunct'.[246]

Fillmore's assumptions that 'one instance per clause' is not applicable to the languages like Bengali or other Indian languages. We can have more than one instance in a clause of a complex or compound sentence.

We disagree with his other assumption that 'a single predicator takes noun clauses of different cases':

> I am warm: Experiencer
> This jacket is warm: Instrument
> Summer is warm: Time
> The room is warm: Location[247]

All the noun phrases in the above-mentioned examples should be labelled as the same 'case' considering the verb, i.e., the sentence semantics indicates the same relation of the noun phrases with the same verb.

It seems almost amusing to see that Fillmore assigns 'experiencer', 'instrument', 'time', and 'location' to the above nominals which occur with a similar link verb and a similar adjective *warm.* One need not give too much emphasis on the real world event and word semantics in labelling the grammatical relation such as roles of the nominals. We consider that the link verb *is/am* indicates a state (warm) of the different subjects such as *I, this jacket, summer* and *the room.* And nothing more is expressed by the examples given by Fillmore. His analyses follow the way he perceives the meaning: *I feel warm* (which admittedly is closer to *I am warm*), *this jacket makes me warm, it is warm in summer, it is warm in this room.* Fillmore points out that it is

...one thing to see if there is a stopping place in the attempt to list the semantic functions that go with any given predicator, another thing to see if the list of semantic function found for different predicators have enough overlap to make it believable that there is a small list for grammatical theory in general.'[248]

Fillmore provides the analogous examples:

> John was sad (emotion experiencer role),
> I am warm (sensation experiencer role)

[246]Chatterjee, pp. 95-96.
[247]Fillmore, p. 9.
[248]Fillmore, p. 10.

The movie was sad
This jacket is warm } experience-eliciting role

In these four examples, he distinguishes between emotion, sensation and experience eliciting roles. However, we are not convinced that these roles are needed in grammar (although what he says may refer to facts of the real world and probably to features which are needed in word semantics).

And he shows how in 'comparative construction' and co-ordinate conjunction construction two experiencers or two instruments can occur, but mixture of cases is not possible.

'When the instrument role is occupied by a sentence, that sentence identifies an event which is understood as having some other event or state as its consequence. The object case is that of the entity which moves or which undergoes change and I still use it as a waste basket. Sentences embedded to objects can serve to identify, for example, the content of a psychological event, as with verbs of judging or imagining. Source and Goal are used in the ways I suggested earlier, and in a few other ways as well. Since the Goal case is used to indicate the later state or end result of some action or change, it can absorb what I used to call 'Resultative' or 'Factitive'; that is, it specifies the end result role of a thing which comes into existence as a result of the action identified by the predicator, as in (I wrote a poem) or (I constructed a bridge). A sentence embedded as goal therefore is one which identifies the resulting state or event in a Causative construction.'[249]

Fillmore also suggests 'the possibility of positing a new case "Force" as unnecessary, since this putative Force case never occurs in contrast with either Agent or Instrument'.[250]

In the way he reasons, if he wanted 'force' to be accepted he would find contrast, and if he would not want it he would not find any contrast. He prefers to absorb 'force' into 'instrument' case, and considers the semantic properties of the verbs to be taken as very important. He suggests to solve the problem of *push*, *hit*, *drop* in sentences such as 'I hit the ball over the fence' by syntactically transforming deep structure into surface structure. The deep structure would be represented by *I hit the ball and the ball went over the fence*—'the two clauses embedded to a higher predicate that has a meaning suggested by the word cause, predicating the event—causation relation between the two clauses'.[251]

This is indeed a good example of confusion of grammar and the real world situation. Moreover there is an added imaginary clause.

[249]Fillmore, p. 13.
[250]Fillmore, p. 16.
[251]Fillmore, p. 21.

Other cases like Benefactive are established:

Benefactive constructions occur only in sentences with Agents and only when the Agent's role is thought of as being deliberate or voluntary. To add Benefactive to the list of cases would thus require that the theory be complemented with a system of redundancy principle regarding the selection of cases for sentences, and would require furthermore that an understanding of the expression of intentional or voluntary acts be accounted for within the case apparatus.[252]

The assumption, according to which the *sampradāna kāraka* is not accepted by the Bengali scholars, is that if voluntary action is to be accounted for, then, all actions—angry, pleasing, emotional, sorrowful, greedy etc.—should be accounted for, and to do this each and every verb should have different cases. In Bengali we have more than eight hundred verbs. Most of them should have different cases since they express different types of activities.[253] Similarly, in Sanskrit there are two thousand and five hundred verb roots, and perhaps a 'casegrammar' of Sanskrit should account for two thousand and five hundred cases for all these different verbs.

Bengali scholars believe that *sampradāna* (benefactive) which is related to voluntary action should be absorbed in *karma* (object). Scholars like Ramendrasundar, Haraprasad and Rabindranath strongly support this view and favour the establishment of a *neutral case* for Bengali, which would be different from *kartṛ* (agent) and *karma* (object). The neutral case is related to the predicator in a way which may be explained as adjunct to the predicative verb. It may be *instrument*, *locative*, *ablative*, or it may simply be called adverbial, they suggest.[254]

Prof. Fillmore's discussion on the conceptual aspect of cases seems very complicated, and it confuses grammar and the real world event to some extent.

If linguists have to think of a cut-off point 'in the attempt to list the semantic functions that go with any given predicator', the traditional '*kāraka* notion' and verb classification can be taken into consideration.

The semantic relation which is called 'role' should be considered different from other adjectival, manner adverbial, clause adverbial, etc. expressions. For instance, *krɔme* 'gradually', *rātri hoilo* 'the night fall', the expression *krɔme* is not a 'role'. A semantic group of words may or may not coincide with a semantic group at the level of sentence semantics.

[3.16] It may be appropriate here to discuss to what extent semantics should come under the domain of grammatical analysis. We use the term grammar in its traditional sense: the study of (phonology) morphology and

[252]Fillmore, p. 31.
[253]Chatterjee, pp. 92-93.
[254]Chatterjee, pp. 100-103.

syntax are included in grammar. To some extent these three levels are conditioned by semantics which could also be a level of grammar. We assume that no one would dispute the statement that 'the word and its meaning are completely identified in our usage'.[255]

Prof. Hammarstrom says:

In a wider sense of the term, meaning can include syntactic functions, the effects of some prosodemes and prosodes, because not only how something is said but also idiolect, sociolect and dialect mean some thing to the listener. Even the context of situation, when in interselection with language facts, contributes to meaning.[256]

He continues: 'When there is interselection between syntax and semantics it seems clear that the problem is authentically linguistic'.[257]

From the above statement it appears that a portion of semantics automatically comes under the domain of grammatical analysis, but the exact position is not clear.

In ancient times the Indian grammarian, philosophers, logicians, disputed over the problem of the relation between a word and its meaning. There was no end and no final conclusion. The grammarians argued: 'Sabda (word) and artha (meaning) are totally dissimilar and discrete and the identity between two such dissimilar and discrete entities cannot but be unreal, and is caused by an illusory superimposition (adhyasa) of the former on the latter.'[258]

The philosophers (mimāṅsaka philosophers) had other views, and they used to argue that the expressiveness was the property of words which had conventional relation and function in a related sequence. A word (sound unit) is a linguistic expression. Even though it is arbitrary in nature, the mutual merger of the word and its meaning is taken for granted.

We think that it is very difficult to determine how much semantics (meaning) should be taken into account in a grammatical analysis, and what should exactly be considered as linguistic problem regarding meaning.

Prof. Hammarstrom explains:

A syntagm may, on the one hand, be thought of as having basically a syntactic function. It 'realizes' a certain construction or, in other words, belongs to some syntagmeme. On the other hand, considering everything realized when a syntagm is produced, one may say that it has also a much wider menning, a total meaning......The syntagm in this sense could be called 'total syntagm'. If one uses this term one would say that a total syntagm has a meaning rather than saying that it has a total meaning....

[255]Bishnupada Bhattacharya, *A Study in Language and Meaning*, p. 19.
[256]Hammarstrom, *Linguistic Units, Acts and Items* (first draft), p. 61.
[257]*Ibid.*, p. 68.
[258]Bhattacharya, p. 33.

'It is often difficult to determine to what extent many problems about meaning and combinations of meanings belong to linguistics or not.

There seem, however, to be cases which should clearly not be dealt with in linguistics. Treating the unacceptability of *two and two equals five*, *the elephant in the zoo weighs one gramme*, or *the sky is always purple* involves problems of mathematics, biology, meteorology, or is perhaps rather just a question of 'common sense'. No linguistic problem would be involved (if the three periods just quoted had been thought of as linguistic problems, they would have been problems of purely semantic horizontal interselection as they do not offer any syntactic problem; in this respect none of them is objectionable). As a matter of fact, periods similar to the three just mentioned would not be of great interest to anybody except for an expert on literature if found in a poem or for a psychiatrist if coming from the mouth of a patient.

'In other instances, where syntax is not either involved in any significant way, there is, however, semantic horizontal interselection to be dealt with by linguists. The adjective *blonde* has a component 'to be said about human hair', which accounts for the normal speaker's correct use: *blonde hair* but not *blonde car*. If however, a child or a foreigner saw a table with the colour he had previously heard referred to as *blonde* (in the case of somebody's hair) he might say *the car is blonde*. If so, one would naturally think that his language was imperfect but not that there was anything wrong with his common sense or his knowledge of reality.

'When there is interselection between syntax and semantics it seems clear that the problem is authentically linguistic. Although this principle may help us to see if a problem should be treated at all in linguistics, it is not always adequate as it may be difficult to determine how much should be included in syntax. It seems, however, to be a linguistic problem to determine that a subject has allofuncts and also which sets of lexes are in interselection with different allofuncts. In *the mother may admire the boy* the lex *mother* belongs to a set which has vertical interselection with subjects with the diallofunct experiencer of the allofunct agent. This diallofunct is required by the predicate verb *admire*. If instead, one tries out the period *sincerity may admire the boy*, *sincerity* is not a word in interselection with the diallofunct experiencer.'[259]

This long quotation has been given to show the difference between a Western and an Indian scholar. The argument of Prof. Hammarstrom about the three periods, *two and two equals five*, etc. and *blonde car*, may be acceptable. His explanation of *the mother* and *sincerity* in connection with the verb *admire* seems inadequate. The set of lexes are differentiated on the basis of their semantic features. Word semantic features, which most Western scholars include, are not taken as the criterion for establishing

[259]Hammarstrom, pp. 154, 165-66.

grammatical relations (on the level of sentence) in Indian grammar.[260] The allofuncts of a subject are identified on the basis of the total meaning of the sentence and not mainly on the basis of the semantic component of the lexes.

One can say that the total meaning of a sentence may be obtained in either of the ways mentioned. The approaches may be as follows:

(*a*) Sentence semantics in which word features (detail semantic component of the lexes) are rather dominant; and
(*b*) Sentence semantics in which word features are less dominant.

In the Western approach we find the sentence semantics with dominant word semantics, whereas in Indian approach it is found that the sentence semantics with less dominant word semantics.

Furthermore, I should like to point out that *sincerity may admire the boy* and *blonde car* may both be called imperfect use of language, because we have argued before that a syntactical unit should be semantically relevant and acceptable to the language user. The very definition of a sentence in Indian grammar implies that a sentence should be semantically relevant,[261] a sentence is considered as a synthetic whole made up of its constituents which are interrelated. Hence every (unit) constituent should be semantically relevant to become a constituent of that particular construction. Semantic relevancy should exist at the sentence level; in other words, the selection of one item by the other is on the basis of collocation (acceptable association with one another both in regard to meaning and grammatical order).

In Indian grammar, either in establishing syntagmatic relations such as 'role' or in identifying allofuncts of a subject such as 'agent' non-agent including subfunctions such as object, independent factor, etc., the meaning of the lexical items are only taken into consideration in an indirect way. The total meaning is the resultant information communicated through the meaning of the lexes and their related meaning in that particular given construction. On the other hand, if one goes to the detail of word semantic components, the investigation automatically goes down from the higher level of sentence to the lower level of word.

Prof. Hammarstrom means that *blonde car* should be considered as (*a*) 'language error', which is a linguistic problem, whereas *the elephant weighs one gramme* or *the sky is always purple* would be considered as (*b*) being 'against reality', which is not considered by certain linguists as linguistic problem at all.

As in the Bengali example *āgun ṭhāṇḍā* (fire (is) cold), an expression can be both 'language error' and 'against reality'. The sequence of words is unacceptable because it is against the rules of collocation.

260Chatterjee, p. 83; Acharya, p. 95.

261Chatterjee, pp. 291-93, 300-301; Vidyabhushan, pp. 120-22; Bhattacharya, pp. 128-57.

As a sentence is a combination of both structure and meaning, we think the unacceptable meaning or the semantic irrelevance need not be considered as a linguistic problem. Like the sentence just mentioned above, the period *sincerity may admire the boy* can be considered as an example against reality. Sincerity cannot admire anything, it is a quality. About the word *fire* in the example just quoted, one can say that fire itself includes the quality of heat and coldness is not a quality of fire. There is no conventional association between these two pairs of words i.e., sincerity-admire and fire cold.

Many structuralists and other linguists do not seem to bother about such disparity in conventional association between the lexical items in a sentence. But they do bother about the grammaticalness of the sentence.

Some of the modern Western linguists are rather philosophers when they take into account reality, when they establish distinctive features (semantic components) of the NU and establish such roles as 'experiencer', 'benefactive' and so on. Also they paraphrase a sentence in various ways considering the possible reality of the proposition. When the type of 'roles' mentioned is established and 'reciprocity of actions' is understood by linguists such as Fillmore, Jackendoff, etc. it seems that the factual content of the proposition is given primary concern.

Bhattacharya says:

'All theorists belonging to rival camps as they are do maintain that mere juxtaposition of any and every two or more terms cannot make a sentence... The component words to constitute a sentence must satisfy the triple requirements of expectancy (ākāṇksa), competency, or propriety (yogyatā) and proximity or contiguity (āsatti or sannidhi)...these three factors that together constitute the formal validity of all sentential utterances.'[262]

We have discussed briefly the semantic theory of India in Chapter II. From the above quotation it seems obvious that even for formal syntactical validity of an utterance the required factors were the three qualities mentioned. Here formal validity means the grammaticalness of the syntactic construction. Another quotation may be given here:

'Syntactical expectancy is nothing but the non-completion of the relational sense intended to be communicated by the speaker. A particular term is said to have propositional expectancy with reference to another term, if the non-cognition of the latter is responsible for the absence of the resultant relational judgment of which the former is one of the constituent relata. Keeping this in view this criterion of propositional expectancy it is possible to assert that a substantive, a declensional suffix, a radical stem and a conjugational suffix—all these are mutually expectant having semantic

2 2Bhattacharya, pp. 128-29.

interdependence on each other for the communication of a particular relational thought-unit, so that they constitute the basic requirements of a proposition that is asserted to be the vehicle of judgmental cognition. Thus to communicate the idea, viz., "bring the jar", the constituent concepts must be expressed by their verbal counterparts in such a succession of the stem, the nominal inflexion, the root and the radical suffix, as is capable of making the comprehension of the particular relational thought psychologically possible. And in the case of the judgment referred to above, viz., "ghaṭam ānaya" (bring the jar), the particular sequence would be as follows, viz., ghaṭs-am (denotative of the accusative case), ā-vni and -hi (expressive of the second person Imperative). Thus in the ultimate analysis, propositional expectancy is reduced to a particular sequence (anupurvi) of stem and roots and verbal and nominal suffixes—that is fixed insofar as the comprehension of a particular relational thought-unit is concerned. And when this basic requirement of syntactical expectancy is fulfilled a string of verbal utterance is said to constitute a formally valid proposition.'[263]

One must also consider the 'syntactical possibility' and syntactical contiguity. We believe that the grammarians postulate the sentence as a logical unit of expression. A sentence we mentioned in the previous paragraph is considered as a synthetic whole made up of its constituents which are interrelated.

Avoiding all kinds of controversy one can say in a simplified way that the interdependence of syntax and semantics is fairly dealt with in *kāraka prakarana* in Sanskrit grammar, where the concord (i.e., a kind of agreement with the forms which is expressed by overt maker) and government (i.e., a kind of relation between the nominal and verbal which is called *kāraka*) are dealt with.

Kale says:

'Syntax deals with the mode of arranging words in sentence. Of the three divisions of syntax—concord, government and order, the syntax of Sanskrit is mainly concerned with the first two ... ... Sanskrit syntax also takes further into account the meaning and use of a participles, the various tenses and moods and participles.[264]

It seems that semantic relations of syntagms, different uses and meanings of the elements, and all such things are included in grammar.

Further, we assume that the semantic references can be maintained at two levels in grammar: (*a*) word level, and (*b*) sentence level. The different classes of words (such as noun, verb, etc.) and their detailed components (such as animate, inanimate, etc. classification) are to be considered at the word semantic level. The grammatical relations such as roles and syntactic

[263]Bhattacharya, pp. 138-39.
[264]Kale, p. 468-69.

functions such as subject predicate are considered at the sentence semantic level. The cross-reference of the two levels is shown in voice category.

We argue that the portion of semantics which is concerned with the meaning of the units such as *pada* or syntagms such as a noun phrase or a verb phrase and a sentence which may be called period come under the domain of a grammatical analysis.

The agent, object or subject, predicate functions are identified by the meaning of the items and the units as a whole. This kind of interdependence and interrelation of semantics and syntax is our concern.

We do not think that this part of semantics can be relegated from a grammatical analysis, although semantics is 'viewed as an autonomous sub-discipline of linguistics'.[265]

The word in a sentence is not 'the word as such' but the word as an 'isolated' unit exists in the mind (or brain, perhaps). The things as understood in one's language are more real than the unknown things as such.

We do not think that semantics is to be 'thought of as being a higher level than syntax'.[266] In the Indian grammar semantics and syntax cannot be separated. In one sense, all the levels of grammar phoneti cs, morphology and syntax are to some extent conditioned by semantics.

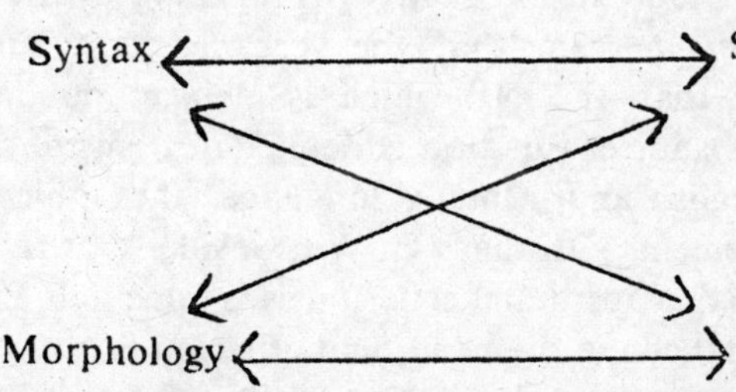

We suggest that this can be shown in the following way when syntactic-levels are described:

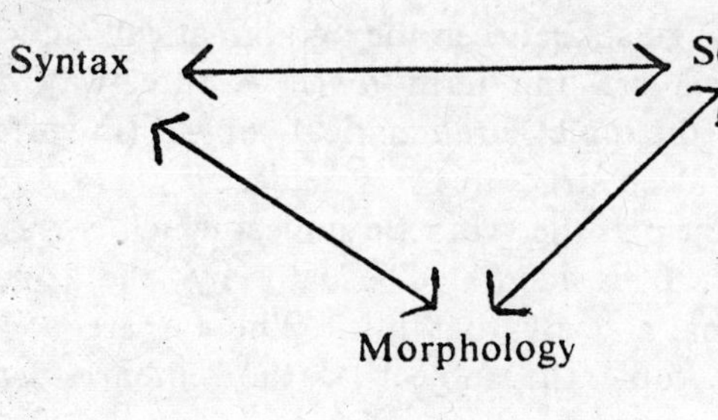

[265]Karin Aijmer, *Psychological Predicate*, p. 12.
[266]Hammarstrom, p. 139.

[3.16.1] Though a given sentence structurally is a particular combination of elements or sequences of words and though it is bound by a certain intonation (a prosodeme pattern), this does not imply that the sentence is semantically relevant.

Very often one can observe that the syntactic criterion alone is not good enough. For instance, to identify 'object' one can consider the following examples:

I see you
I love you
I told you
I beg you

Not all the expressions of *you* in the above English sentences can be called object of the respective verbs, although syntactically they behave similarly. We believe that the term object must be defined basically in semantic terms.[267]

Object implies the semantic function of a nominal, and it belongs to the same rank as agent, instrument, etc. This notional criterion is often confused, when in so many grammars it is said that the object of an active sentence can be the subject of a passive sentence.

The syntactic conversion such as causative, passive from non-causative and non-passive is possible due to the change of meaning of the verb, insertion of some units, etc. It seems that the verb selects its subject and object. When it is said that the NP which is subject dominates the sentence, we think that the subject function is defined in terms of semantics rather than syntax. In English and in many languages the subject implies that NU which is in agreement with the VU. We consider that this implies a syntactic function. Also the positional criterion is syntactic in nature. In many sentences in Indian language the positional criterion is not valid. We suppose that in English the positional criterion is applied to identify direct object also, but the agreement criterion is invalid in the case of direct object which is identified on the basis of a relation to the verb.

Many linguists distinguish between the 'grammatical' and 'logical' subject.[268] Many linguists use the term *topic*. A three-way distinction of psychological subject (the topic), grammatical subject (in surface structure) and logical subject (in deep structure)[269] is made.

We use the term subject as the syntactic subject which corresponds to the 'grammatical subject'. It is identified usually by the concord when a sentence has a nominal and a verbal unit. Where there is no copula or verb unit, we call the topic the subject of the sentence considering the meaning of the whole sentence.

[267]Chatterjee, pp. 86-88. Prof. Chatterjee considers *karma* corresponds to object, and it should be notionally defined.

[268]Karin Aijmer, *Psychological Predicate*, p. 12.

[269]Lyons, pp. 343-44.

In our analysis we favour five basic relations:

(1) *Kartṛ*, which we think corresponds to 'agent';
(2) *Karma*, which we think corresponds to 'object';
(3) *Apādāna*, which we think corresponds to 'ablative';
(4) *Karana*, which we think corresponds to 'instrumental';
(5) *Adhikaraṇa*, which we think corresponds to 'locative'.

We should like to provide the following comments:

(1) *Karma* can accommodate the 'role' of *sampradāna* which corresponds to the term 'benefactive'. Both 'dative' and 'benefactive' should be included in the more basic idea of object which corresponds to *karma*.
(2) The *apādāṇa* can accommodate 'source', 'cause', and 'sign'.
(3) The *adhikaraṇa* accommodates 'time', 'place', matter (subject).

The 'source' seems a borderline case. 'Source' in one sense includes the meaning *place of origin*.

Syntactically the agent and the object can be the subject of a sentence but the other cases can not be the subject in a Bengali sentence. The other cases are always to be considered as belonging to the predicate part. Therefore, it is subordinate to the verbal syntagma. One may say that it behaves like modifier to the verb syntagma. Considering this function syntactically it can be said to be comparable to that of an adverbial.

Compare the following expressions:

(*a*) *jore bɔlo*
loudly speak = you speak loudly

(*b*) *kāje jāo*
to work go = you go to work
(*i*) go to the place of work (location)
(*ii*) go for the work (aim, objective)

(*c*) *hāte kɔro*
with hand do (make) = you make (it) by hand

The expressions, *jore* in (*a*) is an adverb; *kāje* may be paraphrased as (*i*) the place of work, or (*ii*) the purpose, then either it should be (semantically) locative or perhaps purposive; *hāte* is instrumental. Therefore, syntactically it may not be unlikely to consider them as adverbial although they have different semantic functions.

We understand that the adverbial is defined in terms of syntax. And the type of relationship we termed 'roles' is defined in terms of semantics.

Note that we are referring to what Lyons terms sentence-adjuncts:

'A modifier attached to a head upon which it is dependent and from which it can be 'detached' without any consequent syntactic change in the sentence. We are here concerned with what are normally regarded as sentence-adjuncts, rather than with the modifiers of lower-level constituents (such as adjectives, modifying nouns within the noun phrase, adverbs modifying verbs within the verb phrase, etc.). Examples of sentence-adjuncts...(*in Central Park* and *on Sunday* in the sentence *John killed Bill in Central Park on Sunday*).

'Sentence adjunct may be of various ranks (clause, phrases or words). For example, the clause *as soon as his wife arrived*, the phrase *three hours later*, and the word *immediately*, can all be attached as adjuncts to the nucleus (which is itself a complete sentence) *John left for the office*. Furthermore, adjuncts fall into various classes according to their semantic function: they may be adjuncts of time, of place, of purpose, of result, of condition and so on. Not all these different classes are manifest at all rank'.[270]

Some of our Bengali locatives, ablatives and instrumental units can be explained as sentence-adjuncts or sentence adverbials, and can be detached from the sentence without causing any essential syntactic change. Cases where the verbal construction is impersonal and the subject is an object: subject may pose problem. For instance:

āmār kāj bhālo lāge
to me work pleases (suits)
= Work suits me/I like to work.
tomār ekhāne sɔjjho hɔe (jɔlhaoa, 'climate')
your (to you) here tolerates (suits)
= This place (the climate of this place) suits you.

Although the nominal functioning as *locative* (to me, to you), *āmār tomār* may be detached, somehow the meaning is affected, the meaning would not be clear if the unit is deleted. It would seem that something is missing. There may arise another question: whether the expression *āmār* or *tomār* can be appropriately labelled as locative or it should be instrumental in the sense 'by me' or *adverbial of agent* in the sense *in relation to me*?

However, the syntactic construction is not much affected. So one may say that except *kartṛ* and *karma* other semantic relations of the nominals may be called sentence-adverbial considering their syntactic behaviour only. They may be labelled as 'neutral case' since they have this type of meaning and the type of overt marker. They are not included in the verb unit even though they are a part of the predicate of a sentence. The term predicate here means 'the term used ordinarily for the whole of a (normally constructed) sentence minus the subject'.[271]

[270]Lyons, pp. 344-45.

[271]Jespersen, *Analytic Syntax*, pp. 38-39. He further says: 'It may be doubtful whether the bipartition of a sentence into subject and predicate found in most books on the theory

Lyons differentiates cases such as 'grammatical' and 'local'.[272] Also he distinguishes between an adjunct and a complement.[273]

To us it seems that the distinction of cases such as 'grammatical' and 'local' is irrelevant. We would like to consider any syntagmatic relation as grammatical. Therefore, the *adhikaraṇa* (locative), *karaṇa* (instrumental) and *apādāna* (ablative) are as grammatical as the *kartṛ* (subject, agent), *karma* (object including *sampradāna*) are. The difference lies in their meaning which is based on the relation between the different NU and the VU. It is obvious that sentence semantics should belong to grammar and not to the lexicon.

Case is primarily considered as the inflexional category of the noun in traditional Western grammar. Quotations can be given from Jespersen and Lyons.

Jespersen suggests:

'As I have said on several occasions, we should not, in treating of the grammar of any language, recognize more cases, or other cases, than are clearly distinguished by formal criteria; thus we have no dative in English or Danish, no ablative in Greek, etc. A case is always a "morphoseme" in the sense defined above. As a matter of fact we rarely have one form only, and as rarely one notional use only; generally several forms go together to produce one case, which again serves to express more than one notion. Where thus several form-classes meet with several notional classes there is never the slightest correspondence between any one of the A divisions and any one of the C divisions.'[273a]

All this is explained in a chart which is reproduced in the following. The chart shows the marker, function of the form and notion indicated by it:

(A) Form, (B) Function, (C) Notion, one example. The English preterit:

A	B	C
-ed (handed))		(past time
-t (fixed))		(unreality in present
-d (showed))		(time (if we know; I
-t (with inner change)	preterit	(wish we know)
(left), kernel unchanged)		(future time (it is
(put), inner change (drank),)		(time you went to bed)
different kernel (was))		(shifted present time
		((how did you know I
		(was a Dane?)
		(all times (men were
		(deceivers ever).'[274]

of grammar has any great value'. Jespersen differentiates between predicate and predicative for which he uses the abbreviations P (in the case of predicative of result he uses PR).

She is an actress; SVP
He is angry; SVP
She is young and pretty; SVP & P
This is not good; SVNP
This is no good; SVP

Predicative of result
He gets angry; SVPR
Adverbs and prepositional group
The rain is over; SVP

[272]Lyons, pp. 295-304.
[273]Lyons, p. 345.
[273a]*Jespersen, Analytic Syntax*, pp. 107-08.
[274]*Ibid.*, p. 95.

Jespersen further defines 'morphoseme' in the following manner:

'As a matter of fact much or all of what is placed in C would be reckoned as "function" by most scholars. In column B we have the meeting ground of outer and inner—but this meeting is the essential characteristic of all linguistic activity, and column B might therefore be superscribed "linguistic centre" or "linguo-centre": what we meet there are units which, as I said, Janus-like face both ways, towards form, and towards notion. A new word seems to be wanted, and I venture to propose Morphoseme: I should define a morphoseme as a linguistic unit standing at the inter-secting point where form and notion meet. A morphoseme may have one form, but generally has two or more forms; similarly it corresponds generally not to one notional idea only, but to several. It belongs to one definite language alone.'[275]

The above quotation from Jespersen may be compared with Lyons' definition below:

'Case was the most important of the inflexional categories of the noun, as tense was the most important inflexional category of the verb. It is significant that the term 'case' (originally more or less synonymous with what was later called 'inflexion') was restricted to one particular inflexional category. The reason for this would seem to be that most of the other categories—gender, number, tense, person, etc.—could be related to a principle of semantic classification. Although each case of the noun was given a label suggestive of at least one of its principal semantic functions (e.g., the 'dative' was the case associated with the notion of 'giving', the 'ablative' was the case associated with 'removal', etc.), it was impossible to give a satisfactory general definition of the category of case itself in semantic terms. In effect, traditional definitions of the category of case for Latin and Greek (and other Indo European languages) say little more than the following: of the two inflexional categories of the noun, one is number (definable in semantic terms and relatable to the Aristotelian category of quantity), the other is case. The category of case was, as it were, the most peculiarly grammatical of all the traditional categories of inflexion, for it had no counterpart in the sister sciences of logic, epistemology and metaphysics.'[276]

The above quotations from Jespersen and Lyons, make one thing clear to us, and that is that 'case' was considered as having above all formal criteria in Western grammar. Jespersen proposed to consider the notional idea also, and Lyons remarks about the syntactic function. Fillmore and other recent authors have used the term case for content units.

[275]*Ibid.*, pp. 97-98.

[276]Lyons, *Introduction to Theoretical Linguistics*, p. 289.

In traditional Indian grammar, the syntactic function of the other *kāraka* except the *kartṛkāraka* is not mentioned. We have mentioned before that Bengali scholars like Ramendra Sundar suggests to classify 'cases' (which corresponds to the term *kāraka*) in Bengali considering their syntactic behaviour. Following Western grammar he calls *adhikaraṇa* (locative), *apādāna* (ablative) and *karaṇa* (instrumental) as adjunct. He prefers to label them as neutral, since their relation to the verb syntagm is not as direct as the other (*kartā*, *karma*). The definition of adjunct given by Lyons[277] is more or less suitable to Bengali constructions. But Lyons' definition of complement is not suitable to Bengali constructions. The syntactic requirement for both adjunct and complement seems the same in a Bengali construction. They may be compared with English in the following way.

with locative phrase:

rāṭrite condrodɔe hoilo
at night the rising of the moon occurred
(locative)

English example:

John killed Bill *in Central Park on Sunday*[278] (adjunct)

an ablative phrase:

kukɔrme birɔtohɔo
in misdeed/from misdeed (you) desist

English example:

You desist *from misdeed.*

an instrumental phrase:

āmrā cokkhe dekhi
we by eyes (through eyes) see

English may be:

we see *through our eyes.*

Syntactically the above mentioned locative, ablative and instrumental phrases may be called adjunct in Bengali also.

But the English distinction between 'complement' and adjunct is not applicable to Bengali. The two examples given by Lyons may be translated in Bengali as follows:

[277]Lyons, pp. 344-45.
[278]Lyons, pp. 345.

senṭral *parke* *pæreḍ* *chilo* (hoechilo)
(at) in Central Park the parade was
or *robibare* *ḍəmonstrəsan* *chilo* (hoechilo)
on Sunday the demonstration was

Lyons says:

'The predicative complement is syntactically required, in order to 'complete' the structure of the predicate (hence the term 'complement'). More particularly the term 'complement' is used of such 'adverbial' expressions as *in Central Park* or *on Sunday* in sentences like *the parade was in Central Park* or *the demonstration was on Sunday*. The temporal and locative phrases in these two sentences are obviously not adjuncts (since *The parade was* and *The demonstration was* are syntactically incomplete). The difference between an adjunct and a complement is, in principle, quite clear: the former is an optional (extranuclear) constituent, and the latter an obligatory (nuclear) constituent of the sentence. In practice, the distinction between sentence-adjuncts and predicative complements is often far from clear. As we have just seen, the same class of words or phrases may occur as a locative or temporal adjunct in one set of sentences and as a complement (of the copula) in the other.[279]

Lyons further tries to shows the syntactic distinction between temporal adjuncts and temporal complements with 'first-order nominals' and 'second-order nominals'. Then he describes the 'surface-structure' and underlying constituent structure.

It seems to me that the unit division in Bengali construction perhaps differentiates the complements from the adjuncts. It may be said that complement occurs within the unit, and adjunct itself is a separate unit having modifying relation to other unit of the sentence. It also seems advantageous to consider locative units or nominal phrases (instrumental, ablative, etc.) as 'cases' defined in the way we set up other cases (roles) in semantic terms. We believe that the semantic function or the 'case' and syntactic functions such as adjunct, complement, etc. should not be confused, and they should be defined in the two levels of semantics and syntax. In Bengali the same lexical items may occur in different constructions and they may occur in the same positions also. For instance:

(*i*) *āmrā boi pori* and
we book read
(*ii*) *āmrā boie poṛi* or
we in book read
(*iii*) *āmār boi poṛi*
my book read

[279]Lyons, pp. 345-46.

In (*i*) *book* is object, in (*ii*) *in book* is locative, in (*iii*) *amar-boi* is also an object unit where *āmār* is the complement of *boi.*

We establish that a lex together with the marker in combination with other lexes contribute to express the total meaning of a given sentence. And the total meaning implies the type of relation which we call (case) role. The syntactic criteria of determining such relations (between the NU's and the VU) do not seem to be satisfactory in all languages.

Considering the syntactic criterion one can say that the distinction between predicative complement, adjunct and sentence adjunct is 'often far from clear' in English. In Bengali constructions the distinction between predicative complement and the adjunct does not exist. What we mean by complement is that the lexical element which modifies the other one and occurs in one single unit. Further, the definition of adverb in English grammar is not always clear. Sometimes it is said that adverbs are 'those words which modify the verb'.[280] Here adverb seems to mean adverbial. In this sense we think complement, adverb, adjective, attribute all give some meaning, these are modifier elements either to the verb or to the noun.

Possibly, one can group the basic roles in two groups considering their syntactic behaviour. The *kartā* and *karma* (in which we include *sampradāna*) can constitute one group. The other group comprises *apādāna*, *karaṇa* and *adhikaraṇa*.

We believe that the term adjunct includes the subject adjuncts, predicative adjuncts and sentence adjuncts, whereas the term adverbial is appropriate to the unit which modifies the verb only.

We think that it is better not to use such terms as adjunct, complement, adverb, etc. when we set up the semantic functions of the NU's, i.e., the 'roles'. We follow the binary division of a sentence which is structurally NU, VU. We have said before that a sentence can be structurally NU, NU (AU) or VU also.

The references and interselection between syntax and semantics can be diagrammatically presented.

[280]Ian Michael: *English Grammatical Categories*, pp. 443-51.

THE BINARY DIVISION OF A SENTENCE

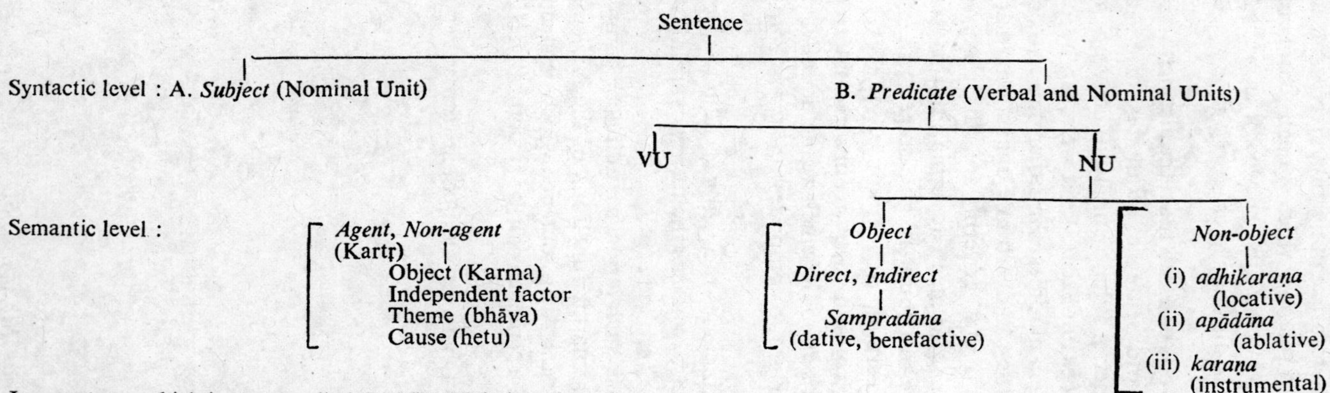

In a sentence which is structurally NU, NU (VU) the subject is labelled as Independent factor (topic). It is established on the basis of meaning and for this unit the question of grammatical agreement does not arise.

[3.17.0] We are doubtful about the way in contemporary linguistic analysis distinctive features are treated in syntax. To us, the distinctive features of nominals such as animate, inanimate, etc. should be explained in the word level description. We differ with the idea of rigidity, the rigorous formalization and the process of transformation. In most cases transformations seem to be counter intuitive.

To the generativists and transformationalists a grammar of a language should describe explicitly the system of rules. They take into account the ideal speaker-hearer in an abstract sense. They are concerned with the question what linguistic knowledge should be presupposed in a native speaker to produce and interpret sentence, whereas the traditional analysis objectively depicted the language characteristics, we believe that synchronic description should be 'neutral in relation to speaker and hearer' in a completely homogeneous speech community.

Let us consider in some detail about Chomsky's remark. His discussion in the *Current Trends in Linguistics* (vol. 3, p. 3-6) makes the following points clear:

(*a*) A linguistic grammar aims to discover and exhibit the mechanisms 'that make the achievement' of producing and understanding speech possible.

(*b*) 'The problem for the linguistic theory is to discover general properties of any system of rules that may serve as the basis for a human language.

(*c*) It is difficult to see how performance can be seriously studied except on the basis of an explicit theory of the competence that underlies it.

(*d*) They (traditional grammarians) do not actually formulate the rules of the grammar....They do not provide an analysis of the 'faculate de language'....

(*e*) The fundamental importance of this creative aspect of normal language use has been recognized since the seventeenth century at least, and it was at the core of Humboldtian general linguistics.

(*f*) Normal use of language involves the production and interpretation of sentences that are similar to sentences that have been heard before only in that they are generated by the rules of the same grammar.... fixed formulas of one sort or another.

(*g*) All these points were underestimated even by a linguist such as Jespersen. This is evident from the common description of language use as a matter of grammatical habit.

(*h*) A generative grammar is a system of rules that relate signals to semantic interpretations of these signals.

(*i*) Let us then introduce the neutral technical notion of 'syntactic description' and take a syntactic description of a sentence to be an (abstract) object of some sort, associated with the sentence, that uniquely determines its semantic interpretation (the latter notion being left unspecified pending further insight into semantic theory) as well as its phonetic form.

(*j*) A particular linguistic theory must specify the set of possible syntactic descriptions for sentences of a natural language.

(*k*) Notice that a... (SD) may convey information about a sentence beyond its phonetic form and semantic interpretation.

It is doubtful how far it is possible to differentiate between 'competence' and 'performance' in grammatical analysis. And it is not clear how 'the creative aspect' (creativity in language) of normal language use in rigid formalization can be analysed in grammar. Considering that synchronic description should be 'neutral in relation to speaker and hearer', we find that the traditional Indian grammar satisfies some of these points. The three tables shown in this analysis would make it clear that the syntactic description has cross reference with semantics.

If semantic interpretation refers to the meaning of the sentence, i.e., the intended information which would be conveyed, then it is doubtless that one would have to know the dictionary meaning of the lexical item and to understand the relational meaning of the items of that particular construction. This cannot be described in any formula, unless sentence is defined in the way we defined it. It is difficult to believe how a relation between words and their meanings can be acquired and be used properly in appropriate situations by a normal human child or adult unless the appropriate language habits had been developed in them.

Chomsky further suggests that a descriptively adequate grammar should express 'degree of deviation', and should be 'factually correct in variety of respects'. It should show 'the ambiguity of a sentence', 'distinct SdS' of a particular sentence, 'each of which specifies the system of grammatical relations that underlies one of the distinct semantic interpretations of the sentence'.

Then comes his remark:

Hence the SD must (*i*) determine a semantic interpretation, and (*ii*) determine a phonetic representation. Let us define the 'deep structure of a sentence' as that aspect of the SD that determines its semantic interpretation, and the 'surface structure of a sentence' as that aspect of the SD that determines its phonetic form'. A grammar then must consist of three components: a syntactic component, which generates SD's each of which consists of a surface structure and a deep structure; a semantic component, which assigns a semantic interpretation to a deep structure; a phonological component, which assigns a phonetic interpretation to a surface structure. Thus the grammar as a whole will associate phonetic representations and semantic interpretations, as required, this association being mediated by the syntactic component that generates deep structures as elements of SD's. This notion of 'deep structure' and 'surface structure' are intended as explications of the Humboldtian notions 'inner form of a sentence and outer form of a sentence...' There is a good reason to suppose that the surface structure of a sentence is a labelled bracketing that segments it into its continuous constituents categorizes these segments the constituents into further categorized constituents, etc.[281]

We would like to say again that we do not see the need for separate deep and surface structures.

We agree however with Chomsky when he remarks that 'a sentence has an inherent grammatical structure; this structure provides it with a certain range of potential semantic interpretations'.[282] But we cannot agree with him when he says:

'In particular the rules of English grammar that constitute the competence of the native speaker, provide the sentences (4), (5), (11), (12) with alternative syntactic descriptions each expressing its network of semantically significant grammatical relations. In a particular situation, the hearer may use information that goes well beyond grammar to determine which of the potential interpretations was intended (or whether, perhaps, something was intended that goes beyond the explicit semantic content of the utterance that was actually used). Absolutely nothing of any significance is known about this use of extra-grammatical information in interpretation of sentence, beyond the fact that it exists and is an important characteristic of performance.'[283]

However, these problems do not directly belong to grammar which concerns expression structure and its meaning structure. An 'ambiguous' sentence is mostly really two sentences with at least somewhat different structure (but with the same lexical items).

When a sentence with similar lexical items gives two meanings (readings), it should usually be considered as having two different constructions: the grammatical unit division, stresses, pause or break (prosodic feature) differ in two constructions with same phonetic representation. In many cases the context indicates which reading is desired. Therefore, it is no synonymity at all. In other words 'the one sentence' is actually more than one sentence.

We agree that 'the problem for the Grammarian is to discover' the system of a language. Various rules can be formulated for the regularities in a language. But the way Chomsky and other generativists establish the rules,

[281]Current Trends in Linguistics, Vol. 3, p. 7.

[282]*Ibid.*, p. 12.

[283]*Ibid.*, (4) They don't know how good meat tastes (p. 6); (5) What disturbed John was being disregarded by everyone (p. 6); (11) (*i*) Old men and women; (*ii*) They are flying planes (p. 14); (12) (*i*) The shooting of the hunters; (*ii*) John was frightened by the new method (p. 14).

it seems that they in general have in mind a dummy human, a computer or a machine, even though they always refer to the term 'normal use', 'natural language', etc.

Both in theory and in practice, the Indian traditional Grammarians' target was living human beings. So they formalized rules following inductive processes. Even though these were not represented in tree diagrams, there are rules at various levels: the levels of phonetics, morphology, semantics and syntax in traditional grammar. For instance, the derivative rules, the description of *krita, taddhite suffixes* (declension and derivative rules), the *sandhi rules* (morphophonemic rules), the *conception of kāraka and vācya*, the *notion of uddesya vidheya*, etc., the various morphological representations of different case relations and the restrictive occurrence of different cases in the subject and predicate part of a sentence, etc. are to be found in Indian traditional grammars, which describe the language comparatively and adequately. However, traditional Grammarians were not influenced in their grammatical thinking by the idea of producing a model or mechanism of language acquisition.

The attempt to surpass the boundary of grammar and connect linguistics with psychology, physiology, mathematics, computer science, so on and so forth automatically may be dangerous, as irrelevant speculations may enter into linguistics. However, the search of a model for language acquisition and production together with a model for understanding language may be fascinating. In this case knowledge of psychology will certainly be important.

In our opinion Chomsky and the generativists to some extent often confuse the grammar and a description of real world events. Quite different sentences (with different grammatical description) are relatable to the same event in the real world. So we do not support the idea of 'deep structure'.

Also, we are not sure about the specific importance of one level only as one can start with any level in grammatical analysis. Different levels of grammar are related, so in analysing one level there arise cross references to other levels also. And we think that it is sensible to remain within the limit of grammar when one deals with grammar. We do not believe that we have an 'entirely erroneous' idea, if we accept the use of the term 'generalization' in grammatical analysis. We believe that some kind of generalization must be accounted for in syntax and semantics. Otherwise, no rules at any level can stand, nor can they be learnt from listening to speech.

When linguists represent sentence as NP+VP, we think it is also a kind of generalization of sentence structure. It is the interest of the Grammarians or linguists to investigate the regularities in language, to analyse the facts of languages, and to define and describe them in different levels of grammar. Also, the speaker has unconsciously made a generalization. But the way generativist-transformationalists emphasise that a linguistic grammar should only depict 'the underlying system of rules that has been mastered by the native speaker-hearer, seems not convincing to us. Their descriptive technique and presentation can not be taken as a completely satisfactory conceptual representation of all language phenomena in any sense of finality.

We intend to point out the weakness of the transformation rules as we think that Chomsky's claim that 'the role of grammatical transformation in syntax and phonology seems hardly disputable' is challengeable. Also the claim for universality is questionable. If creativity and language differences are recognized, then how far is mechanistic formalization be applicable.

However, everyone will agree with him that 'linguistics is a living subject' and 'any theory of grammar that can be formulated today must be highly tentative'. We also assume that any preconceived and arbitrary theory will fade away in course of time.

It is doubtless that the most basic regularities of a language system can be described in a rather precise and succinct manner, but we think that the principle of economy in linguistics should not be allowed to oppose more elaborate descriptions when necessary. The 'surface' and 'deep' structures idea has cumbersome consequences in the high number of inter-related rules. However, the new theoretical framework has been vigorously employed in linguistic analysis recently. Whether it is Chomsky's 'transformation', Chafe's 'symbolization processes', or Lamb's 'realization rules'[284] for relating different sentences, they are crippled with cumbersome rules of a kind which does not seem adequate. We have a strong feeling that experiment has a secondary place in social science.

The model theory of acquisition has rules which can hardly be usefully applied by a normal human being in normal language communication. Instead of following these theories, we believe in a more traditional multi-dimensional theory of grammar.

Even though Fillmore does not find any fruitful solutions in Pāṇiṇi's *kāraka* theory,[285] we believe that the semantically oriented theory of traditional Indian grammar shows a good way of describing syntactic and semantic properties of a language system at different levels of description. We have already mentioned that we consider that sentences are definitely structurally different where grammatical meaning is different, even though they may be affiliated in basic sentence meaning. We also said before that 'sentences having two readings' are often structurally two different sentences. We believe in the intuition of the native speaker. We assume that grammar is concerned with the ideal representations of the speaker-hearer's knowledge. 'Such ideal representations' can be called 'phonetic representations of expressions'. Likewise, grammar 'is not concerned with particular idiosyncratic connotations of the speaker-hearer's knowledge of what the meaning of the expression ought to be like relative to normal usage in

[284]Fillmore, 'Case for Case', *Universals in Linguistic Theory*, pp. 8-9.

[285]Chomsky, *Aspects of the Theory of Syntax*; *Syntactic Structures*; Lamb, Outline of *Stratificational Grammar*.

the speech community. Such ideal representations are called semantic representations of expressions.'[286] A grammar of a language couples the expression side of that specific language with its content side. To quote from the same author:

'The goal of the theory of grammar is to determine (a) the universal principles by which grammars are structured (morpho-syntax and phonology) and (b) the universal rules by which speakers generate semantic representations (semantics). In order to understand the function of phonological and morpho-syntactic rules we need to know first the nature of the structures which are their input, i.e., phonetic representation on the side of the hearer (perception and interpretation) and semantic representations on the side of the speaker (production).'[287]

However, we also need to know the specific structure of some given language. We agree with the above opinion and believe that a speaker 'generates semantic representation' intuitively, and that he can do so because he acquires language habits. To quote further from the same source: 'What one would expect is that a grammar is developed as a rule system which takes semantic representations as input and converts them into phonetic representations and conversely.'[288] We believe that the abstract syntactic structures can be established by investigating the regularities of the actual expressions. Every expression has a meaning or semantic representation. The actual expression contains lexical items related in meaning (together) in a given construction.

As we have done ourselves, the author from whose work the above quotations have been given distinguishes between sentence semantics and word semantics:

'The sentence semantics of a sentence represents the meaning of the surface syntax of a sentence in logical syntax without reference to the meaning of any particular word of the sentence. The following are the aspects of a sentence which contribute to its sentence semantics: the categorical (including subcategorical) information of constituents, morphological markers, word order and intonation. These aspects of a sentence allow the listener to reconstruct such information as declarative, interrogative, tense, sentence connection, sentence embedding, topic-comment relations, focus formation and presuppositions......whereas we treat sentence semantics entirely in the syntax, we treat word semantics entirely in the lexicon.'[289]

[286]Renate Bartsch, *Theo Vennemann*, 'Semantic Structure', 1972, p. 3-4.
[287]*Ibid.*, pp. 3-4.
[288]*Ibid.*, p. 6.
[289]*Ibid.*, p. 39.

Although we would not like to contradict the idea mentioned in the above quotation in any major way, we include further the total meaning of the whole sentence which includes the specific meaning of a word in some context (lex seme), the meaning of the lexical items and their related meaning in a syntagm of the sentence, etc.

We do not believe in any deletion rules or other extrinsic rules to project a surface structure. The expression side or the surface structure, whichever may be the term used seems to provide directly all sorts of grammatical information necessary for a complete description. The syntactic structure and the semantic structure provide all kinds of necessary information. Therefore, we reject any idea of 'deep structure'. We say that semantics and syntax are interrelated. Chomsky's diagram (1967, p. 420):

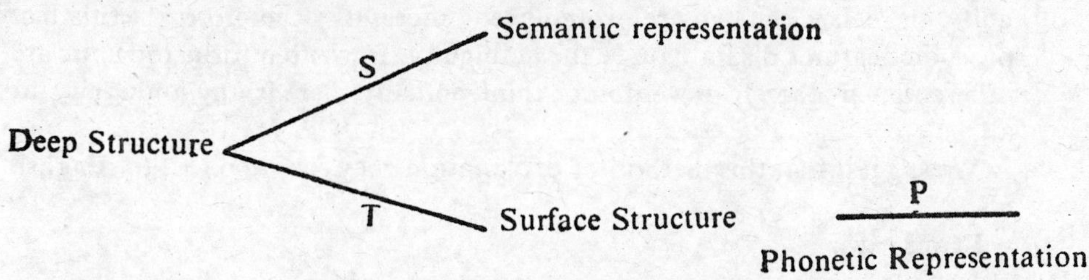

It does not seem to account well for basic language facts.

[3.17.1] Further, we intend to discuss in some detail some points regarding the ambiguity of sentence and the ergative transformation. The type of ambiguity taken into account in many recent analyses can sometimes be explained as a double meaning of a homophonous utterance; sometimes quite differently it may be described as difference in unit division, in prosodic feature or in context.

A phrase in Bengali can be reduced to a compound word which is characteristically similar to word. Therefore, this type of ambiguity found at the phrase level may be treated as a word having different meanings. In the following way ambiguity can be disambiguated.

A sentence which can be interpreted in different ways usually is called ambiguous sentence. Modern linguists commonly employ the term two readings of one sentence or phrase. The ambiguity of the sentence arises from the ambiguity of phrase or a word.

loker *nindā*
of people criticism
= criticism of people/criticism made by people

This ambiguous Bengali phrase can be reduced to a word such as *lok-nindā* and this word is also ambiguous. However, in the sentences below, the context disambiguates the meaning.

(*a*) *lok nindā* *bipɔdjɔnok*
criticism of people (is) dangerous

(*b*) *mānus lok nindā* *bhɔepae*
people criticism of others are frightening

In recent analyses this type of ambiguity is dealt with. Chomsky's examples: *the shooting of the hunters, the flying planes*, etc. and examples given by Lyons: *it is the love of God which inspires men to work for their fellows*, etc. are of this type.

But in both languages the ambiguous phrase (word) can conceivably be disambiguated by the reference of the context.

Note that the same syllables in the same order can be written and pronounced in two different ways. In this case one should not speak of ambiguity. In reality, the two are pronounced differently; therefore the distinct prosodic features disambiguate the ambiguity. In written form the units are differentiated; therefore we do not think actually there is any ambiguity at all.

We suggest that this method of explanation may be applied to English also.

Lyons says:

'One of Chomsky's most famous examples, the phrase *flying planes* (in a sentence such as *flying planes can be dangerous*), is ambiguous for much the same reasons as the *love of God* is ambiguous. Under one interpretation *flying planes* is related to a sentence in which planes is the subject of *fly* or *are flying*, under the other in which planes is the object of *fly* (cf. Planes fly v. John flies planes).

'In traditional grammar, there is a distinction drawn between the 'participle' and the 'gerund'. Insofar as this distinction applies to English (and there are situations in which it is unclear) it might be formulated as follows:

(*a*) A participle is a word which is derived from a verb and used as adjective.

(*b*) A gerund is a word which is derived from a verb and used as a noun.

This distinction is clearly relevant to the analysis of an ambiguous phrase like *flying planes*. If we consider the following two sentences (in which the principles of subject-verb concord "disambiguate" the phrase in question)

(1) Flying planes are dangerous

(2) Flying planes is dangerous

the difference between the "participle" and the "gerund" comes out clearly. The verb *are* in (1) is plural because its subject is *planes*, a plural noun, which is the head of the endocentric phrase, *flying planes*; moreover in (1) *flying* is distributionally equivalent to an adjective (e.g., supersonic). The recognition of a head and a modifier in *flying planes* in (2) is more problematical, but *flying* is nominal and the whole phrase is the subject (cf. flying is dangerous). Traditional statements about the participle and the 'gerund' are transformational in nature.'[290]

If Lyons' use of the term 'transformational in nature' simply meant convertibility or derivability, then what he says is understandable, although a traditional account is usually worded in such a way that transformations are included. Lyons' statement does not seem to be correct.

However, he justifies the deep structure hypothesis:

We can interpret them to mean that a particular word (in the sense of "lexeme") may be verbal in one sentence and adjectival in a transformationally-related phrase, or 'verbal' in one sentence and nominal in a transformationally-related phrase. Without, for the moment, considering the nature of the rules which might account for these relationships, let us merely say that in (1) the phrase *flying planes* is to be derived by a rule which 'transforms the structure underlying a sentence like *planes are flying* and assigns to the resultant noun-phrase the derived structure of adjective+noun; and that in (2) the phrase *flying planes* is to be derived by transformational rule from the structure underlying a sentence like *John flies planes* and assigns to the resultant noun-phrase the derived structural description noun+noun (the first of the two nouns, if any, being the one that controls concord). If we now assume that the rules of the grammar generate sentences like (1) and (2) with both an underlying ('deep') and a derived (surface) structural description, we have in principle explicated the 'subjective' and 'objective' interpretations of noun phrases like *flying planes*.[291]

Obviously, we differ, because we believe that language provides more directly all indications needed for interpretation of sentences. We cannot see either that Lyons' way of 'explicating' subjective versus objective is superior to the traditional way of defining more directly these terms.

We have already said that we disagree with the idea of the ergative transformation. We do not think that Lyons means by the term ergative transformation, the transitive and intransitive use of the same verb. The idea of ergative transformation includes many things. It is described by Lyons in the following way.

We will consider the relationship between transitivity and ergativity in some greater detail. The first point to be made is that there are many verbs in English which may combine with either one or two nominals in sentence-nuclie (move, change, open, etc.). Consider the following sentences:

[290]Lyons, pp. 249-50.
[291]Lyons, p. 250.

(1) The stone moved.
(2) John moved.
(3) John moved the stone.

In (1) and (2) *move* is intransitive, whereas in (3) it is transitive. Moreover there is an important relationship between (1) and (3). With reference to the information conveyed by (1), we might well ask 'who moved it?', i.e., who was the "actor" or "agent" responsible for the movement of the stone? And if this question is put explicitly, the answer might be "John did" (an utterance derived from the sentence (3) *John moved the stone*). The term that is generally employed by linguists for the syntactic relationship holds between (1) and (3) is "ergative": the subject of an intransitive verb "becomes" the object of a corresponding transitive verb, and a new *ergative* subject is introduced as the 'agent' (or 'cause') of the action referred to. This suggests that a transitive sentence like (3) may be derived syntactically from an intransitive sentence like (1) by means of an ergative or causative transformation...It will also be observed that the causative or ergative agent in (3) is an animate noun. We have already noted the tendency for the subjects of transitive verbs to be animate.'[292]

We think that the type of explanation Lyons gives to establish *ergativity* does not concern grammar. The question such as 'who moved it (stone)' cannot arise out of the sentence *the stone moved.* Many intransitive verbs can be used transitively any *vice versa* in many languages. But this type of occurrence in two different constructions which are independent cannot be considered as a syntactic relation at all.

As a matter of fact, we would say that (1) and (3) are related also (2) and (3) are related semantically, because of the expressions *the stone* and *John* respectively. In (1) and (3) the stone occurs in different functions. Perhaps Lyons includes 'agent' and 'object' in syntax. But we consider these as semantic functions. Anyhow, the expression *the stone* occurs in different positions. The (2) and (3) are related in the sense the expression *John* occurred in both as agent. The thre esentences are independent. The expression *thestone* occurs as subject [potential object of the verb (transitive) *move*] in (1) and the same expression occurs as object in (3). This relation gives stress to the transitive and intransitive use of the verb rather than stressing the ergative or causative subject.

One may add that *the stone* (1) is the subject of (intransitively used) the verb *move*, *the stone* (3) is the object of the transitive verb *move*.

We have pointed out before that the function of agent, object of a nominal is semantic in nature and not syntactic. We think that the difference indicated by these independent sentences can be called the difference in

[292]Lyons, pp. 351-52.

subject focus by the intransitive and transitive use of the same verb and this is a point (topic) of voice. To us it seems unnecessary to say (1) and (3) are syntactically related.

It seems fallacious to say that the sentence (3) is 'derived syntactically from an intransitive sentence like (1)', because the idea of ergative or causative transformation would be superimposition here. There is no point in asking further question about the sentence 'the stone moved'. The information is completely conveyed by the sentence. If, however, one asks Lyons' question, the answer 'John did' can never be derived from this sentence. How can the question arise: who was the 'actor' or 'agent' responsible for the movement of the stone if the expression is just 'the stone moved'? And if one asks the question the real word perhaps, but not sentence (1), can give an answer. We think that no relation can be established between a verb and an imaginary acting person.

As a matter of fact, a new word can be formed by adding a suffix or prefix or some other element to a root or stem. Similarly, one can think that one sentence can be formed from another by combining or discarding bits and pieces of it. There may be differences in numbers of units, in the existing form of a unit (morphological or phonetic) in the verb construction, in allosemes of the same verb in intransitive and transitive use of the same verb in the function of the different units, etc. However, whether one speaks of derivation or transformation (in syntax) this way of describing is (on the whole) not the way we are using in our study.

A portion of the predicate, i.e., the nominal unit functioning as object, has the potentiality to be changed into the syntactic subject, i.e., a syntactic interchange occurs in two semantically affiliated independent sentences.

[3.17.2] Lyons refers to the term 'ergativity' to mean the conflict between criteria. A kind of parallelism is observed in many languages where the subject of an intransitive verb takes a marker similar to the one of the goal of the transitive verb. 'This syntactic parallelism between the 'goal' of a transitive verb and the subject of an intransitive verb is generally referred to as ergativity.'[293] Curme also has this idea of ergativity.

We have objected to the idea of considering the ergative relation as syntactic rather than semantic. And we do not consider either 'lexicalization or 'zero-modification' of causative transformation at the syntactic level because in these changes the meaning is bound to change.

We have repeatedly pointed out that in the real world a hearer may 'feel obliged to infer in order to understand the sentence'. But this should hardly mean that one is allowed to infer the real world situation in grammatical analyses in the way it has been done in the case under discussion.

[293]Lyons, p. 342.

The hypothetical 'object deletion' or introduction of an 'ergative-subject' leads to the confusion of the real world situation and grammar. This inference results in establishing a hypothetical 'underlying structure' which seems very close to the event of the real world, but far from the meaning of the language.

Let us quote from Aijmer:

'A grammar must, for instance, be able to provide an explicit and descriptively adequate account of the ambiguity of the now hackneyed "the shooting of the hunters" (Chomsky 1957:88) by giving the two meanings (they shoot the hunters or the hunters shoot (something) distinct underlying "kernel sentences". A formal explanation of such ambiguities is thus outside the scope of, for instance, immediate constituent analysis.'[294]

In the footnote the author explains that it can be solved 'by the definitions of traditional grammar', but he points out that the aim is different.

This is also generative in that it aims to give the rules for generating all the grammatical sentences of a language, but is not explicit. The fact that structural ambiguity cannot always be discovered by a native speaker by introspection does not retract from its validity as data for which the grammar must account. To establish whether sentences have the same or different meaning in fact requires considerable ingenuity and sophistication in the linguist in constructing paraphrases. Compare in this respect Chomsky 1965:21:

But consider such a sentence as

(5) *I had a book stolen.*

Few hearers may be aware of the fact that their internalized grammar in fact provides at least three structural descriptions for this sentence. Nevertheless, this fact can be brought to consciousness by consideration of subject elaboration of sentence (5), for example.

(*i*) '*I had a book stolen form my car when I stupidly left the window open*', that is someone stole a book from my car;

(*ii*) '*I had a book stolen from his library by a professional thief who I hired to do the job*', that is 'I had someone steal a book';

(*iii*) '*I almost had a book stolen, but they caught me leaving the library with it*', that is 'I had almost succeeded in stealing a book'.

In bringing to consciousness the triple ambiguity of (5) in this way, we represent no new information to the hearer and teach him nothing

[294]Aijmer, *Psychological Predicate*, p. 12.

new about his language but simply arrange matters in such a way that his linguistic intuition, previously obscured, becomes evident to him.'[295]

It is difficult to understand why the generative approach is more explicit' than the traditional one. This seems to be an empty claim by Aijmer. Typically, a traditional linguist would call *the hunters* in *the shooting of the hunters* an 'object' (if the hunters were shot). He would also call *the hunters* 'object' if one said *I shoot the hunters*. He would have defined 'object' and he would often provide a paraphrase to make things clear (but the paraphrase is not made part of the final description). The type of psychological question and the type of paraphrases given by Aijmer seems to tempt the modern linguists to set up 'deep structures' following Chomsky and others.

We would like to give two more quotations from Aijmer:

'A theory of semantic interpretation introducing projection rules operating on the sentence and its structural description was expounded by J. Katz and J. Fodor in 1963 (Katz and Fodor 1964). It was assumed in their work that the semantic interpretation was also dependent on the transformational history of the sentence. In the following year the publication of Katz and Postal's *An Integrated Theory af Linguistic Description* signals a new conception of semantics: all that is needed for the interpretation of a sentence is contained in its underlying structure and, consequently, transformations are not allowed to change meaning. These innovations are with certain modifications, incorporated in Chomsky' *Aspects of Theory of Syntax* (1965). The grammar is here described as a system of rules. The syntactic rules generate an underlying phrase marker (the deep structure of the sentence). The semantic interpretation is given by projection rules which, with the syntactic deep structure as input, derive readings on the basis of the semantic specification of the lexical entries and the constituent structure.

'The meaning of the lexical elements and their selectional restrictions are formulated in terms of semantic components. We define a semantic component (feature) as the minimum contrastive elements into which the meaning of a lexical item can be broken down.

Features can also play a role for subcategorization and for formulating selection rules constraining lexical insertion. In Katz and Fodor's article *The Structure of a Semantic Theory* (1964), selectional restrictions are stated in the semantic component and are functions of the so-called semantic markers. Chomsky replaced the semantic (and syntactic) markers by distinctive features in analogy with the use of features in phonology. The use of subcategorization features prevents the generation of syntactically and semantically deviant sentences by the base rules. The features are syntactic and introduced by the phrase structure rules of the base (features which are

[295]*Ibid.*, p. 13.

not referred to by any syntactic rules are, however, semantic). Examples of such syntactic features are (count), (animate), (human). A feature like (count) subcategorizing the noun, is probably needed to ensure the proper distinction...in the same way the distinction human/non-human be made by a syntactic feature in order to account for the distribution of the relative pronoun who and which...

'A theory with the conception of semantics described above can for instance account for semantically deviant sentences (resulting from a relaxation of the selection rules) and for ambiguity (one sentence with two readings) as well as analyticity (bachelors are unmarried) and contradiction (bachelors are married) (cf. Katz 1966:188).[296]

And the author's comment:

'The grammar envisaged in *syntactic structure* is an inventory of rules which mechanically generate all the grammatical sentences of the language. Subsequent developments in transformational-generative grammar aimed at constructing grammars of particular languages or writing the rules generating certain syntactic construction...One outcome of the discovery that the generative capacity of the transformations was too powerful for ordinary language and resulted in ungrammatical sentences was the interest in formulating constraints on transformation.'[297]

We admit that this procedure may have elements which are useful in machine translation. It certainly looks impressive when represented in chart diagram or in various "formalized" ways. The main criticism would, however, be that "deep structure" and transformations seem to be quite counter intuitive.

[3.17.3] It is a matter of choice whether someone will describe anything in inductive or deductive processes. No native speaker is consciously aware about any grammatical rules when he uses language in normal language communication. We have pointed out that, if semantic features of the lexical items are accounted for in identifying semantic roles, then the number will be high. And if this high number is to be represented in a rule structured grammar it would be unnecessarily complicated without yielding any gainful results, and such purposeless rules often result in confusions of the grammar and the real world in linguistic description.

We may say that the theory of transformation is often coupled with superimposition, because the linguist often applies certain items which are not in the given sentence. We believe that in grammatical analysis one should analyse what is given in the 'closest' possible way. We restrict our-

[296] *Ibid.*, pp. 14-16.
[297] *Ibid.*, p. 16.

selves to a method where as much as possible philosophical and certain psychological implications are avoided.

We do not rely on the theory of projection (semantic projection rule, etc.) which is used in grammar (in word of generativist or transformationalist), but perhaps do not intuitively suit language in human mind. We believe that meaning and form are associated conventionally (which is cognized by the human mind) and that the associated units are used both in producing and interpreting language.

After Chomsky's remark that there is no aspect of linguistic study more subject to confusion and more in need of clear and careful formulation than that which deals with the points of connection between syntax and semantics" in *Syntactic Structure* (1957), many books were written referring to this topic and a 'standard theory' was formulated.[298]

In 1972 Chomsky presented a 'revision' of the standard theory to an 'extended standard theory (EST)'. And he confirmed the status of deep structure saying that 'further evidence is presented leading again to the conclusion that a level of deep structure (in the sense of the standard theory and EST) must be postulated'.[299] He considers the deep structure as central: '...the grammatical relations of the deep structure remain fundamental for syntactic interpretation, determining what have been called "thematic relation" or "case relations" but other aspects of meaning are determined by surface structure'.[300]

Note that Chomsky just claims that his grammar, including deep structure, is correct.

Chomsky defines:

A grammar of a language, in the sense in which I will use this term, can be loosely described as a system of rules that expresses the correspondence between sound and meaning in this language......Let us assume further that the grammar in some manner specifies an infinite class of surface structures, each of which is mapped on to a phonetic representation by a system of phonological rules. I assume further that the grammar contains a system of grammatical transformations, each mapping of phrase markers on to phrase marker.[301]

Chomsky further elaborates:

Surface structures are mapped into phonetic representations by the phonological rules. Post-lexical structures are mapped into semantic representations by the semantic rules. In this formulation, the post-lexical structures are called deep structures. The deep structures contain all lexical items, each with its complement of grammatical features. Furthermore, the con-

[298]See Preface of Noam Chomsky's *Studies on Semantics in Generative Grammar*, 1972, pp. 62-63.
[299]*Ibid.*
[300]*Ibid.*
[301]*Ibid.*

figurations of the phrase-marker P, which are preserved in the deep structure, can be taken to define grammatical relations and functions in a straightforward manner. It is natural (though I shall argue, only in part correct) to suppose that the semantic interpretation of a sentence is determined by the intrinsic semantic content of lexical items and the manner in which they are related at the level of deep structure. Supposing this (following in essence, Katz and Postal, 1964), it would follow that deep structures determine semantic representation under the rules of semantic interpretation.

'Thus the deep structures in this theory, are held to meet several conditions. First, they determine semantic representations. Second, they are mapped into well formed surface structure by grammatical transformations (without any subsequent insertion of lexical items). Third, they satisfy the set of formal conditions defined by the base rules; in particular, the rules of the categorical component define the grammatical functions and order of constituents and the contextual features of lexical entries determine how lexical items can be entered into such structures'.[302]

First of all, we would say there is no necessity for a grammar to set up deep structure in the sense of EST. Considering the way Chomsky gradually extends his theory of syntactic structures from 1957-72, we believe that in the long run he might abandon the deep structure hypothesis considering it a superficial exaggeration.

'Consider next the following modification of the standard theory. We consider a new set of structures C (for "case system") which represent semantically significant relations among phrases such as the agent-action in (4) and of instrument action as in (5):

(4) John opened the door.
(5) The key opened the door.

Suppose we were to assume, in a realization of the standard theory, that the deep structures of (4) and (5) are identical except for lexical entries. Then these deep structures, it might be argued, do not represent the required relations. For example, as grammatical relations are defined in Chomsky (1965), the subject-predicate relation is the relation that holds between *John* and *opened the door* in (4), and between *the key* and *opened the door* in (5); hence the relation of agent-action and instrument action are not differentiated. Let us therefore construct the structures C1 and C2 of C as follows:

(6) C1: [(v, open), (agent, John), (object, the door)].
(7) C2: [(v, open, (instrument, the key) (object, the door)].

Are case systems, so described, empirically distinguishable from the standard

[302]Noam Chomsky, *Studies on Semantics in Generative Grammar*, pp. 65-66.

system? It is not at all obvious. Thus consider the example just given. It was argued if (4) and (5) have the same deep structure, apart from lexical entries (let us put aside the questions whether this is correct), then the relations indicated in (6) and (7) are not represented in deep structure. However, this argument depends on an assumption, which need not be accepted, regarding rules of semantic interpretation. In fact, the rules mapping C1 and C2 on to the deep structures of (4) and (5) respectively, can be interpreted as rules of semantic interpretation of these deep structures. Thus one rule (probably universal) will stipulate that for verbs of action, the animate subject may be interpreted as the agent, etc.; various qualifications are needed whether we interpret these rules as rules of semantic interpretation or as rules mapping C on to S; I see very little difference between them, at this level of discussion, and the same seems to be true in many more complex cases. It might be argued that the case system expresses these facts in a "direct way", whereas the standard system does so only indirectly. The distinction seems to be meaningless. Without principles of interpretation, a formal system expresses nothing at all. What it expresses, what information it provides, is determined by these principles.

'A good part of the critique and elaboration of the standard theory in the past few years has focused on the notion of deep structure and the relation of semantic representation to syntactic structure. This is quite natural'.[303]

Chomsky explains that Fillmore's case representation and the standard theory are not very different. Chomsky then concludes that 'properties of surface structure play a distinct role in semantic interpretation. It seems to me that these ideas suggest a line of investigation which though still unclear in many respects, may prove quite promising'.[304]

We have pointed out before that 'case' is realized in terms of semantics in traditional Indian approach. It differs from the Western modern approach in many aspects. In the Indian approach the verbs are classified differently, and the semantic features of the nouns are not taken into account when 'cases' are established.

The deep structure notion of the modern Western approach is complicated, but it is not yet sufficiently comprehensive to incorporate the grammatical relations and functions held by noun phrases. The total meaning of the given sentence is taken as the criterion to label such relations and functions of the phrases in traditional Indian grammar. The problem of agent: subject, object: subject, instrument: subject, etc. that is, the subject of intransitive or transitive verb is explained in voice category.

[303]*Ibid.*, pp. 73-75.
[304]*Ibid.*, p. 117.

On the one hand, the interchange of agent, object in active and passive constructions and the change of their position are explained as the subject focusing by the verb; on the other hand the problem of agent (or object subject) versus instrument (or instrumental subject) can also be explained as subject focusing by the transitive and intransitive verb respectively. Thus, there is no need for an abstract structure to co-relate these sentences.

[3.18.0] It may be a matter of choice if one follows Chomsky's suggestion (the generative transformational approach in general). The basic issue seems to be if a grammar should attach great importance to language acquisition, phenomena of the real world, experience and psychological aspects (which are, no doubt, related to the language) or if a grammar should more exclusively aim at a description of language as a means of communication, providing information on how the different elements interact in the system.

In our opinion, the former may be the subject matter of a different branch of linguistics, and the latter should be the main aim of grammar or general linguistics. Note that hypothetical deep structures and arbitrary abstractions are not common in traditional descriptions as those in the following pages. Instead, the description is close to what seems to be 'facts'.

In Indian grammar the verbal classification and derivation of different words and their interaction were described. Using the Pāṇinian terminology we can say that there are mainly two kinds of roots: (A) *dhātu* 'verb root', (B) *name* 'nominal root'; and also the following basic syntagmas that can occur in a sentence independently or severally (together with the other):

(1)	*tiŋɔntɔpada*	'finite verb form'
(2)	*kridantapada*	'nonfinite, nominal, adjectival form, etc.
(3)	*avyaya pada*	'which cannot be declined, or Indeclinable'

If the (1) and (2) type units are segmented one may get either A or B root (or stem). We have already given the structural classification of verbs. Semantically and syntactically, derivative verbs are of different types:

(*i*)	*nijɔntɔ dhātu*	'causative verb'
(*ii*)	*sannanta dhātu*	'desiderative verb'
(*iii*)	*yananta dhātu*	'frequentative verb'
(*iv*)	*nāma dhātu*	'denominative verb'
(*v*)	*karmavācya dhātu*	'passive verb'[305]

[305]Kale, pp. 367-99; Vidhyabhushan, pp. 63-65; Chatterjee, pp. 134.

The above mentioned (*ii*), (*iii*) and (*iv*) are borderline cases and they may be just described, according to their structural differences. But (*i*) and (*v*) and the finite verb in addition to their structural description have to be defined in terms of semantics and syntax.

Verbs can also be classified on the basis of their capacity to take an object in addition to the subject, that is, the transitive-intransitive differences of verbs are relevant. Many verbs can be used both in transitive and intransitive in several independent constructions.

Further, in Sanskrit there are two uses of verbs: *Ātmanepada* and *Parasmaipada*. In Bengali the verbs are described in a similar fashion (except for *Ātmanepada* and *Parasmaipada* use, because in Bengali there is no such use).[306]

The semantic syntactic properties of the verb (including the context) indicate active, passive and causative differences in sentences. We have already pointed out that such establishment of, syntactic relation, either of ergative or of causative-non-causative relation between two independent constructions, is questionable, and we have given our arguments. We have argued that this kind of relation is based on superimposition. We have also pointed out that the active-passive sentences are related in meaning in the sense the real event is expressed in the two different constructions of active and passive. But the grammatical meaning of the items occurring in these two different constructions is changed. So we think the main principle of transformation (meaning does not change) is not maintained. Even though the causative sentence may be taken as structurally partly similar to the passive, the causative has an interesting difference from active-passive. In a three-place construction of a causative sentence, an indirect object can become a subject, if the three-place causative is reduced to a two-place construction of non-causative by applying a deletion T-rule. If so, then the established syntactic characteristic that only the direct object becomes the subject in passive, fails. The ergative and causative transformations introduce new items which are not at all present in a given sentence. A causative verb is structurally different from the non-causative and a passive verb from a non-passive. Either at syntactic level or at semantic level there occurs a change by application of any transformation. Therefore, it seems contradictory to say that transformation does not change meaning.

[306]Kale, pp. 288-468; Chatterjee, p. 133-80.

CHAPTER FOUR

NOMINALS AS SUBJECT AND AS PREDICATE

[4.0] The syntactic structure of the Bengali sentence negates the well-known definition to English that the subject NU is determined by virtue of its particular position. The structure of the Bengali sentence also makes it evident that the binary division into subject and predicate cannot be a universal feature of the sentence. Some quotations may be given.

Lyons describes: 'Thus we might define the topic of the sentence as the left most NP immediately dominated by S in the surface structure, and the comment of the sentence as the rest of the string...'.[1] But he thinks this cannot be the final word and he continues:

'Consideration of the examples given in this section that there are far more distinctions involved than can be accounted for by the simple dichotomy of 'grammatical' and 'logical' subjects. Even a three-way distinction of 'psychological' subject (the topic), 'grammatical' subject (in surface structure) and 'logical' subject (in deep structure) fails to capture all the distinctions which at one time or another, have been associated with the notion of 'subject' in grammatical and logical theory'.[2]

Jespersen defines:

'The subject is the primary which is most intimately connected with the verb (predicate) in the form which it actually has in the sentence with which we are concerned; thus *Tom* is the subject in (1) Tom beats John, but not in (2) John is beaten by Tom; in the latter sentence *John* is the subject because he is the person most intimately connected with the verb *beat* in the actual form employed: is beaten. We can thus find out the subject by asking who (or what) followed by the verb in the form used in the sentence (1) who beats (John)? Tom; (2) who is beaten (by Tom)? John—subject as a grammatical term can thus be defined only in connection with the rest of the sentence in its actual form'.[3]

We consider that only a complicated definition will be capable of identifying the complicated function of noun phrase which is called subject in grammar.

[1]Lyons, p. 343.
[2]Lyons, p. 344.
[3]Jespersen, *Analytic Syntax*, p. 126.

First of all, subject NU can be signalled in a sentence which is structurally NU, VU by its agreement with the VU, which is overtly manifested by the concord.

The *Encyclopaedia of Linguistics* says:

'Functional relations such as subject and object have also been called categories but these are essentially relational terms. In a simple English active sentence of the structure noun phrase+verb noun phrase, the subject is the noun phrase which is immediately constituent with the rest of the sentence (the predicate)....English subject and objects are not therefore categories of units in the sense in which noun phrases are a category, but represent different relations between noun phrases, verb and sentences. This covert (constituency) relation may be overtly reinforced by concord.[4]

Fries considers 'subject' as a

'...formal linguistic structural matter; it is a particular construction for a class I word; it is not a matter of the meaning of the word with reference to a real situation. It is true that the structural meaning of many 'subjects' is 'performer' but the meaning of performer is signalled by many other devices and there are many 'subjects' which have other meanings than that of performer.[5]

We also maintain that 'subject' is a technical term for a noun phrase having a particular function in a construction. Fries further says:

'Subjects represent at least five different meanings:

The *dean* approved all our recommendations (521)
(subject is performer)

One *difficulty* is the size of the trees (253)
(subject is that which is identified)

The *abstract* is very bulky (200)
(subject is that which is described)

The *requisition* was sent over a week ago (540)
(subject is that which undergoes the action)

Mr. W- was given the complete file on-(552)
(subject is that "to or for" which the action is performed)

Although the "subject" structure may in various sentences carry any one of these five meanings, the formal arrangements of any particular sentence will determine which of these meanings the "subject" signals'.[6]

[4] *Encyclopaedia of Linguistics, Information and Control*, p. 206.
[5] Fries, The Structure of English, 1952, p. 176.
[6] *Ibid.*, pp. 177-78.

From the above-mentioned quotations it seems obvious that even though the formal criteria, the grammatical device of agreement-concord, the syntactical position and relation with the verb are considered to be the factors for identifying a 'subject', the meaning criterion is not abandoned, rather most other criteria are conditioned by meaning. But that meaning is not the reference of the real world event, that is made clear by Fries. Lyons differentiates between 'grammatical' and 'logical' (semantic) subjects. In praise of generative grammar, the *Encyclopaedia* defines:

'A distinction needs to be drawn between the "grammatical" subject and object and the "semantic" (or logical) subject and object (i.e., the "actor" and the "goal" of the action). If the subject in English were defined as the noun phrase in concord (or potential concord) with the verb, then in a sentence like *he frightens the children,* the "grammatical" subject is also the actor. In a passive sentence *the children are frightened by him* the grammatical subject (children) and the actor (him) do not coincide. Nor do they coincide in a sentence like *he scares easily,* when the "grammatical" subject can hardly be regarded as actor. In more complex sentence, the relation between the "grammatical" and "semantic" subject and object can become very involved....

'It is the inability of grammars which confine their attention to the surface structure (so-called taxonomic grammars) to provide any explication of the relationship between the latent deep structure and the patent surface structure which has stimulated the development of generative grammars containing a transformational component.'[7]

We have already shown in diagram which roles can function as subject in a Bengali construction. It is observed that not all sentences have NU, VU structure. Linguists such as Jespersen point out that a sentence may be without subject [*Analytic Syntax*, p. 127]. Commonly the imperatives are subjectless. In English also it is often subjectless (Gleason Tr., *Linguistics and English Grammar*, p. 317).

[4.1] In this framework it is observed that in the subject part of a sentence, the NU holding agent relation occurs frequently. It is shown statistically that 80 per cent of all sentences contain a subject NU in Bengali.

Considering the sentence semantics (the total meaning of the sentence), we observe that a performer (which we use as a grammatical term) may be animate or inanimate.

In some cases the *agent* (animate) and the doer in the real world coincide. In some cases one can consider an animate noun as *cause*, if the alloseme of the verb and the other related noun phrase occurring in the sentence,

[7]*Encyclopaedia of Linguistics, Information and Control*, p. 206.

signal the cause meaning of the subject noun, which is animate in its semantic feature.

The inanimate NU referring to the physical objects, machines and other things may be termed as agent-inanimate. Some of the inanimate agents may be the originator, source or cause in the real world. Recall the English example quoted from *The Grammar of Contemporary English*: 'The avalanche destroyed several villages.' The agent (including subfunctions), the *hetu*, the object, *the independent factor*, *the theme* occur as subject in Bengali constructions. These labels (given to the subject NU) are defined in semantic terms in our study. Other semantic functions held by the NU's are normally found in the predicate part of a Bengali sentence.

We believe that the idea intended to be expressed by the speaker is perfectly communicated to the listener through these examples which have structure either NU, NU (including AU) or VU.

One may be tempted to posit a hypothetical VU or NU which is found in other structures such as NU, VU. We think to add such NU or VU in the structure of VU and NU would be unnecessary. It seems appropriate to remark that, in Bengali and possibly in many other languages, the sentence structures are as follows:

(*i*) NU, VU.
(*ii*) NU, NU.
(*iii*) VU.

Thus NP, VP should not be taken as the universal characteristic of sentence structure. Secondly, we suggest that the binary division of subject and predicate is appropriate to the structure of NU, VU. But the sentences which have NU, NU or VU structure would preferably be called sentence building sequence. The subject predicate division is not syntactically appropriate to these structures of sentences.[8]

[4.2] Assuming that the subject-predicate division is a characteristic feature of some sentences which are structurally NU, VU, we shall divide further the subject and the predicate below. The subject may be presented as:

[8]Consider a few *sentences* :

ākās nil
the sky (is) blue
kālṭi sɔrotkāl
the time (is) autumn (season)
jābo
will go (I/we)
dekhi
Let me see

subject NU (NU. . .)

(modifier NU) subject nominal

(modifier element) head nominals (s)

Syntactically and semantically, the subject part of a sentence is one unit which is segmentable.

prithibir *kono des-i* | *sɔrgo* *nɔe*
of the world any country heaven is not
modifier—modifier-head[9]

It may be a longer syntactic unit or smaller; in turn it may be either simple or complex. Complex units are (obviously) segmentable.

If an expanded longer single syntactic unit (subject) of Bengali is translated into English it may contain several relative clauses, whereas in Bengali the sentence with such unit may not have any relative clause at all. For instance, a Bengali sentence like below:

(1) *oije sei* *āmār-bɔṛobh āier* *grāmer-bāṛir*
that-that-that my elder brother's country house-of
(emphasizer-particular) (modifier) (modifier)
bhāŋā-jānlāṭā
broken window that
(subject nominal)

SUBJECT PART

(2) *sārātehɔbe*
has to be repaired (fixed up)
(verb unit)

The subject nominal expression *jānlāṭā* 'the window' has the modifying element *bhāŋā* and three preceding modifiers. It can be translated into English as: that particular broken window of my elder brother's house, which is in the country, has to be repaired. Note the *which* clause in English construction and the markers in Bengali construction.

The longer syntactic unit like the one just mentioned, which consists of several elements (lexical items), may be adequately described in *pada* concept rather than the English type expanded noun phrase unit. The underlined portions of the subject unit cannot appropriately be called noun

[9]Chatterjee, p. 329.

phrases. Even though there is a link marker -r in various items occurring in the long expression *āmār...jānlāṭā*, the nominals linked by the marker do not constitute a compound. The marker shows the link between the preceding and following nominals. In this study the whole subject unit is considered as a single complex NU. The segments such as *oije sei*, *amārbhāier grāmerbāṛir* are attribute to the head NU *bhāyā-jānlāṭā*. Semantically, the three smaller segments are in attributive relation to each other and jointly to the head of the longer unit. The initial segment has no link marker, syntactically, it precedes and shows relation to the other. Therefore the *oijesei* segment is to be considered as a separate attributive segment.

It can be said that the structure of *āmār...jānlātā* has the genitive construction,[10] and in Bengali the genitive precedes the (head) governing noun. The whole unit is a combination of discrete elements connected with certain markers. There is no obvious reason to consider that this long expression in Bengali consists of a few underlying relative clauses. Syntactically, they constitute one single complex unit, because they are semantically relevant and connected directly with each other.

[4.3] We note that a subject NU can hold roles (relations, semantic functions) as follows:

Roles *(semantics)*	*Subject NU* *or katṛpada* *(syntax)*	*(Kāraka :* *Semantic relation)*	
(*i*) agent	subject	(*kartṛ*)	
(*ii*) object	subject	(*karma*)	
(*iii*) topic	subject :	independent factor	(savatantrah)
	subject :	theme (*bhāva*)	
(*iv*) cause	subject :	(hetu)	

All types of subjects are focussed by the VU in NU, VU sentences. Where the action is highlighted as topic, we call it theme and the corresponding Bengali (Sanskrit) term is *bhāva*. In the latter sentence the doer (of the real world) occupies a neutral position in the subject part like an attribute to the subject nominal. Its positional occurrence is unlike the adverbial of agent in passive construction. We believe that the above-mentioned function of the subject NU, i.e., the agent, non-agent distinction (including their subfunctions) can be identified on the basis of sentence semantics.

[4.4] The predicate part of a Bengali sentence can contain one or more than one NU. The predicate may be presented as:

Predicate

VU NU (NU. . .)

[10]Greenberg, *Universals of Language*, 1966. for some universal of grammar with particular reference to the order of meaning elements, see p. 2.

The predicate NU may be either simple or complex. A complex predicate NU can have modifier(s) and a head nominal. The predicate can be further divided showing the VU and other NU(s) apart. This shows a possible non-combinability of the two or more units. The VU is headed by a verb and the NU or AU can be headed by a noun or adjective. The NU(s) have different types of relations with the VU. The NU(s) holding roles such as object, cause, instrument, locative and ablative can occur in the predicate part. Except the NU holding object role, other NU(s) occur with obligatory markers.

However, the sentence modifiers are doubtful cases. Expressions like fortunately, occasionally, perhaps, etc. often modify a whole sentence. In that case it seems inappropriate either to include that syntagam in the subject part or in the predicate part of the sentence. Some linguists prefer to call it 'sentence outer'. Another problematic unit is the provoked agent in causative sentences. Syntactically, one can tempt to put the NU under the predicate part in case of adverbial of agents. One can call the 'provoked-agent an object-agent. It seems that the unit having 'provoked-agent' role in causative sentence offers a syntactic problem. It is difficult to know if it should be part of the subject or part of the predicate.

Thus, it can be remarked that even though in many cases the subject-predicate division seems quite appropriate, this binary division does not apply to many other sentences. The two specific problems just mentioned are cases which go against the universality of the subject, predicate division of sentence.

The notion of phrase has not been well defined by any grammarian. It seems doubtful whether the unit like 'sentence outer' can be called a phrase. In our opinion, it seems appropriate to call such a syntactic unit a phrase (as the smallest unit). A nominal phrase which has discontinuous elements can also be called discontinuous nominal phrase. In English a verb phrase can be discontinuous, such as, did they go? Usually, the expression *did-go* is described as a discontinuous verb phrase.

[4.4.1] Considering the word order of Bengali constructions, the predicate NU(s) cannot be described as the NU which occur after the VU or copula or a verb considered to be similar to the copula. Notice that Bengali is a verb final language like Hindi and other languages of India, and that the usual order of the words in Bengali is subject—object—verb. This order is not fixed even though it is very common. The subject and object can be juxtaposed. Likewise, *adhikaraṇa*, *apādāna* can be juxtaposed with subject. In other words,

S O V
S A V etc.

can easily be juxtaposed as O S V or A S V. For stylistic purposes the V may also occur in initial position to make the expression lively and forceful. Thus, the word order is not always the relevant criterion for the definition of the subject or predicate in Bengali. The sentence semantics play a distinct role.

The subject focus by the verb is categorized in four different types of *vācya* which seems partially to correspond to the English term voice or one may consider to set up sub or sub-sub functions of the basic semantic functions we set up.

[4.5] In addition to what is already mentioned about the items and their arrangement in a Bengali active construction, a few remarks can be added:

(1) Two nouns or more can be conjoined by a conjunction and the whole expression is to be considered as an expanded NU, and this NU can occur in the subject part. For instance;

CONTINUOUS

rām lakkhon o sītā/bone colilen
= Ram, Lakshmana and Sita went to the forest.

The three proper names are head nominals. In such a case the last one can take a marker. It is found that in the subject and the object the NU marker is not always obligatory.

An example of a discontinuous phrase:

(1)	(2)	(3)
ṭhlæāgāṛite	*iŋrāj-rɔmoni*	*o ɔssopriṣṭhe*
in a pushcart	English women and	on the horseback
(4)	(5)	(6)
iŋrājpurusgɔn	*bāyu-sebɔne*	*bāhir-hoiāchen*
English men	to breathe fresh air	have come out

The two long segments *thælā...romoni* and *ɔsso....purusgɔn* are conjoined with a conjunction *o*. The subject NU's *iŋrājrɔmoni* and *iŋrājpurusgɔn* are discontinuous because of the insertion of a noun phrase *ɔssopriṣṭhe* which modifies both the following nominal and the verb. The expressions (2) and (4) are subject nominals which are connected with the connector *o*.

In the subject part of a sentence there may be more than one subject nominal with one attribute only, and the subjects are connected with one another by a conjunction and divided into various sense groups through the prosodic feature of a certain break between them. For instance:

(1)
tãhār uccobɔŋso *o pɔdomɔrjādā*
his noble family and high prestige

(2) (3)
bidyā o buddhi *cɔrittro o kɔrtobbonisṭhā*
education and intelligence character and dutifulness

(4) (5) (6)
ebŋ *sɔkolersohit* *ɔkrittim* *o* *ɔmāik-bɔbohār*
and with all sincere and polite behaviour

(7) (8) (9)
ei sɔmosto miliā *tãhāke* *biśeṣbhābe*
all these together him particularly

(10)
jɔnoprio-kariātuliāche
popular-made (Chatterjee, p. 311)

Nos. (1), (2), (3) and (6) have a conjunction between them and (1), (2), (3); these segments are conjoined with (5) and (6) through a conjunction. All these segments are divided by a kind of break. No. (7) and the initial morpheme *tãhār* seem to be the attributes of these segments. The whole portion beginning with *tãhār* and ending with *milia* is to be taken as subject. No. (8) is object (target), (9) is adverb and (10) the verbal unit. So (8), (9) and (10) should constitute the predicate part. The subject may be considered to have cause function.

An extremely expanded subject part can be like the following:

(*i*) *āmāder sei roudro tɔpto srānto dɔridra bhārotbɔrso*
our that hot tired (weary) poor India

(*ii*) *āmāder sei dhɔrāprāntoborti ɔporicito*
our that cornered, unknown

bismrita nibhrito nodikɔloddhoni supto baŋlādesh
forgotten (lonely) quiet, river murmured sleepy Bengal

(*iii*) *āmārsei ɔkɔrmonno grihoprio bāllokāl*
mine that idle home loving childhood

(*iv*) *āmārbhālabāsā lālāyita kɔlponā kliṣṭojoubɔn*
my (love longing) imaginative youth

(*v*) *āmārnisceṣṭo niruddɔm oti bæthito jiboner smriti*
my inactive effortless very painful life's recollection

(*vi*) *ei surjo kirone*
in this sunshine

(*vii*) *eitɔpto bāyu hillole*
in this hot wind wave

(*viii*) *sudur moricikār mɔto*
distant mirage like

(*ix*) *āmār Swapnabhārnɔto dristir Sāmne*
my dreamy sight before/in front of

(*x*) *jege uṭhche*
are appearing (coming)
(Tagore, 'Europe Yatrir Diary', 23rd October 1890, in *Ravindra racanāvali* centenary vol. 10, p. 457.

Every NU from (*i*) to (*v*) may be considered as a sentence in their own right if it occurs separately. In the above example they all function as the subject of the VU No. (*x*); No. (*vi*), (*vii*) and (*ix*) may be considered as having cause and (*ix*) having locative functions. They are part of the predicate portion. No. (*viii*) is the attribute to all the subjects. Therefore, it should go to the subject part of the sentence. Even though the whole portion consisting of (*i*) to (*v*) NU(s) together with No. (*viii*) should be considered as subject part, the whole subject part is divided into various segments.

Two or more (expanded) NP(s) (usually with markers) can follow each other in which case one is attribute to the other. For instance:

(*i*) *porikkhāte sāphollolābhe kritosɔŋkolpo*
in examination—to attain success firmed in mind

(*ii*) *rāmbābur sāntosiṣṭo bɔro cheleṭi*
Rambabu's goodnatured elder boy

(*iii*) *dibārāttro*
whole day and night

(*iv*) *ækmone*
attentively

(*v*) *ɔbisrām*
without any break (rest)

(*vi*) *poṛiteche*
is reading (Chatterjee, p. 299)

The NU(s) No. (*i*), (*ii*), should constitute the subject part. The (*i*) as a single NU functions as the attribute of the subject noun *cheleti* 'boy'. Other items in No. (*ii*) are also attributed to the same noun. No. (*iii*), (*iv*) and (*v*) are to be considered in the predicate part because they are modifying the VU No. (*vi*).

(2) *Predicate NU.* Like the subject part of a sentence, the predicate part can have NU's which may be conjoined by a conjunction or a conjunction may occur within a single NU of a predicate part. For instance,

(*A*)	(1)	(2)	(3)	(4)
	oder ghɔre	*bhāt*	*ache*	*ebŋ*
	in their possession	food	exists	and

(5)	(6)
oder hāte	*procur pɔesā*
in their hand	plenty of money

No. (2) and (6) are subjects of the VU No. (3). No. (4) is a conjunction, No. (1) and (5) are in the predicate part, both may be considered functioning as locative.

(*B*)	(1)	(2)	(3)
	roge o soke	*se bhāŋiā*	*poṛiāche*
	(by) illness and sorrow	he has broken	down

In the above example, No. (2) is the subject of the VU No. (3). NU No. (1) functions as the cause and it belongs to the predicate part of the sentence. There are two items in the NU No. (1) and there occurs a conjunction. Recall our example (B) of type (1). The two expressions *thælāgāṛite* 'in (on) the pushcart', *ɔssopriṣṭhe* 'on the horseback', even precede the other NU's *iŋrājrɔmoni* and *iŋrajpurusgɔn* respectively, but these locative phrases do not belong to the subject part, rather they modify the VU, in other words they function as manner adverbial, therefore they are part of the predicate. The sentence can be translated into English as:

(*a*) The English women and the English men have come out.

(*b*) They come out in a pushcart and on the horse(s) back respectively.

There occurs no corresponding term 'respectively' in Bengali constructions, but there is a conjunction *o* and it simultaneously conjoins the subject NU(s) and the predicate NU(s). In paraphrase (*b*) the adverb 'respectively' appears, without which the meaning would be unclear. On the other hand, in the Bengali phrase the meaning is clear without a word corresponding with respectively because of the conjunction *o*.

(3) Two independent clauses can be conjoined with a conjunction:

(*a*) *se tomār sɔŋge dækhākoribe boliā ājrātre āsiteche*
he you with will meet so today night is coming
= He is coming tonight because he wants to see you.

(*b*) *rāg hoiāchilo boliā bokiāchilām*
anger appeared so scolded

mone dukkʰo korionā
in mind sorrow do not do
=(I) got angry and scolded (you), don't mind please.

In both the above-mentioned examples the expression *boliā* occurs as a connector between the two clauses. The two different clauses could form two independent sentences.

[4.6] Some units contain a nominal and a non-finite verbal item which functions as the modifier both to the verb and to the nominal. For instance:

(1)	(2)	(3)
ghɔre thākte	*bābui*	*bʰeje*

in nest being a bird gets wet
(being in the nest)
=A babui (kind of bird) gets wet even though it is in the nest.

The unit (1) modifies the nominal in the sense that the modifier indicates the state of the bird. However, it also modifies the verb in the sense it expresses the condition or the manner of the action when it takes place. Either one can put the expression (1) into the subject part as the subject modifier or one can put it into the predicate part as adverbial. Or, which may be the best solution, it could be an 'outer' adverbial (see above). For instance:

(A) *tumi gāṛi ānte ānte āmār*
you car to bring (while bring) to me (my)
sājgoj hoejābe
dress will be finished
=While you bring the car I shall dress up (dressing will be finished in relation to me).

For the two clauses, there is only one finite verb, *hoejābe*.

Compare a relative clause:

(B) *āmi dekhlām ki (je) tomār gāṛi okhāne āche*
I saw that (which is) your car is there

We think the grammatical relation held by the preceding clause in (A) has the dependent relation to the following clause, in particular to the finite verb of the sentence, whereas the grammatical relation held by the following clause in (B) is an object relation to the verb.[11]

[11]K.V. Subbarao, 'Phrase Structure Rule for Noun Phrase in Hindi', Indian Linguistics, Vol. 35, No. 3, September 1974, pp. 173-80. He thinks relative clause and the clause like (A) can be described as embedded structure.

In our opinion, the expression with non-finite verb form should be included in the predicate part of the sentence. Another suggestion would be that when a group of items fulfils certain conditions such as occurrence in successive order and holding modifier (attributive) relation to the following items, they can be called a phrase. Prof. Chatterjee mentions that the non-finite verbal expression corresponds to the term 'participle', and the whole unit with nominal and verbal infinitive as an 'adverbial phrase'.[12]

We agree that semantically the whole syntactic unit (the syntagm) is modifying the finite verb. Thus, it holds the adverbial relation. But, syntactically, it seems doubtful whether the term phrase is appropriate to label the whole syntagm. The syntagm consists of both inflected nominal and inflected verbal items. They do not constitute either a nominal or a verbal phrase, even though they occur in a successive order. Although semantically the two can be linked up, syntactically they do not constitute a single unit. In a phrase usually one element occurs as the attribute to the other. They should either be related to each other in attributive relation (genitive relation), or they may be considered as more than one head nominal in a phrase, where the last element takes the marker; in other words, the phrase is usually bound by a marker. The above-mentioned syntagm does not fulfil these conditions. In the Western grammar the syntactic hierarchy is usually as follows (from the highest to the lowest): (*a*) sentence, (*b*) clause, and (*c*) phrase; whereas in traditional Indian grammar we find the two-way syntactic divisions:

> *vākya* (which corresponds to sentence);
> *pada* (which corresponds to the inflected form including compound).

The intermediate divisions such as expanded phrase and clause have no equivalent in traditional Indian grammar.

Consider the following expressions in English:

> The new French car. . .
> The new French car in the garage. . .

Both the shorter and the longer expression may be called phrase in English. They can be defined as nominal groups. It is impossible to consider these nominal groups as sentences in English.

Compare the Bengali equivalent of the above-mentioned two English expressions:

> (*ekṭi*) *notun phɔrāsi moṭor gaṛi* (*ti*)
> (one) new French car
> *gæreje* (*ekṭi*) *notun phɔrāsi moṭor gaṛi*(*ti*)
> in the garage (one) new French car

[12]Chatterjee, pp. 174-77.

Intuitively, a native speaker can relate the corresponding terms of *new* and *French* with *car*.

An article is not an obligatory element with a Bengali nominal expression. If the expression *one* is to be taken into account, syntactically it would be an attribute to *the car* which it would precede. The English example is a phrase, and in Bengali we may say in this particular example that the phrase and sentence coincide.

Although the other expression is described in the same fashion, *in the garage* is a separate unit; therefore, there are two phrases, which constitute either a sentence in Bengali (translation) or a phrase of a sentence.

In an English sentence like 'Wally kisses Sally' 'He met her', etc. one might think that one should posit reciprocal action of the verb. But this idea seems to be based on confusion between the event of the real world and the grammar.[13] Semantically, the initiative comes from *Wally* and *he* in respective sentences; syntactically, the pronominal form *her* signals its object function, also the position of *Sally* and *her* signal their object function. From the view point of sentence semantics, *Sally* and *her* are not more involved in the action that any other object, e.g. *the stone* in *I threw the stone*.

[4.7] Some verbs can be used both transitively and intransitively. For instance, a verb *ṭɔl-*, 'move':

intransitive use: *pāhāṛ ṭɔle*
the mountain moves

intransitive use with a cause nominal:
bʰumikɔmpe pāhāṛ ṭɔle
in earthquake the mountain moves

transitive causative use with an agent nominal:
bʰumikɔmpo pāhāṛ (-ke) ṭɔlāe
the earthquake the mountain cause to move

From the point of view of the origin and segmentability Bengali verbs can be classified mainly in two groups. Even though Prof. Chatterjee and N. Vidya Bhushan and others have classified them into three groups, we think the third group is basically considered as a variety of the second one.[14] Instead of saying simple, complex and compound, it can be said *simple* and *non-simple*.

Kale describes Sanskrit verbs mostly in terms of two, and we follow him: 'primitive' and 'derivative' are the two main classifications of the verbs. 'Primitive verbs or roots are those which originally exist in the language,

[13]Extra Linguistic fact influences the grammatical analysis.
[14]Chatterjee, pp. 134-38; Vidya Bhushan, pp. 63-67.

while derivative verbs are those which may be derived from a parent stock —a root or a noun.'[15]

It seems that both 'primitive' and 'derivatives' exist in the language.[16] The difference is that one may be called a simple verbal root, and the other may be called a complex verbal or non-verbal root. For instance:

(A) *Primitive roots which cannot be segmented further*

(*i*) cɔl- 'move'
bɔl- 'speak'
pɔṛ- 'read', 'fall'

(*ii*) From an onomatopoeia:
hãc, 'sneeze' = *hãc-e* 'he/she sneeze'

(B) *Derivative roots are those which can be segmented*:

(*i*) From a verb: cɔl+a = *cālā* 'cause to move'

(*ii*) Many nouns or adjectives can be used as verbs in combination with another verb such as *hɔ-* 'be', *kɔr-* 'do', *thāk-* 'live, stay', *pā-* 'get' etc.

ekmɔt 'agree' = *ækmɔt+hɔ* 'be agree'
lābʰ 'gain' = *lābh+kɔr* '(you) obtain'

(iii) This group has another variety: infinitive verb form combined with an auxiliary:
gāite-thāk 'go on singing'

B(*i*), (*ii*) and (*iii*) are to be considered as derivative. Nos. (*ii*), (*iii*) are compound in nature; the two morphemes having two independent meanings form a verb. The passive verbs in Bengali come under this class. It is derivative and compound in nature. For instance:

dʰɔr- 'hold', 'catch'
dhɔrā 'you fix it'/cause to catch (hold)
Passive *dhɔrā+pɔṛ* 'be captive', 'caught'

Generally the following points should be taken into consideration when verbs of any language are described:

(1) *Origin*
A. *Primitive*
(*i*) verb root
(*ii*) non-verbal root

[15]Kale, p. 239.
[16]Their primordial roots are found.

B. *Derivative*

(*i*) verbal root
(*ii*) non-verbal root

(2) *Tense* (*aspect*)

Present habitual (indefinite)
Present progressive (continuous)
Present perfect
Present imperative
Past indefinite
Past habitual
Past progressive (continuous)
Past perfect
Future simple
Future imperative

(3) *Mood*

Indicative
Subjunctive (with intention condition)[17] and obligation
Imperative (present is identical with the stem, future is identical with simple future partly)

(4) *Structure*

A (*i*), (*ii*): the structure is simple.
B (*i*), (*ii*): the structure is complex or compound (compound means an infinitive, a noun or adjective word used as verb in combination with another verb).

(5) *Construction and Voice*

In active construction any type of verb can occur. In passive and causative constructions verbs may be complex or compound.

The tense (aspect) and mood of a verb are expressed by means of inflexion in Bengali. Besides these Bengali verbs are conjugated by the use of personal markers. In addition to all these complexities, verbs can be either transitive or intransitive. Usually, verbs such as *hɔ* -'be' *thāk-* 'live', 'remain', *āch-*'exist' *ghɔṭ* 'happen', *ās-* 'come', *ja-* 'go', etc. are intransitive. Some can be used both as transitive and intransitive. Some verbs are considered to be potentially transitive. The transitive-intransitive uses of a verb are basically dependent on the (*i*) meaning of the verb, and on the (*ii*) environment of its occurrence in a given sentence. Thus, it seems that the transitive or intransitive meaning of a verb is understood on the basis of the total meaning of the sentence;

[17]Lyons, p. 308 (scale of attitude); Chatterjee, p. 146.

in other words, the sentence level analysis is valid in explaining the transitive-intransitive use of the verb.

The subject NU in active, passive and causative construction with any verb takes the same marker except in certain moods of the verb. Recall our example,

> *Jhunkā-ke jete hɔe*
> Jhunka has to go

(see appendix). The subject NU appears with *-ke* marker and the verb seems to be impersonal. Besides this, *-ke* marker occurs with provoked agent which is syntactically object:subject in a causative sentence.

The subject NU appears with *-ke* (*-r*, *-e*) marker (*i*) when combined with the obligatory mood of the verb, and (*ii*) when it occurs in a causative sentence. The subject NU appears with *-r* marker in singular and *-der* in plural with verbs such as *bʰālo lāgā* 'like'/*mondo-lāgā* 'dislike', etc. Otherwise a subject NU occurs with *ϕ* marker or other singular and plural markers which can indicate definiteness, etc.

Likewise, a predicate NU occurs with *ϕ* marker or (*i*) plural markers with or without *-ke*; (*ii*) singular marker with *-ke*; (*iii*) and other morphological as well as postpositional markers. Any nominal unit such as complement phrase to the verb, adverbial, any kind of manner or the type of semantic roles we set up such as object, instrument, locative, ablative, etc. function as predicate NU's. Keith Allan considers that 'complement noun phrases and prepositional phrases, adjectives and verb'[18]—all these function as predicators in English and in many languages as well.

It does not seem very significant to differentiate between a full verb such as *kɔr-* 'do', *bɔl-* 'speak', etc. and a verb such as *hɔ-* 'be' (is, am, are), *āch-* 'exist', etc. because we think that in a higher (sentence) level analysis a particular meaning of a lexical item cannot dominate the sentence meaning. Also we consider that the semantic and syntactic function of NU's and the transitive intransitive use of a verb are to be understood on the basis of sentence semantics which belongs to a higher level than word semantics level.

It may be interesting to consider the definition of sentence in terms of Indian traditional grammar. B.K. Matilal describes:

(*i*) Sentence or vākya may be initially defined as any word complex. In order to account for only those sentences which are accepted intuitively as both grammatical and meaningful, the definition has to be qualified by introducing such notion as competency (yogyatā) expectancy (ākāṅkṣā), and contiguity (āsatti).

[18]Keith Allan, 'Complement Noun Phrases and Prepositional Phrases, Adjectives and Verbs' in *Foundations of Language*, Vol. 10, No. 3, September 1973, p. 377.

(*ii*) For a sentence to be meaningful means that it can be understood by the hearer, which in its turn means, according to the Indian theorists, that it can generate a corresponding cognition in the hearer. Such a cognition called sabdabodha, can be represented by a paraphrase.

(*iii*) This cognition can only arise from a sentence which is syntactically well formed (as already suggested by the notion of ākānkṣā) i.e. in which the elements are interrelated in accordance with syntactic and inflexional rules.

(*iv*) The paraphrase which represents the sabdabodha can be analysed in terms of the qualificand-qualifier structure.

(*v*) The notion of sabdabodha thus explicated, may be taken to correspond with the notion of meaning of a sentence.[19]

It is noticeable that both semantic and syntactic criteria are effective in the definition of sentence. It has been said before that both syntactic and semantic criteria are effective for the idea of *pada* (phrase). Even though traditionally these two are defined in syntax, i.e. the *vākya* (sentence) and *pada*, the expanded noun phrase can also be explained in terms of *pada*. Therefore, we think that the subject noun phrase and the predicate noun phrase are to be understood in terms of semantics and syntax. Although word order is not fixed in the language under discussion, the syntactic device of inflexion and the sentence meaning adequately indicate the subject and predicate function of the nominal units which occur in NU, VU structure.

[4.8] There are more than one basic structure in Bengali sentences (in most Indian languages). There are more than two types of basic constructions, viz. active, passive and causative. These three types of constructions can be either in affirmative or negative and can either be interrogative or non-interrogative.

Normally affirmative and negative sentences occur in an even intonation, that is, the beginning and the ending remain on the same intonation level. But the usual pattern of an interrogative sentence end in high intonation. Also the negative and interrogative sentences are signalled by a negative morpheme and an interrogative morpheme respectively. For instance,

Affirmative, non-interrogative:
āmi jābo
I shall go

Negative, non-interrogative:
āmi jābo nā
I shall go not

[19]B.K. Matilal, 'Indian Theories on the Nature of the Sentence (Vākya)', *Foundations of Language*, No. 2 (1966), p. 393.

Interrogative, affirmative:

āmi ki jābo
I (interrogative morpheme) shall go
= shall (should) I go?

Interrogative, negative:

āmi ki jābo nā
I (interrogative morpheme) shall go no
= shall (should) I not go?

The interrogative morpheme may either occur before or after the verb. The negative morpheme usually occurs after the verb, normally in the final position. The morpheme *nā* can occur in non-final position, in such case the *nā* may not express the negative meaning. For instance:

āmi jābo nā ki
I shall go (?) interrogative

The *nā* can either be joined with the preceding verb and constitute a negative verb, or it can be joined with the following interrogative particle and constitute a unit with *ki*. It depends on the speaker or writer's intention, i.e. which of the above meanings is desired in a particular context. In the first case the sentence would be translated as: *I shall not go*? In the second case the sentence would be translated as: *Shall I go*?

Beside this, in some stylistic expressions or in relative sentence, the *nā* can occur in non-final position. For instance:

na kɔre, na kɔruk
not does, not let do
= If (he/she/they) do not wish

If he/she does (they do) not wish to do it, he/she does (they do) not have to do it.

jodi nā kɔre/nā korle, āmi ki korbo
if not does, not do (relative particle) I what shall do
= If (he/she/they) do not do, what can I do?
(How can I help?)

In final position the morpheme *nā* can express politeness. For instance;

āpni sedin asun nā
you that day come please
= Please you come on that day

or *nā* in final position of a sentence may be paraphrased in two sentences;

> *ami bolbo ki nā*
> I shall say if (or) not
> = Should I say (tell) or should I not?

[4.9] We have mentioned before that Bengali is a 'verb final language' like Hindi.[20] Normally, in most cases the subject precedes the verb, and it usually occurs in the initial position. Even though SOV is the usual pattern, the VU or the predicate NU can occur in the initial position (i.e. in S position), which may be due to emphasis, request, question, command. Sometimes the locative/ablative instrumental NU occur in that position, even though they can never be the subject of a Bengali sentence.

We have mentioned before that basic roles held by the NU's are few. We set six (subsets included). Note that there may be other expressions which can be called nominal expressions but which should not be considered as role units. In one way or other, this latter type of nominal expression may be indirectly connected either with the verb or with the whole sentence. They may be adverbials, modifiers to the subject or modifiers to the whole sentence.

[4.10] In a Bengali construction a simple sentence can contain more than one predicate NU. It contains only one finite verb[21] but there may be other non-finite verbal form(s).

For instance, consider a simple sentence containing eight arguments (NU's) in the predicate part which fulfil the requirements of noun phrase:

(*i*) *grisme, bɔrsae, site, hemonte, sɔrote*
in summer in rain in winter in dew in autumn
bɔsonte proti ritu poribɔrtone
in spring, in every season change
bivinno gɔromdese
in various tropical countries

(*ii*) *bicitro-d*^{h}*ɔroner phul phɔler gāch*
various kinds of flower and fruit plants

(*iii*) *jonmāe*
grow

The part (*i*) is containing predicate NU's, (*ii*) is the subject NU, (*iii*) is the verb. Consider another example:

[20] K.V. Subbarao, *Indian Linguistics*, Vol. 35, No. 5, September 1974, p. 174.
[21] Chatterjee, p. 304.

āmi jɔl-die ghɔr dhue
I with water (applying water) washing the floor (cleaning the floor)
phultulte bāgāne gelām
to pluck flower to the garden went
=I went to the garden to pluck (collect)
flowers after cleanin g (washing) the floor with water

In English there occurs a relative clause. In Bengali (above-mentioned) constructions there are no relative clauses, but one can get two sentences out of the one mentioned if the non-finite verb form (*dhue*) is being separated and given the status of a finite verb.

CONCLUSION

THE ANALYSIS of Bengali noun phrases has concerned both the expression side and the function side. It has been attempted to restrict this investigation to the levels of syntax and semantics, although morphological markers have had to be included.

It is felt that aspects of the noun phrase such as functions and focus can be adequately dealt with in the framework of the traditional Indian theory. Sentence-level semantics seems crucial in identifying the roles of noun phrases. In our analysis the range of theoretical and descriptive ideas is mapped out. We tried to give an account of the traditional explanation for some aspects of Indian languages, in particular, Bengali.

Examples are collected from different sources and some examples are constructed by the present author. Our results concern:

(*a*) Different types of markers on the noun phrase;
(*b*) Roles of noun phrases; and
(*c*) The four voices of the verb which focus four types of subject noun phrase.

Not all basic roles can occur as the subject of a Bengali construction.

The voice category is mainly defined in terms of the subject focusing by the verb.

It has been suggested that all kinds of words occurring as a separate syntactic unit in a sentence can be given phrase status. The term phrase is considered to correspond to the term *pada* (item with or without inflexion) but not in its extended form. The term sentence corresponds to the term *vākya*.

A sentence outer may be an adjective or an adverbial expression consisting of one word. An indeclinable word may be a single phrase in a sentence, and this phrase cannot necessarily be expanded.

English has discontinuous verb phrases. Bengali, on the other hand, has discontinuous noun phrases.

The following are those of our more general conclusions which are believed to be of interest:

(1) It is suggested that roles are to be established on the semantic axis of the noun and verb relation. More specifically the involvement is based on *sentence semantics*. We believe that the sentence outer, the NU expressing distance, duration, degree of comparison, etc. should not be considered as having the same type of relation to the verbal syntagm as roles such as

agent, object, instrument, etc. Consequently, they are not considered as roles.

(2) The verbs of a language can be classified in a simplified manner as full verbs, *be*-verbs and intransitive or transitive verbs. The semantic features of the nominals may not be taken into account when labelling roles to the NU(s). Only in this way can one establish a reasonably limited number of roles in a language. Thus, it is claimed that a 'cut-off point' in labelling roles to the NU(s) can be achieved.

(3) It is felt (p. 145-58, 249-50) that additional terms are required to label different types of noun phrases which have different relations or involvement with the verb: the *provoked agent*, the *independent factor subject*, and the *theme subject*, (we believe that the term *independent factor* is more appropriate than the term *neutral*).

Although in this study a sentence without a verb is not dealt with in detail, it is found that the dominant noun phrase in this type of construction can also be labelled as *independent factor*.

(4) We cannot see why one sentence structure should be derived from another. However, two structures can have a kind of semantic and syntactic affiliation. Any hypothetical underlying structure seems here to be inappropriate and is often based on the confusion of the grammar and the real world. A language expression certainly refers to the real world. But extra linguistic fact such as cultural conditioning often is the cause of confusion in grammatical analysis which is supposed to be abstract. Following the Indian tradition we understand that a grammar should directly describe the language and not the real world event.

(5) There are many sentences in many languages where either the subject or the predicate part does not occur. In such cases neither a ϕ-verb nor a ϕ-subject seems necessary. However, if deep structures are established in an arbitrary way, NP VP sentences can certainly be postulated everywhere, but this does not mean that they really exist in all languages.

(6) In addition to the subject-predicate sentences, a given language may have several other kinds of sentence structures: NP, VP and NPVP when the NP of this latter structure is not a subject NP.

It is suggested that, in cases where the subject predicate labels are not relevant, either the nominal or the verbal unit (as the case may be) should be considered as having sentence building function. In cases where a sentence has more than one NU, the subject and the predicate can be identified through the following criteria:

(*i*) By position in many languages;

(*ii*) By the device of concord and agreement between the subject NU and the VU;

(*iii*) In some cases the interpretation of the whole sentence (sentence semantics) provides the subject and predicate relation of the NU(s).

(7) The ergative and causative transformations are unacceptable if one assumes that transformations should 'not change the meaning'. It is certain that ergative and causative both change the meaning quite considerably.

(8) Ambiguity is not just two meanings of an expression. If it is a written expression one might think that items are similar, even though two meanings depend on two different readings of the expressions having the same orthographic shape. When the so-called ambiguous sentence is spoken, the prosodic feature differences are often very clear. If so, the alleged homophony is just a mistaken assumption. Also the context can disambiguate the ambiguity of a sentence.

(9) There is no sharp line between syntax and semantics.

(10) In our investigation we have preferred the multidimensional approach of traditional grammar to the undirectional approach of the modern generative-transformational approach. By multidimentional approach we mean that facts of languages are basically to be described at four levels: semantics, syntax, morphology and phonetics. These levels are connected and interrelated. One can start with one level and give a detailed description of that level. However, facts at one level are often 'conditioned' by facts from the others, and the description 'will have to have many cross references'. It must also be admitted that at a higher level description of syntax and semantics very little morphology and no phonetics are involved.

We assume that the basic description should be 'neutral', i.e. it does not describe explicitly the activity of a speakar or a hearer. However

'A neutral basic description would presumably describe the language that an individual uses both when speaking (or writing) and when understanding spoken text (or reading). It should not be denied that one can imagine a 'deep structure' that would be universal in relation to all languages. Every language could be transformed into this universal system and each language could be derived from it in a specific way. This would be an economic procedure in machine translation as soon as several languages are involved. This problem is however, marginal in linguistics. One might think that it is outside linguistics if linguistics is thought to be the study of normal, natural language.[1]

We are of the opinion that, whatever representation of syntax and semantics may be adopted by the linguist it is his responsibility to make it believable that the rules he establishes are of the kind that is used by speakers in natural communication and which seems natural and intuitively acceptable.

[1]See Hammarstrom, 1972, Preface.

However, we may conclude the present work with the expectation that our description and discussion will revitalize the analysis and understanding of some theoretical assumptions in Linguistics. We also hope that the semantic syntactic explanation given in the *kāraka vācya*, *pada* configuration and the structural characteristic of Bengali language presented in this study would be of some interest to scholars researching languages other than English.

APPENDIX ONE

NOMINALS WITH DIFFERENT MARKERS

In the following are the examples of Nominals with different markers. They have been collected at random from a children's magazine SANDESH (Vo. 5, April 1972)

(1) *N+O*

1.	(āmi ækbār tākiei) *cokh* bũje-phellām '(having had a look) I closed my eyes'	p. 325, line 9, col. 2
2.	(dādur) *nāk* ḍākche '(grandfather's) nose was snoring'	p. 326, line 19, col. 2
3.	(bāṛir sāmnepraei) *gāṛi* dāṛie thākto '(in the front of the house often) a car used to stand'	p. 324, line 23, col. 1
4.	(dunɔ, mbore) thākten *ḍāktārohārā* '(in no. 2 apartment) lived Dr. Ohara' —Dr. Ohara used to live in no. 2 apartment	p. 324, line 30, col. 1
5.	(ɔgottā bāddho hoe) *dārogā* uṭhlo '(being compelled) the police officer stood up'	p. 322, line 11, col. 2
6.	(māndāloe sṭimār thāmte) *mɔŋ* nāmlo '(as soon as the steamer stopped at Mandalay) Mong got down'	p. 322, line 26, col. 2
7.	(noile je) *buṛo* noṛbe nā '(otherwise) the old fellow will not move'	p. 322, line 11, col. 2
8.	(ætoṭuku) *kritɔgõtā-bodh* nei (loktar) '(a little) there is no sense of gratitude (of the man)'	p. 319, line 4, col. 1
9.	bɔṛobɔṛo *gāch* gojieche (carpase) 'big tree(s) have grown up (all around)'	p. 319, line 9, col. 1
10.	(tār) *driṣtisokti* bes kome gæche '(his) eyesight much has fallen' =his eyesight is not good (not like that as it was before)	p. 319, line 19, col. 1
11.	(kāche kono) *boṛopāhāṛ* nei '(near about/nearby any) there is no big rock'	p. 319, line 23, col. 1
12.	(uttejɔnāe) dhɔkdhɔk kore uṭhlo (tār) *hridpinḍo* '(in excitement) terribly heated (his) heart'=his heart began to beat terribly in excitement	p. 320, line 4, col. 1
13.	ṭukṭuke lāl sɔccho *pāthor* 'very red transparent stone (copula omitted)'=the very red transparent stone	p. 320, line 5, col. 1
14.	prithibir śerā *moni* (no copula) 'of the world best gem' = the best gem of the world	p. 320, line 6, col. 1
15.	oti durlob^{h} *bostu* 'a very rare material' (no copula) = it is a very rare material	p. 320, line 7, col. 1
16.	mɔŋer sɔŋkhipto *jɔbāb* (no copula) 'of Mong precise answer'=that was the precise answer of Mong	p. 320, line 24, col. 2

17. *tumi* jācāi korte pāro — p. 321, line 5, col. 1
'you can testify'

18. *māthār ṭhik* chilonā (āmār) — p. 321, line 13, col. 1
'of the head sense there is not (mine)' =I had no sense/I was off my head

19. **sɔrbonās*[1] hoegælo (bæbosār) — p. 321, line 15, col. 1
'failure occurred (to the business)' = I have failed in my business/my business failed

20. (ækhon) *ki* kɔrājāe — p. 321, line 24, col. 1
'(now) what is to be done'

21. (na) *khide* nei — p. 321, line 25, col. 1
'(no) appetite have no'=there is no appetite/I have no appetite

22. *keu* jāne nā — p. 321, line 34, col. 1
'anybody knows nothing'=no-one knows

23. (tāke dekhe) *sɔbāi* hɔtobhɔmbo — p. 321, line 35, col. 1
'(seeing him) everybody (all) astonished' (no coupla)

24. usko khusko *cehārā* (no copula) — p. 321, line 36, col. 1
'untidy appearance'=he was looking untidy

25. *cokh* lāl (no copula) — p. 321, line 36, col. 1
'eyes red'= his eyes were red

26. (hāte) mosto dhārālo *kāṭāri* — p. 321, line 37, col. 1
'(in hand) big sharp knife' =a big sharp knife in hand/There was a big sharp knife in his hand (no copula)

27. ki *bæpār* (no copula) — p. 321, line 38, col. 1
'what matter' = what is the matter?

28. lɔmbā lɔmbā segun *gāch* (no copula) — p. 319, line 24, col. 1
'tall tall teak wood tree(s)' = there were tall (teak wood) trees

29. kothāo bā kālce koṭhin grānāiṭer *ḍhipi* — p. 319, line 26, col. 1
'somewhere, blackish solid granite rock' = there was blackish solid granite rock

30. prāe tiris phuṭ gobhir *khād* (no copula) — p. 319, line 32, col. 1
'about thirty feet deep ditch'=there was a ditch which was about thirty feet deep

31. *bʰāggo* phereni — p. 318, line 1, col. 1
'fortune did not appear (come)'=he was not lucky/he could not make fortune

32. (pher) *ɔbhāb* dækhā dieche — p. 318, line 1, col. 1
'(again) scarcity has felt (has come)'

33. (kintu buṛo bɔyese) hāṛbhāŋā khāṭuni ar sorire sɔenā — p. 318, line 32, col. 2
'(but in this age) hard labour is not tolerated by the body'

34. *kɔmpāni* bɔndho hoegælo (bɔchor dɔsek pɔre) — p. 318, line 35, col. 1
'the company was closed (after ten years)'

35. (puronodiner sei) *chobi* mone bhāse , — p. 318, line 4, col. 2
'(of old days that) picture in the mind comes'

36. ebār *bɔrsā* bujhi kāṭena — p. 318, line 11, col. 1
'this year rain seems would not go'

[1] *S* represents palatal sound except in cluster (unless otherwise indicated).

37. cārmuṭho *cāl* ɔboṣiṣṭo āche — p. 318, line 26, col. 2
'handful of rice remains left'

38. oportheke ækphāli *rod* esepoṛeche — p. 319, line 36, col. 1
'from the up a flash of sunlight has fallen'=a flash of sunlight has fallen from the sky

39. cinte sekho pāthorer *jāt* — p. 318, line 29, col. 1
'learn the quality of the stone'=you should know the quality of the stone

40. prānānto *porisrom* kɔrā (no copula) — p. 318, line 2, col. 2
'serious labour to do'

41. krɔme *nesā* dhoreche — p. 318, line 25, col. 1
'gradually addiction occurs' =gradually became addict

42. **boi** poṛchi
'book reading'=I am reading a book

43. *jɔl** dhɔro
'water fetch'=fetch the water

(2) *N*+*ṭā*

44. *māchṭā* kisundor chilo — p. 326, line 23, col. 1
'the fish how good was'=how tasty was the fish

45. æmonki *ghoṛāṭāo* ɔggæn hoegiechilo — p. 326, line 30, col. 1
'even the horse became fainted'

46. dekhiki kālker sei *lokṭā* — p. 326, line 27, col. 2
'what (I) saw, yesterday's that man'
=what (I) saw, that man, whom I saw yesterday

47. *khɔborṭā* roṭe gæche — p. 321, line 22, col. 1
'the news has spread'

48. *bæpārṭā* ɔcirei jānā gælo — p. 321, line 38, col. 1
'the matter soon disclosed'
=the matter was known quickly

49. *sāmnerṭā** khāli (no copula)
'the front one (is) vacant'

50. *āmārṭa* purono (no copula)
'mine one (is) old'

(3) *N*+*ṭi*

51. *kɔldoel sɔhorti* bʰāri sundor kholā mælā (no copula) — p. 342, line 12, col. 1
'the Coldoel city (is) very beautiful and open'

52. *hā̃siṭi** bɔṛo misṭi (no copula)
'the smile (is) very sweet'

53. '*cheleti** bʰalo (no copula)
'the boy (is) good'

54. 'tar *monṭi** bɔṛo sādā (no copula)
'his mind (is) very clear'

* indicates examples taken from author's own dialect,

(4) *N+khānā*

55. '*bʰabkhānā** bʰalo nɔe
'the attitude is not good' (the negative
element incorporates copula)
56. '*kāpoṛkhānā** khub dāmi (no copula)
'the cloth (is) very costly' expensive

(5) *N+khāni*

57. *mōlākhāni* cɔmotkar hoeche
'the garland looks very beautiful'

(6) *N+gachi*

58. *hārgachti*'* notun (no copula)
'the chain (is) new'

(7) *N+rā*

59. *orā* pā̃cṭāe cole elo... p. 312, line 15, col. 1
'they at five o'clock came'
=they came at five o'clock
60. odeser hipi *chelemeyerā* eije dɔledɔle āsche... p. 325, line 10, col. 2
'of the other country the hipi boys and girls are
coming group by group in such way'...

(8) *N+gulo*

61. *pāthorgulo* bhāŋte hɔbe p. 319, line 33, col. 1
'these stones should be broken'
62. *kāṛāgulo* duṣṭu āche p. 310, line 29, col. 1
'the buffalos are naughty'
63. bechebeche *pākākulgulo* pāṛlām p. 310, line 12, col. 1
'carefully ripe plums picked up'
=I picked up the ripe plums carefully

(9) *N+der*

64. *tāder* sikkʰā ei rɔkom p. 324, line 13, col. 2
'their education (training) (is) like that' (no copula)

(10) *N+er/r*

65. *goru bʰæṛār cāṣ* khub besi (no copula) p. 323, line 18, col. 2
'cow and sheep breeding very much'
=they do cow and sheep breeding
66. ekhāne *duṣṭu loker* ɔbhāb nei p. 321, line 27, col. 1
'here bad fellows are not scarce'
=there is no lack of bad fellows here

67. *cunir* kintu kono hodis millonā 'of the ruby but any trace was not' =there was no trace of the ruby/the ruby was not found out p. 321, line 18, col. 2

68. *māer** āche
'mother has got it'

69. *āmār** lāglo
'to me pain'=I feel pain/I am hurt/it wound me

(11) *N+te*

70. *tomāte āmāte* korbo
'you and I will accomplish' (you and me)

71. *churite** keṭeche
'knife has cut (by knife cut)' =it is cut by the knife

72. *gāṛite** jeo
'by car go'=you go by car

73. *boite** āche
'in the book exists=it is written in the book

74. *soktite** kulāe na
'in capacity cannot be done'=it is beyond the capacity

(12) *N+e*

75. *cokhe* dekhi
'through the eyes (we) see'

76. *kolkātāe** thāke
'at Calcutta (he) lives'

77. *bhāie bhāie** culoculi (no copula)
'among the brothers quarrel'
=a dispute occurs among the brothers

78. *kāne** suni
'by ear (we) hear'

79. *pāe** coli
'with feet (we) walk'

80. *eibhābe dese** phirlām
'in this manner to the country return'
(came back)=I came back to the country in this way

81. *māse māse** agām dii
'every month (I) pay in advance'

82. *bikāle** khelo
'in the afternoon play (you)'
=you play in the afternoon

83. *mone** āche
'in mind exists'=remember

84. *poṛāsunāe** bhalo (no copula)
'in study good'=he is good in study

85. *muskile** poṛechi
'in difficulty here fallen (I)'=I am in trouble

86. *ānonde** geechi
'in pleasure sang (I) (in joy)'=I sang in pleasure

87. *tār sāhitye** khub ɔnurāg (no copula)
'his in literature very interest'
=he has much interest in literature

88. *porjɔṭone** beriepɔrā
'for visit to come out' (no copula)=to be out for a travel

89. tār *sukhe-dukhe** sɔmobhāb (no copula)
'his in worries and ease same feeling'
=he does not move either in sorrow or in happiness

(13) *N+ke*

90. (bāddho hoe ābār hɔeto) *tāke mojuri* khāṭṭe hɔbe ('being compelled again, perhaps) he has to work in daily wages' p. 318, line 18, col. 2

91. *jhunkāke* jete hɔe
'Jhunka has to go' p. 310, line 39, col. 2

92. *ḍāktārke** ḍāko
'the doctor call'=call, the doctor

93. *oke** de
'him give'=give it to him

94. *nijeke** bojhāi
'myself pacify'=I pacify myself

95. *bāccuke* eki jɔntronāe phele gælo Jhunkā
'Jhunka has put Bacchu in such a pain' p. 311, line 2, col. 1

96. *tākei* uṭhe cā korte hɔbe
'(him/her) he/she has to make tea' p. 315, line 25, col. 2

97. (....) runur monṭāke pāthor kore dieche
'Runur's mind became hard' p. 316, line 10, col. 1

98. jenechen ār jāniechen *āphrikāke*
'(he) knew and made known Africa' p. 332, line 24, col. 1

99. bā̃dor mā...*Chānāke* khõje
'the mother monkey the little one searches'
=the mother monkey searches the little one p. 330, line 1, col. 2

100. *churiṭāke* bā̃hāte rākhlam
'the knife in left hand (I) kept'
=(I) kept the knife in my left hand p. 331, line 5, col. 1

From the above examples it seems clear that the nouns in Bengali take different suffixes. Some of them indicate plurality, singularity, definiteness; and in some there is no indication as such.

Markers such as *ke*, *-te*, *-e*, *-er/r* in particular together with the *ra*, *der*, *ta*, etc. indicate some other functions of the noun (different than singularity, plurality or definiteness, etc.),

It is also observed that there is no restriction of occurring of any such markers with animate, inanimate, abstract nouns. However, there is a constraint with plural markers and definite markers.

Beside these thirteen types of morphological markers there occur postpositional markers.

APPENDIX TWO

NOMINALS WITH POSTPOSITIONAL MARKERS

Below are examples of postpositional markers on the nominals collected from the Bengali literary magazine DESH *children's magazines* SANDESH *and* KISHOR BHARATI, and Bengali daily newspaper ANANDA BAZAR PRTRIKA.

(1) *N+theke*

		Ananda Bazar Patrika,
1.	*mājh khān theke* nitis-i kɔthā utthāpon korechilo 'in the meantime Nitish (himself) conversation (word) started' =In the meantime Nitish started talking	March 19, 1961 p. 3, line 56, col. 1
2.	*dādārhāttheke* gelās ulṭeche 'from the hand of elder brother (a) glass was spilled' =a glass (of water) was spilled by the hand of the elder brother	p. 3, line 90, col. 1
3.	*jā ekhān theke*, birokto korisne 'go here from disturbance do not do' =do not (disturb) vex (me), go away from here	p. 3, line 18, col. 2
4.	*ālok tɔroŋgo thekei* āmāder...roŋer dhāronā jɔnmae 'light wave from our colour consciousness develops' =our colour consciousness develops from the light waves	p. c, line 40, col. 1
5.	*ditioṭa-theke* prothomṭā biogkore āmrāpāi...kolor indeks 'second from first distracting we get colour index' =distracting the first from the second we get....a colour index	p. c, line 61, col. 3
6.	ei toṛit probāher *sokti thekei...* 'this lightning wave power from' =from the power of the lightning wave...	p. c, line 88, col. 3
7.	kintu *tārāgulo theke...* 'but stars from'....=but from the stars....	p. c, line 92, col. 3
8.	*tārāder rɔŋ-thekei*, sthir korte pāri 'of stars colour from decide can' =(we) can decide from the colour of the stars	p. c, line 29, col. 4
9.	*tārāder bɔrnāli-theke...* (of) stars flow from'=from the glow of the stars	p. c, line 30, col. 4
10.	ei sokti ase *tārāder phɔṭosphiārertāptheke* 'this power comes of stars photosphere's heat from' =this power comes from the heat of the photosphere of the stars	p. c, line 58, col. 4
11.	*tā-thekei* āmrā ... 'that from we'=from that we...	p. c, line 140, col. 4
12.	*ɔdhyapɔk hæmpḍener kāch-theke...* 'professor Hampden from'=from Prof. Hampden...	p. c, line 6, col. 5

13. mānuser gæn-i ækdin tāke *sɔŋskārtheke* mukto korte pāre 'man's knowledge one day him prejudice from free can make' =one day man will be free from prejudice by his knowledge	p. c, line 27, col. 5
14. *lāunjer kɔridor theke...* 'lounge corridor from'=from the corridor of the lounge...	p. c, line 33, col. 5
15. *...prithibir itihas theke* gælo 'world history from gone (wiped out)' =it is removed from the history of the world	p. c, line 51, col. 5
16. ār *sɔmādhisthɔl-theke..* 'and graveyeard from'=and from the grave...	p.c., line 77, col. 7
17. tārsɔmostoi jānlām *mritohuḍsɔner ḍāiri theke* 'his all about knew dead Hudson's diary from'=I knew all about him from the diary of the dead Hudson.	p.c., line 19, col. 8
18. *rāsel-theke* oi pātār-rɔs nie āsen 'Rassell from that leaf juice brought (he)'=he collected the juice out of that leaf from Russell (place name)	p.c., line 30, col. 8
19. *ghɔrer bāire theke...* 'room outside from'=from the outside of the room	p.c., line 34, col. 8
20. *āmāder prithibi-theke...* 'our earth from'=from our earth	Kishor Barati, October ,1972 p. 242, line 15, col. 1
21. ..ta *er-theke* bojhā jetepāre 'that this-from understand can' =that could be understood from this...	p. 242, line 18, col. 1
22. ei chāyā-poth *dokk^{h}in-ākās-theke* arɔmbhokore... 'the milky-way southern sky from beginning'=...the milky way beginning from the southern sky...	p. 242, line 33, col. 1
23. *oi jāegā-theke..* 'that place from'=from that place...	p. 242, line 1, col. 2
24. *ei ghār-theke...* 'from this shoulder'	p. 242, line 17, col. 2
25. *oi sophius nɔkk^{h}ɔttro-theke...* 'that sophius star from'=from the Sophius star...	p. 242, line 18, col. 2
26. *birāṭ puruser nāb^{h}ikɔmol-theke ɔrthāt* beṭelg *tārār kāch-theke* 'great[1] man's navel area from that is Betelg star from'=from the great figure's navel, i.e. from the Betelg star	p. 242, line 30, col. 2
27. *ei ɔbosthā-thekei* 'this condition from'=from this condition	p. 242, line 36, col. 2

[1]Betelgeuse/Betelgeux.

28. *chelebælā-theke* sune āschi 'childhood from are told'=since childhood we have been told — p. 244, line 1, col. 1

29. *pāṛ-theke* nodi ācomkā prāe kuṛi phuṭ neme gæche 'bank-from river suddenly about twenty foot slope'=the river suddenly rushes down about twenty feet at the bottom of the bank — p. 246, line 16, col. 2

30. *rākhāler-kāch-theke* āmrā ā̃c peechilām 'Rakhal-from we guessed'=we guessed from Rakhal — p. 247, line 6, col. 1

31. *ɔndhokār bāgān-theke*.. 'dark garden from'=out of the dark garden... — p. 250, line 25, col. 1

32. *gāṛitheke* neme pālāte 'vehicle from get down to flee' =to get down from the vehicle and flee — p. 260, line 40, col. 1

33. biplobira *jānlā-theke* ũkimere dekhtepelen 'revolutionaries window-from peeping saw'=the revolutionaries peeping through the window, saw — p. 260, line 6, col. 2

34. *ɔnusɔronkārider hāt-theke* tobuo tā̃ra rehāi pān ni 'pursuers hand from still they could not get rid of' = they still could not (get rid) escape from their pursuers — p. 261, line 2, col. 1

35. ..*tār hāt-theke* bonduk kere nie... 'his hand from the gun snatch'=having snatched the gun from his hand — p. 261, line 6, col. 1

36. *sekhān theke* sese lukie kolkatae asen 'there-from at last in disguise at Calcutta came'=from that place they came at last to Calcutta in disguise — p. 261, line 27, col. 1

37. *oi bāṛir-jānlā theke lāphie*.. 'that house window-from jumping' =jumping out of the window of that house — p. 261, line 14, col. 2

38. āgneogirirmoto *gɔnesghoser mukh-theke* 'volcano like Ganesh Ghose's mouth-from' =Ganesh Ghose's speech (was) like a volcano eruption — p. 265, line 18, col. 2

39. *er-theke* mukto hotehɔbe 'this from free would be' =(we) must be free from this — p. 268, line 8, col. 2

40. tā *āj-theke* ṭhik dumaser-moddhe ses korte hɔbe 'that today from just two months within finish to be'=that must be finished within two months from today (has to be finished) — p. 268, line 10. col. 2

41.	*ciṭhitheke jā jānā gælo...* 'letter from what known was' =what was known from the letter (which)	Sandesh, May-June 1972 p. 4, line 12
42.	*tā̃r bāṛi-theke* berie colejān 'his house from being out went away' =he went away from his house	p. 4, line 14,
43.	*tārpɔr-theke* tār ārkono khõj pāoājāeni 'after from his again any notice could not be get'=since that time his whereabouts have not been known	p. 4, line 12
44.	ciṭhiṭā sāmārvil likheche *irākliɔn-theke* 'letter that Samarvil has written Iraklian-from'=Samarvil has written the letter from Iraklian	p.4, line 22
45.	eibhāsā nie ḍimetrias naki *beskichudin-theke* cɔrcākorchen 'this language with Dimetrias possibly sometimes from have been working'=possibly Dimetrias have been working on that language for some time	p. 5, line 25, col. 1
46.	hɔeto eikhātāe pracin *silālipi-theke...* 'perhaps this notebook in old stone inscription from'=perhaps in this notebook (there is some important information) from an old inscription...	p. 5, line 26, col. 1
47.	sekhāne pā̃c sāt din kore *theke*[1] 'there five seven day being staying'=having stayed there for five or seven days	p. 5, line 29, col. 1
48.	seṭā āse *pichoner pāhāṛer dik-theke* 'that came behind mountainside from' =that came from the mountainside, which was behind (the camp)	p.5, line 34, col. 1
49.	se dupurbælā *jɔŋgoler dik-theke* bagher gɔrjon sunechilo 'he at noon forest side from howling of the tiger heard'=he heard the howling of the tiger from the forest at noon time	p. 5, line 2, col. 2
50.	*ɔtodur-theke* se gɔndho pābenā jāni 'so far-from he smell could not get, I know'=I know that he could not smell from such a distance away	p. 5, line 19, col. 2
51.	prosnoṭā *āpnā-thekei* āmār *mukhdie*[2] berie gælo the question spontaneously my mouth from came out'=spontaneously[3] uttered the question	p. 5, line 35, col. 2
52.	kāero jābār kāronṭā *e-theke* poriskār hoeche 'Cairo going cause that this from clear'=from this (his) reason for going to Cairo is clear	p. 6, line 5, col. 2

[1]Homophonous morpheme here is used as an independent word rather than a bound morpheme like postposition.

[2]This can be taken as an example for $N+die$. It can be translated as 'through, from, out of', etc.

[3]The homophonous morpheme is a verb with participle.

53. gɔto ægārodin ɔnekei e-ghɔre *theke*-gæche- p. 6, line 15, col. 2
'last eleven days many in this room lived'=in the past eleven days many people have stayed in this room.

54. *ekhān-theke* uni... p. 6, line 37, col. 2
'here from he'=from here he...

55. *rumbɔer kāch theke* p. 7, line 2, col. 1
'room boy from'=from the room boy

56. ei banij-jo cole-āsche ækebāre *ād-dikal-theke* p. 7, line 13, col. 2
'this trade has been going since ancient time from'=this trade has been going on since ancient times

57. pɔthe āsār somɔe *jhop ghāṛer bʰitor-theke* p. 8, line 9, col. 1
'on the way coming time (bush) wood inside from'=on our way (while we were coming) from the woods

58. *se-dik-theke...* p. 8, line 23, col. 1
'that side from'=from that side...

59. āoājṭā mone hɔe *māṭirtɔlā-theke* āsche p. 8, line 40, col. 1
'sound that seems ground bottom from is coming'=it seems that the sound is coming from the bottom of the earth

60. *ājbhor chɔṭā theke* sāṛe āṭṭā porjonto... p. 8, line 24, col. 2
'today morning 6 o'clock half past eight till'=this morning from 6 o'clock till eight thirty...

61. ei uṭālā ārekṭi *kærāvæn-theke...* p. 8, line 42, col. 2
'this camel driver another caravan from'=this camel driver from another caravan...

62. *āpnā-thekei* moreche ki p. 8, line 43, col. 2
'naturally dead is it'=is it a natural death?

63. *sokunirdɔl-theke* dɔshat dure... p. 9, line 2, col. 1
'vultures from ten cubit distance'=about five yards away from the flock of vultures

64. *uṭ-theke* neme... p. 9, line 3, col. 1
'camel from getting down'
=getting down from the camel

65. *āmrā ḍhipiṭār-theke* p. 9, line 30, col. 1
'we mound from'=from the mound we...

66. *tā̃bu-theke...* p. 10, line 18, col. 1
'tent-from'=from the tent...

67. *dur-theke* dekhle p. 10, line 26, col. 1
'distance-from to see'
=if you see from the distance

68. *cuṛo-theke* poscim-dike p. 10, line 27, col. 1
'summit from western side'
=from the western side of the summit

69. *bāli-theke* jebhābe jinisṭā beriechilo p. 10, line 1, col. 2
'sand from in that manner that thing was visible'=the thing was visible (in that manner) in the sand

70. (āmi) *ājtheke* tin diner moddhe — p. 14, line 9, col. 1
'(I) today-from three-day within'
=within the next three days

71. phebruāri māser mājha-mājhi *ileksɔn ɔphis-theke* ciṭhi elo — p. 18, line 6, col. 1
'February month middle election office from letter came'
=by the middle of February the letter came from the election office

72. conḍibābu *āmāke-nie*[4]...kolkātāe *theke-gelen*[5] — p. 15, line 20, col. 1
'Chandibabu (proper name) me-with in Calcutta remained'
=Chandibabu stayed with me in Calcutta.

73. *bɔṛo-rāsta-theke* kichu bhetorer dike — p. 19, line 5, col. 1
nurmɔhɔl cinema hɔl (no copula)
'main street-from a little inside Nurmahal cinema hall'
=a short distance in from the main street is the Nurmahal cinema hall

74. stri bodripākhi sādhārɔnɔto *pā̃c-chɔmās bɔyes-theke* ḍim pāṛte surukɔre — p. 24, line 25, col. 2
'female budgie bird generally five to six months age from egg lay began'=the female budgie generally starts laying eggs from the age of five to six months

75. *nirākārpur sṭesɔner kāch theke* purboghāṭ pāhāṛer sār suru — p. 36, line 4, col. 1
'Nirakarpur station from eastern ghat mountain ranges begin'
=at the Nirakarpur (railway) station the eastern Ghat mountain ranges begin

76. *cārpās-theke* jāegāṭi nicukinā (no copula) — p. 36, line 24, col. 1
'four sides from that place hollow whether or not'
=whether the place is lower than the other sides or not

Ananda Bazar Patrika January 3, 1962

77. *kompānir lābʰer-theke* — p. 9, line 11, col. 3
'company's profit-from'
=from the profit of the company

78. hæ *mænejiŋ ejenṭ- theke*[6] tɔphāt kothāe kothāe tāi boli — p. 9, line 27, col. 3
'yes managing agent-from different where that I say'
=yes, now I shall point out where this is different from managing agent

79. *obʰiggõ mænejiŋ ejenṭder*[7] *sāhājyo-theke* boncito holo — p. 9, line 54, col. 3
'experienced managing agent's help-from deprived'
=they are deprived of the help of the experienced managing agent

80. *prostābito bæe-er poriman* 87 *koṭiṭākā-theke*[8] — p. 9, line 95, col. 2
'proposed expenditure's quantity 87 crore rupees from'
=of the proposed expenditure of 870 mill. rupees

[4]It is an example of *N+nie.*

[5]The homophonous morpheme is a verb in participial form.

[6]It is interesting to note that the suffix *theke* is used with a loan word to indicate the function of the nominal.

[7]The plural marker *-der* is used with a loan word. The whole underlined unit can be taken as a noun phrase.

[8]The long underlined portion can be taken as a noun phrase.

81. khāddo drobyoke *bikrɔe-kɔr-theke* ɔbyāhɔti diechen — p. 9, line 99, col. 2
'foodstuffs sale tax-from exempted'
=some foods are exempted from sales tax

82. ...*du-tɔrphākɔr-theke*... — p. 9, line 102, col. 2
'double duty from'
=(exempted) from the double duty...

83. ...*misɔr-theke*... — p. 9, line 98, col. 3
'Egypt-from'=from Egypt...

84. *gɔto ɔgɔsṭ mās-theke* — p. 9, line 110, col. 3
'last August month from'
=since last August

85. *sɔb rɔkomer sujog subidhā-theke* bɔncito chilo — p. 9, line 7, col. 4
'all kinds of privileges-from were deprived'
=they were deprived of all kinds of privileges and advantages

86. *bɔlobɔnto rāo meṭā kɔmiṭir ripoṭ-theke*... — p. 9, line 24, col. 6.
'Balabanto Rao Meta Committee's report from'
=from the report of the Balabant Rao Meta Committee...

87. ...*sedinkar-mojuri-theke* — p. 9, line 41, col. 6
'of that day wages from'
=from the wages of the day...

88. srɔmdāner poribɔrte *grām-theke* āhārjer-sɔŋsthān kɔrā prɔojɔn (no copula) — p. 9, line 46, col. 6
'labour in exchange village from food arrangement to do necessary'
=it is necessary to arrange food (for the labourers) in exchange of their labour.

89. iŋlænḍer sresṭhotto *bohukāl-theke* sikrito (no copula) — p. 8, line 2, col. 1
'of England superiority longtime from admitted'
=the superiority of England is admitted for (since) a long time

90. *sær henri arbʰiŋ o mises siḍan-theke* suru kore — p. 8, line 8, col. 1
'Sir Henry Arving and Mrs. Sidan from beginning'
=beginning from Sir Henry Arving and Mrs. Sidan...

91. tɔbe tar khɔroeer porimān *pā̃c-theke*[9] dɔsgun beṛe jāe — p. 8, line 39, col. 2
'but its expenditure's quantity five from ten times increases'
=but (then) its expenditure increases from five to ten times

92. gɔṛe tæroti nāṭṭosālā *probes muller āetheke bẽce-āche* — p. 8, line 52, col. 2
'on an average thirteen theatres box-office collection from survive'
=on an average thirteen theatres manage on their box office earnings

93. *kolikātā, krisnɔnɔgor, Cũcuṛa o onnānno sthān-theke*[10] — p. 8, line 49, col. 3
'Calcutta, Krishnanagar, Chinchura and other places from'
=from Calcutta, Krishnanagar, Chinchura and other places

94. *dosrā januari-theke* — p. 8, line 42, col. 3
'second January-from'
=as from the second of January...

[9]The homophonous morpheme appears with the numeral noun does not indicate the function of the nominal but degree.

[10]The long nominal phrase contains more than one place name. It can be taken as an example of co-ordinated or plural subject.

95. tobu tārā kāche *thekeo*[10a] ekṭu durotto rɔconā kɔren 'still they near being a little difference make' =even though (they) are within the society, they differentiate themselves from the others	Ananda Bazar Patrika January 18, 1963 p. 1, line, 8, col. 3
96. āpātoto sɔkɔrmonisṭho *thekeo*[10a] 'for the time being (at the present moment) in own business being loyal' =at the present moment being loyal to their own work	p. 1, line 32, col. 3
97. *ɔŋgonā potrikār pokk^{h}o theke*[11] 'Angana magazine's part-from' =on behalf of the Angana magazine	January 4, 1962 p. 10, line 1, col. 7
98. utkɔl *kɔŋgres-theke berie* āstonā 'utkal congress-from (they) did not come out' =they did not leave the utkal congress party	Desh, Saturday 17th June, 1972 p. 735, line 31, col. 1
99. ...pɔton ghoṭlo koalison *dɔl-theke* bhāŋālo bole '(it) fell off, coalition group from (they) cause to break away' =(they) caused (the M.L.A.) to break away from the coalition group (it) fell off.	p. 735, line 34, col. 1
100. ...*ɔnekdin-thekei*...bhābchen 'many day-from (they) are thinking' =for many days (they) have been thinking	p. 735, line 36, col. 2
101. ...khuner māmlā ruju hɔoār *pɔr-theke*... 'murder case file being after' =after the murder case had been filed...	p. 737, line 35, col. 1
102. puliser *tɔrɔph-theke* bɔlāholo... 'police side-from it was said'... =it was announced by the police department...	p. 737, line 26, col. 2
103. *chɔddobese-thekeo*... 'in disguise being' ... =even being in disguise...	p. 737, line 21, col. 2
104. *tārpɔr thekei*... 'after-from' =from that time onward/since that time	p. 737, line 29, col. 2
105. ...'des *bides-theke*...jɔṛokore chilen country foreign country from (he) collected (them)' =from different countries (he) collected (them)	p. 741, line 5, col. 1
106. je *bāibel-theke*...niechi 'the (same) bibel-from...(I) have mentioned' =from the (same) Bible...(I) have mentioned	p. 741, line 32, col. 2
107. sɔmobetokorlen rājotter b^{h}inno b^{h}inno *prodes-theke* '(then) assembled kingdom different province from' =(he) assembled (them) from the different provinces of the country	p. 741, line 34, col. 3

[10a]The homophonous morpheme is a verb in participial form.

[11]It is doubtful whether the marker indicates any function like role.

108. panjābi, paṭhān, belucder *bɔbosthā-theke*... p. 742, line 1, col. 1
'panjabi, pathan, beluch method from'
=(it is different) from the methods of the Panjabis, Pathans and Belucies...

109. ...*mɔhāpāp-theke* nijeke rokkhākorte sɔmɔrthohɔn p. 742, line 2, col. 3
'great sin from himself save to was able'
=(he) was able to avoid the great sin

110. se tar dhɔrmobuddhi *bāibel-theke* soŋgroho kɔrenā p. 742, line 7, col. 3
'she her religious sense Bible—from collect do not'
=she (India) did not take over her humanitarian principles from the Bible.

111. ...bohu bicittro *ghɔṭonā-theke* p. 744, line 24, col. 1
'many various event-from=from various events'

112. *riksā-theke* māl nāmāte surukorlo ɔsit p. 745, line 37, col. 1
'rickshaw from beggages to unload began Asit'
=Asit began to unload the things from the rickshaw

113. *dur-theke*...ābār...sɔbdoṭā sonāgælo p. 749, line 14, col. 3
'distance-from...again...the sound could near'
=again (they) could hear the sound from the distance

114. ...kɔrmosuci *ækhonthekei* toirikortehɔbe p. 752, line 38, col. 3
'programme now from prepared has to be'
=...the programme has to be prepared right now

115. *sāmontrotɔntro ār jāegirdāritheke*... p. 753, line 33, col. 1
'feudalism and overlord from (land tenancy)'
=out of feudalism and rule by overlords...

116. ...sei jā̃kerdin *duniā-theke* uṭhe gæche p. 753, line 14, col. 2
'that gorgeous day world from has gone'
=those gorgeous days have gone from the world

117. moŋgolrā bɔlen *bʰarot-theke*...eseche p. 753, line 7, col. 3
'mongols say India from...has come'
=the Mongols says that (it) has come from India

118. khɔdok bā cŋgobɔstro bā uttorio...*bʰārot-thekei* giechilo p. 753, line 6 col. 3
'khadok or angabastra or uttorio...
India from reached (there)'
=(it seems) that the khadok or angabastra or upper garment was introduced from India

119. næsnæl *phədəresɔn-theke* dujon mohilājāben p. 754, line 47, col. 3
'national federation from two ladies will go'
=two ladies will go on behalf of the national federation

120. *sekhān-theke* ār ekṭu egie... p. 755, line 19, col. 1
'there from a little further'...
=a bit further from there

121. ...osudʰṭā nie āsbo *boskompānir-theke* p. 755, line 22, col 1
'medicine taking (will come) Bose company from'
=I shall pick up the medicine from the Bose company

122. tebiler *odʰār-theke* tār jiggāsā p. 756, line 11, col. 1
'of the table that side from his enquiry'
=he enquired from the other side of the table

123. *tor-theke*...b^{h}āṛā ādae kɔrāi kāj dā̃ṛalo tāder — p. 756, line 1, col. 2
'you from rent collection work came to them'
=it is their job to collect rent from you

124. ...sei *kābulioalār thekei*...tā̃r protisṭhā — p. 756, line 34, col. 2
'that kabulioala from...his establishment'
=he became famous because of "kabulioala" (name of a short story)

125. *kāgojer hɔkār theke*...lekɔh hɔoā — p. 757, line 47, col. 1
'newspaper seller from...writer to become'
=from a newspaper seller (he) became a newspaper writer

126. *lekhɔk-theke* ābār sɔmpādɔk hoejāoā — p. 757, line 51, col. 1
'writer from again editor to become'
=then from the writer (he) became the editor

127. tār deo *ṭākār-theke*...coddoānā dileo *tār-theke*...lābh piṭechi — p. 757, line 42, col. 2
'his due from...three-quarters if given that from (I) have gained'
=(I) have made a profit even if he pays back (only) three-quarters of his debt

128. *okhān thekei* purbosurira sɔb rājotto korechen — p. 759, line 20, col. 1
'there from predecessors all governed'
=all the predecessors governed from that place

129. pāthor elo *jɔepur-theke*, *Cunār-theke*, *gɔeā-theke* — p. 759, line 28, col. 1
'stone came Joypore from Cunar from Goya from'
=stones were brought from Joypore, Cunar and Goya

130. purono *kella-thekei* rājkārjo colchilo — p. 759, line 9, col. 2
'old fort from the state service was carried out'
=the administration was carried out from the old fortress

131. *sekhān-theke* ḍhākā bib^{h}ager komisɔnər...pāṭhkore sonān — p. 760, line 33, col. 2
'there from of Dacca Presidency Commission read'
=the Commissioner of the Dacca Presidency... announced from that place

132. bes kichu *din-thekei* jāhāje bimānekore soino āschilo — p. 760, line 8, col. 3
'some day since by ship by plane army were arriving'
=for a long time soldiers were arriving by ship and by plane

133. pinḍir ghātokra *kæntɔnmenṭ-theke* berie elo tæŋknie — p. 760, line 12, col. 3
'of Pindi murderers cantonment from came out tank with'
=the murderers of Pindi came out of the cantonment with their tanks

134. ...koikeir irsa tār pāribārik *poribes-thekei* udb^{h}uto — p. 761, line 18, col 1
'of koikei envy her family environment from developed'
=Koikei's jealousy grew out of her family environment

135. ...ei ukti tārkik *dik-theke*... — p. 761, line 7, col. 2
'this utterance logical point from'
=from the logical point of view this utterance

136. ...*jekhān theke* rāmen sottokār jibon āromb^{h}oholo — p. 761, line 18, col. 2
'where from of Ram real life began'
=from that portion where the active life of Ram began

137. kintu ajodd^{h}ā kānḍer *pɔrtheke*... — p. 762, line 3, col. 1
'but Ajoddha (chapter) canto after'
=but after the Ayodha-canto...

138. ...bʰɔroddāj munir *āsrɔmtheke...* p. 763, line 1, col. 1
'Bharadwaj saint hermitage from'...
=from the hermitage of the sant Bhardwaj

139. ...sei *dāitto theke...* p. 763, line 14, col. 1
'that responsibility from'
=from that responsibility

140. judhisṭhirke dækhājāe *prothomtheke* p. 763, line 31, col. 1
'Judhisthir could be seen beginning from'
=from the beginning Judhisthir could be seen

141. ...bʰoggo bostur *tālikā-theke...* p. 764, line 9, col. 1
'enjoyable thing list from'
=from the list of enjoyable things...

142. judhisṭhirer *mukh-theke...* p. 764, line 38, col. 1
'of Judhisthir mouth from'
=from the mouth of Judhisthir...

143. ...ɔnobɔroto *nānādik-theke...* p. 765, line, 9 col. 1
'perpetually different direction from'
=perpetually from different directions...

144. māllogɔndhādir *upobʰog-theke* boncito hote hɔe p. 765, line 78, col. 2
'of garland and perfume enjoyment from deprived to be'
=(the unfortunates are) deprived of the enjoyment of garlands and perfume

145. ...*kothā-theke* æktā lok-ke dʰore nie elo p. 767, line 28, col. 1
'where from one man caught and brought'
=(he) brought someone from somewhere

146. ...mrittur *hāt-theke...* p. 767, line 15, col. 3
'of death hand from'
=from the jaws of death...

147. ...bier *din-thekei...* p. 768, line 6, col. 2
'of marriage day from'
=since the day of marriage...

148. hɔṭhāt *kothā-theke* p. 768, line 8, col. 2
'suddenly where from'
=suddenly from somewhere nowhere

149. ...*bāire theke* kārgɔlā kāne elo p. 769, line 11, col. 1
'outside from somebody's voice came'
=from outside somebody's voice could be heard

150. ār *kothā-theke* tomāke suiedilo p. 769, line 32, col. 1
'and somewhere from you...were laid out'...
=and (someone) from somewhere caused you to lie down

151. rāji thāko to *theke*[12] jao p. 769, line 10, col. 2
'agree if you then remain'
=if you agree, stay

152. ...*ekhān theke...* p. 770, line 2, col. 1
'here from'
=from here...

[12]It is a verb form.

153. ...bātāsi nijer *gā̃ṭ-theke* debenāki — p. 770, line 6, col. 1
'Batasi own pocket from should pay'
=should Batasi pay out of her own pocket?

(2) *N+nie*

154. *nānā-bisɔe-nie...* — p. 735, line 18, col. 1
'various subjects with'
=with many subjects/with various kinds of topics...

155. *ækhon dɔl tyāgider-nie* — p. 735, line 13, col. 2
'now group-resigner with'
=now, with those who have relinquished the group

156. *je ghɔtonā-nie*, mamla... — p. 737, line 51, col. 1
'that event—with, the litigation (occurs)'
=the event (affair) for which the litigation occurs

157. *se rāe mene-nie bicārpoti* — p. 737, line 49, col. 1
'that verdict accept-with the judge'
=accepting (admitting) the verdict, the Judge

158. *bæpārṭā-nie sārā āmerikāte...* — p. 737, line 13, col. 2
'that matter-with whole America'
=with that matter, in whole America...

159. *je bondukṭā-nie* jonathan marṭin... — p. 737, line 15, col. 2
'that gun-with'
=with that gun which Jonathan Martin

160. *...coritrodos-nie gɔbesɔnā kɔrār jonno* — p. 741, line 13, col. 2
'debauchery-with to research'
=to research on the debauchery (blemish in character)

161. *...ebŋ tāi-nie...* — p. 783, line 5, col. 1
'and that-with'
=and with that matter...

162. *tāi-nie æto-khob*ʰ *mānāynā* — p. 813, line 28, col. 1
'that-with such disappointment does not look nice'
=it is not sensible (unreasonable) to be so much disappointed for that matter

163. *hindurnām-nie bipɔde poṛechen* — p. 813, line 32, col. 1
'Hindu name with in difficulty has fallen'
=(he) is in difficulty with a Hindu name

164. *...mānɔsikɔtā-ṇie* — p. 815, line 2, col. 1
'mentality with'
=with that mentality

165. *prokāsɔkrā nisṭhā-nie ɔŋsogrohon korechen* — p. 815, line 10, col. 1
'The publishers sincerity with have taken part'
=the publishers have taken part with sincerity

166. *kobitā pāṭhyo ki srabyo ei-nie ækṭā torko ache* — p. 819, line 37, col. 2
'the poem to be read or to be heard that with an argument exists'
=it is debatable (there is an argument) whether a poem (poetry) is to be read or to be heard (is readable or audible)

167. *prosɔngo-theke chĩre-nie...montobyo ālgābʰābe tule-nie* — p. 819, line 23, col. 3
'from the context detached...the remark loosely taking up'
=detaching the remark from the context...

168. *robindoranāther gɔdyonie...ālaconā* korechen — p. 820, line 16, col. 3
'Rabindranath's prose-with...has discussed'
=(he) has discussed Rabindranath's prose (style)

169. *bʰāsa āndoloner-dike nie-jāe*[13] — p. 822, line 25, col. 2
'language movement-towards has directed'
=(it) has directed towards the language movement

170. *khælārbʰālomondo-nie* bondhuder sɔnge ki *bitɔrko-kɔre*[14] — p. 823, line 40 col. 1
'of playing good or bad with friends argument does'
=(he) had arguments with his friends with the future of (playing) game

171. *...jātioprerona-nie* phuṭboler jonno — p. 825, line 16, col. 1
'with national pride (inspiration) for football'
=having encouraged (national pride/having national inspiration) for football game

172. *eibār-nie...pɔrpɔrtinbār...* — p. 825, line 21, col. 2
'including this time (taking this time)...consecutively thrice'

173. *university institute* ekṭi ālādā oitijhyo *toiri kore nite*[15] pereche — p. 827, line 5, col. 1
'university institute a separate tradition has made'
=the university institute has developed a different tradition

174. ...okhān theke *diploma-nie*[16] — p. 827, line 8, col. 1
'there from diploma taken'
=having taken the Diploma from there

175. sikkʰārthider toiri *chobi-nie* sɔmāloconā bānchonio noe — p. 827, line 18, col. 1
'learner's painting with (film) criticism is not desirable'
=it is not desirable to criticise the student's (painting) film

176. ...sensɔr borḍ kɔtoṭā *udārbʰāb-nie* dekʰben — p. 828, line 6, col. 1
'censor board how much open mind with will look at'
=(it is doubtful) how much sympathy will be shown by the censor board

177. ...jārā *rāstār kukur-nie...* — p. 828, line 21, col. 1
'who street dog with'
=those who...with the street dog

178. *...sɔrod-nie* bosechen — p. 831, line 5, col. 1
'sarod with sat'
=(he) sat with the Sarod

179. *...dhrupodi soŋgitinie-to* ānondor kājkārbār nɔe — p. 831, line 3, col. 3
'classical music with Ananda does not work'
=Ananda does not deal with classical music

180. *ebɔŋ rɔk bit spiricuāl kok, pɔp, jaj-nie* — p. 831, line 6, col. 3
'and rock beatnik spiritual coke, pop, jazz, with'
=and with the rock bit spiritual coke, pop, jazz...

[13]This expression is not a postposition, it is a homophonous verb form with participle.
[14]It is an expression of verb and not postposition.
[15]It is an expression of model verb and not postposition.
[16]It is an expression of verb form.

181. *...dɔlkenie* — p. 832, line 6, col. 1
'the group with'
=with the group

182. *...golāṭi-nie* — p. 832, line 43, col. 1
'ball-with'
=with that ball

183. *...tai-nie...* — p. 832, line 43, col. 3
'that with'

184. *ɔnnyo je bisɔeguli-nie* ālocanā hɔe — p. 751, line 27, col. 3
'other which subjects with were discussed'
=the other subjects which were discussed

185. *ei bisɔeguli-nie...* — p. 751, line 32, col. 3
'this subjects with'
=with these subjects

186. *ātmio-sɔjon sɔŋgenie* pākā[17] dekhār jonno āsben — p. 754, line 5, col. 3
'relatives friends with final visit for will come'
=(he/they) will come accompanying the friends and relatives for final selection

187. cɔl, toke æk jāegae *nie jāi** — p. 756, line 44, col. 1
'come you one place will take'
=let me take you to a place

188. ei bole, *se niegælo** āmāe... — p. 756, line 5, col. 2
'this said, he took me'...
=having said this (saying this) he took me...

189. (se usulkore nilo) seṭa *keṭe-nie** bākiṭā dilo — p. 756, line 13, col. 2
'(he repayment took) that deducted, the rest gave'
=he adjusted the payment deducting that (having deducted) he gave the rest

190. sāhājādā ājam bāŋlār *sāsonbʰār-nie* dḥākāe ese põucholen 1677 sale — p. 759, line 17, col. 1
'the Prince Ajam Bengal of reponsibility to govẽrn at Dacca came on 1677'
=The Prince Ajam came in 1677 at Dacca to govern Bengal

191. nirdes elo dillicole eso *sipāhi sāntri-nie* — p. 759, line 35, col. 1
'the order came Delhi come back the soldier and army with'
=the command came for coming back to Delhi with his soliders and army

192. gorāpɔltonerā mritodeho guloke *ṭene nie**... — p. 760, line 19, col. 2
foreign soldiers the dead bodies having pulled...

193. pinḍir ghātokrā kæntonmentheke berie-elo *tæŋko kāmān-nie* — p. 760, line 12, col. 3
'Raulpindi's murderers from the cantonment came out with their tanks and cannons'
=The murderers of Raulpindi came out with their tanks and cannons from the cantonment

[17]It means to select a bride or groom finally.

*Indicates verbal expressions.

194. mɔhotterdārā *monḍitokore nie** — p. 761, line 28, col. 2
'with greatness mixed up having'
=having covered with greatness/generosity...

195. jekhāne b^{h}ɔe ɔthobā hɔtāsā, ɔthobā prolob^{h}oner *murti-nie...* — p. 764, line 52, col. 2
'where fear or disappointment or temptation with'
=where with fear, disappointment or temptation...

196. ...*bodle-nie* — p. 765, line 9, col. 2
'changing'=having changed

197. droupodike sɔb^{h}ästhɔle *ṭene-nie** elo — p. 765, line 22, col. 2
'Droupadi at the meeting place pulled down'
=(he) brought Droupadi by force at the open place

198. ekhāne *nie-esechilo** tāke — p. 767, line 12, col. 1
'here have brought him/her'
=he/she was brought there

199. e kothāe *nie-ele** tumi āmāke — p. 767, line 15, col. 1
'(this) where did bring you me'
=where did you bring me?

200. ...bāṛite *nie-gie** *uṭhechilo* — p. 767, line 18, col. 1
'at home having brought went'
=he have brought (her/him) at home

201. kothā theke ækṭā lokke *dhore nie** *elo* — p. 767, line 28, col. 1
'from where one person caught'
=he brought someone from some place

202. ...kothāe *nie-elo** — p. 768, line 2, col. 3
'where brought'

203. ...nijeke *sāmle nie** — p. 769, line 16, col. 1
'herself/himself having checked'
(controlled)=having controlled herself/himself...

204. ...āmāke ækb^{h}ɔ drolok *nie-eseche* ekhāne* — p. 769, line 28, col. 1
'me one gentleman have brought here'
=someone has brought me here

205. nie-āe, nie āe b^{h}etore ḍeke nie-āe* — p. 772, line 25, col. 3
'bring, bring, inside call'
=bring him (her) inside of the house

206. ...sɔdāke *nie esechi*[17a] didi — p. 775, line 23, col. 1
'sada (proper name) have brought elder sister'
=I have brought Sadā/I have come with Sadā

207. boumāke[17a] *nie...* — p. 775, line 8, col. 2
'the daughter-in-law accompany'
=(he) will accompany the daughter-in-law

208. *boumāke-nie*[17a] kesṭonogore colegæche — p. 775, line 4,1 col. 2
'the daughter-in-law with Krishnanagar went'
=(he) went (has gone) to Krishnanagar
with the daughter-in-law

[17a]These can be segmented differently; in one case it may be the part of verbal expression or in other segments it may mean 'with'.

209. ɔtokɔsṭokore sɔdāke *chāṛie nie-elum** p. 775, line 43,
'with such effort Sada having relieve has brought' col. 2
=I have caused relief of Sada by such an effort

210. āmi *ḍeke nie esehi** p. 775, line 3,
'I having called bring him' col. 3
=I call him back

211. *bæpārṭā nie* ses muhurto porjonto p. 778, line 8,
'matter with till the last moment' col. 1

212. uni jɔkhon *sobʰājātrā-nie* rājpɔthe ɔgrosɔr hocchilen p. 778, line 1,
'he when the procession with on the main road was proceeding' col. 3
=when he was proceeding through the main road with
the procession

213. submerin *jātrā-nie* p. 778, line 34,
'submarine travel with' col. 3
=with the travel in a submarine

214. ekṭu *bʰebe-nie* p. 780, line 3,
'a little having thought' col. 2
=having thought for a while

215. kæpṭen *gāṛi-nie* p. 780, line 8,
'captain with the car' col. 3
=the captain with his car

216. *prostābito ruprekhā o kɔrmosuci-nie*[18] p. 752, line 14,
'proposed framework and plan with' col. 3
=with the proposed framework and the plan

217. gāṛi *sɔkolke nie* collo p. 781, line 3,
'the car taking them started' col. 1
=the car started with them

218. ...*phirie nie jābe** p. 781, line 51,
'take back' col. 2
= (it) will take them back

219. ...*ki nie* jæno hā̃sahā̃si korche p. 781, line 55,
'something with seems lạughing' col. 2
=seems (they/he/she) someone were laughing for something

220. ...tɔkhon sāhājjer *āssās-nie* elen p. 785, line 8,
'then help assurance with came' col. 3
=then he came with the assurance of help

221....*phā̃pā kore nie* p. 788, line 28,
'hollow making (having made)' col. 3
=having made a hollow

222. ...ālādā ɔŋse ḍhālāi *kore nie* p. 788, line 42,
'separate half having poured in' col. 3
=having poured in a separate half

223. *nijeke-nie* porikkhā korchen p. 765, line 10,
'himself with test (has examined)' col. 1
=he tests himself

[18]The words in italics can be taken as a unit.

224. *notun dhæn dhāronā-nie* grāme phire jābar *du bɔchorer moddhei*[19] — p. 789, line 29, col. 1
'new ideas and imagination with village return within two years'
=within two years of returning to the village with new ideas and imagination in mind

225. ...*utsāho-nie* phire āsben — p. 797, line 33, col. 1
'energy with will return'
=will come back with energy (storing energy) enthusiasm

226. mānuske *niskriɔtār gonditheke*[20] kɔrmer ghurnite *egie-nie-jāe** — p. 797, line 37, col. 1
'man lethargy from to work push forward'
=(it) pushes forward man from inactiveness to the ceaseless activity

227. se...*nijeke nie* mosgul thake[21] — p. 805, line 4, col. 1
'he himself with keeps busy'
=he keeps busy with himself

228. ...*tir dhonuk-nie* — p. 805, line 21, col. 1
'bow and arrow with'
=with bow and arrow

229. se *cākri-nie* niruddes jātrāe jābe — p. 805, line 9, col. 3
'he taking a job will go to some unknown place'

230. *ki kɔtha-nie* — p. 805, line 23, col. 2
'what word with'
=with some argument...

231. surjo prāy hiṛhiṛ korei ṭene *nie gælo** — p. 806, line 4, col. 3
'Surya (proper name) about to pull and haul
'srilekha (proper name)'
=Surya pushed and pull and haul (Srilekha)

232. surjo srilekhar hāt dhore *ṭene-nie** jābār pɔr... — p. 808, line 24, col. 1
'Surya of Srilekha by hand pulling after going'
=after taking Srilekha's hand and pull and haul her by Surya...

233. surjo srilekhāke nijer ghɔre *nie-ese** — p. 808, line 40, col. 1
'Surjo Srilekha in his room having brought'
=having brought Srilekha in his room, Surya...

234. Srilekhā hāt chāṛienie... — p. 808, line 42, col. 1
'Srilekha having snatched her hand'...

235. Srilekhā surjor cokh-theke *cokh sorie nie*[22] bollo, nāo — p. 809 line 1, col. 1
'Srilekha Surya's eyes from looking other way said take'

236. Surjo ciruni-ṭā *nie-i*... — p. 809, line 2, col. 1
'Surya the comb taking'
=Surya having taken the comb

237. ekṭu k^{h}ɔner moddhei *nijeke sāmle nie* srilekhā dure sore gælo — p. 809, line 5, col. 2
'few minutes within herself having controlled Srilekha distance went (has gone)'

[19]An expression with *N+moddhe*.

[20]An expression with *N+theke*.

[21]There is a slight phonetic difference in this verb form.

[22]This expression and other expressions such as *khe-e nie, jone nie, ni/eke sāmle nie, nie-i, cokh sorie nie* are adverbial expressions.

=Within few seconds Srilekha having controlled herself went away in a distance

238. ā̃colṭā bʰālokore *jorie nie*... p. 809, line 7, col. 2
'the end of the sari tightly having tied up'

239. ...āmi ekkʰuni *khe-e nie* berubo p. 809, line 21, col. 2
'I shortly having taken meal will go out'

240. *siggir nie-āe** p. 809, line 25, col. 2
'quickly bring'
=bring (it) quickly

(3) *N+die* (*moddho-die*)

241. khɔbordār āmār *nām-die* æmon kɔthā... p. 735, line 15, col. 1
'be cautious my name with such word'
=be cautious, do not blame me

242. *nijer bonduk-die* cælāke tini pāṭhie-chilen p. 737, line 32, col. 2
'own gun with the follower he sent'
=he sent his disciple having given his own gun

243. *uriɔrer-hāte-die* pāṭhāilen p. 741, line 2, col. 2
'through Uriar/by Uriar has sent (it)'
=he has sent (it) through Uriar

244. *ḍrɔiŋ-er-moddʰo-die* tā prokās korechen p. 811, line 17, col. 3
'drawing through that has (been) expressed'
=(he) has expressed that through his drawing

245. *litho o uḍkāṭer-moddho-die*... p. 812, line 8, col. 2
'litho and woodcut through'
=through litho and woodcut...

246. *nānā rɔŋer moddho die-i*... p. 812, line 8, col. 3
'various colour through'
=through various colour

247. ...*rɔŋer-ṭāner moddhodie*... p. 812, line 17, col. 3
'the colour touch through'
=through the touch of the colour

248. ...*rāstār namkɔroner moddho-die* p. 817, line 1, col. 1
monisismɔron hote pāre nā
'the road name through remembrance of the great men cannot be'
='it is not a good idea to remember the great men by naming a road after their names

249. nānā rɔkom robindranāth *sironam-die*... p. 819, line 14, col. 3
'different Rabindranath heading with'
=with the caption (heading) of different Rabindranath...

250. *utsāho-die** bollen p. 823, line 31, col. 3
'having given encouragement said'
=encouraging him (he) said

251. biswa olimpike *jog-die** p. 825, line 11, col. 2
'the world Olympic joining'
=having joined/joining the Olympic...

252. jubɔk ätmohottā korlo *ṭrentheke jhā̃p-die* p. 827, line 31, col. 3
'the young man committed suicide train from jumping'
=the young man committed suicide jumping from a train

253. jodilāmā mɔt *die thāken*[22a] p. 754, line 3, col. 3
'if Lama opinion has given'
=if the Lama has given consent (permission/opinion)

254. *tāi-die* dābie rākhi *āgertheke* p. 755, line 8, col. 3
'that with checked beforehand'
=(it) is controlled (with that) applying that beforehand

255. osudhṭā *korte-die*[22a] p. 756, line 2, col. 1
'that medicine to make (prepare) have given'
having requested to prepare the medicine

256. tā *ṭākāṭā-die*[22b] tumi ar pherot naiba nile p. 756, line 39, col. 1
'the money given you again if would not take back'
=say, having given the money you would not take back again

257. sudhu sud *die-gele*[22b] hɔe p. 756, line 52, col. 1
'only interest continue to give (may)'
=only the interest may continuously be given

258. jæno tāke *die āsi gie*[22b] p. 756, line 16, col. 2
'seems him/her should be given (I)'
=as if I should give it to him/her, being present there

259. *se-dhār-die bolchine* p. 756, line 30, col. 2
'that side from not saying'
=(I) am not saying from that point of view

260. je kono dāme *die-dii*[23] p. 757, line 20, col. 1
'any price in gave/will give/has given'
=I gave (have given) (it) in any price

261. tāder khātāe *soi-die* deṛsoṭākā dhār korlām p. 756, line 8, col. 2
'their notebook in signing one hundred
fifty rupees I borrowed'
=signing (having given signature) on their book, I
borrowed one hundred and fifty rupees

262. *ijārā-die-dilen* p. 760, line 42, col. 1
'lease out'
=(he) (gave) lease out

263. *jibɔner sɔb ɔniscɔo tār modʰde-die...* p. 763, line 28, col. 2
'life of all uncertainty through'
=through (all) the uncertainties of life

[22a]It is observed that these expressions are verbal forms and express various aspects. Even though these occur after nominal in a sentence, these do not constitute unit with nominals.

[22b]It is observed that these expressions are verbal forms and express various aspects. Even though these occur after nominal in a sentence, these do not constitute unit with nominals.

[23]We have noticed that often the homophonous morpheme is a verbal form and expresses aspects; it is observed here that such differences in tense—past, future, present perfect—are neutralized. The desired tense is understood from the context, i.e. either from the previous or the following lines of the discourse.

264. *sokreṭiske-die* proyojon chilo — p. 764, line 18, col. 2
'Socratis need was'
=there was a need for Socratis

265. ...*dustɔr mɔtobʰeder moddʰo-die-o* — p. 764, line 27, col. 2
'far disagreement through'
=through impassable (immense) disagreements

266. *āmāder doinondin obʰiggõtā-die* bicār kāleo — p. 764, line 42, col. 2
'our everyday life experience with judge'
=even though (we) judge with our everyday life's experience

267. *majh khān-die* soru soru goli rāstā — p. 767, line 20, col. 1
'middle through narrow lane(s)'
=there are narrow lanes through the middle

268. *ghɔre rekhe-die* āmi *tālā-die-debo* dɔrojāe — p. 774, line 16, col. 3
'room in having kept I lock will give on the door'
=having kept (it) in the room I will lock the door

269. khete-bose *nɔyontārārcokh-die ṭɔsṭɔskore* jcl porte lāglo — p. 775, line 1, col. 1
'while eating Nayantara's eyes through in drops tears roll down'
=tears roll down drop by drop (from) through Nayantara's eyes while she sat for a meal

270. *tini sĩri-die...* — p. 775, line 26, col. 1
'she through the staircase'

271. gāṛi bʰāṛātā *konorɔkome die* — p. 775, line 41, col. 1
'the fare anyhow given'
=anyhow, having given the fare of the car

272. didike khɔborṭā *die asige* — p. 775, line 44, col. 1
'(to the) elder sister the news should give'
=(I) should give the message to the elder sister

273. *sɔkoler-kāche sonā ṭukro ṭukro ghɔṭonar moddho-die* — p. 778, line 10, col. 1
'all persons from heard bit and piece events through'
=through the bits and pieces of events, which were heard from others

274. *netājir-sāmne-die* erā mārchpast koregælo — p. 778, line 9, col. 2
'leaders front through they march did'
=they march before the leader

275. *beter cilte di-ei* toiri hoto — p. 785, line 26, col. 3
'cane fibre with made'
=(these were) used to make with the fibre of cane

276. ...*prolep-die...* — p. 786, line 26, col. 3
'apply as an ointment (having smeared)'
=having given the ointment/smearing it...

277. eibʰābe *bʰitorer kāth bār-kore die...* — p. 788, line 9, col. 1
'in this manner (the) inner juice having squeezed out'

278. *toiri kore-die thāken* — p. 788, line 46, col. 3
'used to make'

279. kāj jɔthesṭo porimāne *jogār kore die...* — p. 789, line 9, col. 1
'(work) job sufficient having made arrangement'
=having arranged for sufficient (job) work...

280. *tārpɔr bʰustɔrer moddʰo-die...* p. 794, line 41, col. 1
'after the through'
=after that through the layers on the earth

281. *bʰustɔr dʰātɔbrāsta bɔṛobāṛi-die ḍʰākā* p. 794, line 30, col. 1
'the outer layer, metal road, big houses with covered'
=the surface (outer) layer of the earth is covered with metal road and big houses

282. *bālirstɔrer moddho-die-i* mukkhoto *bʰugɔrbʰerjɔl ānāgonākɔre* p. 794, line 52, col. 1
'the sand layer through generally underground water flows'
=generally the underground water flows through the sand layer

283. *ekṭi udyogrup dɔnḍo die* p. 797, line 14, col. 1
'one zealous stick with'
=with a zeal...

284. beskore *bæṛātæṛā-die* p. 800, line 37, col. 1
'nicely fencing given'
=nicely (carefully) giving a fencing

285. *dɔrojā-die* mukh baṛie hā̃k dilo p. 805, line 9, col. 1
'door through face peeping called'
=(he) called peeping once through the door

286. chader *sīṛidi-e* neme elo bādol p. 805, line 13, col. 1
'roof is staircase through came down Badol'
=Badol came down stepping on the staircase from the roof

287. egie gælo *bārāndā-die* p. 805, line 14, col. 3
'proceed (forward) veranda through'
=(he) proceeded through the verandah

288. *...cokhe āŋgul-die* p. 807, line 45, col. 1
'eyes in finger with'
=...openly/made it clear

289. priyɔranjan sāph hukum-die-rākhlen p. 808, line 15, col. 1
'Priyaranjan (proper name) clear order having given keep'
=Priyaranjan gave a clear order

290. suprobʰā *uttornā-die* ekṭukhən cupkore roilen p. 808, line 26, col. 1
'Suprobha (proper name) answer not giving a moment quite keep'
=Suprobha remain quite for a while without giving any answer

291. thutnite *āŋgul-die* p. 809, line 17, col. 1
'on the chin finger (with)'
=putting a finger on the chin

292. *ækṭā kāpoṛer phāli die* p. 809, line 25, col. 1
'one cloth's piece with'
=with a piece of cloth

293. edike keu ele *jānlā-die* prothome dækhājābe p. 809, line 45, col. 1
'on this side anyone if comes (the) window through first would be seen'
=if anybody comes on this side he/she would be visible through the window

294. *dɔrojā cheṛe-die* bollo p. 809, line 20,
'door leaving said' col. 2
=being off from the door (he) said

295. ...*surjor pās-die* p. 809, line 20,
'Surya side by' col. 2
=by the side of Surya

296. *jinisṭā-die* ki-hɔbe p. 809, line 24,
'that thing with what would happen' col. 2
=what would happen with that thing?

297. *eidhɔroner sāŋghātik jinis-nie* p. 809, line 36,
'such dangerous thing with' col. 2
Surjo nāṛā-cāṛā kore
Surya handles
=Surya handles with such dangerous thing

298. Surjo *ækdhɔmok-die* bollo jā ekʰhuni nie-āe p. 809, line 45,
'Surya one scold (with) said, go just now bring' col. 2
=Surya scolding her said, go and bring it immediately

299. khɔpkore ...*jhā̃kuni-die*... p. 809, line 2,
'suddenly shaking with' col. 3
=suddenly giving a shake...

300. ḍhukie-die, bāiretheke tālā bɔndho kore... p. 775, line 9,
'pushing from outside locked' col. 2
=(he/she) locked from outside, pushing him/her in

301. *sādhāron hātiār-die*... p. 788, line 6,
'common weapon with' col. 3

302. ...*mom-die* toiri-kore nen p. 788, line 23,
'wax with made (he)' col. 3
=(he) made (it) with wax

303. *ækṭā ribeṭ-die* p. 815, line 43,
'one rebate giving' col. 1
=having given a rebate...

304. je hetu *bɔṛo bɔṛo klāber khæloāṛder-nie*... p. 824, line 25,
'because big clubs players with' col. 1
=because with the players of the big clubs...

305. ...*kolki nāṭikā-die* surukore... p. 829, line 12,
'Kolki drama with beginning' col. 3
=beginning with the drama named 'Kalki'...

306. surute *ækṭā orijinal-die* āsor bosechilo p. 831, line 5,
'beginning one original with meeting start' col. 2
=the meeting started with an 'original' at the beginning

307. *em, el, e, der soi-jālkore...sṭamp-die*... p. 832, line 21,
'M.L.A.'s signature forged...stamp giving' col. 1
=forging the signatures of the M.L.A.'s and giving stamp...

308. Cin *erjonno* bajardɔrer besidam-dite raji p. 832, line 51,
'China for (that) if market price more to give agree' col. 3
=China is ready (agree) to pay more than the
market price for it

309. sekhāne *hānā-die*... p. 735, line 13, col. 2
'there raiding'
=having raided there

310. *puliser cokhe dhulo-die*... p. 735, line 16, col. 2
'police of eye dust through'
=throwing dust to the eyes of the police

(3) *N+moddhe*

311. tāte *pɔncojojonār moddhe-i*... p. 752, line 15, col. 2
'in it five year plan in'
=in it...within the five year plan

312. *dhoni o goriber moddhe pārthokko* p. 752, line 18, col. 2
'rich and poor in difference'
=the difference between the rich and the poor

313. *āgāmi septembɔr māser moddhe* prokāsito hɔbe p. 752, line 35, col. 2
'coming September month within publish will be'
=it will be published within the next September

314. *ɔrthonitibidder moddhe* p. 752, line 44, col. 2
'economists among'
=among the economists

315. *mānusgulir-moddhe* nānā dhɔron āche p. 753, line 25, col. 1
'people among many types exist'
=there are many types among the people

316. *nānā koutuker-mājhe* otithira promān kɔren p. 754, line 33, col. 3
'many fun among guests proved'
=the guests proved (that) in various kinds of fun

317. *erimoddhe* itihāser ɔnekghɔṭonār nirɔb p. 759, line 15, col. 1
sākhkhi lālbāg kellā dā̃ṛie-āche
'this among history of many events silent observer'
=among these, the Lalbag Fort is (standing) still
existing as the silent observer of many events of the history

318. ...*dubɔchorer moddhei*... p. 759, line 37, col. 1
'two years within'
=within two years

319. *kellār moddhei*... p. 760, line 15, col. 1
'the Fort in'
=in the Fort...

320. *lālbāg kellār-moddhe*... p. 760, line 49, col. 1
'Lalbag Fort in'

321. ækhon *pārker-moddhe*... p. 760, line 30, col. 1
'now park in'
=now in the park

322. *duṭo ghɔṭonār-moddhe* sɔmoer bæbodhān tinsobɔc^{h}or p. 760, line 28, col. 3
'two events in time's difference three hundred years'
=between the two events the gap of time is for
three hundred years

323. *er-moddhe*... p. 760, line 29, col. 3
'this in'
=in this/in the meantime

324. koikeir *muṛoh-ācorɔner-moddhe...* p. 761, line 16, col. 1
'Koikeyi's foolish behaviour in'
=in Koikeyi's foolish behaviour

325. kintu *sɔptakāṇḍɔputhir-moddhe...* p. 761, line 1 col. 2
'but seven canto of the book in'
=but in the seven cantos of the book

326. *tār poribār-bɔrger-moddhe...* p. 761, line 22, col. 2
'his family members in'
=among his family members

327. *coturbɔrger-moddhe...* p. 763, line 1, col. 2
'four stage in life in'
=among the four stage in life the desired end

328. sudhu *dhɔrmācarini b*^{h}*ārjār-moddhe* p. 764, line 31, col. 1
'only married and pious wife in'
=only among the pious married wife...

329. *...droupadi o judhisṭhirer-moddhe-o* bhāb binimɔy... p. 764, line 40, col. 1
'Draupadi and Judhisthir in discussion
and exchange of opinion'
=the discussion and exchange of opinion (occurred)
between Draupadi and Judhisthir

330. *bhāeder-moddhe...* p. 764, line 1, col. 2
'brothers among'
=among the brothers

331. niguṛ^{h}o ākorsɔn chilo *dujoner-moddhe* p. 764, line 15, col. 2
'deep understanding was two between'
=there was a deep understanding between the two

332. *coturāsrɔmer-moddhe sresṭho* p. 764, iine 40, col. 2
'four stage in best'
=(it is) the best among the four stages

333. b^{h}obosɔŋsārer ækebāre *moddhikāne*[24] p. 764, line 50, col. 2
'worldly life just middle'
=(it is) just in the middle of the worldly life

334. *ābɔrter-moddhe...* p. 764, line 51, col. 2
'whirlpool in'
=in the whirlpool

335. *oder-moddhe...* p. 807, line 22, col. 1
'them among'
=among them...

336. *ei sɔmpɔrker-moddhe...* p. 807, line 26, col. 1
'this relation in'
=in this relation (between them)

337. *bæpārṭār-moddhe...* p. 807, line 42, col. 1
'matter in'
=in that matter.

338. *ækdiner-moddhei...* p. 774, line 9, col. 2
'one day in'
=within one day

339. *doinondin kājermoddheo* p. 774, line 11, col. 2
'every day work in also'
=even in everyday work

[24]The homophonous morpheme is a word and not a marker here.

340. *eri-moddhe* jodi kānnā pāe... p. 775, line 14. col. 1
'this in if weeps'
=if she feels crying so early

341. *edik-theke netājir khub bæstotār-moddhe* keṭe chilo p. 778, line 6, col. 1
'that side leader very busy in passed'
=from that point of view, Netaji passed (those days) in work (very busy with work)

342. āmi khub sɔmbhɔbɔto *tomāder-moddhe* thākbonā p. 778, lne 4, col. 2
I very likely you among will not be
=it is very likely that I may not be present among you

343. jodi tæmon bipɔd *pɔther-mājhe* uposthit hɔe p. 779, line 18, col. 1
'if such danger way in come up'
=if such danger appears on the way

344. *eder moddhe ɔnekei...* p. 781, line 18, col. 1
'them among many'
=many among them

345. *oder-moddhe* dekhechi p. 781, line 22, col. 1
'them among saw'
=I saw among them

346. *oder-moner-moddhe...* p. 781, line 23, col. 1
'them mind in'
=in their mind

347. *nijeder-moddhe* kɔthābārtā bolche p. 781, line 53, col. 2
'themselves among conversation were speaking'
=they were talking among themselves

348. *chæcer-moddhe...* p. 788, line 3, col. 2
'mould in'
=in the frame (mould/dice)

349. *koŋkriter suṛoŋger majhe mājhe*[25] ciṛ p. 791, line 12, col. 1
'concrete hole in crack'
=in some places in the concrete tunnel, there are cracks

350. 1961-*er-moddhe...* p. 795, line 59, col. 2
'1961 in'
=within 1961...

351. *kɔek miniṭer-moddhe...* p. 795, line 6, col. 3
'a few minutes in'
=within a few minutes

352. krome *tār-moddhe...* p. 795, line 4, col. 1
'gradually its in'
=gradually during this time/gradually in it/ gradually by this time...

353. *bibʰinno rājjyer-moddhe* khudrò silper dik-theke p. 797, line 3, col. 2
'various states in small industries side'
=from the point of view of small industries in the different states/among the different states...

[25]The morpheme is not a bound morphene, it is a word,

354. *khudro silper swārtho sɔŋghāter-mājhe* p. 797, line 2, col. 2
'small industries of interest in'
=in the rivalry of the small industries/
for the interest of the small industries

355. *tāder-moddhe...* p. 811, line 9, col. 1
'them among'
=among them (these)...

356. *bhāskɔrjo nidɔrsoner-moddhe...* p. 811, ine 1, col. 2
'sculpture sample in'
=among the sample of the sculptures

357. '*di phrut selər*'*-chobiṭir-moddhe...* p. 811, line 9, col. 3
'the fruit seller painting in'
=in the painting nāmed the fruit seller

358. *graphik printer-moddhe...* p. 811, line 26, col. 3
'graphic printing in'
=in the graphic printings...

359. *ɔpɔrāpɔr nidɔrsɔner-moddhe...* p. 811, line 31, col. 3
'other illustrations among'
=among other illustrations

360. *oti ɔlpokāler-moddhei...* p. 812, line 38, col. 2
'very short time in'
=within a very short time

361. *ānondoucchāser-moddhe* p. 817, line 21, col. 1
'joyous activity in'
=through the gayful movement

362. kintu *jɔnosādhāroner moddhe* (kobita p. 819, line 7,
pāṭher probrittijāgiechilen Eswar Gupta)
'but common people'
=but among the common people (Iswargupta
created interest in reading poetry)

363. *pɔncɔmdɔsoker-mājhāmājhi...* p. 819, line 17, col. 1
'the fifth (tenth) middle'
=in the middle of this century...

364. *prothom chɔṭi khælār-moddhe...* p. 823, line 24, col. 3
'first six play (games) in'
=among the first six games (matches)

365. *chɔṭi goler-moddhe...* p. 823, line 12, col. 3
'six goal in'
=in the six goal

366. *dillirbiruddhe cāriṭir-moddhe...* p. 823, line 13, col. 3
'Delhi's against four in'
=in the four matches against Delhi...

367. *bāroṭi dɔler moddhe...* p. 825, line 26, col. 1
'twelve groups in'
=among the twelve groups...

368. *duṭi khælāe āṭṭi gole-er-moddhe...* p. 825, line 2, col. 2
'two matches eight goals in'
=among the eight goals in two matches

369. *isṭbeŋgɔl ebŋ mohomeḍansporting-er-moddhe* p. 825, line 14, col. 3
'East Bengal and Mohamadan sporting in'
=in between the East Bengal and Mohamadan sporting

370. *tælenṭed khæloāṛder-moddhe...* p. 825, line 52, col. 3
'talented players among'
=among the talented players

371. *nijeke...prithibir moddhe* phirepāe p. 829, line 19, col. 1
'himself earth in got back'
=he got himself back in the worldly life

372. *sɔcchɔl jiboner-mājhkhāne* hā̃pie oṭhār p. 829, line 26, col. 1
cehārāṭi poricālok spɔsṭokore dækhāte perechen
'smooth life in board being director
clearly able to show (shown'
=the director has clearly shown the picture of
being board in the middle of smooth life

373. *oitijhyer-moddhe...* p. 829, line 40, col. 1
'tradition in'
=in the tradition

374. *dɔrsok ebŋ obhinetāder-moddhe* p. 829, line 19, col. 3
jogsutro sthāponer uddesse...
'the audience and the artists between
a link to put in the purpose of'
=in the aim, to put a link between the audience
and the artist

375. *silpider-moddhe* prosoŋsā pāben p. 830, line 22, col. 3
'artist among praise will get'
=those will be praised among the artists (who)...

376. *...mājhemoddhe-* p. 831, line 18, col. 1
'sometimes'
=sometimes/in some intervals

377. *jār-moddhe...* p. 831, line 44, col. 1
'who in'
=among whom...

378. *braj ebŋ ānondor bājnār mājhkhāne...* p. 831, line 16, col. 2
'Braj and Ananda's music in between'
=in between the musical performance of Braj and Ananda...

379. *...du æk diner moddhe...* p. 832, line 10, col. 1
'two one days in'
=within one or two days

380. *æk māser-moddhe...* p. 832, line 15, col. 1
'one month's in'
=within one month

381. *tāder moddhe...* p. 832, line 42, col. 1
'them in'
=among them

382. *ponero diner moddhe* pɔthe eso p. 832, line 26, col. 3
'fifteen days in way come'
=come in terms within fifteen days

(4) *N+kore*

383. *bāʰlo-kore*[25a] bhebe-dækhā ucit — p. 735, line 48, col. 1
'carefully think should'
=should think carefully (well, rightly)

384. *bises-kore*[25a] tārāi... — p. 735, line 49, col. 1
particularly they

385. *bises-kore* prottokkhckɔr ɔnusandhān kɔmiṭir... — p. 751, line 2, col. 1
'particularly direct tax research committee'
=particularly to the direct tax and research committee

386. krɔmobikās *cchinnokore*[25b] pɔroborti — p. 741, line 10, col. 2
'gradual development breaking, the next'
=breaking the gradual chain of development, the next...

387. *rājār-nikɔṭe probes-koriā*[25b] *tāhār-kāche* — p. 742, line 42, col. 1
'the king near entering him to'
=entering to the king to him

388. lāmāke nā *jiggāsā kore* — p. 754, line 4, col. 2
'the Lama not asking'
=not (without) asking the Lama...

389. Lāmā jɔnmo lɔgno ittædi *bicār-kore sthir-kore* deben — p. 754, line 5, col. 2
'the Lama birth the moment, etc. counting decision will give'
=the Lama will give decision consulting the birth moment, etc.

390. dinkhɔno lāmāi *ṭhik-kore*[26] deben — p. 754, line 1, col. 3
'the date the Lama fixed will'
=the Lama will fix the date and time

391. māke *bhālokore dekhe sune* oimixṭurer — p. 755, line 1, col. 2
'mother carefully examine that mixture'
bɔbosthā-kore gechlen 'prescribed'
=(he) has prescribed that mixture,
carefully examining my mother

392. *sukhbʰog nāgāler bāire bole sādh-kore...* — p. 755, line 24, col. 2
'pleasure beyond the capacity since willingly'
=since the enjoyment is beyond my capacity, willingly...

393. æmonki *tinṭe-koreo* otrāte hɔe — p. 757, line 7, col. 1
'even three (in) is to be passed'
=one has to cover (pass, do) at least in three

394. ɔnkeguli boi *ei- korei* beriejāe — p. 757, line 22, col. 1
'many books in this manner publish'
=in this way many books come out (published)

395. ār *emni-korei* jctsāmānno jā āmār protisṭhā — p. 757, line 23, col. 1
'and this manner in a little that my establishment'
=the little reputation that I have acquired in this manner

[25a]The morpheme *kore* with both noun and adjective function as manner adverbial, sentence outer.

[25b]Both are expressions of verbal form. In example 387 there are three expressions with morphemes such as *nikɔt(e)*, *koriā*, *kāche*.

[26]Manner.

396. jāihok *je koreihok*... p. 757, line 44
'however, in any case' col. 1
=however, anyhow

397. *bājeāpto-kore nilen sɔrkār* p. 757, line 8,
'ceased (forfeits) the government' col. 2
=the government (ceased) forfeited

398. *jɔbordɔkhɔl kore neoā* āmār p. 757, line 25,
'perforce taken mine (by me)' col. 2
=I have taken forcibly (by force)

399. *jɔbordɔkhɔl-kore* pāoā? p. 757, line 26,
'by force obtained' col. 2
=it is obtained by force?

400. nɔeto *jor-kore ādāekore* p. 757, line 29,
'by force collected (received)' col. 2
=otherwise having collected by force

401. jānlā *pāthor-khodāi-kore* jāphri kāṭā p. 760, line 23,
'the window stone engraved latticework' col. 1
=the lattice of the window is stone engraving

402. ke *ākromon-kore bɔse* p. 760, line 34,
'who invades' col. 1
=who knows who invades

403. tāi ātmorokkhār sɔbbɔbosthā *pākā-kore* rākhāi bhālo p. 760, line 35,
'so self-protection arrangement col. 1
finalized to make wise (better)'
=so, it is better to make final arrangement
for self-protection

404. *ki-kore* e sɔmb^{h}ɔbpɔr holo p. 760, line 47,
'how this possible was' col. 1
=how was it possible?

405. sipāhi bidroher ḍheu *emni-kore*... p. 760, line 35,
'Sipohi mutiny's wave this manner in' col. 2
=in that manner the wave of the Sipohi mutiny

406. *jemni-kore* tinso-bɔchor-āge... p. 760, line 9,
'the way three hundred years ago' col. 3
=the way (they did) before three hundred years

407. se-dino *jemni-kore*... p. 760, line 17,
'that day also in the similar way' col. 3
=the sameway, in that day also

408. i-pi-ar bāhinir lokerā *mɔronpɔn-kore*... p. 760, line 19,
'E.P.R. army people sacrificing life' col. 3
=sacrificing their life, the E.P.R. personnel

409. *āsārucched-kore*... p. 765, line 11,
'hope uprooted' col. 1
=uprooting the hopes

410. sāmājik o manobik mullo *upolobdhi koreo*... p. 765, line 22,
'the social and human values being perceived' col. 1
=perceiving the social and human values...

411. *hæmon-kore*[27] ɔsoŋkho khudrotār upɔre... p. 765, line 28,
'how countless mean-ness on' col. 1
=how, avoiding the countless mean-ness...

412. *kɔrnopāto kɔre*[28]*nāi* p. 765, line 16,
'paying attention did not' col. 2
=did not pay attention (he)

413. sāl-brikkhoke lɔtā *jæmon besṭɔn kɔre*[28a] p. 765, line 29,
'the sal tree the creeper as embrace (enclose)' col. 2
=as the creeper surrounds (enclose, embrace)
the teak wood tree

414. supto siŋhoke jāgroto-kore[28a]... p. 765, line 30,
'the sleeping lion make him awake' col. 2
=awakening the sleeping lion

415. bhimsenke *āliŋgɔn-kore*[28a]... p. 765, line 33,
'the (second brother) Vima embracing' col. 2
=embracing Vimasen

416. *ālocɔnā-korei*[28a]... p. 765, line 42,
'having discussed' col. 2

417. jodi keu tā *kore-thāken*[29] p. 765, line 50,
'if anyone that has done' col. 2
=if anybody has done it

418. *māthā-nicu-kore* ghɔrerbhetor ḍhukte hɔe p. 767, line 23,
'head bending (inside) to the room has to enter' col. 1
=one has to enter the room bending his/her head

419. dā̃ṛā āge *khābār bɔbosthā-kore āsi* p. 767, line 26,
'wait first food arrangement doing came' col. 1
=wait, first let me make arrangement for food

420. *bhālokore* bā̃cārjonne p. 767, line 11,
'well living for' col. 3
=to live well

421. sɔbāi *khilkhilkore* hē̃se uṭhlo p. 769, line 41,
'all giggle laughed at' col. 1
=everybody giggled

422. ṭikiṭ *punc-kore...* p. 802, line 1,
'ticket punched' col. 1
=having punched the ticket

423. *ekṭu ekṭu kore* dānābē̃dhe uṭhbe p. 802, line 13,
'slowly (gradually) crystal will form' col. 1
=bit by bit (gradually) the crystal will form

424. tār upɔr *nirbhɔr-kɔre*[29a] p. 802, line 26,
on it depends' col. 1
=it depends upon it

[27]The morpheme is expressing manner.
[28]The morpheme is a main verb.
[28a]The morphemes are participial verb forms.
[29]The participial form is expressing aspect of the verb.
[29a]The morpheme is an auxiliary verb form.

425. āmdāni *bɔndho-kore...* p. 802, line 44, col. 1
'import close down'
=stopping (controlling) the import (goods)

426. deske *sɔyɔmbhɔr-kɔre*[29a] p. 802, line 47, col. 1
'country independent make'
=(that) makes the country independent

427. *emnikorei* porikɔlponār ekṭi bolisṭho adol p. 802, line 2, col. 2
dhɔra-chɔ̃ar-moddhe esejabe
'this way the plan and programme a
strong form take shape will develop'
=in this way the plan and programme
will take a strong shape in reality.

428. ɔnurup-pustikā *prokās-kɔre* p. 803, line 13, col. 2
'similar booklet publishes'
=(they/he) publish the similar type of booklet

429. bibʰinno porikalpanā *rɔconākɔre* p. 803, line 26, col. 2
'various kinds of plan (they) make'
=(they) make various kinds of plan

430. *ekṭu cɔkcoke kore-neoā jete pāre* p. 803, line 44, col. 2
'a slight' (bright) shiny can be made'
=(it) can be made a bit shiny

431. *ṭrəḍ representəsɔn-theke suru-kore...* p. 803, line 47, col. 2
'trade representation from beginning'
=beginning from the trade representation

432. *kebol jogāṛ-kore* nijergænbʰānḍār p. 803, line 48, col. 2
sɔmridʰo-kore nite pārlei holo
'only collecting our knowledge'
=only to make our knowledge luxuriant
by knowing things of the world

433. *snānkore ese* surjo ciruni khũje pācchenā p. 805, line 6, col. 1
'bathing after Surjo comb does not get'
=Surjo was not finding out the comb finishing his bath

434. *khɔ̃jā khũji-korei* se biroktohoe gælo p. 805, line 8, col. 1
'having searched he disgust felt'
=he felt disgusted having searched (it)

435. kāṭher misṭiri sudhu *ghæsghæskore* meda cālācche p. 805, line 12, col. 1
'the carpenter only making a monotonous
sound carpenters plane using'
=the carpenter uses the plane and makes a monotonous sound

436. se hironnokosipu *mone-kore...* p. 805, line 3, col. 2
'he Hironyakasipa thinking'
=then he thinking (him) Hironyakasipa

437. tārpɔr *tɔrtɔr kore...* p. 805, line 4, col. 3
= 'then quickly'

438. se osɔb *toākkā-kɔrena* p. 807, line 8, col. 1
he that bother does not
=he does not bother that

439. *dekhini dekhini b^{h}āb-kore* colegiechilo onnodike p. 807, line 38,
'did not see did not see so pretending col. 1
went on the other side'
=(he) went on the other side pretending
that (he) did not see

440. *bises kore* tār choṭojā p. 807, line 54,
'particularly her younger sister-in-law' col. 1

441. suprobhā tɔkhon *surjor pokkho sɔmɔrthɔn korei...* p. 807, line 7,
'Suprobha then Surjo defending him' col. 3
=Suprobha then defending Surjo

442. suprobhā tobu *protibādkore* bollen p. 808, line 5,
'Suprobha still objecting said' col. 1
=Suprobha still raised an (objection) protest and said...

443. puruschele konodos *kɔrenā* p. 808, line 11,
'men do not do any misdeed' col. 1
=men do not do any wrong/men do not commit a fault

444. tāders*pɔrsokɔrenā* p. 808, line 12,
'nothing them touch' col. 1
=(nothing/anything) can touch them

445. jārā *kɔsṭokore* lekhāpɔṛā sekhe māthārghām p. 808, line 12,
pāe phelā ṭākā *rojgār kɔre* col. 1
'who by effort study dropping the sweat earns bread'
=those who work hard for study (education)
and earn bread by the sweat of their brow...

446. *cul subinyāsto-koreo seāenār-sāmne-theke* sore elonā p. 809, line 4,
'the hair combing well he from the col. 1
mirror from did not go away'
=he did not go away from the mirror even though
he finished combing his hair well

447. nijeke sāmlābār *cesṭā koreo* pārlonā p. 809, line 10,
'herself controlled try though did not stop' col. 1
=she could not control herself even though she tried

448. *gum gum-kore* kil mere... p. 809, line 11,
'with the fist blowing' col. 1
=giving blow with her fist

449. *kono didhā nā kore* p. 809, line 31,
'any hesitation not doing' col. 1
=without any hesitation

450. hāt dukhānā *buker-kāche joṛokore...* p. 809, line 42,
'hand two on the chest folding' col. 1
=folding both hands on the chest

451. surjo ekṭuk^{h}ɔn *cupkore* dā̃ṛie roilo p. 809, line 16,
'Surjo a little silently stood' col. 2
=for a while Surjo stood silently

452. ā̃col *b^{h}edkore* p. 809, line 9,
the end of the cloth piercing col. 3
=through the cover of the cloth

453. *cæcā meci-kore* kono subidhe hɔbenā — p. 809, line 21, col. 3
'noise making any gain would not be'
=there will be no gain by howling

454. *æto-kore* — p. 772, line 1, col. 2
'by such effort'

455. nɔyɔntārā *cup-kore* bosechilo — p. 773, line 26, col. 1
'Nayantara silently sat'

456. *mɔsto ghoṭā-kore* — p. 773, line 37, col. 1
'much pomp with'
=with much pomp and grandeur

457. *māmlā korekore...* — p. 774, line 2, col. 3
'litigation doing (several times)'
=occasionally filing a suit

458. behulā *kæmon-kore...* — p. 774, line 28, col. 3
'Behula how'

459. ækrɔkom *upos-kore...* — p. 775, line 18, col. 1
'a kind of fasting'
=as a matter of fact, fasting

460. khokājodi *ghɔrtheke pāliejābār cesṭākɔre*[30] — p. 775, line 25, col. 2
tumi jæno oke *jor-kore* dhore rakhte bʰɔe pẹona
'Khoka if room from go way tries you
him forcibly to hold fear do not'
=if Khoka tries to flee from the room,
I suggest do not hesitate to hold him forcibly

461. o jodi tomāke kichu *kɔre...*[31] — p. 775, line 28, col. 2
'he if to you anything does'
=if he does anything to you

462. bole, *tālā bɔndho-kore*[32] — p. 775, line 32, col. 2
'locking (the door)'
=saying that, having locked (the door)

463. ei dinṭi *kæmon-kore*[33] pālon kɔra hɔbe — p. 778, line 2, col. 2
'this day how observe will (be)'
=how this day will be observed?

464. bojhābār *cesṭā-kore*[34] bærtho hoten — p. 778, line 22, col. 3
'(to make) understand having tries fail did'
=he did fail (even though) having tried
hard to make (them) understand

465. *submerine-kore*[35] jāoār somoe... — p. 778, line 24, col. 3
'submarine by going time'
=while travelling by a submarine

[30]Here is an expression with an auxiliary *-kɔre.*

[31]The morpheme is a main verb.

[32]It is a participial form expressing aspect.

[33]The morpheme is an expression of manner.

[34]Expresses aspect.

[35]The morpheme is an affix to the noun and gives the meaning with, by.

466. abid-hāsānke-o *bæsto-kore*[36] rākhten p. 778, line 31, col. 3
'Abid Hasan also keep engaged kept (use to keep)'
=also he used to make Abid Hasan engaged (busy) in work

467. bārāndāe bose *ṭhuk ṭhuk-kore*[36a] p. 781, line 47, col. 1
'on the veranda sitting slowly'
=slowly while sitting on the veranda

468. hāter āŋgul kā̃pche *ṭhɔk ṭhɔk-kore*[36a] p. 781, line 29, col. 2
'hands finger was trembling' (hesitatingly)
=the fingers were shivering (all over...)

469. molin bibɔrno photograph *sɔŋgrohokore*...[37] p. 782, line 6, col. 1
'gloomy faded photograph having collected'
ānā esɔber sārthokɔtā ki
'to bring of these utility what'
=what is the utility to collect and
bring faded photograph

470. ṭegore bɔṛo *sundor-kore*[37a] bolechen p. 783, line 6, col. 1
'Tagore very nicely has said'
=Tagore has said very nicely

471. ækbār nijer-mone *gungun-kore*[37a] ge-eo uṭhlen p. 783, line 12, col. 1
'once in own mind humming sang'
=once he sang with a low hum

472. *sɔŋ grohokore*... p. 783, line 4, col. 2
'having collected'

473. kāler bʰrukuṭi *upekkhā-kore*... p. 783, line 24, col. 2
'(the) times frown having (avoided) ignored'
=having ignored the threatening of the time...

474. ta e-kɔthāi *proman-kɔre* p. 783, line 33, col. 2
'that this proves'
=that proves it...

475. ei silporitiṭi *poritæg-kore* tārā... p. 783, line 4, col. 3
'this type of art having forsaken, they (giving up)'
=giving up this system of art, they...

476. *bises-kore* se sɔŋsthār poricalok sri Probhas sen... p. 783, line 9, col. 3
'particularly that institution's
director Sri Probhas Sen'
=particularly Sri Probhas Sen,
the director of that institution

477. probhriti *toiri-kore*[37b] *thāken* p. 786, line 10, col. 3
'etc. used to make'
=(they) used to make

478. *bæbohār-kore-thāken*[37b] p. 786, line 16, col. 3
'used to utilise'
=(they) used to utilize

[36]The participial form is expressing causative meaning.
[36a]Expression of manner.
[37]Expresses aspect.
[37a]Expression of manner.
[37b]The morpheme *kore* in these expressions gives the habitual aspect of the verb.

479. mɔḍel *toiri-kore neoā hɔe*[37b] — p. 786, line 18, col. 3
'(the) model used to make'
=the model is used to be made...

480. *phuṭo bɔndho-kore...* — p. 788, line 1, col. 2
'(the) whole having closed'
=having closed the whole...

481. murtiṭi *bārkore ānā hɔe*[37b] — p. 788, line 5, col. 2
'the idol used to take out'
=the idol is being taken out

482. *sukkmo-kore* goṛte ɔsubidhe hɔenā — p. 788, line 26, col. 3
'finely to make inconvenience there is no'
=there is no inconvenience to make (it) finely

483. procɔnḍo cāp *sriṣṭi-kɔre* — p. 791, line 8, col. 2
'severe pressure make (create)'
=it creates severe pressure

484. *bæbohār-kore-thāken* — p. 788, line 38, col. 3
'used to utilize'
=(they) used to utilize (they) make use of (it).

485. *gie āghāt-kɔre* — p. 791, line 10, col. 2
'having gone, hits'
=(it) hits (that)

486. *sɔrbɔrāho-kore-eseche* — p. 791, line 12, col. 2
'has been supplied'
=(it) has been supplied/(it) used to be supplied

487. ei kendre *sɔŋgroho-kore...* — p. 791, line 14, col. 2
'this centre in having collected'
=having been collected in this centre

488. *ete-kore* — p. 791, line 15, col. 2
'such (doing) having/in it'
=by such effort/as such

489. pɔre kloriner sāhājje *bisodhito-kore...* — p. 791, line 17, col. 2
'afterwards, chlorine with having purified'
=afterwards, having purified with chlorine

490. māthāpichu *kɔmkoreo* jɔl dɔrkār doinik 20 galon — p. 792, line 6, col. 2
'per head minimum water needed every day 20 gallons'
=minimum 20 gallons of water is needed per head daily

491. *kotri pokkher-kāche ceṣṭā-koreo...* — p. 792, line 4, col. 3
'(the) authority near having tried'
=having requested the authority

492. jɔl *pump-kore* tule neoār dorun — p. 794, line 14, col. 1
'water having pumped taking out because'
=because the water is being pumped out

493. bɔchore *æk-phuṭ-kore...* — p. 795, line 18, col. 2
'yearly one foot about'
=yearly about one foot

494. ɔnek *pɔddʰoti-ber kore phelechen* p. 795, line 16, col. 3
'many system has been invented'
= various kinds of system have been invented.

495. *emni-kore...* p. 798, line 3, col. 2
'in this manner/in such a way'

496. sei sārtho holo *silperdik-theke*
'that interest is from the point of view of the art'.

497. niyɔmito bʰābe kāj *kɔre*[38] p. 811, line 6, col. 1
'regularly work does'
= (it) does the job regularly.

498. stɔrbʰed-ke *kendro-kore...* p. 811, line 18, col. 1
'strata difference taking centre'
= taking the different strata as centre.

499. rɔconā khetrer upɔr *ɔbotāronākɔre* p. 811, line 23, col. 1
'the writing on comes up'
= (it) comes up on the writing (painting/drawing).

500. rɔŋer māyā jāl *srisṭi-kɔre* p. 811, line 28, col. 1
'colour world of illusion creates'
= (it) creates the world of illusion of colour.

501. sādā o nil rɔŋ-ke *kendro-kore...* p. 811, line 41, col. 1
'white and blue colour centreing'
= centreing the white and blue colour.

502. rɔŋ *bɔbohār-kɔre* p. 811, line 45, col. 1
'colour use (make use)'
= (they) make use of the colour.

503. nāri o sisuke *kendro-kore...* p. 811, line 52, col. 1
'woman and child centring'
= centring the woman and the child.

504. ɔneker drisṭi *ākɔrson-kore...* p. 811, line 6, col. 2
'many sight has attracted'
= has attracted many...

505. *bises-kore, graphik silpa corcā kore...* p. 811, line 12, col. 2
'particularly, graphic art having cultured'
= particularly having cultured the graphic art.

506. rekhā-jāl *srisṭi-kɔre* p. 811, line 21, col. 3
'illusion of lines creates'
= (it) creates an illusion of lines.

507. du-æk sthɔle coturbʰujke-*kendrokore* æk *rɔŋer opor* ɔnno rɔŋ *bɔbohār-kɔre* p. 812, line 11, col. 2
'one or two places in four taking as centre one the colour on other colour make use.'

508. ekṭi rɔŋer opor ār ekṭi rɔŋ *superimpoje-kɔre* p. 812, line 16, col. 2
'one colour on another one colour superimposes'
= (he/they) superimpose one colour on the other.

[38]A systematic vowel change is observed in the morpheme between the used main verb or auxiliary and the participial or manner, etc.

509. ākār o *bises-kore kɔmpojisoneropor*... — p. 812, line 22, col. 2
'the form and in particular composition on'
= the form (shape) and in particular on the composition .

510. sɔkoler drisṭi *ākɔrson-kɔre* — p. 812, line 37, col 2.
'all attracts'
= attracts (the sight of all) all.

511. ekṭi bisisto-sthān *ɔdhikār-kore phelechen* — p. 812, line 40, col. 2
'one special place occupied has'
= (he) has occupied a special place.

512. ākārer-rup *dān-kɔre* — p. 812, line 42, col. 2
'the form give shape'
= it takes (gives) shape.

513. *nisṭhā sɔhokāre silpocɔrcā-kɔre* — p. 812, line 3, col. 3
'attention with art cultures'
= (he/they) culture art with sincere attention.

514. pārtho-bābu mohommād ke sudd^{b}okore mohammod likhechen — p. 813, line 2, col. 3
'Mr. Partha Mohammad correcting Mohammod has written'
= Mr. Partha has written Mohammad correcting Mohammod.

515. sɔbāi *cɔṭkore*... — p. 813, line 6, col. 1
'all short time in'
= everybody, within a short time.

516. lutphurke *sɔŋsodhɔn-kore* lutphɔrke sikhie... — p. 814, line 17, col. 1
'Lutfur having corrected Lutfor taught'
= (he) has taught Lutfor having corrected Lutfur.

517. tɔkhon tāder-mone eimānosikɔtāo kāj-kɔre — p. 815, line 4, col. 2
'then their mind in this psychological feeling works'
= then, this psychological feeling appears in their mind.

518. Prokāsɔk seimāphik-kore utsāhi kretāke sāhājyokɔren — p. 815, line 7, col. 2
'(the) publisher in that manner interested (enthusiastic) buyer helps'
= in this manner the publisher helps the enthusiastic buyer.

519. debendranāth ṭhākur-theke *ārɔmb^{h}o-kore*... — p. 821, line 11, col. 1
'Debendranath Thakur from beginning'
= beginning from Debendranath Thakur.

520. bɔrtomān grɔnthoṭi sɔŋkɔlon-kore... — p. 821, line 30, col. 1
'(present book) having edited the present book.'

521. jhopjhāṛ-theke *ārɔmbho-kore*... — p. 821, line 5, col. 3
'bush and wood from beginning'
= having started with the bush and shrub.

522. mānnādāi *bɔbosthā kore dilo* — p. 823, line 29, col. 1
'Mannada arrangement made'
= brother Manna made arrangement.

523. grāmer sɔŋskār tæg-kore... — p. 822, line 2, col. 1
'village prejudice abandoning'
= abandoning the village prejudice.

524. *drisṭi-ākɔrsɔn-kɔre* p. 822, line 2, col. 2
'attracts the interest'
= (it) attracts (their) interest.

525. *chelebæla-thekei* monimālā nijeke *nirasrɔe bodh-kɔre* p. 822, line 5, col. 3
'childhood from Monimala herself insecure felt'
= Monimala felt herself insecure from her childhood.

526. kāhinir-gotibeg-ke *ucchɔl-kore* tuleche p. 822, line 26, col. 3
'story flow make speedy/has made speedy'
= (it) made speedy the flow of the story.

527. sɔbāitāder-kɔthā *alocɔnā-kɔre* tāder *tāriph-kɔre sɔŋgopābār cesṭā-kɔre* p. 823, line 24, col. 1
'everybody them discuss them appreciate their company try to get' = everybody discusses them, appreciates them and tries to get their company.

528. nijer *jāegā-kore-nite-pārbe*[39] p. 823, line 49, col. 3
'own room (place) can make (would be able to make)'
= (he) would be able to make a room for himself.

529. āge *ghɔrer-unnoti-kore*... p. 825, line 6, col. 2
'first room (house) (better off) improve'
= at first having improved (the own property (home)) yourself.

530. *bises-kore*... p. 825, line 14, col. 2
'particularly'

531. campiɔnsiper prosno prodhanɔto *nirbʰɔr-kore* thāke p. 825, line 33, col. 3
'championship question mainly depends'
= mainly the question of championship depends on (it).

532. cāridiker ɔnnāe ɔsāmmo tāke kichuṭā *bikkʰubdho-kore-tole* p. 829, line 15, col. 1
'surrounding injustice in equality him to some extent unhappy make'
= the surrounding injustice and inequality make him sick.

533. echobiṭi-o monke ākɔrsɔn-kɔre p. 829, line 32, col. 1
'this picture also the mind strikes'
= this picture also strikes in the mind.

534. *bises-kore* phɔṭographi o sɔmpādanā p. 829, line 24, col. 2
'particularly, the photography and edition'
= particularly, the photography and edition.

535. æk-dɔl jubɔker ārto-hāhākārke *upojibbo-kore*... p. 830, line 4, col. 1
'a group of young people pitiful cry supporting'
= depending (taking as the theme) on the tragedy of a group of young men.

536. æksrenir-netārā *kæmon-kore*... p. 830, line 9, col. 1
'a group of leaders how'
= how a group of leaders.

537. ār dekhlām *ki-kore*... p. 831, line 13, col. 2
'and saw how'
= and I saw how...

[39] The morpheme expresses the aspect of the verb.

538. ɔbʰiggotār *ullekh-kore...* p. 832, line 12, col. 2
'the experience mentioning'
= having mentioned the experience.

539. su-nirdiṣṭo obʰijog-kore *mukkʰo montrir-kāche* p. 832, line 25, col. 2
'specific complain chief minister to'
= having complained specifically to the chief minister.

(5) *N+jonno*

540. *sɔjātir-jonno* onurodh-kɔren p. 743, line 43, col. 1
'countrymen for requested'
= (he) requested for the countrymen.

541. *bærtho-koribār-jonno* lekhā houk p. 743, line 2, col. 2
'make unsuccess for write let'
= let it be written to baffle (it).

542. kɔr-phā̃ki *bɔndho-kɔrār-jonno* p. 751, line 18, col. 1
'tax evasion stop for'
= to stop the tax evasion.

543. kāloṭākār-bridhi *protihɔto-kɔrār-jonno* p. 751, line 2, col. 2
'black money increase resist for'
= to resist the increase of the black money.

544. *rājosser pariman-bāṛābār-jonno ebŋ sɔmpɔder-kendrikɔrɔn protihoto kɔrārjonno* p. 751, line 7, col. 3
'revenue quantity increase for and wealth centralization resist for'
= to increase the quantity of the revenue and to resist the centralization of wealth.

545. sɔmājbād *protiṣṭhār-jonno* sɔrkār bɔddʰo porikor p. 751, line 12, col. 3
'socialism establish for government determined'
= the government is determined to establish socialism.

546. āe-kɔr-phā̃ki *bɔndho-kɔrār-jonno* p. 751, line 14, col. 3
'income tax evasion stop for'
= to stop the income tax evasion.

547. sɔṃājbāder-pɔthe *egobār-jonno* p. 751, line 17, col. 3
'socialism path proceed for'
= to proceed towards the path of socialism.

548. binioge *utsāho-prodāner-jonno* p. 751, line 30, col. 3
'invest to encourage giving for'
= encouraging to invest/to give encouragement to invest.

549. *jātio-sɔncɔe bāṛābār-jonno* p. 752, line 5, col. 2
'national savings increase for'
= to increase the national savings.

550. *...deser-kolyāner-jonno* p. 752, line 21, col. 3
'country's benefit for'
= for the development (benefit) of the country.

551. *jibɔn-dhāroner-jonno* p. 752, line 24, col. 3
'life hold for'
=for living.

552. bʰɔbissɔt *culoculir-jonno nɔe* p. 754, line 38, col. 3
'future quarrel (dispute) for not'
=(it is) not for the dispute (quarrel) in future.

553. jæmon *sukher-jonno* tæmoniābārjæno *ɔsukherjonno-o* p. 755, line 19, col. 3
'as happiness for so again as if illness for also'
=as (it is) for the happiness, so again seems also for the illness.

554. sɔbāimile *tār-jonno* p. 755, line 23, col. 3
'all together that for'
= everybody (all) together (do) for that.

555. mārāpɔṛe ɔnek sɔmɔe *sei-jonnoi* p. 756, line 1, col. 1
'feels difficulty many times that for'
= because of that sometimes (they/one) feels difficulty.

556. jini *toruni potnir mānbʰɔ njoner-jonno* p. 761, line 11, col. 1
'who young wife make happy for'
= who to appease amorous anger, coax and cajole of the young wife.

557. bʰɔrɔter-mɔnobʰab *porikkʰa-kɔrār-jonno* p. 763, line 2, col. 1
'Bharat's mind test for'
= to test Bharat's mind.

558. jār *khoniker-jonno* dækhā p. 763, line 13, col. 2
'whose moment for look (saw/met)'
= who met for a moment.

559. sudhu prosno o proās o dāitto ache *tār-jonno* p. 763, line 24, col. 2
'only question and effort and responsibility exist him for' = he has problem (question), effort and responsibility to accomplish
= only the question, effort and responsibility exist for him (to be done).

560. *dhārtɔrāṣṭrɔder-jonno* p. 764, line 6, col. 1
'Dhritarastra's sons for'
= for the sons of Dhritarastra.

561. ɔnno *kāro-jonno* dāi-non tini p. 765, line 2, col. 1
'another any for responsible not he'
= he is not responsible for anybody else.

562. ei *āloconār-sɔmpurnotār-jonno* p. 765, line 31, col. 1
'this discussion completion for'
= for the completion of this discussion.

563. *ɔstrc sɔŋgroher-jonno* p. 765, line 36, col. 2
'weapon collection for'
= to collect the weapons.

564. *æk-diner jonnei* p. 767, line 4, col. 3
'one day for (only)'
= only for one day.

565. *temni morbār-jonnei* p. 767, line 6,
'so die for' col. 3
= so to die only.

566. *b͠ācār-jonnoi* khāe p. 767, line 30,
'life for eats' col. 3
= eats to live.

567. *khābār-jonnoi* b͠āce p. 767, line 29,
'eating for alive' col. 3
= we are alive because we eat.

568. sudhu *khābār-jonnoi* p. 768, line 1,
'only eating for' col. 1
= only for eating.

569. *colejābār-jonno* p. 771, line 14,
'going for' col. 2
= for going away.

570. *khudro-silper-jonno* p. 803, line 17,
'small industry for' col. 1
= for small industry.

571. *sāhājjo kɔrār-jonno* roeche p. 803, line 30,
'help doing for exists' col. 1
= it is there to help.

572. *tɔdārokir-jonno* p. 803, line 1,
'inspection for' col. 3
= for inspection.

573. *t͠āt-silper-jonno* p. 803, line 2,
'handloom industry for' col. 3
= for the handloom industry.

574. *hɔstɔ o kāru silper-jonno* p. 803, line 4,
'handcraft industry for' col. 3
= for the handcraft industry.

575. *resɔm-silper-jonno* p. 803, line 5,
'silk industry for' col. 3
= for the silk industry.

576. *nārkel* *͠ās-silper-jonno* p. 803, line 6,
'coconut fibre industry for' col. 3
= for the coconut fibre industry.

577. *khādi ebṇ grām-silper-jonno* p. 803, line 7,
'khadi and village industry for' col. 3
= for the khadi and village industry.

578. *lākkhājāto-silper-jonno* p. 803, line 8,
'lac industry for' col. 3
= for the industry of lac-product.

579. *nijer-jonno*-nɔe, *surjor-jonno* p. 809, line 35,
'own for not Surya for' col. 2
= (it is) not for herself, (but) for Surya.

580. *ālnār-kāche jāmāporbār-jonno* gie p. 810, line 3,
'rack to shirt wear for having' col. 3
= having gone to the rack to wear shirt.

581. *sāmānno sɔmɔer-jonno-o* — p. 781, line 15, col. 1
'little time for even'
= even for a little while.

582. *tāder-jonno* proyojon āche-kina jāni-nā — p. 782, line 1, col. 2
'them for needed whether do not know'
= I do not know whether (it is) needed for them.

583. *din-gujrānor-jonno* — p. 785, line 9, col. 2
'day pass for'
= to pass the day.

584. *chā̃cerbʰitore* phā̃pā ɔŋso *srisṭi-kɔrbār-jonno* — p. 786, line 10, col. 3
'mould in hollow portion create for'
= to (create) make a hollow portion inside the mould.

585. ækjon *uccomāddhomik-porikkhār-jonno prostut hocche* — p. 790, line 3, col. 1
'one higher secondary examination for being ready'
= one is being ready (prepare) for higher secondary examination.

586. kintu *se-jonno* — p. 790, line 4, col. 1
'but that for'

587. *mokābilā kɔrār-jonno* — p. 790, line 1, col. 3
'face that for'
= to face that.

588. *tār-jonno* sɔrkārer sɔtɔrkɔdrisṭir-prɔyojon — p. 795, line 33, col. 3
'that for the government careful watch necessary'
= it is necessary for the government to havewat chfuleyes for that.

589. rɔkeṭ-ke jæmon *moddʰākɔrson brittotheke* — p. 797, line 35, col. 1
ṭhele *mɔhākās gāmi kɔrār-jonno* ...
= as (it is necessary) to push the rocket from the centre of gravity to run towards the sky.

590. ei birāṭ dese khudro-silpobāhini-*poricālonār-jonno* — p. 799, line 43, col. 1
'This vast country in small industries direct for'
= to direct the small scale industries in this vast country.

591. *sɔmossā-sɔmādhān-kɔrār-jonno* roechen — p. 800, line 17, col. 1
'problem solve doing for there is'
= there exist (it) to solve the problems.

592. tāke dhonnobād *ei-jonno* — p. 814, line 44, col. 1
'him thanks this for'
= thanks to him for that.

593. *sɔkoler-jonno* — p. 815, line 6, col. 1
'everybody for'
= for everybody.

594. *ɔthɔco jāder-jonno* — p. 815, line 11, col. 1
'but whom for'
= but for whom.

595. *bidɔgdha-hɔoār jonno* p. 815, line 36,
'enlighten being for' col. 1
= for being enlightened/to become enlightened
since (they/he/she) is enlightened.

596. nibɔndhoti *prokāser-jonno* p. 816, line 4,
'(the) article publishing for' col. 1
= to publish the article/for publishing
the article (it is for publication).

597. isam *jomidār-bābu-der-jonno gɔtor dieche* p. 822, line 22,
'Iswam zaminder's for health has given' col. 1
= Iswam has worked for the zaminders
(landlords).

598. phokir sāheber mālotir-jonno je p. 822, line 32,
'Phakir (Mr.) Malati for that' col. 1
= Phakir's that (affection) for Malati.

599. ei āsrɔe-hinotāke *bhɔrāṭ-kɔrār-jonnoi* p. 822, line 7,
'this insecurity fill up for' col. 3
= to fill up this feeling of insecurity.

600. *dɔl-gɔṛār-jonno* p. 823, line 4,
'group made for' col. 3
= to make a group.

601. *ghɔrer-jonno* p. 824, line 21,
'country (home) for' col. 1
= for home (country).

602. *āntorjātik phuṭbɔler sɔŋge poricitohɔbār-jonno* p. 824, line 36,
'international football with acquainted for' col. 1
= for being acquainted with the
international football.

603. ebār *mardeka kæmper-jonno* p. 825, line 1,
'now Mardeca camp for' col. 1
= now for the Mardeca camp.

604. *nicumāner-jonnoi* p. 825, line 12,
'low standard for' col. 1
= for the low standard.

605. porikkhār hɔle chāttroder ṭokaṭuki p. 827, line 17,
dhorbār-jonnoi sikkhɔk churikāhɔto col. 3
'examination hall in students copying detect for teacher stabbed'
= to detect the copying practice of the students at
the examination hall, the teacher was stabbed.

606. *cākri-pābārjonno, porikkhāpāser-jonno* p. 827, line 18,
'job get for examination passed for' col. 3
= to get a job to pass an examination.

607. *bikɔlpo montri-sɔbhā gɔṭhoner-jonno* p. 832, line 8,
'alternative ministry make for' col. 1
= to make an alternative ministry.

608. deske *durbɔl-kore phælār-jonno* p. 832, line 55,
'country weak doing for' col. 3
= to make the country weak.

609. tāhole *mān unnɔyoner jonno* khæloāṛdermoddhe 'then standard raising for player among' = then to improve the standard of the play among the player. — p. 825, line 13, col. 1

(6) *N+kāche*

610. æmonækækṭā māmlā *tāder-kāche* āse 'such a particular litigation them to comes' = such particular type of litigation comes to them. — p. 737, line 21, col. 1

611. sidhānto-gulo pes-korten *hujurer-kāche* 'concluding decisions put (the) authority to' = (he/she) used to put the concluding remarks to (him) the authority. — p. 741, line 7, col. 3

612. seguli sɔbi *ɔrthonitibidder-kāche* 'those all economists to' = all those are to the economists. — p. 751, line 8, col. 1

613. āmito *āpnār-kāche* kono... 'I you to any' = I (did not brorrow) owe anything to you. — p. 755, line 5, col. 1

614. sesomɔe jæno *āmār-kāche*... 'that time as if me to' = I wish that time to me. — p. 756, line 23, col. 2

615. oi *kāblir-kāche* 'that kabuli to' = to that Kabuli (the man from Kabul). — p. 756, line 29, col. 2

616. *tār-kāche* ami jārpɔrnāe kritõggo 'him/her to I very grateful' = I am very grateful to him/her. — p. 757, line 25, col. 1

617. sthānio æk-*protisṭhaner-kāche* 'local one institution to' = to a local institution. — p. 760, line 40, col. 1

618. *ibɔn-dukhter-sɔmādhir-kāche* 'Iban Dukhat tomb near' = near (to) the tomb of Iban Dukhat. — p. 760, line 12, col. 2

619. *tār-kache* 'her/him to' = to him/her. — p. 761, line 30, col. 2

620. ækbār dhɔrmo *bɔker-kāche*[40] 'once Dharma crane to' = once the Dharma to the crane/once to the pious crane. — p. 763, line 53, col. 2

621. ārækbār *krishner-kāche* 'and once Krishna to' = and once to Lord Krishna. — p. 763, line 53, col. 2

622. *grihother-kāche* āsrɔepāe 'householder to shelter gets' = gets shelter to the householder. — p. 764, line 38, col. 2

[40]The two readings depend on the unit division.

623. *eder-kāche* — p. 764, line 45,
'them to' — col. 2
= to them.

624. kono *bisuddho-adorsher-kāche* — p. 765, line 26,
'any pure (high) ideal to' — col. 2
= to any high (pure) ideal.

625. *bhimsener-kāche* — p. 765, line 26,
'Bhimsen to' — col. 2
= to Bhimsen.

626. prithibi krɔmoso *kāche*[40a] sore-āsche — p. 803, line 15,
'earth gradually close comes' — col. 3
= the earth comes closer gradually.

627. sɔb sɔmoe *kāche kāche*[40a] peeche — p. 805, line 11,
'all time close has got' — col. 3
= every time (he) has got (him/her/it) nearby.

628. *dɔrojār-kāche* — p. 805, line 24,
'door to' — col. 3
= to the door/near the door (doorway).

629. *āro kāche-ene* — p. 807, line 34,
'more close bringing' — col. 1
= bringing more close.

630. *kā̃dh o buker-kāche* — p. 809, line 1,
'shoulder and the chest near (on)' — col. 2
= on the shoulder and the chest.

631. *surjor-kāche* — p. 809, line 33,
'Surya to' — col. 2
= to Surya (proper name).

632. *jāder-kāche* — p. 809, line 39,
'whom to' — col. 2
= to whom...

633. *srilekhār kāch-theke* — p. 809, line 26,
'Srilekha from' — col. 3
= from Srilekha (proper name)/to Srilekha.

634. eito sɔbe *bāper-kāch-theke* elo boumā — p. 775, line 46,
'only just father from came daughter-in-law' — col. 2
= the daughter-in-law came back just few days from her father's house.

635. *sɔmobeto dɔrsɔkder-kāche* uni bɔrnonākorlen — p. 778, line 17,
'assembled observers to he described' — col. 2
= he described (it) to the (whole assembled) audience.

636. eder-kāch-theke õr ses ob^{h}ibādan — p. 778, line 13,
'them from his last reception' — col. 3
= it is the last reception (salute) to him from them.

[40a]The morphemes are not bound morphemes but function as separate words.

637. sekɔthā *nāmbiārer-kāche* bises-bhābe sunechi — p. 778, line 36, col. 3
'that Nambier from minutely heard'
=(I) have heard that minutely from (to) Nambier.

638. *uttorsurider-kāche* cirontɔn preronā hɔbe — p. 783, line 21, col. 2
'the next generation to (constant) eternal inspiration will be'
= that will be an everlasting inspiration to the following generation.

639. kintu *āmār-kāche* — p. 785, line 7, col. 1
'but me from (to)'
= but to me (near me).

640. *mɔhājonder-kāche* — p. 785, line 8, col. 2
'merchants to'
= to the moneylenders (from the moneylenders).

641. *probhās-sen-mɔsāier-kāche* sunechi — p. 789, line 16, col. 1
'Probhas Sen Mr. to have heard'
= (I) have heard from Mr. Probhas Sen.

642. stɔr ɔnek *kāchākāchi* — p. 795, line 1, col. 1
'the level very close'
= the levels (are) very close.

643. *kolkātār phoṭ viliamer-kāche* — p. 795, line 10, col. 1
'Calcutta of Fort William near'
= near the Fort William at Calcutta.

644. *kretāder-kāche* — p. 815, line 41, col. 1
'buyers to'
= to the buyers (purchasers).

645. *tāder-kāche* — p. 815, line 46, col. 1
'them to'
=to them.

646. eri *kāchākāchi* — p. 819, line 23, col. 1
'its near (close)'
=close to that...

647. *gɔbesɔkder-kāche* oti prɔojonio dolil — p. 821, line 19, col. 2
'researcher to very important document'
=it is a very important document to the researcher.

648. *bijoy-māmār-kāche* — p. 822, line 11, col. 3
'bijoy uncle to'
= to uncle Bijoy/from uncle Bijoy.

649. *bɔrmār-kāche* — p. 825, line 27, col. 1
'Burma near'
= near Burma/close to Burma/to Burma.

650. *israiler-kāche* — p. 825, line 33, col. 1
'Israel to (near, close)'
= to Israel, near Israel, close to Israel, etc.

651. *durbɔl dɔler-kāche* — p. 825, line 35, col. 3
'weak team to'
= to a weak team/from a weak team.

652. *durbɔler-kāche*
'weak to'
= to a weak (person), from a weak person.

653. *netār kāch-theke* p. 830, line 20, col. 1
'leader from (to)'
= to a leader/from a leader.

654. *rajyopāler-kāche* p. 832, line 2, col. 1
'governor to'
= to the governor/from the governor.

655. *puliser-kāche* p. 832, line 24, col. 1
'police to (from)'
= to the police/from the police.

656. *jāder-kāche* p. 832, line 37, col. 1
'whom to'
= to whom/to them/from whom/from them.

657. *sekh-mujibur-rahamāner-kāche* p. 832, line 31, col. 3
'Saikh Mujibur Rahaman to'
= to Saikh Mujibur Rahaman/from Saikh Mujibur Rahaman.

658. *kocib^{h}ɔ ktoderkāche* p. 823, line 4, col. 1
'young followers to'
= to the young followers/from the young followers.

(7) *N+Nikɔṭ*

659. *saŋbādikder-nikɔṭ* p. 823, line 26, col. 1
'journalists to'
= to the journalists/from the journalists.

660. deser loker *nikɔṭ-hoite* p. 817, line 11, col. 1
'countrymen from'
= from the countrymen.

(8) *N+hoite*

661. *ɔnno sɔkol jātir bɔbosthā-hoite* p. 742, line 6, col. 3
'other all races customs from'
= (it is) different from the customs of all other races.

662. *ɔnnokono sthān-hoite* p. 744, line 20, col. 1
'other any place from'
= from any other place.

663. lālbāg kellā lālkellā *hote pāreni*[41] p. 760, line 1, col. 1
'Lalbag Fort (red) Lal Fort (red) cannot be'

664. cālculo-hin *bāunḍule hote*[41a] p. 763, line 45, col. 2
'shelter less vagabond to be'
= to be a homeless destitute.

[41]The morpheme is a participial form of the verb, and does not constitute a unit with the nominal *lāl-kellā*.

[41a]The morphemes are verbal expressions.

665. *boncitohote hɔe*[41a] p. 765, line 18,
'to be deprived of' col. 2

666. kār *sthān-hote-pāre*[41a] tā sɔhɔjei phuṭe uṭhbe p. 802, line 11,
'whose room may be that easily be clear' col. 1
= it will be easy to understand who will get the place
(chance/will be mentioned).

667. *bʰiṭe chāṛā-hoite hɔe nā* p. 790, line 1,
'ancestral home abandon become would not have' col. 1
= (he) would not have to abandon the ancestral home.

668. sɔrbodā *protārito hote hote*[42] mon ɔto sɔŋkucito hoe poṛeche p. 815, line 5,
'always being deceived mind such hesitant that' col. 3
= (I/am) such hesitant, since being deceived always that...

669. ālocɔnādi *prokāsito-hote* dekhini p. 816, line 6,
'discussions being published did not see' col. 2
= (I) have not seen any published article on that.

670. kobi-sɔnmelɔn *jukto-hote thāke* p. 819, line 37,
'poetic society being joined in' col. 1
= the poetic society is being joined in (it).

671. ekṭu *ɔswosti-hote-thāke* p. 819, line 19,
'little uneasy felt' col. 3
= (I) felt a little bit uneasy.

672. āmi ɔrɔnnodeb *hote cāi nā* p. 826, line 2,
'I Aranyadev to become do not want' col. 1
= I do not want to be a Forest God.

673. silpike *kɔkhɔno kɔkhɔno nirāsɔkto-hote-hɔe* p. 829, line 21,
'the artist sometimes (aloof) detached to be' col. 2
= sometimes an artist should have a detached feeling.

674. *ihār pɔscāt-hoite* soriā jāo p. 741, line 5,
'its behind from get away' col. 2
= get away from its behind.

675. *deser citto-hoite* bilupto hoiā-chilo p. 819, line 16,
'country's heart from wiped out' col. 1
= (he) had been wiped out from the country.

(9) *N+dārā*

676. *dʰābokgɔn-dārā* p. 743, line 21,
'pursuers by' col. 1
= by the pursuers.

677. *dhābɔkgɔner hɔsto-dārā* p. 743, line 12,
'pursuers hands by' col. 2
= by the hands of the pursuers.

[41a] The morphemes are verbal expressions.

[42] The morpheme is a participial form of verb and expresses continuous action. Compare with *N+kore* (adverbial) such as *kɔto jɔtno kore kore kobita porte hɔe* 'how carefully, poems are to be read'.

678. tārā *ɔsuār-dārā* p. 764, line 7, col. 1
'they envy (jealousy) by'
= they by envy (jealousy)/
because of jealousy (envy) they...

(10) *N+rupe*

679. tini *judhisṭhirer-b^hārjā-rupe protib^hātohote thāken* p. 764, line 7, col. 2
'she Judhisthir's wife as depicted being'
= she is being depicted as the wife of Judhisṭhir.

(11) *N+dhore*

680. *tæro hɔptā-dhore*[43] bicar collo p. 737, line 18, col. 3
'thirteen weeks long case ran'
= the court case continued for thirteen weeks (long).

681. *bes-kichudin-dhorei* p. 760, line 1, col. 3
'well some days (from) long indeed'
= indeed for (sometimes) few days.

(26) *N+proti*

682. *bālmikir-proti* ɔbicār korbo p. 761, line 7, col. 1
'Balmiki to injustice will do'
= I shall do injustice to Balmiki.

683. *bhrātā o b^hātribodhur-proti* p. 761, line 22, col. 1
'brother and brother's wife to'
= to the brother and sister-in-law.

684. *mone mone ɔrjuner-proti* p. 764, line 17, col. 1
'mind in Arjun to'
= mentally, to Arjun (she was attached).

685. *proti-din notun-kore* bojhāpāṛā korte hɔbenā p. 765, line 4, col. 1
'every day as new consideration have not been made'
= (I/we) do not have to consider (realize, understand)
every day (with the same topic) taking as new.

686. *griher-proti poribārer-proti* bimukh hoeoṭhe p. 765, line 23, col. 1
'home to, family to unfavourable to be'
= turn away from home and the family.

687. *proti-pɔde pɔde* sāhājjo nin p. 803, line 37, col. 1
'every step in help take'
= (you) take help in every step.

[43]Even though in our collected examples there is no form like verbal participle or a separate word, the morpheme *dhore* can function as participial, main or auxiliary verb, adverbial and a separate word in the language, such as: *tākedhore* 'holding him'/'by his recommendation'; *dhorenilam* 'I take it granted'; *dhɔro* 'suppose'; *dhore dhore* 'holding', 'supporting'; *dhɔro* 'catch'; *dhɔre-nā* 'cannot contain'; *dhār dhore* 'along the beach'.

688. *poscim bɔŋger lok-silper-proti* p. 785, line 11, col. 3
'West Bengal's folk art to'
= to the folk art of West Bengal.

689. *soisɔb-kāl-thekei chobiā̃kār-proti* meeṭir jhõk chilo p. 812, line 47, col. 2
'childhood from drawing picture to the girl has interest'
= the girl has interest towards drawing from her childhood.

690. *tāder-proti* p. 815, line 12, col. 1
them to
= to them

691. *ækjon monisir krito kɔrmer proti sroddhā nibedɔner moddho-die* amra smɔronkori p. 816, line 5,
'one great man's work to respect showing through we remember'
= we remember the great man through showing (casting) our respect towards his work.

692. bidhān sobhā dɔler-proti p. 832, line 91, col. 1
'to the assembly members group'

693. *bicitro-bisɔer-proti* p. 822, line 12, col. 2
'various subjects of to'
= to various kinds of subjects.

694. *sɔntāner-proti* p. 822, line 16, col. 3
'child to'
= to the child.

695. *proti-khælātei* p. 823, line 26, col. 3
'each play in'
= in each play show indeed.

696. *gāner moddhe* phuṭe uṭheche *nārir-proti* purusercirontonpremer kɔthā p. 783, line 7, col. 1
'song in has expressed woman to man of eternal love'
= In (Tagore) song the eternal love of man to woman has been expressed.

(26) *N+upor* (*upor theke hāte*)

697. jāte, *goriber upor-theke* p. 751, line 25, col. 3
'however, poor on (from)'
= however, from the poor.

698. jhā̃pie porlo *rājārbāgerpulisbærākerupɔr* p. 760, line 13, col. 3
'jumped Rajarbag police barrack on'
= they (swamped) jumped on the Rajarbag police barrack.

699. *heḍkoāṭarer-upor* p. 760, line 14, col. 3.
'headquarter upon'
= on the headquarter.

700. *ādhunik-sɔmājer upor* tibro kɔsā ghāt p. 811, line 12, col. 3
'modern society upon strong criticism'
= (it is) a strong criticism on the modern society.

701. *ghɔrer phuṭbɔler sārther upɔre noe* p. 824, line 1, col. 2
'country football interest than not'
= it is not important than the interest of the football team of the country.

702. din din *upore* uṭhche p. 825, line 35, col. 1
'day by day high is going'
= it is increasing higher day by day

703. ekṭikisoṛer *oibɔoser nisɔŋgotār-opor*[44] p. 892, line 4.
ekṭi porikkha mulɔk chobi
'of a teenager of that age loneliness upon an experimental picture'
= it is an experimental movie of a teenager boy on the loneliness of that age.

704. *obʰiggõ prokāsɔkder-opor* p. 832, line 9, col. 2
'experienced publishers upon'
= on the experienced publishers.

705. *sarat-sāhitter-upor* p. 815, line 24, col. 1
'Sarat literature on'
= on the literature of Saratchandra.

(12) *N+bhitɔr (bʰetɔre)*

706. *kellār bʰetɔre* p. 760, line 11, col. 1
'fort inside'
= inside the fort.

707. tɔbe *bhitore bʰitore* phũschilo p. 760, line 44, col. 2
'but in wordly (in mind) was (angry) burning'
= but in mind (they) were burning.

708. mɔḍelṭi *dhātur-ācchādoner-bhitore* theke-jae p. 788, line 6, col. 2
'the model metal sheet in remains'
= the model remains inside the metal cover.

709. *bhitore* ækjoṛā phɔrseph theke-jāe p. 832, line 41, col. 3
'inside one pair of forceps remains'

710. *bhitor-theke* bɔle uṭhlo p. 772, line 19, col. 3
'from inside (she) said'

N+bāhir (bāhire/bāire)

711. hɔṭhāt *bāire-theke* p. 775, line 22, col. 1
'suddenly outside from'
= all on a sudden from the outside.

712. *bāire-theke* p. 774, line 10, col. 1
'outside from'
= from the outside.

[44]This morpheme can function as a separate word such as *opor opor* 'outwardly', 'superficially', etc.

713. *kellār-bāire* p. 760, line 25, col. 1
'fort outside'
= outside the fort.

(13) *N+pokk*^{h}*e*

714. *sɔmɔgro sāmrājyer-pokk*^{h}*e* p. 797, line 5, col. 3
'whole kingdom to (on behalf)'
= to the whole kingdom (country/state).

715. jā sāstho abɔŋ silpo *ubʰɔer-pokk*^{h}*ei* p. 795, line 5, col. 1
'what health and industry both for (to) harmful'
= which is harmful both to the health and industry (art).

716. *sɔnnāsir-pokk*^{h}*e* p. 764, line 5, col. 1
'Sanyasi to'
= to the ascetic.

717. *droupadir moto dhɔrmācrinir-pokk*^{h}*eo* p. 764, line 15, col. 1
'Draupadi like religious minded for even'
= even to the pious woman like Draupadi.

718. *krittibāspottrikār pokk*^{h}*o-theke* p. 819, line 45, col. 1
'Krittibas magazine behalf from'
=on behalf of the journal named 'Krittibas'.

719. *tār-pokkhe* p. 767, line 9, col. 2
'him for' (to)
= for him/to him.

720. *pɔltār-pokkhe*[45] p. 791, line 3, col. 3
'Palta for'
= for Palta/to Palta.

(14) *N+khettre*

721. *kutir silper punorujjibɔner-khettre* p. 790, line 2, col. 2
'cottage industry revival matter'
= in the topic (matter) of the revival of the cottage industry.

722. *ɔnnānno silper-khettreo* p. 790, line 5, col. 3
'other industries matter also'
= also in the matter of the other industries (as well).

723. *silper-khettreo-tāi* p. 799, line 16, col. 1
'industry to true'
= it is true to the field of industry/it is applicable to the field of industry.

The above-mentioned morphemes either occur as the bound element or as an independent word or as a participial form of verb. Often the bound element modifies the nominal in the sense a preposition does in English.

[45]The morpheme can also give the meaning 'on behalf of' such as: *kompanir-pokk*^{h}*e darie* 'standing on behalf of the company, *amar pokk*^{h}*e* 'on my part', etc.

Even though the bound element functions sometimes as preposition, the meaning of the nominal unit does not express roles of the nominal in the sense it does not show any relation to the verbal syntagma in the given sentence. For instance:

724. tāder bɔyes *dɔsmās-theke* ponerobɔchor — p. 832, line 41, col. 1
'their age ten months from fifteen years'
= they are between ten months to fifteen years.

725. *sɔdɔssoder mɔtāmɔt-theke* — p. 832, line 6, col. 3
'members opinion from'
= from the point of view of the members.

726. *gouhāṭite cobbise-jun-theke* — p. 829, line 5, col. 3
'Gauhati at 24th June from'
= from 24th June at Gauhati.

727. sei *ɔsthir sɔmɔe thekei* nāṭoker arɔmbʰo — p. 830, line 13, col. 1
'that transition period from drama begins'
= the beginning of the drama is from that difficult period onword.

728. *āiner-hāt-theke nijer bibeker hāt-theke* — p. 829, line 4, col. 1
'law hand from...own consciousness hand from'
= from the law, from his own consciousness.

729. *bāroi julāi-theke* — p. 824, line 11, col. 1
'12th July from'
= since 12th July.

730. *bises drisṭikon-theke* — p. 822, line 35, col. 2
'particular point from'
= from the specific point of view.

731. *pitār snehɔbhālobāsā-theke* — p. 822, line 1, col. 3
'father's love and affection from'
= from the point of view of father's affection and love.

732. *gæn hɔoār pɔr-thekei* — p. 820, line 8, col. 3
'knowledge having after from'
= after having attained the maturity/since attaining maturity.

733. *bohudin-theke* bohusɔŋkhɔk-*robindro songitānurāgir-kāche* — p. 820, line 16, col. 2
'long time since innumerable Rabindra song lovers to'
= to the Rabindra music lover since long time.

This expression with *kāche* can be substituted with *nikɔṭ* or *nikɔṭe*. Similarly, the expression with *theke* can be substituted with *hoite*, *jābot*, *dhore* which respectively indicate the same meaning. Probably, the expression with *kāche/nikɔṭ/nikɔṭe* may be said to be expressing a role like locative, whereas such role may not be appropriate to the expression with *theke/hoite/jābot* in the above example (No. 733).

The same type of problem can also be observed when the nominal indicates a situation or state of affairs or condition.

734. *tini bipɔd-theke* kāukekāuke uddʰār kɔren — p. 821, line 31, col. 1
'he danger from some saves'
= he saves some people from danger.

The expression with *theke* can be substituted with a morphological marker *-e* or morpheme such as *hoite*. It seems to be a borderline case whether *from danger/in danger/to danger* can be assigned as locative.

735. protijogita *arombʰo hɔoār pɔr-theke* — p. 824, line 18, col. 1
'starting after from'
= after starting the tournament/since the tournament starts.

It seems also to be a doubtful case.

736. tobu uttejɔnār-ɔbokās *thekei-jāe* — p. 828, line 5, col. 1
'then to be agitated remains (the room for being agitated/the room for agitation)'

This is a verbal expression. We observe such homophonous morphemes in many examples. In this case no question of assigning any role arises.

737. ɔnekkichuɔjānā *theke-jāe* — p. 803, line 13, col. 3
'many things remain unknown'

738. *porikirno biruddʰotār-moddhe* bẽcethākār... — p. 822, line 19, col. 3
'surrounding adversity in being alive'
= being alive in the midst of adversity.

It seems doubtful whether locative role is applicable.

739. *āge-theke* prostut-hoe-neoār-prɔojonāche — p. 819, line 9, col. 3
'beforehand to be ready necessity exists'
= it is necessary to be ready beforehand.

It seems there is no relation between the expression *āge-theke* and *prɔojon-āche.*

740. khudrɔ silpoke *brihɔt-silper-āotā-theke āgle rākhār-ceṣṭā* — p. 800, line 38, col. 1
'small industry big industry shadow from'
= it is the attempt to protect the small industry from the shadow of big industry.

741. sei sārtho-holo *silper-dik-theke* deske *sābolombi-kore tolā* — p. 800, line 1, col. 1
'that interest is industrial point of view country make independent'
= the interest is to make the country independent in industrial sphere.

742. tā āgei *thik-kore* nā dile — p. 799, line 3, col. 1
'that beforehand specified not giving'
= if it is not specified beforehand.

743. *āj-theke* ponero bɔchor-pɔr — p. 794, line 11, col. 1
'today from fifteen years after'
= after fifteen years from today.

It does not seem appropriate to assign locative or such role to any of the above-mentioned expressions with *theke* in 740–43.

744. *chobiṭi-theke* dækhā-jābe — p. 786, line 28, col. 3
'picture from will be seen'
=it will be seen in the picture.

745. *chobiguli-thekei* protiomānhɔbe — p. 786, line 2, col. 3
'pictures from will be understood'
= it would be understood from the pictures.

746. *dhātumurtir-gɔṭhon-prokɔron-theke* — p. 785, line 21, col. 3
'metal idol shape from'
= from the shape of the metallic idols.

These expressions with *theke* in 743–45 may be assigned as source from the total meaning of the sentence.

747. *goṛā-theke* — p. 807, line 4, col. 1
'beginning from'
= from the beginning.

748. *tɔkhon-theke* — p. 806, line 5, col. 2
'then since'
= since that time/since long time.

749. *kɔlponā-theke* tāke ṭene nāmān rāstār dhulote — p. 803, line 36, col. 1
'imagination from it pull down dusty reality'
=(he) pulled it (him) down to the dusty reality from the level of imagination.

Maybe these expressions are assigned as the adverbial since the total meaning of the sentence indicates that the nominal expressions with *theke* function as the attribute to the verbal unit. In one way or other it modifies the verb.

750. *mānuser-pokk*^{h}*e* eijibon ki jɔtheṣṭo — p. 765, line 25, col. 1
'human being to this life enough'
= is this life enough to human being?

751. ei ukti *tāttik-dik-theke*... — p. 761, line 7, col. 2
'this statement logic point of view'
= from the logical point of view this statement...

It is doubtful whether any role can be assigned to the expression with *theke*.

752. *nichɔk sɔrolɔtārdik-theke* — p. 812, line 12, col. 3
'purely simplicity point from'
= purely from the point of simplicity.

753. *ɔnnānno bæbosāi-theke* pustok bæbosāi b^{h}inno — p. 815, line 50, col. 1
'other traders from booksellers different'
= the booksellers are different from other traders.

The meaning of the sentence indicates that *theke* corresponds to 'than' rather than 'from'. Neither the role of locative nor source seems appropriate to the expression with *theke.*

754. kretārā ei *cɔkro-theke...* p. 815, line 39, col. 1
'buyers this circle from'
= the buyers (be away) from this circle.

It is doubtful if any direct relation can be established between the nominal unit with *theke* and the verb. From the total meaning of the sentence it may be considered as adverbial. It may be substituted with *hoite.*

Besides these there can be expressions such as:

755. *e boiṭā-theke oboiṭā* bhālo
'this book from that book good'
= this book is better than the other one.

Here the expression with *theke* definitely is not expressing any role; it rather expresses the degree.

APPENDIX THREE

STRUCTURE OF BENGALI SENTENCES

The following examples are collected from RAVINDRA RACANAVAL (Vol. 7). *Different structures of Bengali sentences* (NU VU, VU, NU) *are observable.*

	Subject			*Predicate*	
	Noun (Phrase)			*Verb*	*Noun (Phrase)*
	Animate	*Inanimate Object*	*Abstract (including verbal noun)*		
1.			*ghɔṭonā* (the) 'event'	*ɔṅkita-hoito* 'used to draw'	
2.			*duicāridin bāki* 'few days are remaining' =fewdays left	*āche* are (exist)	
3.				*pāṭhkorite pārite* 'could read' (you)	
4.			*nobin siter batas* (the) 'new winter air' = fresh cold air	*āniāditeche* 'is bringing'	
5.		*toru pallab* (the) tree(s) and plant(s)		*sihoriā uṭhi-teche* 'are trembling' 'are moving' 'are shivering'	
6.		*cāriṭi mātro dhap* only four steps		*jāgiā-āche* 'awake' = is over the wa-ter level	
7.		*kacu bon* 'vegetable'		*jonmiāche* 'has grown'	
8.		*gɔngārjɔl* 'Ganges water'		*giāche* 'has reached'	

9.		*noukāguli* (the) boats		*bhāsiauṭhiā* 'having floated' *tɔl mɔl* *koriteche* 'are moving'
10.		*seguli* those (boats)		*bā̃dhāchilo* 'were anchored'
11.		*joārer jɔl* (the) tide water = the tidal wave		*āghāt* *koriteche* 'is hitting'
12.		*roudra* sunlight		*poṛiāche* 'has fallen'
13.		*kāśphul* (a kind of) flower		*phuṭe nāi* 'not blossom'
14.	*mājhirā* 'boatmen'			*khuliādilo* 'opened', 'untied', 'unfastened'
15.	*pākhirā* 'birds'			*uṛiāche* 'have flown'
16.		*noukāguli* 'boats'		*bāhir hoiāche* 'have set sail'
17.				*choṛaia giache* 'have been scattered'
18.	*meyerā* (the) girls			*āsiāche* have come
19.	*tomāder* your=you			*mone hoite* *pare* 'in mind can appear' = can think
20.		*diner ālo* daylight *rātrer chāyā* (the) shade of the night		*pɔṛe* 'fall'
21.	*bridhā* 'the old woman'			*jāitechen* 'is going'
22.		*pātāṭā* 'the leaf'		*ghuriā ghuriā* *kæraito* 'used to whirl'
23.			*kɔthā* 'the word'	*āse* 'comes, arises'

24.			*haṭ* 'market'	*bosito* 'used to open, used to sit'	
25.		*golpātār chāuni* 'a shade of leaves'		*chilo* was	
26.		*pātār chāyāguli* 'the shadows of the leaves'		*khælā korito* 'used to move, used to play'	
27.	*ækṭā phiṉe* 'one blackbird'			*bāsā-koriā chilo* 'made nest'	
28.			*sɔmoe* 'the time'	*hoiāche* 'has come'	
29.		*mɔl* 'anklet' bell		*bājite thākito* used to ring	
30.		*gɔngā* 'the Ganges'		*bhoriā uṭhe* 'was full to the brim'	
31.			*ābɔrɔn* a shade	*rɔconākoriā-cilo* 'made'	
32.				*ɔgocɔr chilo* 'was unknown'	*kɔlponār nikɔṭe* 'to the imagination'
33.		*sisirerrekhā* 'a line of dew'		*poriāchilo* 'fell, was visible'	
34.			*āgomɔn bārtā* '(the) arrival news'	*rāṣṭrohoiā porilo* 'was spread'	
35.			*bhiṛ* 'the crowd'	*bāṛite lāgilo* 'began to increase'	
36.			*tāhār proti-potti* 'his fame'	*hoilo* 'appeared (he became famous)'	
37.		*ɔndhɔkār* '(the) darkness'		*nāmiā poṛito* 'used to come down'	
38.		*lālābhā* '(the) red glow'		*bāhir hoiā asito* 'used to come out'	

39.			*sɔbdɔ* 'a sound'	*uccarito hoite thake* 'is being uttered'
40.		*drisyɔpɔṭ* 'scenery'		*poribortito hoiājāe* 'is being changed'
41.		*surjakirɔn* '(the) sun's rays'		*protipholito hoite thākito* 'used to be reflected'
42.			*kã̄sorghɔnṭa bājā* '(the) ringing of the bells'	*ses hoiā gælo* 'was finished'
43.		*joārer-jɔl* '(the) tide water = the tidal wave'		*chɔl chɔl koriteche* 'was murmuring'
44.		*ɔndhɔkār* 'the darkness'		*bosiā āche* 'was seated'
45.	*kusum* 'a proper name (female)'			*bosiā āche* 'was seated'
46.	*bāduṛ* '(a) bat'			*jhuliteche* 'was hanging'
47.	*pẽcɔk* 'owl'			*kã̄dia uṭhiteche* 'was wailing'
48.			*srigāler dhoni* '(the) howling of the jackal'	*uthilo o thāmiā gælo* 'raised and stopped'
49.	*sɔnnyasi* '(the) saint'			*bāhir hoiā asilen* 'came out'
50.		*kapoṛ* '(the) cover = the cloth'		*poriā gælo* fell down
51.		*jotsnā* '(the) moonlight'		*poṛilo* 'fell'
52.			*ubhɔer dækhā* 'meeting of the two'	*hoilo* 'occurred'
53.			*cenāsonā* 'knowing'	*hoilo* 'occurred'

54.		*purbo jɔnmer poricɔe* 'the acquaintance of the former life'	*chilo* 'was (had)'	
55.		*dristi* 'vision'	*prosārito hoiā gælo* 'widen, opened'	
56.		*mlan chāyā* '(the) sorry look (on her face)'	*durhoiā gælo* 'removed, faded away'	
57.		*prophullotā* '(a) cheer-fulness'	*ālokoriātulito* 'used to make (her) glorious (bright)'	
58.	*bɔsonter bātās* 'the spring air'		*dite-thāke* 'began to blow'	
59.	*himer bhālɔo* '(the) cold touch'		*dur hoiājāe* 'faded away, has gone (goes away)'	
60.	*bā̃si* (the) 'flute'		*bājiā uṭhe* 'began to sound'	
61.		*gāner-sɔbdo* 'the music'	*sunite pāoa-jāe* 'could be heard'	
62.		*jouboner sɔncār* 'the accummula-tion of youth'	*hoiteche* 'was occurring'	
63.	*lɔtā gulmo-guli* 'the creeping plants and bushes'		*bikosito hoiā uṭhiteche* 'were blosso-ming'	
64.	*tāhār cokh* 'her eyes'		*bhoriā āsilo* 'were full'	*jɔle* 'with water'
65.		*swapnerghor* '(the) trance'	*bhāŋilonā* 'was not removed'	
66.		*dækhā* 'meeting'	*nā hɔe* 'could not take place'	
67.	*bātās* 'the wind'		*hu hu korite lāgilo* 'began to blow excessively'	

68. *āmi* 'I'		*bolitechi* 'am saying'	
69. *tumi* 'you'		*ɔsɔnmān* 'disrespect' *korio nā* 'do not'	
70. *Isākhān* 'proper name (male)'		*cāhilen* 'looked at'	
71.		*monojogdilen* 'gave attention'	
72.		*hasia uthilen* 'laughed at'	
73. *Rājdhɔr* 'proper name (male)'		*bolilen* 'said'	
74. *Indrakumar* 'proper name (male)'		*probesh* *korilen* 'entered'	
75. *æk konnā* 'one daughter'		*jonmilo* 'was born'	*pā̃c cheler pɔr* 'after five sons' *jokhon* 'when'
76. *bāpmāe* 'the parents'		*rākhilen* 'gave'	*nam* 'name' *tahar* 'her' *nirupama* 'Nirupama'
77.		*sonā-jāe* *nāi* 'has never been heard'	*e gosṭhite æmon* *soukhin* *nām purbe* *kokhono* 'in this family such fashionable name before ever'
78.	*bibāher* *prostāb* 'the marriage negotiation'	*coliteche* 'is going on'	*ækhon nirupomār* 'now of Niru- poma'
79. *tāhār pitā* *rāmendra* *sundar mitra* 'her father Ramendra Sundar Mitra'		*khõjkɔren* 'did effort'	*ɔnek* 'much'
80.		*hɔenā* 'was not'	*monermoto* 'according to his likeness' *pātro kichutei* 'the groom'

81.		*sɔndhān koria bahir koriāchen* 'has found out'	*obosese æk rāebāhadurer ghɔrer ækmātro cheleke* 'at last the only boy of a noble family'
82. *bɔr pokko hoite* 'groom's party from' = the groom's party		*cahiā bosilo* 'has demanded'	*dɔs-hājār tākā pɔn ebɔŋ bohuldān-sāmogr i* 'ten thousand rupees dowry household and other materials'
83. *rāmendra sundar* 'Ramendra Sundar (proper name male)'		*sɔnmɔ to hoilen* 'has agreed'	*kichu mātro bibecɔnā nā koriā* 'without any discrimination' *tahatei* 'in that proposal'
84.	*hāt-chārā* 'be given up'	*kɔrājāena* 'cannot'	*æmon pāttro konomɔte* 'such groom anyway (in any case)'
85.	*ṭākar-jogāṛ* 'the provision of money'	*hɔe nā* 'cannot be done'	*kichutei ār* 'even though did much effort'
86.	*bibāher din* 'the day of marriage'	*nikɔṭ-hoiā-āsiache* 'has come nearer'	*edike* 'while, on the other hand'
87.	*bibāher din* 'the day of marriage'	*uposthit hoilo* 'came, appeared'	*ɔbosese* 'at last'
88. *æk jon* 'someone'		*sikār koriā chilo* 'had agreed'	*dhārdite nitāntootirik-tosude* 'to lend in a high interest' *bākiṭākāṭā* 'the rest amount'
89. *se* 'he'		*uposthit hoilo na* 'did not present (was not present)'	
90.	*ækṭā tumul golojog* 'a serious (violent) disorder'	*bādhiā gælo* 'started'	*bibāho sɔbhāe* 'in the marriage assembly'

91. *rāmendra sundar* 'Ramendra Sundar (proper name, male)'		*bolilen* 'said'	*āmāder rāe-bāhādurer hātepāe dhoriā* 'very humbly to the Raibahadur'
92.	*subhakārja* 'the auspicious ceremony'	*sɔmpɔnno hoiājāk* 'let be finished'	
93. *āmi* 'I'		*sodhkoriā dibo* 'will pay'	*ṭākāṭā niscoe* 'the money certainly'
94. *rāebāhādur* 'the Raibahadur (a title)'		*bolilen* 'said'	
95.	*sabhāsth kɔrā* 'bringing in the assembly'	*jāibenā* 'will not be done'	*bɔr, ṭākāṭā hāte nā pāile* 'the groom if the money is not handed over (if the money is not received)'
96.	*ækṭā kānnā* 'a cry'	*poriāgælo* 'begun'	*ei durghɔṭonāe* 'for this uneasy matter' event *ɔntopure* inside the house
97. *se* 'she'		*bosiā āche* 'is sitting'	*cupkoriā,* 'quietly' *celiporiā* 'having worn the dress' *gɔhonā poriā* 'wearing ornaments' *ei gurutɔro* '*bipɔder je mulkāron* 'who is the root of this serious trouble'
98.	*ækṭā bhokti* 'a respect' '*kimbāɔnurāg* 'or love'	*jonmiteche* 'was developing'	*bhābi-sosur-kuler-proti* 'to the would-be father-in-law's family' *tahar* 'her' *je khub* 'indeed'

99.	*tāhā* 'that'	*bɔlājāe na* 'could not be said'	
100.	*ākṭā subidhā* 'an opportunity'	*hoilo* 'came'	*itimoddhe* 'in the meantime'
101. *bɔr* 'the groom'		*ɔbādhyo-hoiā-uṭhilo* 'became disobedient'	*sɔhosā, tāhār pitrideber* 'suddenly to his father'
102. *se* 'he'		*boliā bosilo* 'said (unexpectedly)'	*bāpke* 'to the father'
103.		*bujhine* 'do not understand'	*kenā bæcā dordamer kɔtha* 'the story of buying and selling and bargaining'
104. *āmi* 'I'		*āsiāchi* 'have come'	*bibāho korite* 'to marry' *bibāh koriā jāibo* 'will return being married'
105. *bāp* 'the father'		*bolio* 'said'	*jāhākedekhilo* 'whom (he) saw' *tāhāke* 'to whom'
106. *mɔhāsɔe* 'gentleman'		*dekhiāchen* 'have (you) seen'	*āj kālkār cheleder bɔbohār* 'the behaviour of the modern boys'
107. *dueækjɔn procinlok* 'a few old men'		*chilo* 'were (there)'	
108. *tāhārā* 'they'		*bolilo* 'said'	
109.	*sāstra sikshā niti sikshā* 'the moral education and culture'	*nāi* 'does not exist'	*ækebāre* 'any more' *kājei* 'therefore, so' *bɔrtoman sikkhar bisɔmɔephɔl nijen sɔntaner*
110. *rāebāhādur* 'the gentleman'		*bosiā rohilen* 'sat (remain sitting)'	*moddhe protto-kho-koriā* 'observing in his own child the

				evil result of the modern education'
111.		*bibāho* 'the marriage ceremony'	*sɔmpɔnno hoiā-gælo* 'was over'	*ækprokār bisɔnno nirānɔndo-bhābe* 'in a cheerless mood'
112.	*bāp* 'the father'		*rākhite parilen-nā* 'could not control'	*cokher jɔl* 'tears' *sosurbāṛi* 'at the time of' *jāibārsomɔe* 'going to the in-law's house' *nirupɔmāke buketania-* 'taking Nirupama' *loia* 'very close'
113.	*niru* 'Niru'		*jigā̃sākorilo* 'enquired'	
114.	*tārā* 'they'		*āstedebe-nā* 'will not allow to come'	*ki āmāke ār* 'me again' *baba* 'father'
115.	*rām sundar* 'Ram Sundar'		*bolilen* 'said'	
116.			*aste-debenā* 'should not allow to come'	*kæno* 'why' *ma* 'mother'
117.	*āmi* 'I'		*nie-āsbo* 'will take back'	*tomāke* 'you'
118.	*rām sundar* 'Ram Sundar'		*dekhitejān* 'goes to see'	*prāei meyeke* 'often the daughter'
119.		*protipotti* 'dignity'	*nāi* 'was not'	*kintu behāi bāṛite tāhār* 'but in the house of the father-in-law of the daughter, his (of him)'
120.	*cākorgulo* 'the servants' (*porjonto*) 'also'		*dækhe* 'see'	*tāhāke* 'him' *nicunɔjore* 'with disrespect'
121.			*dekhite-pān* 'could meet'	*meyeke ɔntopure bāhire pācminiṭer jcnno* 'the daughter

				outside in a separate room only for five minutes'
122.		*konodin* 'some times'	*dekhite-pānnā* 'could not meet'	
123.		*ɔpomān* 'insultation'	*sɔhajaena* 'could not be tolerated'	*kuṭumbo grihe æmon koria* 'in relations house in such a way'
124.	*rām sundɔr* 'Ram Sundar'		*sthirkorilen* 'decided'	
125.			*sodhkorite-hoibe* 'should be paid'	*jāmon koriā houk tākāṭa* 'anyhow the money'
126.		*je rin-bhār* 'that burden of debt'	*cāpiāche* 'has fallen'	*kintu* 'but' *k͠ādhe* 'on the shoulder'
127.			*sāmlāno* 'to evade'	*tāhāri bhār duskar* 'its burden very difficult'
128.			*ɔttontoṭānā-ṭāni pori-āche* 'has fall very short'	*khɔroc pɔtrer* 'of expenditure'
129.			*ɔbolɔmbɔn korite-hoiteche* 'has to take'	*pāonādārder dristipɔth* 'to avoid the creditors' *æṛāibār jonno sɔrbodāi hin kousal* 'always false tricks'
130.			*kh͠ɔṭā-lāgāiteche* 'giving blame'	*odike* 'on the other side' *sosurbari* 'at the in-laws house' *meyeke* 'to the daughter'
131.		*asru-bisarjan* 'tears shedding'	*d͠ārāiāche* 'has become'	*pitrigriher nindā suniā* 'hearing the dishonour of the father's family' *tāhār* 'her' *nitya kriār*-'every day' *modhe* (in) 'matter'

132.			*sāsuṛirakros* 'the grudge of the mother-in-law'	*mete-nā* 'not come to an end'	*bisesato* 'particularly' *ār kichutei* 'in any way'
133.			*khāoā porāro* 'eating and clothing also'	*jɔtno hɔena* 'not take care of'	*æmon ki bouer* 'even of the bride'
134.	*jodi kono dɔā pɔrotɔntro-protibesini* 'if any kind-hearted neighbour woman'			*ullekhkɔre* 'mentions'	*kono truṭir* 'of any fault'
135.	*sāsuṛi* 'mother-in-law'			*bɔle* 'says'	
136.			*oi* 'that'	*dherhoeche* 'is enough'	
137.	*bāp* 'the father'			*dito* 'would give'	*ɔrthāt* 'in other words' *jodipurā dam* 'if (meet up the demand) full price'
138.	*meye* 'the daughter'			*pāito* 'would get'	*to* 'then' *pura jɔtno* 'full attention'
139.	*sɔkɔlei* 'all of them'			*dækhāe* 'show'	*æmon bhālo* 'such manner'
140.	*bodhur* 'of the bride'			*nāi* 'has no'	*ɔdhikār* 'right' *jæno* 'as if'
141.				*probes-koriache* 'has entered'	*phā̃ki-diā* 'by chance'
142.		*bāper kāne* 'to the ear of the father'		*giā-thā-kibe* 'might have gone'	*bodh hɔe konyār eisɔkol ɔnādor o ɔpomāner-kothā* 'perhaps these dishonour and disrespect of the daughter'
143.	*rām sundar* 'Ram Sundar'			*bikrɔer cesṭā kori-telagilen* 'tried to sell'	*tāi ɔbosese bɔsotbaṭi* 'so at last the dwelling house'
144.				*gopone-rākhilen* 'kept in secret'	*kintu cheleder je grihohin korite bosiāchen sekɔthā tāhāder*

				nikɔṭhoite 'but he is about to making the boys homeless that them from' = (he) kept it secret from them that he is making them homeless
145.			*sthiro koriāchilen* 'has decided'	*bāṛi bikrɔe koriā* 'having sold the house' *sei bāṛir bhāṛāloiā* 'having rented the same house'
146.			*bas koriben* will live	
147.			*coliben* will manage	*æmon kousale* such tactfully *je* that *tāhār mrittur purbe* before his death
148.	*chelerā* 'the boys'		*jānite pribenā* 'would not know'	*ekɔthā* the information
149.	*chelerā* 'the boys'		*jānite parilo* 'come to know'	
150.	*sɔkole* 'all of them'		*āsiākā̃diā porilo* 'began to implore'	
151.	*bɔṛotinṭi chele* 'the three elderly sons'			*bisesɔto* 'in particular' *bibāhito* 'married'
152.	*sɔntān* 'child'		*āche* 'has'	*tāhāder kāhāro* 'of them (to) some' = some of them
153.		*tāhāder-apotti* 'their objections'	*hoiādā̃ṛāilo* 'became'	*gurutɔro* 'very serious'
154.		*bāṛibikrɔe* '(the) selling of the house'	*sthogito-rohilo* remain postponed	

155.			*sɔŋsārkhɔroc* '(the) expen- diture (of the family)'	*cɔlena* 'cannot run'	*ar* 'anymore'
156.	*niru* 'Niru (proper name—female)'			*bujhite- pārilo* 'could understand'	*sɔb* 'everything' *baper mukh dekhia* 'having looked at the father's face'
157.			*doino ebŋ- duscinta* 'the poverty and worries'	*prokashoia- porilo* 'were expressed (revealed)'	*briddher pɔkko- kese* '(from) in the gray hair of the old man' *suskomukkhe* 'in his dry face' *ebŋ sɔda sɔŋ kucito bhabe* 'and in his hesitated behaviour'
158.	*bāp* '(the) father'				*meyerkāche* 'to the daughter' *ɔporādhi* '(is an) offender'
159.			*se ɔporādher onutap* 'that repentance of the offend'	*gopon rākhā jāe* 'could be kept in secret'	*tɔkhɔn ki* 'then (interrogation)'
160.	*rāmsundar* 'Ram Sundar' (proper name—male)			*sākkhātlābh- korilen* 'could meet'	*jɔkhon* 'when' *behāibāṛionu moti krome* 'with the permission of the in-laws' *khɔnokāler jonno* 'for a short while' *kɔnnār* 'of the daughter'
161.		*bāper buk* 'the heart of the father'		*kæmonkoria- phāṭe* 'how pains (breaks)'	*tɔkhon* 'then'
162.			*taha* 'that'	*terpaoajaito* 'could be understood'	*tahar hasi dekhilei* 'to see his (pathetic) smile'
163.	*niru* 'Niru (proper name— female)'			*nitānto ɔdhirhoia- uthiāche* 'became very restless'	*sei bæthito pitrihridɔeke sāntona dibār jonno* 'to pacify the worried father' *dinkɔtok bāper bari jaibar*

			jonno 'wish to go to the father's house'
164. *se* 'she'		*durethākite-parena* 'could not stay away'	*ār* 'anymore' *bāper mlān mukh dekhia* 'observing the melancholy face (gloomy face) of the father'
165.		*kohilo* 'said'	*ækdin rāmsun-darke* 'one day to Ramsunder'
166. *bābā* 'father'		*loiājāo* 'take'	*āmāke* 'me' *bari* 'home'
167. *rāmsundar* 'Ramsundar'		*bolilen* 'said'	*accha* 'alright'
168.	*konojor* 'any claim'	*nāi* 'does not exist'	*kintu tāhār* 'but him (in relation to him)'
169.	*sāvābik odhikar* '(the) natural claim'	*āche* 'exists'	*pitār je* 'of the father' *nijer konnār upore* 'on his own daughter'
170.	*tāhā* 'that'	*bɔndhok rākhite-hoiāche* 'has to be mortgaged'	*jæno* 'as if' *pɔner tākār poribɔrte* 'in exchange of the promised money'
171.	*kɔnnār dɔrson* the 'meeting with the daughter'	*vikkhā cāhitehɔe* 'has to be begged'	*æmonki* 'even' *seo* 'that also' *otisɔsɔnkoce* 'very hesita-tingly'
172.	*kohibārmukh* 'to say anything'	*thāke nā* 'remain no way'	*nirās hoile* 'if become disappointed' *sɔmɔebisese* 'sometimes' *ditiokɔthati* 'the second word'
173. *bāp* 'the father'		*thāke* 'remain'	*kikoriā nā āniā tāhāke, meye āsite cāhile* 'how, not bringing her if the daughter wished to come'

174.	*se itihās* 'that history (story)'		*gopon thākā bhālo* 'to be in secret (is) better' = it is better to be in secret
175.	*ækṭā mɔsto curi* 'a big theft'	*hoiā-giāche* 'has occurred'	*hɔre krishnar bāriṭe* 'in the house of Hare Krishnar'
176.	*ækṭā nutan bæmo* 'a new disease'	*āsiāche* 'has come'	*sɔhore* 'in the city'
177.		*ālocɔnā-korilen* 'did discussion'	*se sɔmbondhe* 'about that' *ɔnekājgubi* 'many baseless'
178.		*bolilen* 'said'	*ɔbosese* 'at last' *hukāṭi nāmāiā* 'keeping down the tobacco pipe' *kɔthāe kɔthāe* 'by the way'
179.	*sei tākāṭā* 'that money'	*bākiāche* 'is being unpaid'	*hā hā behāi* 'yes Behai (there is no corresponding word in English for this term)'
180.		*monekori* '(I) think'	*roji* 'every day'
181.		*jācchi* '(I) am going'	
182.		*nie-jāi* '(I) should take'	*kichu hāte kore* 'something (in hand) with me'
183.		*mone thākenā* 'could not keep in mind (cannot remember)'	*kintu* 'but' *sɔmɔekāle* 'in time'
184.		*buro hoe-porechi* '(I) become old' = I am old now	
185.		*bāhirkorilen* '(he) put out'	*oti sɔhoje* 'very easily' *otiobohele* 'with ease' *æmoni æk dirgho*

			bhumikā koriā 'giving such a long introduction *pānjorer tinkhāni* *osthir moto* 'like the three ribs of the chest' *sei tinkhāni not* 'those three notes'
186. *rāy bāhādur* 'The Raybahadur (a title)'		*ɔṭṭohāsyo-* *korilen* 'did a roar of laughter'	*sɔbe mātro tin* *hāzarṭākār not* *dekhibā* 'having seen only three thousand rupees notes'
187.	*bāṛi ānibār* *prostab* 'the proposal to bring home'	*āse nā* 'cannot come'	*eighɔṭonār pɔr* 'after this event' *meyeke* 'the daughter' *kāhāro* *mukhe* 'in any- body's mouth'
188. *rāmsundar* Ramsundar		*bhābilen* 'thought'	*kebɔol* 'only'
189.	*sesɔkol* *kutum bitar* *sɔŋkoc* 'such hesitation of relation'	*sobhāpāenā* 'does not fit'	*āmāke* 'to me' *ar* 'anymore' = such hesitation does not fit to me anymore, thought Mr. Ramsundar.
190.		*pārilen* 'made'	*mɔrmāhɔto-bhābe* *ɔnekkhɔn cup-* *koriā thākiā* 'having been silent for a long time in utter disappointment' *ɔbosese mridu-* *swre kɔthāṭā* 'at last in low voice that proposal'
191. *rāybāhādur* 'the Raybahadur'		*bolilen* 'said'	*kono kāron mātro* *ullekh nā koriā* 'not mentioning any reason at all'
192.	*se* 'that'	*hocche na* 'cannot be done'	*ækhon* 'now'

193.			*coliā-gelen* 'went away'	*eiboliā* 'saying this' *kɔrmopo-lokhe* 'for some work' *stanantɔre* 'in another place'
194.			*protigā̃* *korilen* 'promised'	*mone mone* 'in mind'
195.			*dābi korite-pāriben* 'could claim'	*jɔtodin nā* *sɔmosto ṭākā* *sodh koriā-diā* 'so long paying all money' *ɔsonkoce konmyar upore* 'unhesitatingly on his daughter'
196.			*jāiben nā* 'will not go'	*totodin ār* 'so long any more' *behāibāṛi* 'the relation's house'
197.		*bohudin* 'many days'	*gælo* 'were past'	
198.	*nirupamā* 'Nirupama (proper name—female)'		*pāṭhāe* 'sends'	*loker upor lok* 'one man after another'
199.			*pāenā* 'cannot get'	*bāper dækhā* 'visit of the father'
200.			*bɔndho* *korilo* 'stopped'	*ɔbosese* 'at last' *obhimānkoriā* 'being sensitive' *lok pāṭhāno* 'sending messenger'
201.			*āghāt lāgilo* 'was wounded'	*rāmsundorer mone* 'in the mind of Ram-sundar' = Ramsundar was wounded
202.		*āswin mās* 'the month of Aswin'	*āsilo* 'came'	
203.	*rāmsundar* 'Ramsundar'		*jātrārudyog* *korilen* 'about to start'	*pɔncomi ki sos-tir dine* 'on the day of Puja Festival'

					ābār cādorer prante gutiktok not bādhiā 'again tying up a few notes on the end of the scarf'
204.				*sɔkh hoiāche* 'has wished'	*bohudin hoite* 'for a long time' *tāhār* 'of him' *thælāgāṛite coṛiā* 'boarding on a carriage' *hāoākhāibār* 'to go out'
205.			*miṭibār upāe* 'the way to meet up'	*hoiteche nā* 'has not come'	*kichutei* 'in any way'
206.		*bhālo-kāpoṛ* 'good dress'		*nāi* 'does not exist'	*tāhār* 'to him' *æk khanio* 'a single one'
207.	*rāmsundar* 'Ramsundar'			*jāniten* 'knows'	*tāhā* 'that'
208.	*bridho* 'the old man'			*cintā koriāchen* 'has thought'	*se sɔmbondhe* 'about that' *tāmāk khāite kāite* 'while smoking'
209.			*pujār nimontrɔn* 'the invitation for Puja festival'	*hoile* 'will come'	*rāybāhādurer bāṛi jɔkhon* 'Raybahadur's house when' = When the invitation will come from the Raybahadur family
210.	*tāhār putro bodhugɔnke* 'his daughter-in-law's'			*jāite-hoibe* 'have to go'	*oti jɔt sāmānno ɔlonkāre* 'in a very plain dress' *doridrermoto* 'like the poor'
211.	*tini* 'he'			*ɔnek dirgho-sās pheliā-chen* 'had many deep sighs'	*ekɔthā smoron koriā* 'remembering that' = He felt very sorry, remembering that.
212.			*ārkono phɔl* 'any more	*hɔenai* 'did not	*kintu tāhāte* 'but in it'

			result'	come'	*tāhār lɔlāṭer bārdhokyo rekā gobhirotɔro hɔoāchārā* 'except his sign on the forehead being deep'
213.	*bridho* 'the old man'			*probes-korilen* 'entered'	*tāhār behāi bāṛite* 'to the house of his relation'
214.			*se sɔsɔnkoc-bhab* 'that hesitation'	*nai* 'is no more'	*aj tahar* 'today in relation to him'
215.		*se cokito sɔlɔjjo-drisṭipāt* 'that hesitating modest look'		*dur hoiā-giāche* 'has gone'	*dārrokkhi o bhrittoder mukher-proti* 'to the face of the guards and servants of the house'
216.				*sunilen* '(he) heard'	
217.	*rāybāhādur* 'the Raybahadur'			*nāi* 'was not'	*ghɔre* 'in the house'=the Raybahadur was not present at home
218.				*ɔpekkhā korite-hoibe* '(he) has to wait'	*kichukkhon* 'for some time'
219.	*rāmsundar* 'Ramsundar'			*sākkhāt-korilen* 'met'	*konnyār sohit monerucchās sɔŋbɔrônkorite nāpāria* 'with his daughter, not being able to check his emotion'
220.		*jɔl* 'the tears'		*poritelagilo* 'roll down'	*ānonde dui cokh dia* 'due to excitement through both eyes'
221.	*bāpo* 'the father'			*kā̃de* 'weeps'	
222.	*meyeo* 'the daughter also'			*kā̃de* 'weeps'	
223.	*duijone keho* 'the two of them'			*kohite-parena* 'could not speak'	*ār kɔthā* 'any word'

224.		*kichukkhon* 'sometimes'	*gælo* 'past'	*æmon koriā* 'in such way (manner)'
225.	*rāmsundar* 'Ramsundar'		*bolilen* 'said'	*tārpore* 'after that'
226.			*niejācchi* 'shall be taking'	*ebār toke mā* 'this time you, mother' = this time I shall be taking you home
227.		*ārkono gol* 'any more problem'	*nāi* 'does not exist'	
228.	*rāmsundar jesṭhoputro hɔromohon* 'the elder son of Ramsundar, Haramohon'		*probes-korilen* 'entered'	*æmon somoe* 'at that time' *tār duṭi chele sɔŋge-loiā* 'accompanied by his two sons' *sɔhosā, ghɔre* 'suddenly, in the room'
229.			*bolilen* 'said'	*pitake* 'to the father'
230.	*bābā* 'father'		*bhāsāle* 'throw'	*āmāder tɔbe ebār pɔthe* 'us, then, now, on the road' = father, you throw us on the road now?'
231.	*rāmsundar* 'Ramsundar'		*bolilen* 'said'	*sɔhosā, ogni murti-hoiā* 'suddenly being angry'
232.	*ami* 'I'		*hɔbo* 'would go'	*toder jonnoki, nɔrok-gāmi* 'for you (interrogation) to the hell?'
233.	*torā* 'you'		*dibine* 'will not allow'	*āmake, āmār sotto pālon korite* 'me, to keep my words'
234.	*rāmsundar* 'Ramsundar'		*bikroe koriā bosiā-āchen* 'has sold'	*bari* 'the house' = Ramsundar has already sold the house
235.	*chelerā* 'the sons (the boys)'		*nā jānitepare* 'could not realize'	*kichute* 'anyhow'

236.		*ɔnek bɔbosthā koriāchilen* 'made many arrangements'	*tāhār* 'for that' = for that he made several arrangements = he took much care
237. *tāhārā* 'they'		*jāniāche* 'have come to know'	*kintu tobu* 'but, still'
238.		*ɔttonto rusto o birokto hoiā uṭhilen* 'became very angry and disturbed'	*dekhiā* 'having known that' = having heard that
239. *nirupamā* 'Nirupama'		*kohilo* 'said'	*sɔmosto bujhite-pāriā* 'having understood everything'
240. *bābā, tumi* 'father, you'		*dāo* '(if) give'	*ār æk pɔesā* 'any more farthing' *āmār sosurke* 'to my father-in-law'
241.		*dekhte pābenā* 'could not see'	*tāhole, ār tomār meyeke* 'then, any more your daughter'
242. *āmi* 'I'		*nāditepāri* 'cannot give'	*ār eṭākāṭā jodi tāhole torbāper ɔpomān ebŋ tor ɔpoman* 'and this money if then your father's insult and your insult'
243. *niru* 'Niru'		*kohilo* 'said'	
244.		*dāo* 'give'	*ṭākā jodi tɔbei ɔpoman* 'the money if then insult' = it is an insult if you give money
245.	*kono morjādā* 'any dignity'	*nei* 'does not exist'	*tomār meyer ki* 'of your daughter (interrogation)' = is there no dignity of your daughter?

246.	*āmi* 'I'			*ki ṭākār tholi* 'a bag of money' = am I a bag of money?
247.		*ṭākā* 'the money'	*āche* 'exists'	*jɔtokkhon, tɔtokkhon āmār dām* 'so long that long (is) my value' = should my value be judged by money? = so long the money exists my importance is there?
248.	*tumi* 'you'		*koro nā* 'do not do'	*nā bābā e tākā die āmārɔpomān* 'no father giving the money my insult (disrespect)'
249.	*āmār sāmi* 'my husband'		*cān nā* 'does not want'	*tāchāṛā, e ṭākā* 'besides that, this money'
250.			*debenā jete* 'will not allow to go'	*tāhole tomāke ma* 'then, you mother' = mother then (they) will not allow to go
251.	*nirupamā* 'Nirupama'		*kohilo* 'said'	
252.			*nadæe to* 'if not do' = if they do not	
253.			*kikorbe* 'what you will do'	*bɔlo* 'tell (me)'
254.	*tumio* 'you too'		*ceonā* 'do not ask'	*ār nie jete* 'again to take (me)'
255.	*rāmsundar* 'Ramsundar'		*phiriāgelen* 'went back'	*kompito hɔste* 'in trembling hand' *not bā̃dhā cadorti kā̃dhe tuliā* 'having put the scarf on the shoulder' *bari* 'to home'
256.	*rāmsundar* 'Ramsundar'		*āniachilen* 'brought'	*kintu ei je taka* 'but that this money' = that Ramsundar has brought money

257.				*coliā* *giachen-* 'had return'	*ebŋ konnyār* *nisedhe* 'and due to the prohibition of the daughter' *seṭākā nā diāi* 'not giving that money'
258.			*sekɔthā* 'that story'	*gopon rohilo-* *nā* 'was not remain in hiding'	
259.	*kono sɔbhāb* *koutuholi* *dārlɔgno* *kɔntho-dāsi* 'any sneaky maidservant'			*dilo* 'gave'	*ei khɔbor* 'this information' *nirur-sāsuṛike* 'to the mother- in-law of Niru'
260.			*ākrosersimā* 'the limit of the grudge'	*rohilonā* 'knows no bound'	*suniā tāhār ār* 'having heard (to) her'
261.		*sosurbāṛi* 'the house of the father- in-law'		*hoiā-uthilo* 'became'	*nirupɔmār* *pokkhe sɔrosjjā* 'to Nirupama arrow-bed, thorny bed'
262.	*tāhārsāmi* 'her husband'			*coliā-giāche* 'has gone'	*edike* 'on the other hand' *bibāher ɔlpodin* *pɔrei* 'shortly after marriage' *deputi mæjistrate* *hoiā desāntɔre* 'gaining the position of the Deputy Magis- trate in a distant place'
263.			*hinɔtā* 'meanness'	*sikkhā hɔe* 'would learn'	*pache sɔŋsɔrgo* *dose* 'if (behind) in bad company'
264.			*nirur-* *sākkhātkār* 'the meeting of Niru'	*sɔmpurno-* *nisiddho* 'completely prohibited'	*bāṛir ātmio* *sɔjoner-sohit* 'with her family and relations'
265.			*gurutɔro* *piṛā* 'a serious illness'	*hoilo* 'occurred'	*ei somɔe nirur* *ækta* 'at that time, of Niru (a)'

266.		*sɔmpurnodos* 'complete responsibility'	*deoā-jāe-nā* 'cannot be given'	*kintu sejonno tāhār-sāsuṛike* 'but for that her mother-in-law' = but for that her mother-in-law should not be blamed totally
267. *se* 'she'			*ɔttɔnto ɔbohelā korito* 'neglect very much'	*sorirer-proti* '(to) her health' = she herself neglected her health very much
268.	*māthārdɔrojā* 'the door near the bed'		*kholā* 'remain open'	*kārtik māser himer somɔe sɔmostorāt* 'at (during) the cold season, whole night'
269.	*kāpor* 'proper clothing'		*nāi* 'were not used'	*siter somɔe gae* 'during the winter, on the body'
270.		*niɔm* 'regularity'	*nāi* 'does not maintained'	*āhārer* 'of food' = no regularity was maintained for taking food
271. *dāsirā* 'the maidservants'			*bhuliājāito* 'used to forget'	*jɔkhon mājhe mājhe khābār ānite* 'when sometimes to bring food'
272. *se* 'she'			*bāskoriteche* 'is living'	*pɔrer ghɔrer dās dāsi ebŋ kɔrtāgrihini der onugroher upor* 'on the favour of the non-relations (whim, gratis)'
273.		*ei sɔŋsksār* 'this idea (feeling) (prejudice)'	*bɔddhomul-hoiteche* 'was taking firm root'	*tāhār-mone* 'in her mind'
274.		*erupbhābṭa* 'this attitude'	*sɔjho-hoito-nā* 'was not tolerated'	*sāsuṛir* 'to the mother-in-law' = the mother-in-law could not tolerate this attitude

275.			*dekhiten* 'could see'	*jodi āhārer proti bodhur kono ɔbohelā* 'if the neglect to food of the daughter-in-law'
276. *sāsuṛi* 'the mother-in-law'			*boliten* 'used to remark'	*nɔbāber bāṛir meye kinā* 'since the girl (is) from the Nabab's house!'
277.	*goriber ghɔrer ɔnno* 'the food of the poor family'		*rocenā* 'not become tasteful'	*or mukhe* 'to her appetite' = the food does not seem tasteful to her
278.			*boliten* 'used to say'	*kɔkhonobā* 'sometimes'
279.		*ki chiri* 'how look'	*hocche* 'does'	*dine dine* 'day by day' = how does (she) look day by day
280.			*hoejācche* 'looks like'	*jæno poṛā kāṭh* 'as if burnt wood'
281.		*rog* 'the disease'	*gurutoro-hoiāuṭhilo* 'became serious'	*jɔkhon* 'when'
282. *sāsuṛi* 'the mother-in-law'			*bolilen* 'said'	*or somosto nækāmi* 'everything of her (are) show'
283. *niru* 'Niru'			*sɔbinɔebolilo* 'requested modestly'	*ɔbosese ækdin sāsuṛike* 'at last, one day, to the mother-in-law'
284.			*dekhbo* '(I) shall see'	*bābāke ār āmār bhāider ækbār* 'my father and my brothers once again' = I would like to see my father and brothers
285. *sāsuṛi* 'the mother-in-law'			*bolilen* 'said'	*kebol bāper bāri jāibār chɔl* 'only pretention to go to the parents' house'

286.	*keho* 'anybody'			*biswās-koribenā* 'will not believe'	
287.		*nirur-sās* 'Niru's last gasp'		*uposthithoilo* 'appeared (occurred)'	*jedin sondhār somɔe* 'that day at the evening'
288.	*dāktār* 'the doctor'			*dekhilo* 'checked'	*seidin prothom* 'that day, for the first time'
289.			*dāktārer dækhā* 'the checking of the doctor'	*ses-hoilo* 'was over (finished)'	*ebŋ sei dini* 'and that very day'
290.	*bāṛir bɔṛobou* 'the eldest daughter-in-law of the family'			*moriāche* 'has died'	
291.			*ɔntestikriā* 'the funeral ceremony'	*sɔmpɔnno-hoilo* 'was performed'	*khub dhum koriā* 'with pomp and grandeur'
292.			*protipotti* 'the fame'	*āche* 'exists'	*protimā bisɔrjoner sɔmāroho sɔmbondhe* 'about the immersion of the idol' *jelar-moddhe raecoudhurider* 'of the Raychoudhuri family in the district' = the Raychoudhuri family is famous for their immersion ceremony
293.			*temoni ækṭā khæti* 'such kind of fame'	*rohiā gælo* 'remained'	*bɔro bouer sɔtkār sɔmbondhe* 'about the funeral ceremony of the eldest daughter-in-law'
294.	*keho* 'anybody'			*dækhenāi* 'have not seen'	*kɔkhono æmon cɔndon kāṣṭher cita* 'ever such a funeral pile made of sandal-wood'
295.				*sɔmbhɔb* '(is) possible'	*æmonghɔṭā-koriā srāddho* 'such a pompous funeral ceremony'

					kebol raebahādur bāṛite 'only at the house of Raybahadur (there is a possibility)'
296.				*sunājāe* '(it) could heard'	*ihāte tāhāder* 'in it, of them'
297.			*kincit-rin* 'slight debt'	*hoiāchilo* 'has occurred'	
298.			*tāhār meyer mrittu* 'the death of his daughter'	*hoiāche* 'has occurred'	*kirup somārohe ramsundarke santona dibar somɔe* 'how pompously at the time of consoling Ramsundar'
299.	*sɔkolei* all (everybody)			*korilo* 'gave'	*bohul bɔrnonā* 'vivid description'
300.		*deputi mæejistreter cithi* 'the letter of the Deputy Magistrate'		*āsilo* 'came (arrived)'	*edike* 'on the other hand (in the meantime)'
301.	*āmi* 'I'			*bɔndobɔsto koriā-āchi* 'arrangements have done'	*sɔmosto ekhāne* 'all, here' = here I have made all arrangements
302.				*pāṭhāibe* 'should sent'	*ɔtoeb obilɔmbe amar strike ekhane* 'therefore without any delay my wife here' = therefore please send my wife here without any delay
303.	*rāybāhādurer mohisi* 'the wife of Raybahadur'			*likhilen* 'wrote'	
304.				*sɔmbɔndho koriachi* '(I) have negotiated'	*bābā tomārjonno ār ekṭi meye* 'my boy; for you another girl'
305.				*āsibe* '(you) should come'	*ɔtoeb obilɔmbe chuṭi loia ekhane* 'therefore without any delay, taking leave of absence here'

No.					
306.			*bishājārṭākā pon* 'twenty thousand (is) promised'		*ebare ebŋ hate hate adae* 'this time and collection immediately'
307.	*poṣṭmāṣṭārke* 'the Post-master'			*āsitehɔe* 'has to come'	*prothom kāj ārombhokoriā ulāpurgrāme* 'at the beginning of the job at the village Ulapur'
308.		*ekṭi nilkuthi* 'an Indigo office (farm)'		*āche* 'exists (there is)'	*nikɔte* 'near the village' = there is an Indigo farm close to the village
309.	*kuṭhir sāhib* 'the officer (foreign) of the farm'			*stāponkɔrāiā-che* 'has caused to open'	*tāi ɔnek jogār koria, ei nutɔn postophis* 'so with much effort this new post office'
310.			*jerɔkom* 'as it'	*hɔe* happens	*jɔler māchke dāŋāe tulile* 'if the fish (is) brought out of the water'
311.			*seidɔsā* 'that condition (state)'	*uposthit-hoiache* 'has appeared'	*poṣṭmāṣṭārer eigɔndograme asia* 'to the post-master, having come to this small village'
312.	*kuṭhirgomostā probhriti jesɔkol-kɔrmocari* 'the clerks and workers of the farm'			*āche* 'are'	
313.			*tāhāder phursot* 'their leisure'	*prāe nāi* 'does not exist'	= it seems they have no leisure time
314.	*tāhārā* 'they'			*upojukto nɔe* 'are not fit'	*bhɔdroloker sohit misibar* 'to mix with a gentleman'
315.	*kolikātār chele* 'the boy from Calcutta'			*jāne nā* 'does not know'	*bisesɔto bhālo-koriā misite* 'particularly to make friendship nicely'

316.			*hɔe udhɔto nɔe ɔprotibho* 'either arrogant or confounded'	*hoiāthāke* 'usually (they) are'	*ɔporicito sthāne gele* 'if (they) go to an unfamiliar place'
317.			*tāhār melā mesa* 'his acquaintance (with other)'	*hoiā-utḥenā* 'would not take place (does not occur)'	*ei kārone sthānio loker sohit* 'because of that, with the local people'
318.			*kāj* 'work'	*odhik nāi* 'is not much'	*ɔthoco hāte* 'but in his disposal (there)'
319.				*ceṣṭākɔren* '(he) tries'	*kɔkhono kɔkhono du ækta kobita likhite* 'some-times to write a few poems'
320.				*bækto-koriā-chen* '(he) has expressed'	*tāhāte, æmon bhāb* 'in his poems such attitude (mood)'
321.			*jibon* 'the life'	*kātiājāe* '(could be past) could run'	*je bɔrosukhe somostodin torupɔllober* 'that very happily whole day looking at' *kɔmpon ebŋ ākāser megh dekhiā* 'the clouds of the sky and listening to the murmur of the leaves'
322.	*ɔntorjāmi* 'God' *doitto* 'the demon'			*janen* 'knows' *bānāiā-dæe* 'if would build (construct)'	*jodiāsiā ækrattrer moddhe* 'coming (there) within one night' *eisakhapɔllob sɔmet gach guli katia* 'cutting all the trees with bunches' *paka rasta* 'the metal road'
323.		*sāri sāri ɔṭṭalika* 'the rows of big buildings'		*ruddhokoriā-rākhe* 'keep away'	*driṣṭi pɔthhoite ākāser meghke* 'from the sight, the clouds of the sky'

324.	*ei ādhmɔrā bhɔdrosɔntānṭi* 'this depressed gentleman'			*labhkorite-pare* 'can regain'	*tahahoile* 'then' *punoscɔ nɔboji-bon* 'again (gets) back his energy'
325.				*khāite hɔe* '(he) has to eat'	*nije rā̃dhiā* 'cooking by himself'
326.	*grāmer ekti pitrimātri hin balika* 'an orphan girl of the village'			*koriā dæe* 'does'	*tāhār kājkɔrmo* 'his household work'
327.				*khāite-pāe* '(she) gets to eat'	*cāriṭi cāriṭi* 'some food'
328.				*dækhājāe nā* 'cannot be seen'	*bibāher bises sɔmbhābonā* 'the possibility of marriage'
329.		*dhum* 'the smoke'		*kundolāito hoiā-uthito* 'used to come up rolling'	*sondhār somoe* in the evening *jɔkhon* 'when' *grāmer goāl ghɔr-hoite* 'from the village cowsheds'
330.	*jhilli* 'the crickets'			*ḍākito* 'used to make (noise) sound'	*jhope jhope* 'in every bush and shrub'
331.	*grāmer nesākhor bāuler dɔl* 'the drunken bawls of the village'			*juriāditogān* 'used to start singing'	*dure* 'in a distance' *khol kɔrotal bajaia* 'with the accompaniment of the musical instrument' (drum and cymbal)
			isɔt hrit-kɔmpɔn 'slight palpitation'	*uposthithoito* 'used to appear'	*jokhonɔndhokār dāoāe bosiā* 'when sitting on the dark veranda' *kobi hridɔeo* 'even in the mind of the poet' *æklābosia* 'being lonely' *gacher kɔmpon dekhile* 'if would watch the moving of the trees'

332.	*poṣṭmāṣṭār* 'the postmaster'		*dākiten* 'used to call'	*rɔton tokhon ghɔrerkone ekti dipsikhā jāliā* 'Ratan (proper name) that time in the corner having lit up a lamp'
333.	*rɔton* 'Ratan'		*ɔpekkhākoriā thākito* 'used to wait (expect)'	*dāre-bosiā* 'sitting near the doorway' *ei ḍaker jonno* 'for this call'
334.			*āsito nā* 'would not enter (she)'	*kintu æk ḍāke* 'but with one call' *ghɔre* 'in the room'
335.			*bolito* 'used to say'	*ki go dādābābu* 'hallo! dadababu (respected term of address for a maidservant)'
336.			*ḍākcho* '(you) are calling'	*kæno* 'why'
337.	*tui* 'you (inferior)'		*korchis* 'are doing'	*ki* 'what'
338.			*jete hɔbe* 'have to go (I)'	*ækhoni hẽseler culo dhɔrāte* 'just now, to make fire to the kitchen oven'
339.		*kāj* 'the work'	*pɔre hɔbe* 'has to be done later'	*tor hẽseler* 'your kitchen (work)'
340.			*seje deto* 'make'	*ækhon ækbār tāmākṭā* 'now once more the tobacco pipe (make)' = now once more you make the tobacco pipe
341.			(is)	*rɔtoner probes ghoteɔbilombe duṭi gāl phulāiā kolikāe phũ dite dite* 'the entrance of Ratan without any delay blowing the tobacco pipe'

342. *poṣṭmāṣṭār* 'the postmaster'		*jiggā̃sā kɔren* 'asked (enquired)'	*phɔskoriā* 'suddenly' *hāthoite koli-kāṭā-loiā* 'having taken the bowl which contains tobacco'
343.		*mone pɔṛe* 'can (you) remember'	*ācchā rɔton tor māke* 'hello Ratan to you your mother' = hello Ratan could you remember your mother?
344. *bāp* 'the father'		*āsito* 'used to come (home)'	*porisrom koriā sondhābælāe* 'after days work (labour) in the evening'
345. *bāp* 'the father'		*besi bhālo-bāsito* 'loved (her) more'	*māer cee tāhāke* 'than the mother her' = the father loved her more than her mother
346.		*mone āche* 'she can remember'	*bāpke ɔlpo ɔlpo* 'the father very little'
347.	*duṭiekṭi sondha* 'a few evenings'	*mone oŋkito āche* 'are printed in her mind'	*tāhāri-moddhe chobirmoto* 'among these like pictures' = some of the evenings are drawn in her mind like pictures
348. *rɔton* 'Ratan'		*bosiā-porito* 'used to sit'	*eikɔthā-hoite poṣṭmāṣṭārer pāerkāche krome māṭir upore* 'gradually while they used to talk Ratan sat down on the floor near the feet of the postmaster'
349.		*mone poṛito* '(she) could remember'	*tāhār ekṭi choṭo* 'her a little brother' *bhāi*

350. *duijonemiliā* 'both of them'			*māchdhɔrā-khælā koriā-chilo* 'did fishing (play)'	*bohu purbekār borsārdine ækdini* 'long before one day in the rainy season' *ækṭā ḍobār-dhāre* 'on the bank of a ditch' *gacher bhaŋa-* 'having taken'
351.		*seikɔthātāi* 'that story'	*besiudɔe-hoito* 'used to appear often (in her mind)'	*ḍālke chipkoriā* 'a broken branch as a fishing rod' *ɔnek gurutɔro ghɔṭoner cee* 'rather than many serious events'
352.	*rāt* 'the night'		*hoiā-jāito* 'become late'	*eirup kɔthā-prosɔnge* 'in such way of conversation' *mājhe-mājhe* 'sometimes'
353.	*sɔkāler bāsi-bænjon* 'the vegetable cooked in the morning'		*thākito* 'would remain'	
354.		*rā̃dhite-iccha* 'willingness to cook'	*thākitonā* 'would not remain'	*tɔkhon ālosso krome ar poṣṭ-māṣṭārer* 'then due to laziness to the post-master (there)'
355. *ratan* 'Ratan'			*ānito* 'used to bring'	*unundhɔrāiā taṛatarikhan-kɔtok ruṭi sẽkia* 'making fire quickly a few bread having baked'
356.		*rātrer āhār* 'the meal of the night'	*coliājāito* 'used to be finished'	*tāhātei* 'with that' *ubhɔer* 'of them'
357. *poṣṭmāṣṭāro* 'the postmaster also'			*pāṛiten* 'used to say'	*ghɔrer kɔthā* 'about his home' *ækækdin sondhā bælā sei brihɔt āṭ cālār kone coukir upor bosiā*

					'in some evenings having seated on the chair in a corner of the room'
358.		*hridɔe* 'the heart'		*bæthito-hoiā uṭhito* 'used to be heavy'	*choto bhāi mā ebŋ didir kɔthā porbāse æklāghɔre bosiā jāhāder jonno* 'young brother, mother and the elder sister in a distance place sitting alone for whom'
359.			*sesɔkol kɔthā* all these'	*udɔe hɔe* 'arose'	*sɔrbodāi mone* 'always in the mind'
360.			*jāhā* 'which'	*utthāpɔn kɔrājāe nā* 'could not be spoken'	*ɔthoco nilkuthir gomostāderkāche* 'but to the clerks of the Indigo plantation' *konomotei* 'in any way'
361.			*seikɔthā* 'all those'	*boliājāiten* 'used to speak'	*ekti ɔsikkhito khudro bālikāke* 'to an uneducated little girl'
362.				*mone hoitonā* 'does not seem'	*kichumāttro ɔsɔŋgɔto* 'slightly improper (a bit improper)'
363.			*æmon* 'such'	*hoilo* 'happened'	*ɔbosese* '(at the end) after sometimes'
364.	*bālikā* 'the girl'			*ullekhkorito* 'used to mention (call)'	*kɔthopokɔthon kāle* 'during conversation' *taharghɔrer lọk-digoke* 'his family mentioned' *ma, didi, dada bolia poricito loker næe* 'as mother, sister, brother like a known person'

365.	*bālikā* 'the girl'			*citrito-koriā-loiā-chilo* 'has drawn'	*æmonki tāhār khudro hridoe-pɔte* 'even in (the canvas of her heart) her mind' *tahader kalponik murtio* 'their imaginary figure also'
366.		*isɔt tɔpto su-komol bātās* 'slighty warm pleasant wind'		*ditechilo* 'was blowing'	*ækdin bɔrsā kāler meghomuk-to diprohɔre* 'one day in the clear sky of the rainy season'
367.		*æk prokār gɔndho* 'a kind of smell'		*utthito-hoitechilo* 'was raising'	*roudre bhijā ghās o gāch pālā-hoite* 'in the sun from the wet grass and the trees and plants'
368.				*mone hoite-chilo* '(it) seemed'	*jæno klanto dhɔronir gāer upor āsiā* 'that on the body of the tired earth (soil)'
369.		*usnonissās* 'warm sigh'		*lāgiteche* 'is touching'	
370.	*kothākār æk nāchoṛbāndā pakhi* 'a tenacious bird from nowhere'			*ābritti koritechilo* 'was reciting'	*tāhār ækṭānā surer nalis* 'its monotonous complaint' *prokritir dɔrbare* 'to the nature' *ɔttɔnto korumsɔre* 'in a very pitiful tone' *bare bare* 'again and again'
371.			*kāj* 'work'	*chilonā* 'was not'	*poṣṭmāṣṭārer-hāte* 'in the hand of the postmaster (there was no work)'
372.			*dekhibār-bisɔe* 'worth seeing objects'	*chilo* 'were'	*sedinkar bristi-dhouto mosrin torupɔllober-hillol* 'of that

				day the movement of the rainwashed smooth glowing leaves and the trees' *ebŋ pɔrabhuto bɔrsar bhɔgnabosisto roudro subhra meghostɔr* 'and the glowing brightness of the clouds which were residue of the defeated rainy season'
373.	*poṣṭmāṣṭār* 'the postmaster'		*dekhitechilen* 'was observing'	*tāhā* 'that'
374.			*bhābitechilen* '(he) was thinking'	
375.	*nitānto āponār lok* 'one who very close'		*thākito* 'would present'	*eisomoe ekti keho* 'at the moment, one who'
376.			*mone hoitelagilo* 'seems appear to the mind'	*krome* 'gradually'
377.	*sei pākhi* 'that bird'		*boliteche* 'is telling'	*oi kɔthāi barbar* 'that thing again and again'
378.	*keho* 'anybody'		*bissāskɔrenā* 'would not believe'	
379.			*jāniteopāenā* 'could not know'	*ebŋ* 'and'
380.		*udɔe* 'arrival'	*hoiā-thāke* 'would appear, would come (occurs)'	*eirup ækṭā bhaber* 'of such thought' *chotopollir* 'small village of' *samanno betoner postmastarermone* 'of the postmaster who gets small

		salary (and who lives in that insignificant village)'
381. *postmastār* 'the postmaster'	*dākilen* 'called'	*ektu dirgho nissas phelia, ratan* 'taking a deep breath, Ratan'
382. *rātān* 'Ratan'	*khāitechilo* 'was eating'	*tɔkhon peārā tɔlāe bosiā* 'at that time sitting beneath the trees' *kā̃cā peārā* 'the green guava'
383.	*chuṭiā āsilo* 'came' (quickly, running)'	*probhur kɔnṭho sɔr suniā* 'hearing the voice of the master' *obilombe* 'without any delay'
384.	*hā̃-pāite-hā-pāite-bolilo* 'said panting breathlessly'	
385.	*ḍākcho* '(you) are calling'	*dādābābu* 'hello dadababu (an addressing term)'
386. *poṣṭmāṣṭār* 'the postmaster'	*bolilen* 'said'	
387. *āmi* 'I'	*sekhābo* 'will teach'	*toke* 'you' *ektu ektu-kore-poṛte* 'to read gradually step by step'
388.	*korilen* 'did teaching (he taught her)'	*boliā* 'saying that' *somosto dupurbælā* 'the whole afternoon' *tāhāke loiā sɔ-re ɔ sɔre ā* 'with her (uttered) the vowels'
389.	*uttirno-hoilen*	*ebṇ eirupe ɔlpodinei juk-*

				'passed, completed'	*to okkhor* 'and within a short time the conjunct consonant'
390.			*bɔrsɔner-ɔnto* 'of the pouring end' = the end of the pouring	*nāi* 'there is no'	*srābon māse* 'in the month of monsoon'
391.		*khāl, bil nālā*, 'the canal, ditch, marshy land'		*bhoriā-uthilo* 'were filled up'	*jɔle* 'with water'
392.			*cɔlā cɔl* 'coming and going (movement, communication)'	*bɔndho* 'stopped'	*grāmer rāstāe prae ækprokar* 'on the village road it (is) about to stop'
393.				*jāite hɔe* 'has to go'	*noukā-koriā* 'by boat' *haṭe* 'to the market place'
394.		*bādlā* 'the cloud'		*koriāche* 'prevailed'	*ækdin prātokāl-hoite* 'one day since the morning'
395.	*poṣṭmāṣṭārer-chātriti* 'the student of the postmaster'			*ɔpekkhā-koria-bosia-chilo* 'was waiting'	*dārerkāche* 'near the doorway'
396.	*āponi* 'she herself'			*probeskorilo* 'entered'	*khuŋgi-puthi-loiā* 'with her books' *ghɔrer-moddhe* 'in the room'
397.				*dekhilo* 'saw'	
398.	*poṣṭmāṣṭār* 'the postmaster'			*suiā-āchen* 'was lying down'	*tāhār khāṭiār-upore* 'on his bed'
399.				*bisrām-koritechen* '(he) was taking rest'	*monekoriā* 'considering that'
400.				*jāibar upok-rom korilo* '(she) was about to leave (the room)'	*oti nissɔbde* 'very quietly' *ghɔr-hoite* 'from the room' *punosco bāhire* 'again to outside'

401.		*sunilo* 'heard (she)'	*sɔhosā ratan* 'suddenly Ratan'
402.		*bolilo* '(she) said (replied)'	*tārātāri phiriā-giā* 'having returned quickly'
403.		*ghumoccile* '(you) were sleeping'	*dādābābu* 'dada-babu (address-ing term)'
404.	*poṣṭmāṣṭār* 'the postmaster'	*bolilen* 'said'	*kātor sɔre* 'in a pathetic tone'
405.		*bhālobodh-hocche-nā* 'not feeling well'	*sorirṭā* 'the body' = I am not feeling well
406.		*dækh-to* '(you) check'	*āmār kɔpāle hāt-die* 'touching my forehead with your hand'
407.		*icchā kɔre* '(he) wishes (it appears in the mind)'	*ei nitānto niss-ɔngo probāse* 'in this lonely' foreign place *ghɔno bɔrsāe* 'in this rain' *rogkātor sorire* 'in such ill-health' *ekṭu-khāni sebāpaite* 'to get a warm nursing'
408.		*mone pɔṛe* '(he) could remember'	*tɔpto lɔlāṭer-upor* 'on the sick forehead' *s̃ākha pɔrā ko-mol hɔster spɔrso* 'a touch of soft hand which (is) rounded with bangle'
409.	*jɔnoni odidi* 'the mother and the elder sister'	*bosiā-āchen* 'are sitting'	*pāse* 'on the sickbed' *ei ghor-probāse rogjɔn-tronāe* 'in this lonely distant place in such time'
410.		*icchā kɔre* '(he) wishes'	*eikɔthā mone-korite* 'to think (to imagine) that'

411.	*probāsir-moner obhilās* 'the wish of the foreigner'	*bærtho hoilonā* 'was not in vain'	
412. *bālikā rɔton* 'the girl Ratan'		*rohilo nā* 'would not' 'no longer'	*ār bālikā* 'anymore a little girl'
413. *se* 'she'		*odhikār-koriā-bosilo* 'took (achieved the status)'	*jɔnonir pɔd* 'the place of the mother' *sei-muhurtei* 'at that moment'
414.		*dākiā ānilo* '(she) called'	*boiddo* 'the doctor'
415.		*khāoāilo* '(she) caused to take'	*jɔthā somoe-boṭikā* 'in right time the tablet'
416.		*rohilo* 'sat'	*sārārātri* 'whole night' *siore* 'on the side of the sickbed'
417. *āponi* 'she herself'		*r͂ādhiā dilo* 'cooked'	*pothyo* 'the diet'
418.		*jigg͂āsā-korilo* '(she) asked, enquired'	*ebŋ sɔtobār-koriā* 'and hundred times'
419.		*bhālo bodhhocche* 'better do you feel'	*h͂āgo dādābābu ektukhāni* 'hello dadababu, a little'
420. *poṣṭmāṣṭār* 'the postmaster'		*uṭhilen* 'got up'	*bohudinpɔre khinsorire rogsojja tæg* 'after a long time in a very weak state the sickbed leaving (he left)'
421.		*sthir-korilen* 'decided'	*mone* 'in his mind' *arɔnoe* 'not any more' *ekhanhoite* 'from this place' *bodlihoitehoibe* '(he) has to leave', has to take transfer

422.			*dɔrkhāsto-korilen* '(he) applied'	*sthānio ɔsāsther ullekh-koriā* 'mentioning the unhealthy weather of the place' *tɔtkhonāt* 'immediately' *kolikātāe kotri-pokkoder nikot* 'to the authority at Calcutta' *bodli hoibār-jonno* 'to be transferred'
423.	*ratan* 'Ratan'		*adhikār-korilo* 'took'	*dārer bāhire* 'on the doorway' *ābār tāhār sɔs-thān* 'again her marked place' *rogsebā hoite-niskriti pāiā* 'having been released from her duty to nurse'
424.			*dākpɔṛenā* 'the call does not appear'	*tāhāke purbobɔt* 'to her as it (was) before'
425.			*uki-māriā-dækhe* '(she) poked'	*mājhe-mājhe* 'sometimes (occasionally)'
426.	*poṣṭmāṣṭār* 'the postmaster'		*suiā-āchen* 'is lying down'	*ɔttontoɔnno-monosko-bhābe* 'very unmindfully' *coukite* 'on the chair' *ɔthoba* or *khatiae* 'on the bed'
427.	*rɔton* 'Ratan'		*bosiā-āche* 'was waiting'	*jɔkhon āhɔbhān-prottasa koria* 'when expecting the call'
428.	*tini* 'he'		*protikkhā-koritechen* 'was waiting (expecting)'	*tɔkhon* 'at that time '*ɔdhircitte* 'excitingly' (restlessly) *tāhār dɔrkāster-uttor* 'the reply of his petition'

429. *bālikā* ‘the girl’		*porilo* ‘read’	*dārer-bāhirebosiā* ‘sitting outside’ *sɔhɔsrobārkoriā* ‘a hundred and thousand of times’ *tāhār purono pɔṛā* ‘her old lessons’
430.		*golmalhoiajae* ‘(she) would forget’	*pāche* ‘if’ *jedin* ‘the day when’ *sɔhosā* ‘unexpectedly’ *dākpoṛiā* ‘called for’
431.	*āsoṅkā* ‘worry’	*chilo* ‘was’	*ei tāhar ækṭā* ‘such her one’
432.	*dāk* ‘the call’	*poṛilo* ‘came’	*ɔbosese* ‘at last’ *sɔptāho khānen-pɔre* ‘after one week’ *ækdin sondha bælae* ‘in one evening’
433. *rɔton* ‘Ratan’		*bolio* ‘said’	*udbelito hridɔe-griher-moddhe-probes-koriā* ‘very anxiously having entered into the room’
434. *dādābābu* ‘superior, elder brother (addressing term)’		*ḍākchile* ‘did (you) call’	*āmāke* ‘me’
435. *poṣṭmāṣṭār* ‘the postmaster’		*bolilen* ‘said’	*ratan* ‘hello Ratan’
436. *āmi* ‘I’		*jācchi* ‘am going’	*kali* ‘tomorrow’
437. *dādābābu* ‘(addressing term)’		*jāccho* ‘are (you) going’	*kothāe* ‘where’
438.		*jācchi* ‘(I) am going’	*bāṛi* ‘heme’
439.		*āsbe* ‘will come’	*ābār kɔbe* ‘when again back’
440.		*āṣbonā* ‘(I) will not come back’	*ār* ‘any more’

441.	*ratan* 'Ratan'			*jiggāsā-korilo-na* 'did not ask'	*ār kono kɔthā* 'any more word'
442.	*poṣṭmāṣṭār* 'the postmaster' *apnii* 'himself'			*bolilen* 'said'	*tāhāke* 'her'
443.	*tini* 'he'			*dɔrkhāsto-koriachilen* 'made petition'	*bodlir-jonno* 'for transfer'
444.		*dɔrkhāsto* 'the petition'		*nā-monjur-hoiāche* 'is not accepted'	
445.	*tini* 'he'			*jāitechen* 'is going'	*tāi* 'so' *kāje-jɔbāb die* 'resigning his position' *bāṛi* 'home'
446.	*keho* 'anyone'			*kohilo nā* 'did not speak'	*ɔnekkhɔn ārkono kɔthā* 'for a long time any more word'
447.		*prodip* 'the lamp'		*jolite-lāgilo* 'was burning'	*miṭmiṭ-koriā* 'mildly'
448.		*bristirjɔl* the rainwater		*ṭɔp ṭɔp-koriā poṛitelāgilo* 'was dropping'	*ebŋ ækshāne ghɔrer-jirno-cal bhed-koriā* 'and in one place through the hole of the roof' *ekṭimāṭir sɔrār upor* 'on an earthen pot'
449.	*rɔton* 'Ratan'			*gælo* went	*kichukhon pɔre* 'after some time' *āste āste uṭhiā* 'very quietly' *rānnaghɔre* 'to the kitchen' *ruṭigoṛite* 'to make bread'
450.			*ɔnek bhābonā* 'many thoughts'	*udɔe-hoiā-chilo-* 'appeared'	*bodhkori* 'perhaps' *moddhe-moddhe* 'occasionally' *niathae* 'in her mind'

451. *bālikā* 'the girl'		*jiggāsā-korilo* 'asked'	*poṣṭmāṣṭārer-āhar sɔmāpto-hoile pɔr* 'after the postmaster had finished his meal'
452. *dādābābu* 'dadababu'		*nie-jābe* 'would (you) take'	*āmāke* 'me' *tomāderbāṛi* 'to your home'
453. *poṣṭmāṣṭār* 'the postmaster'		*kohilen* 'said'	*hāsiā* 'smilingly'
454.	*se* 'that'	*kikore-hobe* 'how could be possible'	
455.		*abossokbodh-korilen nā* '(he) did not feel necessary'	*bæpārṭā je kiki-karone ɔsɔmbhɔb* 'why the matter (is) not possible' *taha balikake bujhano* 'that to make her understand'
456.	*hāssodhonir kɔnthosɔr* 'the smiling sound'	*bājite-lāgilo* 'was ringing'	*somosto rātṛi* 'whole night' *sɔpne ebŋ jāgɔ-rone* 'in her sleep and dream' *bālikār kāne* 'to the ear of the girl' *poṣṭmāṣṭārer seki kore hɔbe* 'the word of the postmaster how could that be possible'
457. *poṣṭmāṣṭār* 'the postmaster'		*dekhilen* 'saw'	*bhore uṭhiā* 'rising early in the morning'
458.		*ṭhik-āche* 'was alright'	*tāhār snānerjɔl* 'water for his bath'
459. *tini* 'he'		*jātrākoriben* 'will start'	*kɔkhon* 'when'
460. *tini* 'he'		*snānkoriten* 'used to bathe'	*tolājɔle* 'on fetched water' *kolikātarobbhās onusāre* 'due to the habit of living in Calcutta'

461. *bālikā* 'the girl'		*jiggā̃sā-koṛite-pāre-nāi* 'could not ask'	*sekɔthā* 'that' *kikarone* 'for what reason'
462. *raton* 'Ratan'		*tuliā-āniā-chilo* 'had fetched'	*jɔl* 'water' *ɔtorātre* 'in that late night' *nodi-hoite* 'from the river' *pāche prātokāle ābossok hɔe* 'if (he) needs in the early morning'
463.		*dāk poṛilo* 'the call came'	*snān sɔmāpon hoile* 'after the bath' *ratoner* 'to Ratan'
464. *rɔton* 'Ratan'		*probeskorilo* 'entered'	*nissɔbde grihe* 'without making any sound (very quietly) into the room'
465.		*cāhilo* 'looked at'	*ebŋ ādes-protikkāe ækbār nirɔbe probhur-mukher-dike* 'and in expectation of any work once quietly to the face of the master'
466. *probhu* 'the master'		*kohilen* 'said'	*rɔton āmārjāegāe* 'Ratan in my place'
467. *jelokṭi* 'that man'		*āsben* 'will come'	*tāke bole-die-jābo toke āmeri-moto jɔtnokorben* 'him I shall talk to you like me will look after'
468. *āmi* 'I'		*jācchi* 'am going'	*bole, toke kichu bhābte hɔbenā* 'because of that you do not have to worry for anything'
469.	*eikɔthāguli* 'these words'	*kono sɔndeho-nāi* 'there is no doubt'	*je ɔttonto sneho-gɔrbho ebŋ dɔā-dro hridɔehoite-uttito* 'that very deep affection is mixed with these'

470. *ke* 'who'	*bujhibe* 'will understand'	*nāri hridɔe kintu* 'the woman's heart but'
471. *rɔton* 'Ratan'	*sɔjho kori-āche* 'has tolerated'	*ɔnekdin probhur-ɔnek tiroskār* 'many days many scoldings of the master'
472.	*sohite-pārilonā* 'could not tolerate'	*kintu einɔrom kɔthā* 'but these soft words'
473.	*kohilo* 'said'	*ækebāre uccho-sitohoiā kā̃dia-uthiā* 'being cried loudly'
474. *tomār* 'you'	*bolte-hɔbenā* 'need not speak'	*nānā kāuke kichu* 'no, no, anything about me to anybody'
475. *āmi* 'I'	*cāine* 'do not want'	*thākte* 'to be here (to work here)'
476. *poṣṭmāṣṭār* 'the postmaster'	*rohilen* 'became'	*tāi, ɔbāk-hoiā* 'so surprised'
477. *nutɔn poṣṭ-māṣṭār* 'the new postmaster'	*āsilo* 'came'	
478. *purāton poṣṭ-mastar'* the former post-master'	*gɔmonun-mukh-hoilen* 'was about to leave'	*tāhāke somosto-cārj bujāiādiā* 'having given him the whole charge'
479.	*bolilen* 'said'	*jāibār somoe-rɔtonke dākiā* 'at the time of departure calling Ratan'
480. *āmi* 'I'	*dite pārini* 'could give'	*toke kɔkhono kichu* 'to you never anything'
481.	*die-gelum* '(I) am giving'	*ājjābārsomoe toke kichu* 'today at the time of leaving you some money'
482.	*pāiāchilen* '(he) got (had)'	*ete tor dinkɔtok colbe* 'with this you would manage a

			few days' *pɔth khɔrcā-bādetāhār betonerjɔto ṭākā* 'keeping the travel fare whatever the salary'
483.		*bāhirkorilen* '(he) took out'	*pɔket-hoite* 'from his pocket'
484. *raton* 'Ratan'		*kohilo* 'said'	*tɔkhon dhulāe poṛiā* 'then sitting on the ground'
485.		*pori* '(I) fell'	*tomār pāe* 'to your feet' = I beg you
486.		*dite hɔbenā* '(you) don't have to give'	*āmāke kichu* 'to me anything'
487. *kāuke* 'anybody'		*bhābte hɔbenā* 'has not to think'	*āmārjonne-kichu* 'about my future'
488.		*pɔlāiā gælo* (she) ran away	*boliā* 'saying that' *douraia* 'hurriedly' *sekhanhoite* 'from that place'
489. *bhutopurbo postmastar* 'the former postmaster'		*colilen* '(was going) went'	*nissās pheliā*, 'taking a deep sigh' *hate bæg-loiā* 'taking the bag in his hand' *kā̃dhe chātāloiā* 'taking the umbrella on his shoulder' *muṭer māthāe tiner-pēṭrā tuliā* 'giving the porter his tin box' *dhiredhire noukāɔbhimukhe* 'slowly to the boat'
490.		*uṭhilen* '(he) board'	*jɔkhon noukāe* 'when, on the boat'
491.	*noukā* 'the boat'	*chāṛiādilo* 'started moving'	

492.	*bɔrsā bis- phārite nodi* 'the river full with rainwater'		*chɔl chɔl korite lāgilo* 'began to make sound'	*dhɔronir uccho-* '*lito ɔsrurāsirmoto* like the tears of the earth' *cāridike* 'on all sides of the boat'
493.			*onubhɔb- korite- lāgilen* 'he started feeling'	*tɔkhon hridɔer- moddhe* 'then in his heart' *ækṭā ottonto bedonā* 'a very strong pain (feeling)'
494.	*ekti grāmno- bālikār mukho- chobi* 'a face of a village girl'		*prokāskorite- lāgilo* 'began to express'	*jæno æk bisso- bæpi brihɔt ɔbækto mɔrmobæ- thā* 'as if a very deep unspoken feeling'
495.			*icchāhoilo* '(he) thought'	*ækbār nitanto* 'once'
496.			*phiriā jāi* 'he wanted to return'	
497.			*loiā āsi* 'let me bring'	*jɔgoter kṛoro- cuto sei ɔna- thini-ke sŋge- koria* 'the orphan child with me'
498.	*bātās* 'the wind'		*pāiāche* 'has come'	*kintu tɔkhon-pale* 'but then to the sail'
499.	*bɔrsārsrot* 'the current in the rainy season'		*bohiteche* 'was blowing'	*khɔrotɔro-bege* 'forcefully'
500.	*nodikuler-sosān* 'the crema- tion ground on the bank of the river'		*dekhā-diāche* 'has to be seen (has come in sight)'	*grām otikrom* 'leaving behind the village' *nodiprobāhe- bhāsomān pothi- ker udās hridoe*
		eitɔtter udɔe 'the thought'	*hoilo* 'came appeared'	'in the indifferent mind of the traveller who was sailing on the boat' *jibone æmon kɔto- bicched mrittu āche* 'in life there

arise such kind of departing and death' *phiriā-phɔlki* 'what is the necessity to go back'.

In most cases, in Bengali constructions verb phrases occur at the end. For convenience the verb phrase is shown in between the subject part and the predicate part of a sentence in our table. The adverbial phrase is considered as a part of the predicate. The sentence outer also is shown in the predicate part in our table.

BIBLIOGRAPHY

ACHARYA, P., *Racanā Vicinta*, Calcutta, 1970.

AIJMER, KARIN, *Psychological Predicate*, Stockholm, 1972.

ALLAN, KEITH, 'Complement Noun Phrase and Prepositional Phrases, Adjectives and Verbs', *Foundations of Language*, Vol. 10. No. 3, September, 1973.

ANDERSON, J.M., *The Grammar of Case*, Cambridge University Press, Cambridge, 1971.

APTE, V.S., *The Student's Guide to Sanskrit Composition: A Treatise on Sanskrit Syntax for the Use of Schools*, 1963.

BAHULIKAR, SANDAMINI, *Indian Linguistics*, Vol. 34, No. 2, June 1973.

BANERJEE, S. AND BHATTACHARYA, D., *H.S. Sanskrit Second Paper*, Calcutta, 1969.

BENVENISTE, EMILE, *Problems in General Linguistics*, University of Miami Press, 1971.

BHATTACHARYA, BISHNUPADA, *A Study in Language and Meaning*, Calcutta, 1962.

———, DINESH CHANDRA, *Nyāya Sāstre Bāngāli: Bange Nabya Nyāya Charcā*, Vangiya Sāhitya Parishad.

BRATISLAVA, ANNA RACOVA, 'System of Tenses in Bengali and Their Morphemic Structure', *Asian and African Studies*, VIII, Moscow, 1972.

CARDONA, GEORGE, 'Studies in Indian Grammarians: The Method of Description Reflected in the Sivasutra', *Transaction of the American Philosophical Society*, New Series, Vol. 59, Pt. I, January, 1969.

CHAFE, WALLACE L., *Meaning and the Structure of the Language*, University of Chicago Press, 1970.

CHATTERJEE, S.K., Saral Bhāsā Prokās Bānglā Vyākaran, Vāk-Sāhitya, Calcutta, 1965.

———, *Origin and Development of Bengali Language*, Pt. I & III, London, 1972.

CHOMSKY, N., *Syntactic Structures*, The Hague, 1957.

———, *Aspects of the Theory of Syntax*, 1965.

———, 'A Transformation Approach to Syntax' in J.A. Fodor and J.J. Katz (ed.), *The Structure of Language*, 1964.

———, 'The Logical Basis of Linguistic Theories', *Proceedings of the Ninth International Congress of Linguistics*, 1964.

———, 'Topics in the Theory of Generative Grammar', *Tanua Linguarun*, Series Minor 56, London, 1966.

———, *Language and Mind*, 1968.

———, *Studies on Semantics in Generative Grammar*, 1972.

COLLINDER, BJORN, 'Noam Chomsky Und Die Generative Grammatik', *Acta Univer sitatis Upsaliensis*, Acta Socientatis Linguisticae Upsaliensis Nova Series, 2:1, Uppsala, 1970.

COMRIES, BERNARD, 'The Ergative Variations on a Theme', *Lingua*, 32, 1973.

CURME, *Parts of Speech and Accidence.*

CUTLER, A., 'A Note on a Reference by J.D. McCawley to Adjectives Denoting Temperature', *Talanya*, I, The Hague, 1972.

DAVIDSON, DONALD AND HARMEN, GILBERT (eds.), *Semantics of Natural Language*, 1972.

DIXON, R.M.W., 'A Method of Semantic Description' in D.D. Steinberg and L.A. Jakobovits (eds.), *Semantics*, Cambridge University Press, 1963.

FILLMORE, C.J., 'Case for Case' in E. Bech and R.T. Harms (eds.), *Universals in Linguistic Theory*, 1968.

———, 'Lexical Entries for Verbs', *Foundations of Language*, Vol. 5, No. 4, November, 1968.

———, 'Some Problems for Case Grammar', *Working Papers in Linguistics*, No. 10, The Ohio State University, Columbus, 1971.

———, 'Verbs of Judging: An Exercise in Semantic Description' in E. Bach and R.T. Harms (ed.), *Universals in Linguistic Theory*, 1968.

FODOR, J.A. AND KATZ, J.J. (eds.), *The Structure of Language*, 1964.

FRIES, C.C., *The Structure of English*. 1952.

GEIGER WILHELM, *A Grammar of the Sinhalese Language*, Colombo, 1938.

GLEASON (Jr.), *Linguistics and English Grammar*, New York, 1965.

GOLDIN, MARK, G., Spanish Case and Function, Georgetown University Press, 1968.

GROOT DE, *Classifications of Cases and Uses of Cases*, 1956.

GRUBER, J.S., *Language*, Vol. 43, No. 4, 1967.

HALLIDAY, M.A.K., 'Notes on Transitivity and Theme in English, Part 2', *JL*, Vol. III, 1967.

HAMARSTROM, U.G.E., *Linguistic Units, Acts and Items* (first draft and second draft), 1971.

———, 'On Generative Phonology: A Critical Appraisal', *Phonetics*, Vol. 27, No. 3, 1973.

HARRIS, Z.S., 'Transformational Theory', *Language*, Vol. 41, 1965.

———, 'Two Systems of Grammar: Report and Paraphrase' in *Structural and Transformational Linguistic*, Dordrecht, 1970.

HASLEY, *Colloquiel Hindusthani.*

HOCKET, 'Two Models IA Versus IP', *Word*, 1954.

JACKENDOFF, 'Semantic Interpretation in Generative Grammar', The MIT Press, 1972.

JAN FIRBAS, 'Non Thematic Subjects in Contemporary English', *Travaux Linguistiques de Prague*, Vol. 2, Prague Academia, 1966.

JESPERSEN, OTTO, *Analytic Syntax: Essentials of English Grammar*, London, 1933.

———, 'A Modern English Grammar' (Part III, Syntax).

———, '*Philosophy of Grammar*'.

KALE, M.R., *Higher Sanskrit Grammar* (3rd edn), 1912.

KATZ, J. AND FODOR J.A., A Reply to Dixon's "A Trend in Semantics", *Linguistics*, 3, 1964.

———, *The Philosophy of Language: Semantic Theory*, 1966.

KELLOGG, *Grammar of Hindi Language*, 1965.

KILPARASKY, PAUL, 'Linguistic Universals and Linguistic Change' in E. Bach and R.T. Harms (ed.), *Universals in Linguistic Theory*, 1968.

KUNJUNNI RAJA, K., *Indian Theories of Meaning*, Madras, 1963.

LAMB, SYDNEY, M., *Outline of the Stratificational Grammar*, Washington, 1966.

LANGEONDON, D.T., *Essentials of English Grammar*, 1970.

———, *The Study of Syntax: The Generative Transformational Approach to the Structure of American English*, New York, 1969.

LINELL PER, 'Problems of Psychological Reality in Generative Phonology: A Critical Assessment', *Ruul*, 4. (Reports from Uppsala University, Department of Linguistics), 1974.

LONGYEAR, CHRISTOPHER RUDSTON, Linguistically Determined Categories of Meanings, The Hague, 1971.

LYAS, COLIN (eds.), *Philosophy and Linguistics*, 1971.

LYONS, JOHN, *Introduction to theoretical Linguistics*, Cambridge University Press, 1968.

MEETHAN, A.R. (ed.), *Encyclopaedia of Linguistic Information and Control*, 1969.

MISRA, VIDYA NIWAS, *The Descriptive Technique of* Pāṇini: *An Introduction*, The Hague, 1966.

MORAVESIK, J.M.E., 'Linguistic Theory and the Philosophy of Language', *Foundation of Language*, 3.

MOTILAL B.K., '*Indian Theories on the Nature of the Sentence* (Vākya)', *Foundations of Language*, 2, 1966.

ONIONS, C.T., *Modern English Syntax*, Routledge and Kegan Paul, London, 1971.

PĀṆINI, *Āśtādhyāyī*, Vol. I, II, ed. and tr. Srisa Chandra Vasu, Delhi, 1962.

PAUL MELLEMA, 'A Brief Against Case Grammar', *Foundations of Language*, Vol. II, No. 1, January 1974.

PLATT, J.T., *Grammatical Form and Grammatical Meaning*, Melbourne, 1970.

POP, AURTHER, *Semantics and Necessary Truth*, 1958.

QUIRK, *et al.*, *A Grammar of Contemporary English.*

ROSENBAUM, P.S., *Phrase Structure*, 1967.

RYLE, G., *The Concept of Mind*, London, 1949.

SENGUPTA, S., *Sanskrita Sabda Sāstrer Mulkathā*, Calcutta, 1957.

SPEIJER, J.S., *Sanskrit Syntax*, Kyoto, 1968.

STAAL, J.F., *Word Order in Sanskrit and Universal Grammar*, 1967.

STAROSTA, S., 'Case Forms and Case Relations in Sora', *Working Papers in Linguistics*, Vol. 5, No. 1, January-March, 1973.

SUBBARAO, K.V., 'Phrase Structure Rules for Noun Phrase in Hindi', *Indian Linguistics*, Vol. 35, No. 3, September 1974.

SVARTVIK, JAN, *On Voice in English Verb*, The Hague, 1966.

SWEET, *New English Grammar.*

TAGORE, RABINDRANATH, *Rabindra Racanābali*, Vol. 7, 14, Calcutta, 1961.

TARAPOREWALA, I.J.S., *Sanskrit Syntax*, Delhi, 1967.

VIDYABHUSHAN N., *Bhāṣābodha Bānglā Vyākaraṇa Racanā*, Calcutta, 1971.

DICTIONARIES CONSULTED

APTE, V.S., *The Practical Sanskrit-English Dictionary.*

BASU, RAJSEKHAR, *Calantikā*, Calcutta, 1955.

Dev's Concise Dictionary: Bengali to English, Calcutta, 1955.

MACDONELL, ARTHUR ANTHONY, A Practical Sanskrit Dictionary, Oxford University Press, 1929.

Monier-William, M., *Sanskrit English Dictionary*, 1960.

Saṁsad English-Bengali Dictionary, 1963.

INDEX

ERRATA

Page	*Line*	*For*	*Read*
16	F. note	Langendon	Langeondon
19	19	suffixeg	suffix, e.g.
19	23	*gācha*	*gāchā*
19	29	*gācha*	*gāchā*
22	36	form	form,
30	38	*tebile*	*ṭebile*
43	23	into about	into the about
46	20	*karmadhārayā*	*karmadhāraya*
71	17	figure or speech	figure of speech
76	10	*cād*	*cā̃d*
119	37	*bhāva*	*bhāŋ̥ā*
121	9	*kartṛvacya*	*kartṛvācya*
131	1	*svaṭantra-*	*svatantra*
131	26	*uddesya*	*uddeśya*
165	F. note	Pānini	Pāṇini
171	4	*ache*	*āche*
172	22	s	as
172	34	Syntagma	syntagm
176	20	Syntagma	syntagm
187	18	syntagma	syntagm
199	27	Paṇiṇi's	Pāṇini's
219	30	*bhāva*	*bhāŋ̥ā*
224	16	*thaela*	*ṭhaelā*
237	15	undirectional	unidirectional
237	16	multidimentional	multidimensional